INTREPID SAILORS

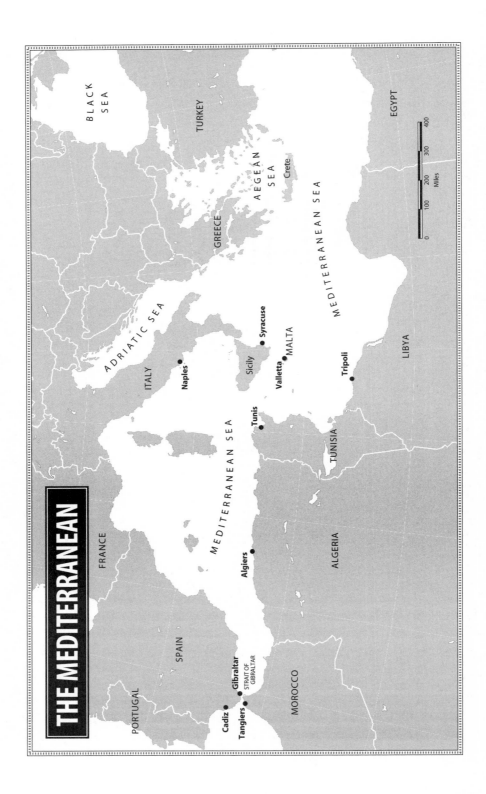

THE MEDITERRANEAN

PORTUGAL

SPAIN

FRANCE

Cadiz
Tangiers
Gibraltar
STRAIT OF
GIBRALTAR

MOROCCO

Algiers

ALGERIA

MEDITERRANEAN SEA

ITALY

Naples

ADRIATIC SEA

Tunis

TUNISIA

Sicily

Syracuse

Valletta
MALTA

Tripoli

LIBYA

MEDITERRANEAN SEA

GREECE

AEGEAN
SEA

Crete

TURKEY

BLACK
SEA

MEDITERRANEAN SEA

EGYPT

0   100   200   300   400
Miles

INTREPID SAILORS

THE LEGACY OF PREBLE'S BOYS AND THE TRIPOLI CAMPAIGN

CHIPP REID

Naval Institute Press
Annapolis, Maryland

Naval Institute Press
291 Wood Road
Annapolis, MD 21402

Library of Congress Cataloging-in-Publication Data

Reid, Chipp.
  Intrepid sailors : the legacy of Preble's boys and the Tripoli campaign / Chipp Reid.
    p. cm.
  Includes bibliographical references and index.
  ISBN 978-1-61251-117-7 (hbk. : alk. paper) — ISBN 978-1-61251-125-2 (e-book) 1. United States—History—Tripolitan War, 1801-1805—Naval operations. 2. Pirates—Africa, North—History—19th century. 3. Preble, Edward, 1761-1807. 4. United States—History, Naval—To 1900. 5. Philadelphia (Frigate) 6. Intrepid (Ketch) I. Title.
  E335.R45 2012
  355.00973—dc23

                                                                                        2012020926

♾ This paper meets the requirements of ANSI/NISO z39.48-1992 (Permanence of Paper).
Printed in the United States of America.

20 19 18 17 16 15 14 13 12   9 8 7 6 5 4 3 2 1
First printing

CONTENTS

MAPS

FOREWORD

FROM THE BEGINNING OF OUR NAVY there were great deeds made by great men. Naval heroes with names that all Americans knew like the father of our Navy, John Paul Jones; Capt. Isaac Hull; Commodores Perry and Preble, not to mention admirals Dewey, Mitcher, Halsey, and Nimitz. All our naval heroes became so because they faced adversity, often against overwhelming odds and their actions won victory for their forces and doing so saved our nation.

A hundred years ago names like Stephen Decatur, William Bainbridge, and Richard Somers were household names as well. Their actions against roaming corsairs of the Barbary Pirates and during the blockade of Tripoli helped free captive Americans and ultimately rid the United States of piracy forever. But there was a time in our country when names like Decatur, Somers, and Stewart were just as common and the feats of these men off the coast of North Africa were fireplace stories . . . they were stories that inspired generations of young men to take to the sea to follow their legacy.

When our fledgling Navy was established, it was done so with antipiracy in mind. And although our Navy has gone on to challenge the great sea powers for supremacy of the seas, the Navy has also had a consistent responsibility that it still fulfills today: freedom of navigation.

The story of *Intrepid* and sacrifice of her brave crews off the shores of Tripoli is legendary. It is a story that is as amazing today as it was two hundred years ago. *Intrepid Sailors* is an inspiring recollection of the events of those times, the actions of our young Navy off the shores of Tripoli, and a historical recollection of events surrounding the sacrifice of *Intrepid* and her brave crew. It pays homage to the Sailors and the Officers charged to lead them. I highly recommend this story be read with the hope that it reminds us not only of our roots as a Navy, but of our obligation to bring our Sailors home.

—*FORCM (AW/SW/NAC) Jon D. Port, USN*

ACKNOWLEDGMENTS

IN ANY UNDERTAKING SUCH AS THE RESEARCHING and writing of a book that covers a topic more than two hundred years old, any number of people contribute.

The staff of the Manuscript Division, Library of Congress, was of immense help and we got to know each other on a first-name basis. Whether it was crawling through back rooms to find "lost" boxes of papers or faxing me a single page that was key to the story, the Manuscript staff was instrumental in my research.

Just as important were the staffs at the Sterling Memorial Library and the Beineke Museum of Western Americana at Yale University. Both libraries contain extensive collections of manuscripts from the Barbary Wars period—many of these documents at Yale are now digital—and, even more important, first-edition books from the period. The Yale staff was more than accommodating and often had as much fun seeing the books I was able to find as I had in finding them.

A third major resource—and one of the best for anyone doing research on any maritime topic—was the entire staff and collections at Mystic Seaport, the Museum of America and the Sea. From the late Don Treworgy, who ran the planetarium, to the staff in the Collections Resource Center, to the staff at the G. W. Blunt–White Library, everyone at Mystic was knowledgeable and as interested in "old records" as I was. The museum's large living history department made it possible to actually see, touch, and, in some cases, execute the same tasks as the officers and men who fought in 1804.

I also must thank the staff at the Nimitz Library at the U.S. Naval Academy for granting me access to the stacks. I am quite sure the librarians all got a chuckle when an old sea dog in shorts and faded hat emerged from the stacks amid legions of freshly washed and properly attired midshipmen!

My deepest thanks to the crew of the tall ship *Quinnipiack*—Kirk Rouge, Drew Kerlee, Paul Cipriani, Jon Wisch, Sarah Herard, and Brandon "Kalmar" Marshall—with whom I sailed and learned old-fashioned marlinspike seamanship. Thank you for answering my seemingly innumerable (and often irritating!) questions. This book was born on the deck of the *Quinny*.

To "my captain" Heijo Knuttel, the call of the sea remains undiminished and, just as you predicted, I have learned how to cope with balancing "real life" with answering that call.

Thanks also go out to Sally Hastings, Mayor Jack Glasser, and City Councilman Greg Sykora of Somers Point, New Jersey. Named for the family of the father of Richard Somers, the folks in this New Jersey city were and are excited about this book and the complete story of Richard Somers. They welcomed me into their town and have allowed me to help in the major project of recovering the remains of the crew of the *Intrepid*. When I am in Somers Point, I feel at home.

Finally, thanks to my mom and dad, who instilled in me a love of history and of our great country, who taught me that patriotism is not bad, and who acted as my early editors and audience. That I finished *Intrepid Sailors* and that it tells a good story is as much their accomplishment as mine. Most of all thank you for supporting me or giving me a swift kick whenever I needed it. Thank you for everything.

—*Chipp Reid*
Annapolis, Maryland

INTREPID
SAILORS

CHAPTER 1

"TO BE PREPARED FOR WAR"

ORE THAN TWO HUNDRED YEARS AGO, on the night of September 4, 1804, a tiny boat crept into the harbor of Tripoli, in what is now Libya. Tripoli in the early nineteenth century was a semiautonomous part of the old Ottoman Empire. Its ruler, the bashaw (or prince), made his money through piracy. Corsairs from Tripoli scoured the Mediterranean, looking for European and, increasingly, American ships to capture. The bashaw would hold the crews for ransom, then extort money from their governments to guarantee safe passage for their vessels. The United States paid its share of "tribute"—diplomatic-speak for protection money—to Tripoli as well as to Morocco, Algiers, and Tunis, the small nations along the North African coast that made up the Barbary States. By 1801, however, the Americans had had enough and President Thomas Jefferson dispatched three different naval forces to Tripoli to quell the pirates.

The first two squadrons failed in their mission, but the third force, which sailed to the Mediterranean in 1803 under Commo. Edward Preble, became the stuff of legend. The officers that served under Preble set the standard of courage and honor to which the United States Navy still holds its commissioned and noncommissioned ranks. For more than a hundred years, Preble's campaign against Tripoli was common knowledge among Americans, who told and retold the story. The campaign contained a little bit of everything. There was ship-to-ship combat, sea chases, daring, desperate hand-to-hand combat, and tragedy.

Among Preble's officers were three men that were almost larger than life—Stephen Decatur Jr., Richard Somers, and Charles Stewart. They were friends since childhood. In an age when rivals tended to settle their differences on the dueling ground, Decatur, Somers, and Stewart grew closer and pushed one another to excel. The friendship between Somers and Decatur became especially well known and celebrated. Young boys grew up learning about the pair and emulating their bond. In 1898 the English writer Molly Elliott Seawell forever enshrined their friendship when she wrote a book especially for children, *Decatur and Somers*. Although Seawell softened some of the harsher realities of their lives, she immortalized the achievements of and the relationship between the two naval officers.[1]

Somers was in command of the small ship that sailed into the unknown the night of September 4, 1804. His was the first ship to carry the name *Intrepid* in the U.S. Navy. Originally a French supply vessel sold to Tripoli, she became part of the American squadron under Preble after her capture in November 1803. Although the smallest vessel in the American flotilla, she played a large role in Preble's campaign before lying all but forgotten at an Italian port. Come the summer of 1804, however, Preble again turned to the *Intrepid* for a special mission, and he turned to Somers to lead it.

For Somers, the mission that night was his shot at the glory that had eluded him throughout the summer of 1804 but that his friends had found. Despite always being on the cusp of the same sort of success, Somers never quite achieved it. He always seemed to miss out when his two closest friends had an adventure or scored a major achievement. When Preble decided to use the *Intrepid* to sneak into Tripoli harbor, Somers jumped at the chance to lead the mission.

Decatur was the clear star of the fleet. Dashing, handsome, and charismatic, Decatur commanded the first special operations mission on which the *Intrepid* sailed. That exploit would earn him a rapid promotion and make him a favorite officer in the squadron. He would earn even more glory during the desperate battles off Tripoli.

Stewart, who started the year as the senior officer of the three, won praise for the way he commanded the blockade of Tripoli harbor in the spring and summer of 1804. Operating under orders from Commo. Edward Preble, Stewart tied a noose around Tripoli with his force of brigs and schooners. He captured several prizes, blasted the city's defenses, and choked off all supplies going into the pirate lair. He was, until Decatur's promotion, the second-in-command of the American squadron in the Mediterranean.

One reason for the closeness between the three men was the way their personalities meshed. Decatur was the leader and had been since childhood. Of the children, it was always Decatur who would take the biggest risks swimming or ice-skating. Stewart was the steadiest of the three. Thoughtful but with his own streak of rashness, he never made the same mistake twice. Somers was the quiet one of the three, but his reticence covered tremendous courage.

The boys grew up during a time of change in America. They watched as the colonies evolved into an independent nation. Their families were staunch patriots; living in Philadelphia allowed them to rub elbows with some of the most famous men in the new country, including George Washington, John Adams and, most important to their careers, Capt. John Barry of the Continental Navy. Their childhood laid the foundation of their burning desire to serve the new United States, and the fledgling U.S. Navy provided them that opportunity. There was something about being part of the first permanent military force in the country, one that would take them to foreign shores, that emboldened them. All three embodied the early American spirit that nothing was impossible, and all burned with a passion to earn glory for themselves and for the new United States Navy. Their passion became the nation's.

"The better feeling of the country was entirely in [the Navy's] favor," wrote novelist James Fenimore Cooper, who enlisted in the Navy in 1807 and earned an appointment as a midshipman in 1811. "Families of the highest social and political influence pressed forward to offer their sons to the service, the navy being the favorite branch. . . . Young and intelligent seamen were taken from the merchant service, to receive the rank of lieutenants. . . . The seaman of the nation joined heartily in the feeling of the day."[2]

Somers was not alone in the *Intrepid*. He had twelve other men, all volunteers, willing to sail with him into the unknown. Four of the men were from the *Nautilus*, the warship Somers commanded: James Harris, William Keith, James Simms, and Thomas Tompline enlisted in Maryland in 1803 when Somers was fitting out the *Nautilus* for the Mediterranean. All four were experienced seamen who, like Somers, had missed the chances for glory earlier in the campaign.[3] The six other enlisted men were volunteers from the USS *Constitution*. Robert Clark, Isaac Downes, William Harrison, Hugh McCormick, Peter Penner, and Jacob Williams stepped forward when Lt. Henry Wadsworth, second-in-command on the *Intrepid*, called for volunteers from among the crew on the U.S. flagship. They were $10-a-month sailors, yet their desire for glory was just as strong as that of their officers.[4] The mission on which they sailed would mark the culmination of Preble's campaign against the Barbary pirates and make the name *Intrepid* synonymous with the United States Navy.

The United States was still a new nation in 1803, barely twenty years removed from its unprecedented declaration of independence from Great Britain. The U.S. Navy was even newer. Although it traced its lineage to the Continental Navy of the Revolutionary War, the actual U.S. Navy did not exist until St. Patrick's Day 1794, when President George Washington signed into law the bill creating the force. The Navy lived a fitful existence for the next four years and did not launch its first vessel until 1797. When the first frigate slid down the ways in Philadelphia, few people harbored the illusion the Navy would suddenly challenge established maritime powers such as England or France for supremacy on the seas.

Congress authorized a force of just six frigates—of unprecedented size and power—but no small ships such as schooners or brigs to work inshore or serve as scouts, and no mammoth line-of-battleships. As far as American naval planners could see, the new Navy needed neither. No one—other than the officers of the infant force—expected the Navy to take on a European power. The main enemy politicians expected the Navy to face was pirates.

When America won its independence from Great Britain, it also won the responsibility of protecting its own ships. The new nation was a maritime country, and its merchant vessels were the lifeblood of an economy that in the 1780s teetered on bankruptcy. America's merchant vessels were the new nation's best economic asset and its main source of revenue.

As early as 1784, merchant vessels from Salem, Massachusetts, were doing a brisk worldwide trade. The *William and Henry*, Benjamin Hodges master, sailed to Canton and back in 1784. She brought back with her 200,000 pounds of tea, coffee, and $4,000 of silks and nankeens. Her duties were $10,000.[5]

The lucrative nature of American's trade fleet was not a secret. Greedy eyes along the North African coast saw fat Yankee merchantmen as easy prey, and they were. When the United States became independent, it lost the protection of the British Royal Navy. Now, instead of flying the Union Jack, U.S. ships flew the Stars and Stripes, and to the semiautonomous states along the Barbary Coast, that flag meant quick money.

Algiers was the first of the Barbary States to start grabbing American ships. In 1786 an Algerian corsair snatched the Boston brig *Celia*. The pirates seized the ship, stole the cargo, and held the captain and crew for ransom. The seizure prompted the United States to follow European custom and pay for peace treaties with the various pirate kingdoms. By 1790 America was paying tribute to every Barbary state.

It was not enough: the more tribute the new nation paid, the more the pirate nations wanted.[6] It was more than President George Washington could take. The nation's first chief executive told Congress in late 1790, "To be prepared for war is one of the most effectual means of preserving peace."[7] Washington began lobbying for a full-time military. It was, at first, an uphill battle.

Until the adoption of the U.S. Constitution in 1789, Congress was essentially impotent when it came to levying taxes; it could barely pay its own expenses, let alone support a military. America sold off its last warship from the Revolutionary War, the 36-gun frigate *Alliance*, in 1785. After

that, the new nation had no means of protecting its commerce. Near bankruptcy combined with the excesses of pre–Revolutionary War British military
policy made many lawmakers reluctant to allow a standing military. The
debate raged for three years as Washington and the New England delega-
tions, except for Vermont, argued with their southern counterparts over the
need for a navy.

Washington quietly took the lead in the debate. In his annual address to
Congress in late 1793, he told lawmakers,

> I cannot recommend to your notice measures for the fulfill-
> ment of our duties to the rest of the world without again press-
> ing upon you the necessity of placing ourselves in a condition
> of complete defense and of exacting from them the fulfillment
> of their duties toward us.
>
> The United States ought not to indulge a persuasion that,
> contrary to the order of human events, they will forever keep
> at a distance those painful appeals to arms with which the
> history of every other nation abounds. There is a rank due
> to the United States among nations which will be withheld,
> if not absolutely lost, by the reputation of weakness. If we
> desire to avoid insult, we must be able to repel it; if we desire
> to secure peace, one of the most powerful instruments of our
> rising prosperity, it must be known that we are at all times
> ready for war.[8]

It was a strong argument, but not strong enough to sway reluctant lawmakers. It took a renewed series of pirate attacks to finally push Congress past
its fears of a standing military and approve the creation of the United States
Navy, and, once more, it was Algiers that caused the uproar.

———————

The ruler of Algiers, the dey, in 1793 declared open season on American
shipping as more and more U.S.-flagged ships entered the Mediterranean.
The outbreak of war between France and England in 1792 had opened the
doors to new trade areas for the United States, and American merchants
quickly capitalized on the vacuum the lack of French and British merchantmen created. American vessels flooded the Mediterranean, carrying dried
fish, pickled mackerel, salt beef and salt pork, boards and shingles, barrel
staves and hoops, cheese, butter, and candles. The homeward-bound cargo
usually consisted of molasses, sugar, coffee, cocoa, cotton, and a few other
articles. The value of these cargoes was a boon, both locally and nationally.

Trade between Salem and Cadiz, Spain, for example, brought in $150,000 in taxes in just three months in 1788.[9]

By late 1793 the dey wanted a higher cut of American riches. He might have received some prompting. Secretary of State Edmund Randolph, on January 20, 1794, wrote to David Humphreys, then U.S. consul to Tripoli, saying he believed the English were behind the dey's renewed belligerence. He also said the British consul in Lisbon was trying to convince the Portuguese to end their patrols just outside the entrance to the Mediterranean. Randolph told Humphreys the same war that opened the Mediterranean to American shipping also removed a major block to pirate attacks—European navies: "By advices from several respectable quarters we daily learn that some one or other of the power of the Mediterranean, who have hitherto contributed to keep the pirates of Algiers in check, are withdrawing by negotiations, terror or actual invasion from hostility against them."[10]

By the time Randolph's letter reached Humphreys, the Algerians had seized 7 ships and held 113 Americans hostage. The dey wanted at least $2,000 per man in ransom, plus a frigate, naval stores, and other "gifts" before he would even consider releasing the Americans.[11]

News of the pirate attacks and the Algerians' harsh treatment of American prisoners began to circulate throughout the country. George Folger, master of the New Bedford brig *Hazard*, told his story to the news pamphlet "Agreeable Intelligence." Folger told of beatings, starvation, and near enslavement at the hands of the pirates. Humphreys, from his post in Tripoli, sent lurid tales home of how the Algerians put their captives in chains, subjecting them to slavery. At the same time, the captives themselves sent plaintive letters to Congress, pleading for help.[12]

It was the last straw. When Washington introduced legislation to create a "naval armament," Congress was ready. The president wanted to build six warships—all frigates—to protect American merchant vessels from the pirates. The House, in a forty-six to forty-four vote on January 2, 1794, agreed to debate the subject. The Senate agreed two days later.[13]

———◆——◆———

As much as they loathed the practice of tribute, purchased peace, and the savage nature of the Barbary pirates, naval advocates owed the seafaring outlaws a debt. If not for the pirates, their dreams of a navy would remain unfulfilled; they made sure to press home their point. When Congress began debating whether to fund a navy, two sides quickly emerged. The merchant states of the north, along with coastal regions of Virginia and South Carolina, favored creating a navy. Lawmakers from New England and the coastal South represented areas that depended on the sea. Lawmakers from the more agrarian states—including Vermont, much of Pennsylvania, and most of the southern states—saw no need to fork over the money.

William Giles, representative from Virginia, was one of the opponents of the navy measure. Six frigates, he argued, were simply not enough to end pirate attacks, "considering the resources of the Algerines and the superior policy of having recourse to negotiations and purchase of peace. The bill contains, in itself, essentially a declaration of war. Our calculations, there-fore, should be extended to the utmost limit of the naval ability of the hos-tile nation." Giles said he believed the Algerians, in concert with the other Barbary nations, could smash such a small flotilla. They were, he said, "long accustomed to naval enterprises and desperate in naval engagements." Giles also said the practice of buying off the pirates was not the national disgrace navy advocates claimed it was, saying, "They had been subsidized for peace by almost every European nation." The Virginian then voiced the darkest fear of navy opponents, that a standing military, especially a navy, was the first step toward a military dictatorship. Giles "viewed the establishment of a navy as a complete dereliction of the policy of discharging the principal of the public debt. History does not afford an instance of a nation which continued to increase their navy and decrease their debt at the same time. It is an operation exceeding the ability of any nation. The naval competition in Europe has produced oppression to their subjects and ruin to themselves. A navy is the most expensive means of defense and the tyranny of governments consists in the expensiveness of their machinery."[14]

Naval advocates had an entirely different perspective. South Carolina Representative William Smith argued the dey would continue to grab American vessels: "As long as our vessels were so easy and so tempting prey to the cupidity of these rovers, it would be vain to expect that they would sell a peace for anything like the price which the government would be willing to give or that a peace, if affected, would have any duration." He believed backing down to Algiers would further encourage the pirates once "the dey should understand that we undertook no measures to protect our trade, and were afraid of the expense of a small armament. Even should a peace be purchased, the temptation to break it would be so great that we ought not to expect that it would be observed. But if the dey knew that we had some naval armament and were resolved to protect our trade, he would find his account not only in making peace with us, but in maintaining it." Smith also ridiculed the idea building a navy would somehow bankrupt the new nation: "This country is peculiarly fitted to a navy, abounding with all kinds of resources, we have within ourselves those means which other maritime nations were obliged to obtain from abroad. The nature of our situation, and the navigat-ing disposition of a considerable portion of our citizens, evinces still more the propriety of some Naval Armament. Sweden, with a population no greater than that of the United States, and with more slender resources, maintained a large navy." The United States, with its increasing population, wealth, and abundant national resources, could not only outfit a squadron, but also could do so with without "an insupportable expense."[15]

In the end, however, it was not national pride or policy that won the argument—it was simple economics. Barbary pirate attacks—even the threat of them—sent insurance costs spiraling out of control and threatened the new nation's main source of income.[16] An added incentive, President Washington pointed out, was any naval construction would take place in several states and put hundreds of men to work. The prospect of jobs in their districts essentially forced congressional representatives and senators to approve the building of the United States Navy.[17] On March 17, 1794, Washington signed into law "An Act to Provide a Naval Armament." It was the beginning of the United States Navy.[18]

Work on the six authorized warships began almost as soon as the ink dried on the new law. Secretary of War Henry Knox enlisted famed shipwrights Joshua Humphreys and Josiah Fox to design the frigates, and their ideas created an entirely new class of warship. The American frigates would be strong enough to blast any comparable vessel out of the water, yet fast enough to escape larger ships of the line.

Congress gave President Washington $688,888 to build the nation's first warships. Many in Congress believed the frigates—even the threat of building them—would scare Algiers enough to stop the attacks. If not, the six warships would be strong enough to smash the pirates. The bill authorized the frigates, but made no mention of any other type of ship.[19]

"An Act to Provide a Naval Armament" also contained a clause Washington included as a way of placating opponents to a navy. Work on the frigates would stop if Algiers agreed to a purchased peace. Cost overruns and problems procuring materials prevented any real work on the frigates until 1795, but once the ships began to take shape, the dey of Algiers became more open to negotiations. On April 25, 1796, David Humphreys reported to Secretary of State Edmund Randolph that in exchange for slightly more than $600,000 in cash and materiel and a 36-gun warship, the dey would sign a peace treaty.[20]

The purchased peace with Algiers seemingly put an end to the navy discussion. Lawmakers pointed to the clause in calling for an end to construction of the warships should America make peace with the pirates as a reason to kill the U.S. Navy before it even hit the waves. The jobs the shipbuilding program created were popular, however, as word of the treaty with Algiers circulated, work continued on three of the frigates.

Washington, much to France's chagrin, declared neutrality when war once more broke out between America's ally and England. Neither country was particularly pleased to see Yankee merchant vessels plying the oceans. In Washington's opinion, the Europeans would only respect strength. "To secure respect to a neutral flag requires a naval force organized and ready to vindicate it from insult or aggression," he told Congress on December 6, 1796. "This may even prevent the necessity of going to war by discouraging belligerent powers from committing such violations of the rights of the neutral party as may, first and last, leave no other option. These considerations invite the United States to look to the means and to set about the gradual creation of a Navy."[21]

And there were problems in the Caribbean. When John Adams won election to the presidency, relations with France were in decline. By 1797 French privateers were seizing American merchantmen working the Caribbean. It was too much for Adams. America's economy depended on its trading fleets while her open shores seemed to invite invasion. He told Congress on May 16, 1797, it was time to act: "With a sea coast of near 2,000 miles in extent, opening a wide field for fisheries, navigation, and commerce, a great portion of our citizens naturally apply their industry and enterprise to these objects. Any serious and permanent injury to commerce would not fail to produce the most embarrassing disorders. To prevent it from being undermined and destroyed it is essential that it receive an adequate protection."[22]

The pirate attacks in the Caribbean, whether or not the French government endorsed them, infuriated America. When word leaked that a group of French diplomats solicited bribes to intercede on behalf of the United States, the American public saw this as little better than the acts of the Barbary Pirates and anti-French sentiment boiled over. Adams ordered the immediate completion of the six authorized ships. Merchants from Boston to Charleston got into the act as well, raising money and hiring shipwrights to build warships they then presented to the federal government. Among the best of these so-called subscription ships were the 38-gun *Philadelphia*, 32-gun *Essex*, and 24-gun *John Adams*.[23] In addition, Congress authorized Adams to outfit merchant vessels as warships as a stopgap measure to protect American merchant vessels in the Caribbean. The first were the leaky frigates *Ganges* and the equally ungainly *Montezuma*.[24]

The arrival of the fledgling U.S. Navy in the Caribbean in 1798 probably did not scare the French, at least not at first. Commo. John Barry, an aging Revolutionary War veteran, was in overall command. Under his guidance, the American ships slowly spread out across the sea, convoying merchant ships while searching for privateers.

Barry established a school at sea so his younger officers could learn their trade. Barry, at fifty-five, had plenty to teach his junior officers but was already suffering from bouts of asthma that would cause his death in 1801.

Decatur, Somers, and Stewart all served under Barry on board his flagship, the 44-gun frigate *United States*. James Barron, who in the future would play a pivotal role in Decatur's life, was the first lieutenant or executive officer. Stewart was the fourth lieutenant. Somers, who spent two years as a merchant seaman, was among the senior midshipmen.[25]

Barry was a genial man who believed in allowing his young charges to find their own way, albeit with some cajoling from the commodore. His senior commander, Capt. Thomas Truxtun, on the 36-gun *Constellation*, had a different approach. A stern disciplinarian, Truxtun looked to America's old enemy for his curriculum. He made no apologies for turning his back on French manuals, which were all the rage in the United States, and using British methods. He did so because, as he put it, the British knew how to win at sea: "Notwithstanding the prejudice that exists in our nation against the British government, for their spoliations and many unprovoked cruelties exhibited on our citizens, yet I think none can be so much so, as not to acknowledge them, at this time, the first maritime power on the globe, with respect to naval tactics, discipline, and the general management of ships of war; they are therefore a proper example for us to imitate in our infancy." He made Royal Navy standards the standards on the *Constellation* and exhorted his junior officers to apply themselves to their studies, especially in the art of gunnery.[26]

Truxtun's moves paid huge dividends when the *Constellation* fell in with the French frigate *Insurgente* on February 9, 1799, and pummeled the French ship into submission. Almost a year later, Truxtun and the *Constellation* pounded the 52-gun French frigate *Vengeance* to the point of surrender, but the French ship managed to sneak off under cover of darkness.

Decatur, Somers, and Stewart did not enjoy the same success. Their frigate, the *United States*, spent most of her time either convoying American trade vessels or searching in vain for French warships. Indeed, other than the *Constellation*, the vaunted American frigates accomplished very little. Instead, it was a pair of small ships, the schooners *Enterprise* and *Experiment*, that won the bulk of the victories in the Quasi-War with France. Together, the two schooners captured more French vessels than all of the American frigates combined.[27]

Lt. John Shaw, who served on the *Montezuma*, took command of the *Enterprise* in 1799. Lt. Charles Stewart left the *United States* to command the *Experiment*. These served as even better classrooms than the frigates for teaching the Navy's young officers how to command a ship. This was no accident. Secretary of the Navy Benjamin Stoddert was a huge advocate of a powerful navy. In a letter to Congress on February 9, 1799, the Marylander set out his own vision of the U.S. Navy: six 74-gun ships of the line, nine 44-gun frigates, three 32-gun frigates, twelve smaller vessels mounting 20–28 cannon, and nine sloops of war of 20 guns or fewer.[28] He also knew, however, that he would never get the money from Congress to build the type of fleet he believed the nation needed. Small ships, the Navy secretary said, not only could aid in the war against pirates and privateers, but also could act as schoolhouses for new officers. Although the senior officers all had experience in the Revolutionary War either as privateers or as regular officers in the Continental Navy, the junior officers were relatively inexperienced, with only merchant marine service under their belts.

Since he knew he would never have the size fleet he wanted, Stoddert wanted officers whose zeal and abilities could make up for a lack of numbers. The Quasi-War gave the Navy secretary the proving ground on which to essentially clear out the less-desirable political appointees and groom those who exhibited the qualities he wanted: "A spirit of enterprise and adventure cannot be too much encouraged. Bravery is a quality not to be dispensed with in the officers. Like charity, it covers a good many defects. If our officers cannot be inspired by the true kind of zeal and spirit which will enable us to make up for the want of great force by great activity, we had better burn our ships and commence a navy at some future time when our citizens have more spirit." The Navy's midshipmen, lieutenants, and lieutenant commandants, Stoddert said, would all benefit from "every day's experience" that would "add to the stock of knowledge" they already possessed.[29]

For Charles Stewart, command of the *Experiment* was his first chance to learn how to lead men on his own. Because the U.S. Navy, out of financial necessity, was relatively small, ships were likely to serve independently for long periods. Officers who could prove their ability to operate on their own were invaluable. Not every officer, however, was quite as sold on commanding a small schooner. Shaw, Stoddert's choice as commander of the *Enterprise*, did everything he could short of resigning to get out of his first independent command. An immigrant from Ireland, Shaw, like Stewart and Somers, was a veteran of merchant service. His service under Capt. Alexander Murray failed to impress on the young lieutenant the need for further learning. It did not take Shaw long to change his mind about commanding a smaller vessel, however. The *Enterprise* racked up win after win in the Caribbean, including the capture of the much larger *Flambeau*, a brig of 14 guns with a crew of 110 men. The *Flambeau* carried 9-pounders (against the *Enterprise*'s 6-pounders) but the skill of Shaw and his crew more than leveled the contest. The French suffered four dead and twenty-nine wounded—more than a third of their crew. The *Enterprise* had just two men wounded.[30]

At first reluctant to command a 135-ton schooner, Shaw soon realized what he could accomplish in the *Enterprise*, and jumped at the chance to have his own ship. He sent a letter off to his former commander, Captain Murray, of his change of heart and the pride he had in his new ship. Murray, in his reply dated January 22, 1800, congratulated his former third lieutenant: "I am very happy you have such a good command and am well convinced that the small fast sailing vessels are the most profitable to the Commanders."[31]

———◆—◆———

Murray would prove to be prophetic, although Congress, ever looking to contain the cost of a still-somewhat unpopular military, tried very hard to get rid of most of the Navy when the United States and France agreed on terms to end the undeclared naval war. By the beginning of 1801, the Navy had twenty-four ships, many of them subscription ships. With the war over, the lawmakers saw no reason for such a large naval establishment. Even Stoddert, who was a proponent of a large fleet, believed the nation should sell off many of its vessels while building more frigates and ships of the line.[32]

The end of the Quasi-War gave Congress and President John Adams the chance to swiftly downgrade America's fleet. The House and the Senate quickly approved the Peace Establishment Act of 1801 and ordered the Navy to sell off all but twelve ships.[33] Public outcry forced Congress to keep the *Enterprise*, bumping the final figure to thirteen, but the Navy duly sold off the *Experiment* and most of the subscription frigates.

The Peace Establishment Act also ordered the Navy to greatly reduce its ranks and put in place a rigid seniority system. Officers could only move up the chain of command as their superiors retired, resigned, or died. The Navy eliminated the Royal Navy–like ranks of lieutenant commandant and master commandant, settling for just three officer ratings—midshipman, lieutenant, and captain. The Act also slashed the total number of officers, sidelining many veterans of the conflict with France. Three officers that made the cut were lieutenants: Stephen Decatur, Richard Somers, and Charles Stewart.[34]

CHAPTER 2

INTO THE FRAY

MERICA FOUGHT ITS FIRST OVERSEAS WAR in 1801 after the ruler of Tripoli, a small-time tyrant with the grand-sounding title Bashaw Yusuf Karamanli, entered the grounds of the U.S. consulate, and chopped down the American flag.

Karamanli was angry about the amount of tribute the United States lavished on Tunis and Algiers to keep those cities from attacking American merchantmen. After hearing rumors of the amount of treasure the Americans gave his neighbors—and rivals—Karamanli summoned U.S. consul James Leander Cathcart to his palace. When the American diplomat arrived, Karamanli launched into a tirade. "The Bashaw observed that the United States made liberal presents to Algiers and Tunis, that he was informed of the particulars of all our negotiations, that he even had a list of the cargo which had arrived at Tunis, that it is worth a treasure," Cathcart told Secretary of State James Madison. He reported that Karamanli demanded to know, "Why does not the United States send me a voluntary present?" The bashaw blustered that he was responsible for the treaties the new nation had with the other Barbary states, saying he intervened on America's behalf with the dey of Algiers and the prince of Tunis. He said America insulted him by paying him "almost nothing in comparison to what I have received from other nations. I have cruisers as well as Tunis and as good Raises [admirals] and sailors," he told Cathcart. "I am an independent prince as well as the Bashaw of Tunis and I can hurt the commerce of any nation as much as the Tunisians."[1]

The threats did not work. The Americans refused to increase the tribute payments to Karamanli, and the Tripolitan leader promptly declared war on the United States.[2] In the past, the threats and belligerent tone were enough to make the American government find a way to fork over more tribute. Karamanli, however, had not counted on Thomas Jefferson.

Unlike George Washington and John Adams, who made overtures of fighting but in the end paid off the pirates, Jefferson actually wanted an excuse to attack them. As early as 1786, when Jefferson was America's minister to France, he conjured the idea of a coalition "of several powers" that would once and for all end the threat of the "piratical states of Barbary."[3]

Now he had his chance. America would not pay tribute. He would use the Navy to "reduce the barbarians of Tripoli to the desire of peace on proper terms."[4]

—◆ ◆—

The Mediterranean world into which the U.S. Navy sailed was a mix of the old and the new. Potentates ruled with the power of medieval lords—locally—while still paying at least lip service to greater powers.

The Barbary States was a collection of Muslim territories that were little more than city-states. Algiers was the largest and most powerful of the Barbary powers. Algerian raids on American commerce brought about the creation of the U.S. Navy, although diplomats managed to buy off the pirates before a shooting war broke out.[5]

After Algiers in size came Morocco. The emperor of Morocco, Muley Soliman, ruled from Tangiers as the head of the lone truly independent nation among the Barbary states. The others, including Algiers, swore allegiance to the sultan—or "Grand Signor"—of the Ottoman Empire. The sultan, however, ruled from Constantinople, and though the Barbary States sent him annual "gifts," he had little real influence over them. Jefferson summed up the relationship between the North African leaders and the sultan, saying they "did indeed acknowledge a certain dependence on the Porte [sultan], and availed themselves of it whenever any thing was to be gained by it, but disregarded it when it subjected them to any demand."[6]

Morocco was the first nation in the Mediterranean to recognize the United States, signing a peace treaty with the new nation in 1786. Although he expected annual tribute, the emperor in Tangiers was more neutral than hostile toward America. Tribute and treaties, however, did little to guarantee the emperor's goodwill, as Commo. Edward Preble would learn upon his arrival in the Mediterranean.

Tunis and Tripoli were the smallest of the Barbary states and among the more bellicose. Petty jealousy drove the princes of those cities—the bey of Tunis and the bashaw of Tripoli—to continually threaten to unleash their corsairs on unarmed American merchantmen. Tripoli was especially hostile to just about any country that did not treat it as well as it treated neighboring states.

When the United States chose tribute over war with Algiers in 1795, it was up to U.S. consul David Humphreys to pay the dey. The former colonel in the Continental Army was not happy with his task. He warned Secretary of State Timothy Pickering the Algiers treaty would no doubt inspire the other states to seek more tribute from America: "I make no comment nor will I attempt to express my feeling because words would do injustice to them. In case the business with Algiers should be finally adjusted, there is little probability the negotiation with Tunis (a State, whose corsairs, like at Oran, would be with Algiers equally dangerous to the navigation of the U.S. in the Mediterranean) could be accomplished for less sum than between $200,000 and $300,000."[7]

For the Barbary States, piracy paid. Whether it was proceeds from grabbing unarmed merchantmen or the tribute nations paid for the promise of unmolested passage in the Mediterranean, piracy made the rulers along North Africa wealthy. It was a long-standing way of earning an income for the Barbary States, one none of the rulers intended to give up.

European nations started paying tribute to the Barbary States in the seventeenth century, believing it was easier to buy off the pirates than it was to fight them. The practice would continue for more than two hundred years, although England, France, Denmark, Portugal, Spain, Sweden, and finally the United States went to war with one or more of the states from time to time.

Commo. Edward Preble got a firsthand look at the convoluted nature of Barbary politics when he arrived on station in October of 1803. While sailing toward the Mediterranean, the commodore passed the Moroccan frigate *Maimona*. The commodore stopped the Arab vessel and checked her papers, which granted a passport for a voyage to Portugal. Since everything was in order, Preble had little choice but to let the 30-gun frigate proceed. However, he knew Muley Soliman, the emperor at Tangiers, was making warlike noises against the United States as he sought better terms for maintaining the peace.

When he arrived in Gibraltar, Preble found two Moroccan ships in American custody, the 24-gun frigates *Mirboka* and *Meshouda*. The *Meshouda* was an old friend of sorts to the Navy and presented a problem for Preble. Supposedly a Tripolitan warship, the *Meshouda* now flew the Moroccan flag. The Americans, however, caught the ship, loaded with war supplies, as she tried to slip into Tripoli.

The emperor wanted both ships back, along with apologies and reparations. It was, the commodore learned, just another day in the political life of the Barbary States.[8]

Preble, however, was not like any other naval officer the Barbary leaders had met. He had a mission and a plan and intended to bring the war right to the Barbary States. He was just the right man for Jefferson who was frustrated with his naval commanders after failures of two previous squadrons to defeat the pirates.

———◆———

Hostilities between Tripoli and the United States broke out officially after Karamanli declared war by entering the grounds of the U.S. embassy and chopping down the American flag on May 14, 1801. President Jefferson, expecting trouble with the bashaw, had dispatched the first squadron of American ships to the Mediterranean two weeks earlier, on May 2, 1801. He put Commo. Richard Dale in command. Dale was the first lieutenant on the USS *Bonhomme Richard* when John Paul Jones captured the British frigate *Serapis*. That, however, had been in 1779. Dale, now forty-seven, no longer had the same fire.[9]

The old commodore arrived on station with the 44-gun frigate *President*, the 38-gun *Philadelphia* and 32-gun *Essex*—both subscription ships—and the *Enterprise*. Dale's squadron spent nearly a year off Tripoli but accomplished almost nothing. He kept the *Philadelphia* and *Essex* busy on escort or guard duty while he used the *President* and *Enterprise* to enforce a blockade of sorts of the bashaw's harbor. Dale prevented Tripolitan ships from grabbing American ships, but failed to scare the bashaw into making peace.

The American campaign against Tripoli did little to improve European, especially British, opinion of the U.S. Navy. Jefferson gave Dale orders—and the leeway—to bring the fight right to the bashaw. He could, the president said, "Chastise their insolence by sinking, burning or destroying their ships and vessels wherever you find them."[10] The old commodore, however, did little to trouble the pirates. The lone bright spot was Andrew Sterrett and the *Enterprise*.

Dale and his fleet set sail from Hampton Roads, Virginia, on June 2, 1801. While the heavy frigates labored across the Atlantic, Sterrett and the *Enterprise* danced across the waves. The squadron commander, rather than hold the schooner back, ordered Sterrett to take the *Enterprise* to Gibraltar and await his arrival.[11]

The *Enterprise* needed just twenty-five days to make it to the gateway of the Mediterranean, arriving at the British bastion June 27. As Sterrett pulled into the harbor, he saw two of the biggest ships in the Tripolitan navy.

The larger of the two was the 28-gun *Meshouda*, which started her life as the brig *Betsey* out of Boston. Moroccan corsairs captured her in 1794 and released her, at which point Tripoli grabbed her. Murad Reis, the high admiral of Tripoli's fleet, turned the *Betsey* into a ship of war, converting her to a schooner and arming her with 28 guns. He also painted her a variety of colors, from green to yellow to white, while painting the muzzles of her guns red. The smaller of the two ships was a 14-gun brig that was only slightly less garish.[12]

The discovery of the two ships created a conflict within Sterrett. His first impulse was to attack both ships. However, since the Tripolitans were in a neutral harbor, he knew he could not. Instead he kept himself ready for action and cruised just outside the harbor entrance, waiting to see if Reis would accept the American's clear challenge to come out and fight.

This was not mere bravado.

Sterrett had served on *Constellation* under Truxtun in the French conflict. When the *Constellation* battled the *Insurgente*, Sterrett commanded a gun division on the frigate. In the heat of the battle, he saw one of his men cringing in a corner. When the seaman refused to fight, Sterrett applied his own brand of discipline, later writing to his brother Charles, "One fellow I was obliged to run through the body with my sword and so put an end to a coward. You must not think this strange, for we would put a man to death for even looking pale on board this ship."[13]

Sterrett established his one-schooner blockade and challenged the Barbary captains to fight him. The Tripolitans refused to move and Sterrett awaited the arrival of Dale's flotilla. He did not have long to wait. Dale reached Gibraltar July 2 and the commodore questioned Reis as to his intentions.

The wily Tripolitan lied to Dale, saying Tripoli and the United States were not at war. Dale, to his credit, did not believe the "admiral." In his report to Secretary of the Navy Samuel Smith, Dale wrote, "From every information I can get here Tripoli is at war with the United States." He ordered Capt. Samuel Barron—James' older brother—and the subscription frigate *Philadelphia* to remain at Gibraltar to keep an eye on the Tripolitan and "take him when he goes out."[14]

The American ships set up their so-called blockade of Tripoli on July 9. For the young lieutenant commandant and the crew of the *Enterprise*, nothing was worse than the boredom of blockade duty. Plus, Dale often used the schooner, with her speed, as a courier and supply vessel, which at least relieved the monotony of sailing back and forth across the mouth of Tripoli harbor but did little else, since there was little chance of action. On August 1, 1801, Dale ordered the quick schooner to head to Malta for water. Sterrett set sail for the British base around dawn.

In keeping with Dale's orders "[n]ot to hoist any colors but English while at sea," Sterrett raised the Union Jack to fool any Tripolitan cruisers into thinking he was a British, not American, warship.[15] It was a common ruse. The rules of war allowed a vessel to fly another country's flag provided it ran up its true colors before opening fire. U.S. ships often flew British and Dutch flags to create confusion among possible enemies.[16]

As Sterrett slipped out of the harbor, he sighted a strange sail on the horizon. Although he could not see what kind of vessel it was in the gloomy predawn light, he could tell she was a square-rigger that was battling headwinds.

The *Enterprise* began a series of easy tacks, using her fore-and-aft rig to quickly make up ground on the unknown vessel. The crew was more than ready. Lt. David Porter, Sterrett's first lieutenant, handled the schooner so well she was within hailing distance of the strange ship in just three hours.

Sterrett, still flying the Union Jack, called out to the mysterious ship, asking her captain who she was and what she was doing. Sterrett quickly noticed the unknown vessel carried 14 guns, 2 more guns than his own command.

Undeterred by the size or strength difference, Sterrett ran in closer when he received no reply to his hails. This time, the mysterious captain replied he was Adm. Rais Mohammed Rous, commanding the 14-gun brig *Tripoli*. Believing Sterrett to be British, the Tripolitan added he was out hunting for American merchantmen but could not find any.

Sterrett's reply was swift.

He lowered the British flag and raised the Stars and Stripes while ordering his men to quarters. Gun crews ran their cannon out while Marines and other sailors seized muskets and rifles and ran to their stations. The *Tripoli* answered with a ragged volley that missed the *Enterprise*. It was 9:00 a.m.[17]

The Tripolitan response was about what Sterrett had expected. Although the *Tripoli* outgunned the American ship 14 to 12 and had a larger crew, Sterrett had little respect for his opponent. Unlike the American skipper, who drilled his crew into shape especially when it came to artillery, the Tripolitans tended to pay scant attention to gunnery. The corsairs preferred to close in and board rather than engage in a slugfest.

After the first Tripolitan volley missed, the *Enterprise* answered with a well-aimed broadside that shook the corsair to the keel. The *Tripoli* attempted to veer off only to have the *Enterprise* tack behind and rake her with broadside after broadside. Admiral Rous then tried to close with the *Enterprise* to board her. The *Tripoli* bore up alongside the *Enterprise*, but just as the Barbary corsairs were about to leap onto the deck, the ship's Marines, led by Lt. Enoch Lane, ripped their ranks with a volley.

The *Tripoli* again bore off as the *Enterprise* continued to pound her with well-aimed broadsides. Sterrett's gunners smashed the *Tripoli*'s masts and punched holes through her hull. Suddenly, the Tripolitans ceased fire and lowered their colors. The crew of the *Enterprise* gave three cheers and closed in to claim their prize. However, just as Sterrett was about to come alongside the *Tripoli*, Rous reraised his colors and attempted to board the schooner.

The tactic enraged Sterrett. He ordered his Marines to sweep the Tripoli's decks with musket fire, which they did to telling effect. The *Enterprise* bore off but continued to hammer away at the brig. The schooner's relatively small guns—just 6-pound cannon—caused damage but failed to completely cripple the Tripolitan ship.

This response did not stop the pirate captain from trying his surrender ruse a second time. Rous again lowered his flag, but this time Sterrett kept his distance. When the Barbary captain raised his colors for a second time and opened fire once more, Sterrett ordered his gunners to pound the *Tripoli* into oblivion.

The *Enterprise* moved off to a distance of about fifty yards and for the next hour mercilessly hammered the Barbary vessel. The little 6-pound guns punched more than eighteen holes into the *Tripoli* at or just below the water-line and toppled her mainmast. Just before noon, Rous again called out for quarter. Sterrett, however, refused until the Tripolitan, in an act of desperation, ripped down his own flag and threw it into the sea. As Lt. David Porter put it, "Sterrett, listening to the voice of humanity, even after such perfidious conduct, ordered the captain to come himself or to send some of officers onboard the Enterprise."[18]

Rous, who was wounded, could not go to the schooner to surrender. The effective fire of the *Enterprise* had smashed every small boat on board his brig. Sterrett ordered Porter to take a boarding party to the Tripoli; what he found there shocked him.

"The crew of the Tripolitans was discovered to be in the most deplorable state," Porter told the *National Intelligencer and Advance*, a newspaper in Washington, DC. "Out of eighty men, 20 are dead and 30 wounded. Among the killed were the second lieutenant and surgeon; among the wounded were the captain and first lieutenant. And so decisive was the fire of *Enterprise* that the Tripolitans were found to be in a most perilous condition, having received 18 shot between wind and water."[19]

The actual toll, according to Sterrett's later report, was higher: thirty dead and thirty wounded.

As for the *Enterprise*, "We have not had a man wounded and we have sustained no material damage to our hull or rigging," Sterrett said.[20]

The *Enterprise* crew made sure Rous and his cruiser could never again threaten American shipping. Dale, in his standing orders to his subordinate, told Sterrett there was just one way to deal with the pirate: "Heave all his guns overboard, cut away his masts and rigging and leave him in a situation that he can just make out to get into some port." Sterrett's crew followed that order with gusto, the *Enterprise* commander reported, telling the commodore, "Agreeably to your orders I dismantled her of everything but an old sail and spar—with heartfelt pleasure." The crippled cruiser limped into Tripoli harbor where the enraged leader of the city stripped Rous of his rank and publicly whipped him.[21]

It was the first, and for that year the only, victory America could celebrate over the Barbary pirates. The credit, Sterrett said, belonged to the "officers and men throughout the vessel [who] behaved in the most spirited and determined manner, obeying every command with promptitude and alertness."[22]

Sterrett's victory over the *Tripoli* was all Dale could call a success during his time in the Mediterranean. The commodore's feeble blockade of Tripoli harbor did little to stop the bashaw from sending shallow-draft craft in and out of his fortress. The *Philadelphia* remained at Gibraltar all summer, keeping an eye on the *Meshouda*. William Bainbridge with the subscription frigate *Essex* was off on his own, trying to shepherd American merchantmen. The squadron commander kept the *President* busy moving from British base to British base, sometimes blockading Tripoli. Dale, meanwhile, returned to the United States in September on the *President*. The frigate, hastily finished in 1799, needed work and his crew enlistment was about to run out.

Dale left the *Enterprise* behind with the two subscription ships. His exit put Samuel Barron in charge of the three remaining vessels. The ineffectiveness of the blockade only increased European snickering at the American force. Britain, France, Portugal, and Spain all paid tribute to the Barbary powers, mostly because it was easier than sending much-needed naval or land forces to fight them. The inability of the American squadron to force Karamanli to the bargaining table seemingly proved to the Europeans it was better to buy off the pirates. In the eyes of the Europeans, especially the British, it showed that the new American Navy was not much of a threat. Morris accomplished even less than Dale during his time in command, turning the American blockade into a farce. The fledgling U.S. Navy was increasingly mocked by both the French and British.[23] Jefferson was becoming increasingly impatient.[24] He was not alone.

William Eaton, the consul in Tunis, chafed at every delay and at every report of a ship entering or leaving Tripoli harbor. He became so exasperated he dashed off a heated letter to Commodore Morris in which he blasted the Navy for not taking strong enough action against Tripoli. "What! Is there no blood in American veins?" he wrote. "Are we incapable of blushing?"[25]

Jefferson was just as eager for progress in the campaign against Tripoli. He took time, however, to pen a congratulatory note to Sterrett after the victory over the *Tripoli*. In it, the president told the young lieutenant, "Too long, for the honor of nations, have those barbarians been suffered to trample on the sacred faith of treaties, on the rights and laws of human nature! You have shown to your countrymen that the enemy cannot meet skill and bravery united. In proving to them that our past condescensions were from a love of peace, not a dread of them, you have deserved well of your country."[26]

Morris' grand tour approach to commanding the squadron worsened the Navy's reputation. The commodore finally blockaded the harbor near the end of the time in command. About the only accomplishment to which Morris and Dale could point that was of any lasting effect was to goad Congress into authorizing smaller ships.

Almost immediately after he returned from the Mediterranean, Dale—along with Morris, who took his time readying the new squadron—lobbied Congress for small ships. Both commodores favored brigs. The two-masted ships were common enough as merchant vessels. However, with the innovations of shipwrights Josiah Fox, James Hackett, and Joshua Humphreys, American-built brigs came into their own as warships. Although square-rigged, the brigs also carried enough fore-and-aft sails to allow them to operate closer to the wind than the larger frigates.

Congress agreed, although, as they always did, the lawmakers saw brigs as a more economical choice rather than as a tactical advantage. Jefferson received authorization for three brigs and made Sterrett his first choice to command one of the new vessels. Jefferson also requested more schooners, seizing on the success of the *Enterprise*. Those decisions would provide the vessels that came to form the backbone of the third U.S. force to sail for the Mediterranean.

During Morris' time in command, it was the little *Enterprise* that again scored the squadron's lone victory, this time with help from the frigate *John Adams*. The *Enterprise*, now under the command of Isaac Hull, was patrolling inside Tripoli harbor when Hull spotted a ship apparently trying to run the blockade. He signaled to John Rodgers on the *John Adams* and on June 22, 1803, the two cornered a 22-gun xebec, a lateen-rigged sailing vessel also equipped with oars; it was among the biggest cruisers in the bashaw's fleet. The *Enterprise* moved in close to shore to cut off landward reinforcements while the *John Adams* opened fire from deeper water. The crew of the Arab craft abandoned ship and the xebec exploded just before 10:00 p.m. The *Enterprise* and *John Adams* suffered no casualties.[27]

The victory was enough to convince the Department of the Navy and Congress of the need for small warships. Robert Smith, who took over as the secretary of the Navy from his brother, Samuel, on July 27, 1801, asked for and received the funds for four new vessels—two brigs and two schooners. The Navy secretary decided to build three of the vessels, the brigs *Argus* and *Syren*, and the schooner *Vixen*. The fourth vessel, the schooner *Nautilus*, Smith bought from a Baltimore merchant.[28]

CHAPTER 3

PREBLE

COMMO. EDWARD PREBLE LOOKED like a sea captain. A shade over six feet tall, trim and muscular, Preble grew up a sailor and a hunter and had a reputation as a no-nonsense but successful mariner. Born on August 15, 1761, in Falmouth, Massachusetts (now Portland, Maine), he was the ninth of twelve children of Brig. Gen. Jedidiah Preble. The Preble patriarch was a veteran of the French and Indian War, where he fought alongside the British. In the years after the war, Jedidiah Preble slowly amassed a prosperous business that included farms, stores, and ships.

As a boy, the younger Preble was prone to temper tantrums and showed at an early age a preference for hunting and fishing over school. His father, however, made sure Edward, like all his sons, received an education. At age fourteen Edward had the choice of going on to Harvard or entering business, but fate, in the form of the Revolutionary War, intervened. Jedidiah Preble by this time was a member of the Massachusetts assembly, where he represented his district of Maine, then part of the Bay State. With his father gone and his older brothers off serving in the war, the job of running the family farm fell to Edward, a job he did not like.

By 1778 farming had driven Preble right to the edge: one day he simply threw down his hoe and headed off to sea. Preble signed on as a deckhand on the privateer *Hope* before sailing in the same capacity on the merchant vessel *Merrimack* working the West Indies trade. Then, with barely two years of experience under his belt and thanks in large part to his father's influence, Preble landed an appointment as an acting midshipman on the Massachusetts State Navy frigate, *Protector*. She was a 26-gun ship and the pride of the Bay State fleet, which Massachusetts ran independently of the Continental Navy.

Preble spent most of the year on the state vessel, cruising the New England coast and the Caribbean. On May 26, 1780, lookouts on the

Protector spotted a strange sail off the coast of Cape Race, Newfoundland. The American approached the stranger. Each flew a British flag. Once in range, however, the *Protector* ran up the American colors and opened fire on the approaching ship, the *Admiral Duff*, a 32-gun armed merchantman out of Jamaica. John Foster Williams, captain of the *Protector*, handled his vessel ably, keeping the wind while blasting away at the British vessel. After exchanging broadsides for nearly ninety minutes, the British vessel caught fire then blew up. The *Protector* then plucked fifty-five survivors out of the icy waters and began to make her way back toward Boston.

For Preble, this first taste of combat ended in victory but its laurels were quickly overshadowed. During that voyage the prisoners passed on a fever to the Americans. By the time the *Protector* reached Boston on Preble's nineteenth birthday, nearly the entire crew was sick with the mystery ailment. Sick with fever, Preble remained on land until December, when he and the *Protector* sailed out on a commerce-raiding expedition. Joining Edward on the voyage was his brother Joshua as an acting midshipman.

The *Protector* sailed first for Nova Scotia then headed south toward the West Indies. On May 3, the Bay State vessel was off Block Island, where she ran into a pair of British frigates, including the 44-gun *Roebuck*. Captain Williams was unable to escape from his much stronger opponents and he struck his colors. The British took Preble and most of the crew captive. The crew found themselves languishing in the notorious prison hulk *Jersey* in New York.

Once more, Preble's family connections came to his aid. His father contacted a well-known Loyalist then living in New York and asked him to intervene on the boy's behalf, and on July 24 the British exchanged Preble for a captive English officer. Preble returned to Boston on July 26, 1781, and remained there until 1782, when he shipped out on the new Massachusetts State cruiser *Winthrop*. Preble served on the *Winthrop* until the end of the Revolutionary War, Among his exploits on the *Winthrop* was commanding a boarding party that snatched an English brig during a raid in Penobscot Bay.

He spent the next sixteen years as a merchant sailor, eventually rising to command his own vessels. When Congress authorized creation of the U.S. Navy in 1794, Preble applied for an appointment as a lieutenant. After the United States bought its peace with the Algerian pirates, work on the Navy slowed to a crawl and Preble remained in merchant service. By the winter of 1797–1798, Preble was a somewhat well-to-do merchant captain with a reputation for running a tight ship and for always making a profit. The lure of profit nearly kept Preble from accepting his commission when it finally came on April 9, 1798. He was supposed to join the *Constitution* under Capt. Samuel Nicholson. His business dealings, however, kept him busy, and instead Preble took command of the brig-of-war *Pickering*.[1]

The *Pickering* made a pair of cruises to the Caribbean under Preble's command, but aside from convoying merchant vessels, the ship saw little action. Preble, however, was impressive enough as her skipper that Congress approved his appointment as a full captain on June 7, 1799. He received command of the newly built 32-gun *Essex*, a subscription frigate the merchants of Salem built for the Navy. His first cruise on the *Essex* took him to the other side of the world. The *Essex* was bound for Java, where she would become the first U.S. warship in the East Indies. Preble had orders to protect the U.S. merchantmen on their way back from the Orient, a small but increasingly valuable segment of U.S. trade.

The *Essex* set out with the frigate *Congress* on January 6, 1800, for the distant Dutch colonies of Java and Batavia in the Pacific Ocean. It would be a long trip. Preble was older than all of his officers save one and had a very low opinion of his subordinates, a sentiment the crew returned. Floggings were common, and the ship's Marine detachment appeared to be a favorite target of the skipper.

Lt. James Porter, commander of the Marines on the *Essex*, told Corps commandant Lt. Colonel William Burrows he believed the Navy should sack the taciturn and volatile captain, questioning many of Preble's punishments and blaming the captain for a high number of desertions: "As a commander he ought to have known better and my remonstrating with him would avail but little. I will venture to say there is not an officer or a man of the [ship's company] that will ever go with him again."[2]

There was, however, another side to the stern sea captain. Before he left on his epic voyage, Preble took time out from his duties to win Mary Deering. To claim the heart of his intended, Preble went right to Mary's mother, a wealthy widow and mother of a close friend. In a letter to Mary's mother, Dorcas Deering, dated December 17, 1799, Preble poured out his heart—and his desire: "You have long known of my attachment to your lovely daughter and I feel truly sensible of the delicacy with which you have ever attended to my feelings. Could my lovely friend know how much I suffer from the thought of so long an absence from her for whom alone I wish to live, I am sure she would pity me. Give my best love to her and tell her the future happiness of my life rests with her and the God of all goodness restore to me the joys of loved society and bless me with her affection." He ended his note with a quick postscript: "Should Mary Deering bless another with her affections, and not me, I am lost forever. For heaven's sake, plead for me."[3]

The *Essex* sailed in unison with the *Congress* for four days until a storm separated the two. The *Essex* was a faster sailer than the *Congress*, and on

January 12, 1800, Preble made course toward Cape Town, South Africa, the prearranged meeting place in case the two frigates became separated. Reaching his destination two months later on March 12, Preble waited for the *Congress* for two weeks, not knowing a storm had ravaged the other frigate. He finally left Cape Town on March 27 and headed toward Java and the East Indies, arriving at the Dutch colony in early May.

Preble soon heard reports of a French privateer prowling the area, the *Confiance*. The *Essex* chased the French ship, even exchanged shots with her, but could never quite catch her. The *Essex* managed to at least scare the Frenchman away, and as May turned to June, began rounding up American merchant vessels to build a convoy for the voyage back to America. The *Essex* left the East Indies on June 24 and finally pulled into New York Harbor on November 28. Three weeks later, Preble left for Falmouth, where he completed his courtship of Mary Deering.

When the *Essex* arrived in Java in May 1800, she was the first American warship to sail into that area of the Pacific. His arrival there also marked the start of Preble's health problems. The thirty-nine-year-old New Englander contracted a stomach illness, most likely a parasite. By the time he returned from a brief honeymoon after marrying Mary in April, Preble could barely move. "The present state of my health . . . is very much impaired," he wrote to Secretary of the Navy Samuel Smith in April 1801. "A vegetable and milk diet and gentle equestrian exercise" seemed, to Preble the most likely path to recovery from his affliction.[4] He was optimistic that he would recover in "three or four" months, but he struggled with his ailment for nearly two years. He did not return to duty until the summer of 1803, when Jefferson put him in charge of the third attempt to end North African piracy.[5]

Charged with this daunting task, the forty-three-year-old commodore had a difficult time just getting his force together and wanted the entire flotilla to set off at one time. President Jefferson, however, ordered the ships to sail one at a time as they became ready for sea, and when Preble took command of the *Constitution* in May 1803, the frigate was barely seaworthy. The 44-gun ship needed a lengthy overhaul and Preble did not arrive on station until September.

As he made the seven-week transit across the Atlantic, Preble took a hard look at the men he commanded, and did not like what he saw. The commodore was an old-school disciplinarian in a new service that was still trying to find its way. Most of Preble's officers had served under either genial John Barry or straight-laced Thomas Truxtun. Barry used a gentle hand to guide his new officers, turning a blind eye when they went a bit overboard with their aggressiveness—toward the French and each other—while shaping them to understand the need for teamwork.[6] Truxtun was a different sort. A privateer during the Revolution, Truxtun looked to the Royal Navy for his inspiration when it came to discipline and how to run a warship. Under him, many of Preble's young officers first learned ways to command men at sea and the intricacies of sailing and fighting a man-of-war. Under Barry, young officers such as Stephen Decatur, Isaac Hull, Charles Stewart, and Richard Somers could ask "Why?" and Barry would explain his reasoning. Truxtun was a bit more straightforward, telling his men what to do and explaining the reason almost as an afterthought. Neither approach worked for Preble.

Preble was similar to Truxtun on board ship, although he lacked the former commodore's deft touch with the men. Under Preble, orders were orders and an officer or seaman carried them out or faced the consequences. He quickly squelched any thoughts among his junior officers that the free-wheeling days of John Barry would survive under his command. He did not care whether his young officers understood the reason for an order, as long as they obeyed. As Midn. Charles Morris put it, "A very violent temper and easily excited temper was one of the prominent characteristics of Commodore Preble, from the undue expression of which, when he was greatly excited, no officer could escape. Irresolution, no less than contradiction, was an offense in his eyes, and decision of action as well as obedience of orders was necessary to preserve his favorable opinion."[7]

Preble's style did not endear him to his officers, not that Preble cared. In a letter to his wife, Preble raged he had "nothing but a pack of boys" to command. "A great disproportion of them are boys lightly deserving of any attention," Preble wrote. "They do not know discipline and do not understand it." To make matters worse, most of his officers came from the mid-Atlantic or southern states. Their accents and mannerisms were all but foreign to Preble, who called Maine home.[8] The young officers were excitable, individualistic, and prone to dueling. During the wide-open days of the Quasi-War, that was fine. Now, however, Preble was in charge and to his officers, the old man was a tyrant.

Preble issued a list of 106 standing orders, among them how the sailors should dress and talk. He outlawed swearing and the *Constitution* logbook is full of descriptions of punishments. The reasons for floggings varied. Marine corporal James Wallace received thirty-six lashes for a botched attempt to fumigate the ship. It was not that Preble was angry about the fumigation attempt: he was angry that Wallace tried to fumigate the *Constitution* on his own hook rather than with the commodore's permission. Wallace nearly set the *Constitution* on fire with his abortive fumigation try and Preble punished him accordingly. The Marine received twelve lashes for "attempting to fumigate any part of the ship without regular orders, 12 lashes for neglect of duty and 12 lashes for causing rope yarns to blaze."[9]

Another crewman to run afoul of the commodore's temper was Able SN Hugh McCormick, who enlisted in New York in July of 1803. During the passage across the Atlantic, Preble found McCormick guilty of neglect of duty and gave him twelve lashes. On October 20, when the *Constitution* was in Gibraltar, McCormick attempted to desert but the ship's guards caught him. Preble clapped him in irons and held him in the brig until December 9, when he allowed McCormick to rejoin the crew.[10]

Irritable and quick to anger, Preble nevertheless was still the same man that romanced his wife, and, in his own way, was fair. Morris discovered just how fair Preble could be while loading supplies on the flagship before her voyage to the Mediterranean. Morris did not have enough men to load the supplies, so he asked the commodore how many more he could pull from the *Constitution*'s crew. He said he "received the reply, in no mild tone: 'None. Get your men where you can find them.' I thought best to take him at his word and engaged 10 or 12 men, and when the work was completed presented to the Commodore for approval an account for their wages. This produced another outbreak, with the inquiry as to how I dared to incur such an expense without his orders; but on being reminded of his former conversation he gave his signature and dismissed me with courtesy."[11]

Like other captains, Preble often prowled the weatherside of the quarterdeck. One of the idiosyncrasies the crew of the *Constitution* quickly came to respect was his tendency to do it alone. His officers knew disturbing him risked earning his wrath, but they were never sure what else might touch off the old man's rage. They also did not know what to expect from Preble once the entire squadron arrived in the Mediterranean.

They found out as they neared Gibraltar. When the *Constitution* rounded Cape Trafalgar on the approach to the British bastion on September 10, she came across a strange vessel. Lookouts told Preble they could see lanterns in the distance and the commodore ran to the quarterdeck.

He grabbed a hailing trumpet and called out, "What ship is that?"

Nothing. The shape in the darkness came closer. Preble hailed again and again received no reply. The commodore's temper rose.

"I hail you for the last time," he shouted. "If you do not answer, I'll fire a shot into you."

"If you fire, I will return a broadside," a voice sang out, but Preble wouldn't back down.

"I'd like to see you do it," Preble said. "I now hail you for an answer. What ship is that?"

The same voice rang out, "This is His Britannic Majesty's ship *Donegal*, 84 guns; Sir Richard Strahan, an English commodore. Send your boat on board."

The reply sparked Preble's rage. No one, not even the commander of a much larger warship, was going to order the Maine native to come or go at a whim. Preble leaped to the mizzen shrouds and thundered back, "This is the United States ship *Constitution*, 44 guns, Edward Preble an American commodore, who will be damned before he sends his boat on board any vessel. Blow your matches, boys." This last command stunned the crews of both ships. "Blow your matches"[12] was the order to his gun captains to prepare to fire. Preble kept the *Constitution* on a constant war footing and her guns were always ready for a fight.

The English ship, it turned out, was not quite as prepared. As the *Constitution*'s gunners blew on their matches—a length of three-eighths-inch-thick rope set on a pole that slowly burned—a boat suddenly appeared alongside.

It was not an 84-gun ship of the line. Instead, the vessel in the darkness was the 32-gun British frigate *Maidstone*. Hailing from the Americas, her officer explained, she was caught by surprise and her captain needed time to clear for action. That explained the initial delay in hailing. *Maidstone*'s captain, Cdr. George Elliot, sent his apologies and congratulated Preble for his readiness.[13]

For the commodore, that ended the affair. For the crew, though, it was an awakening. Preble may have a nasty temper, but he made the *Constitution* into a warship. The crew knew its tasks and did them well. The officers, despite their youth, were learning how to harness their energy.

As for Preble, his junior officers realized the old man had steel in him after all. He was ready to fight a ship twice the size of the *Constitution*. The commodore was quick to anger but just as quick with praise. Here was a commander who wanted action as much as they did.[14]

The men's estimation of their commodore rose even more when midshipmen Ralph Izard and Henry Wadsworth told them how Preble settled affairs with Morocco.

Despite being the first nation to recognize the United States, Morocco, in the autumn of 1803, was making noise as if it planned to plunder U.S.-flagged shipping.[15] The emperor had several warships at sea and Preble's squadron captured two of them. In addition to the *Mirboka*, the Americans grabbed the *Meshouda*, a former Boston-based brig corsair that Tripoli had captured in 1784 and turned into a warship. The bashaw had presented the *Meshouda* to Morocco as a gift in the 1790s, and the emperor wanted it back from the Americans. There also was the curious case of the *Maimona*, the 30-gun frigate Preble believed was already in the Atlantic, hunting American merchant ships.

Preble arrived in Tangiers on September 16 with the *Constitution* and *John Adams*, the frigate *New York*, and the schooner *Nautilus*. He went on shore with U.S. consul Tobias Lear, Capt. John Rodgers, and two other officers to discuss the problem with Morocco. The commodore, however, made sure the emperor knew he was an American naval officer. He refused to remove his sword and refused to kneel in the emperor's presence despite repeated orders to do so. The emperor finally asked Preble, "Are you not afraid of being arrested?" "No sir," the commodore replied, "If you presume to do it, my squadron in your full view will lay your batteries, your castles and your city in ruins."[16]

Preble was not bluffing. He had left orders on the *Constitution* for every ship to remain cleared for action. Sailing Master Haraden recorded the instructions in the flagship's log: "If the least injury is offered to my person, immediately attack the batteries, the castle, the city, and the troops, regardless of my personal safety."[17]

The emperor backed down, pledged his eternal friendship, and showered Preble with gifts. The officers of the squadron took notice. First, the old man was ready to fight a British ship of the line, and now he stared down an entire country. This Preble, they realized, just might be the right man to lead them.[18]

CHAPTER 4

ASSEMBLY POINT

THE U.S. FRIGATE *CONSTITUTION* sliced through the water as she sailed past Sardinia, a large island off the Italian coast in the Mediterranean Sea, on November 24, 1803. The 44-gun flagship of the U.S. Mediterranean squadron was on a westerly heading, and the winds out of the north had her on a broad reach. The moderate breeze filled every sail and pushed the big 44-gun frigate along at nine knots. Commo. Edward Preble stood alongside his sailing master, Nathaniel Haraden, and watched his crew at work.[1]

Preble was on his way to Syracuse on the island of Sicily, where he planned to establish his main base. The commander of the American Mediterranean squadron had just left Tangiers, Morocco, where he had convinced the emperor to abide by his 1786 peace treaty with the United States. After resupplying in Syracuse, he planned to lead his squadron against the pirate stronghold of Tripoli.[2]

Although sailing alone, the 44-gun frigate was part of a larger flotilla. In addition to the *Constitution*, Preble's squadron included the 38-gun frigate *Philadelphia*, the 18-gun brigs *Argus* and *Syren*, the 14-gun schooners *Nautilus* and *Vixen*, and the plucky little 12-gun schooner *Enterprise*.[3] All told, it was a formidable force to bring against the petty despot in Tripoli.

As the *Constitution* plowed through the water, Preble spied a shape in the gathering darkness. He ordered his men to shorten sail and fell off the wind, bleeding off speed. The commodore shivered, but not from the cold. Preble suffered from a stomach ailment and, despite the warmth of the late November evening, pulled his cloak closer around him.[4]

The *Constitution* slowed as she came up on the unknown shape, which came into view as a British man-of-war. Preble kept the *Constitution* on her starboard tack and picked up a speaking trumpet to hail the English ship, which was the 38-gun *Amazon*. The English captain beat Preble to the punch, hailing the American with a tale that made Preble's blood run cold.

"The *Philadelphia* ran on the shoals near Tripoli," the *Amazon's* captain shouted. "She was got off and towed into Tripoli."[5] At first Preble could not believe what he heard. The *Philadelphia*? Captured? If true, it would mean a third of his strength was now in enemy hands.

Angered by the news, Preble issued a flurry of orders. The *Constitution* made sail and came up a bit to catch every breath of wind. Preble changed course from Syracuse and instead ordered his ship to Malta, another British base and one the Americans had used for two years to stage their earlier campaigns against Tripoli. Uncertainty prevailed over the crew. No one knew what Preble's next move might be.

The American squadron arrived piecemeal in the Mediterranean over the course of the summer and fall of 1803. The *Nautilus*, commanded by Lt. Richard Somers, twenty-five, and purchased from a Baltimore merchant, pulled into the British base at Gibraltar on July 27, 1803. The *Philadelphia* under Capt. William Bainbridge arrived August 24. The newly built schooner *Vixen*, under Lt. John Smith, twenty-six, was next, pulling into harbor on September 12. The *Constitution* arrived two days later. The brig *Syren*, under Lt. Charles Stewart, twenty-five, arrived at Gibraltar October 1. The last to arrive was Lt. Stephen Decatur, twenty-four, and another brig, the 18-gun *Argus*, on November 1.

There were three other American ships in the Mediterranean when Preble arrived. The frigates *John Adams* and *New York* were on their way home, so the commodore borrowed them momentarily to scare Morocco into the line. The third was the *Enterprise*, the 12-gun schooner that was already a legend in the Navy and among the public. Lt. Isaac Hull, a Yankee from Connecticut, commanded the little schooner now, adding to her legend with his work outside Tripoli.

Isaac Hull, at thirty the third-oldest officer in the flotilla, took over the *Enterprise* on March 23, 1802. Hull was different from many of his fellow officers, and not just because he was a New Englander. Quiet, almost introspective, Hull was just as happy on land as he was at sea. He had a tendency to gain weight easily—when Preble met him, Hull certainly filled out his uniform.[6]

He might be chubby, but Hull had a reputation as being one of the bravest and most dependable officers in the service. During the Quasi-War, he had plucked a powerful French privateer right out of the Spanish port of Santo Domingo. Before taking over the *Enterprise*, Hull was the executive officer of the *John Adams*. The pudgy New Englander gave that ship its motto one night when the *John Adams* verged on foundering in a storm. Despite his captain's cries of "Rocks!," Hull calmly took charge of the vessel and, though wearing only his underwear, told his commander, "Keep yourself cool, Sir and the ship will be got off." The *John Adams'* crew, under Hull's direction, righted the ship while Hull pulled on his pants. According to his wife, "For a man as chubby as Hull this operation, performed in the presence of most of the crew, required almost as much calm deliberation as bringing the frigate clear of the rocks. But there was not a titter from the men. So impressive had been his act and so inspiring his remark that the watchword of the ship became from then on: 'Keep yourself cool.'"[7]

Preble knew all this, and from the second he met Hull he liked the young lieutenant. Hull could be a bit impertinent, even impolite at times, but he was a capable officer who followed orders. When Decatur arrived with the brig on November 1, Preble put together a mission specifically for the *Argus*, and put Hull in charge of her.[8]

The new brig came across the Atlantic under Stephen Decatur, but the *Argus* was really Preble's ship. The commodore oversaw the brig's construction and knew every plank, every line, every bolt and nail in her. Decatur had his heart set on the *Argus*, but Preble thought Hull would make better use of her.

———— ◆ ————

The commodore and his "cubs," as he called them, grew closer in the weeks following his arrival in the Mediterranean. His actions off Cape Trafalgar and at Tangiers showed he had the stuff the young officers wanted in a commander.

Preble shared at least one quality with all of his officers—his burning passion for the Navy. No one had better insult the United States Navy, at least not around Preble. The commodore proved that on his arrival in Gibraltar. He also gave his young officers a lesson in how to defend honor without the need for pistols.

When Preble arrived at the British base in September 1803, the *Constitution* flew the commodore's long pennant. The sight of the flag made at least one officer's blood boil: After President Thomas Jefferson relieved Commo. Richard Morris of command in the Mediterranean in 1802 and ordered him home, Capt. John Rodgers took over as commodore. Rodgers was twenty-nine, hotheaded and eager for a fight. He attempted to blockade Tripoli with just a pair of ships and even though he could not prevent shipping from entering the harbor, he managed to capture the *Meshouda*.[9]

Rodgers was senior to Preble on the captain's list. The Maryland native was the first lieutenant under Thomas Truxtun when the *Constellation* captured the French frigate *Insurgente*. The victory propelled Rodgers to fame and earned him an immediate promotion, beating Preble to the rank of captain by nearly a year. But now it was Preble in the Mediterranean flying his commodore pennant. It was an affront to Rodgers, who had expected to permanently take over command of the Mediterranean squadron. Rodgers already had his own commodore's pennant flying from the frigate *John Adams* and had no idea Preble would relieve him. "I shall never cease to think myself unfortunate in not knowing your intentions sooner," a dismayed Rodgers wrote to Navy secretary Robert Smith, "as it has prevented me of an opportunity of erecting a lasting monument to the zeal and regard I have for my country."[10]

Preble, as the duly appointed commander of the flotilla, argued he had every right to fly his pennant. Rodgers said he thought it was a direct insult. Preble did not care. To him, settling affairs and keeping the peace with Morocco was far more important than soothing a rival's pride, but at first Rodgers would have none of it. "Permit me to observe that this is not an affair between private individuals, and that my feelings as an officer have been most sensibly injured," he wrote Preble on September 15. "I do insist that, if the date of your commission is subsequent to mine, that is not in the power of the government to place you or any other officer in a situation which could afford an opportunity of treating me with disrespect."[11]

The war of words could have escalated, but Preble, with his New England distaste for dueling, preferred fighting pirates rather than other American naval officers. "I have no disposition to be on such terms with any officer of either the United States squadrons now in these seas as to injure the interests of our country," Preble told Rodgers. "If it possibly can be avoided, I shall with pleasure meet you to consult what measures may be best calculated to keep peace with the Barbary Powers that we are now at peace with, and what measures it will be proper to pursue to bring those powers to terms which are at war with us," the commodore assured Rogers.[12] As a result, Rogers agreed to "cooperate" with Preble in pacifying Morocco before he returned to the United States with the frigates *John Adams* and *New York*. The show of force worked. Morocco pledged peace and Rodgers returned home, angry but without taking the "field of honor" against Preble.[13]

Once more, the young officers under Preble's command watched and learned. The Old Man not only knew how to handle petty dictators, but also understood the idea of honor and how to preserve it without resorting to dueling. Their commander was just as shrewd when it came to foiling the British Royal Navy from engaging in its favorite pastimes—insulting American officers while stealing American crewmen.[14]

American ships had more than a few British subjects among their crews. The British, if they thought they could get a better deal from their own, would desert in droves if they had the chance, Preble said. Rather than pull into a Royal Navy base where his less-than-enthusiastic British-born tars could disappear, Preble decided to establish his base at the ancient Sicilian city of Syracuse, where he could not only prevent desertion, but also more easily procure supplies and keep his officers out of trouble.[15]

After pacifying Morocco, Preble set up his base at Syracuse, where he could keep an eye on his own crews while not worrying about the British. Malta, the massive British base Dale and Morris favored, was closer to Tripoli but also, in Preble's mind, closer to trouble.

———◆·◆———

Preble arrived in the Mediterranean knowing the key to defeating Tripoli rested on his smaller ships and the aggressiveness of his officers. He ordered Bainbridge to take the *Philadelphia* and *Vixen* to Tripoli to establish a blockade while he used the *Constitution* to show the flag at Tangier, Algiers, and Tunis. Preble could either use the smaller craft to keep the other Barbary states in line or send them along to Bainbridge, depending on the situation.

The commodore gave Bainbridge clear orders to keep the *Vixen* with him. He did not want the *Philadelphia* to venture too close to the dangerous reefs that lined Tripoli harbor. That was work for the schooner. Bainbridge could easily cover the smaller schooner with his frigate. He could also take on and defeat anything in the Tripoli navy.

Bainbridge was ready for the chance and set off for Tripoli "to annoy the enemy with all the means in your power," as Preble put it.[16]

The *Philadelphia* and *Vixen* arrived at Tripoli on October 7 and immediately set up a blockade. Bainbridge ordered his lookouts to watch for any ship, no matter how big, trying to sneak out of the harbor. He had no intention of missing a prize. With the *Vixen* working inshore, the *Philadelphia* spent the next twelve days aimlessly sailing off Tripoli. Nothing stirred in the harbor. The lack of action wore on Bainbridge. All he could do, he told Preble, was to sail "on this solitary station, without the good fortune of seeing our enemies, except under the refuge of well-fortified works."[17]

The lookouts on the *Philadelphia* finally spotted a sail on October 19. The frigate gave chase and soon overtook an Austrian brig that was hugging the coastline to evade what her captain said was a Barbary corsair cruising in the Mediterranean. The news started Bainbridge thinking.

The *Philadelphia*, he believed, could cover the harbor. Bainbridge would send Lt. John Smith and the *Vixen* out on a patrol to find the Barbary corsair. Although contrary to Preble's orders to keep the two ships together, Bainbridge told Lieutenant Smith, "By parting company we shall be more likely to intercept any Tripolitan cruisers that may be in our route." He told Smith to "make the best of your way to Malta via Lapidosa, and attend to the orders you received from me" by cruising off Cape Bon, the bulge of North Africa that juts out toward Sicily. Smith dutifully set sail later that day, leaving the *Philadelphia* alone.[18]

For nine days Bainbridge's solo cruise had little effect. A nasty storm blew up off the Sahara, pelting the *Philadelphia* with sand while churning the waters off Tripoli into an angry froth. The storm lashed the *Vixen* as well, driving the schooner well off her ordered path.

———— ✦ ————

The same late-October storm that lashed the *Philadelphia* bounced the *Constitution* around like a cork. Commo. Edward Preble was less happy than usual. The New Englander had enough to deal with when it came to commanding the six ships of his squadron. Now he received word one of them—the *Enterprise*, his most successful—was due to lose its entire crew.[19]

The *Constitution* was on her way to Cadiz Bay, Spain, to ride out the gale. Preble kept his men busy, as usual, but there were no more murmurings against the commodore. He had proved his courage, and every ship in the flotilla over which he could spread his influence benefited. Still, word reached Preble of a promise his predecessor, Commo. Richard Morris, had made to the crew of the *Enterprise*.

The 12-gun schooner was the workhorse of the squadron and the only ship to successfully engage any Tripolitan ships in combat. She was the lucky ship of the flotilla, and a happy one under current commander Isaac Hull. The pudgy New Englander restored the spirits of a crew that came close to snapping under the rigid discipline of former commander Lt. Andrew Sterrett.[20]

Morris, perhaps sensing the needs of the crew, decided to cut short their enlistment period, and promised the sailors they could leave the *Enterprise* just after the New Year. When he found out about that promise, Preble was beside himself with anger, declaring that "In consequence of an imprudent promise made by Commodore Morris to the present crew of the *Enterprise*, entered at Gibraltar last May, that they should be discharged in six months although they shipped for twelve, much difficulty has arisen," Preble wrote to Navy Secretary Smith. "However, they have in consequence of a small advance to each, agreed to remain until April." The need for the *Enterprise* was so acute, the commodore told the Navy secretary, he wanted an additional fifty men to head for the Mediterranean at the earliest possible time. Otherwise, the schooner would "at the time when I shall most want her services, be left destitute of at least half and I think probable more than that proportion of her crew."[21]

The next ship on Preble's mind was the *Argus*, one that had a special connection to the commodore. Preble had overseen the construction of the brig. He took pride in her fine lines and her speed. The *Argus* figured highly in Preble's plans. He had no intention of leaving his rear unguarded and knew he needed a ship to keep an eye on Morocco. He chose the *Argus*, with her eighteen 18-pound carronades and sleek lines, for the job. However, he also wanted the brig to support his operations off Tripoli and wrote to Secretary of the Navy Robert Smith on November 8, "The *Argus* is so fine a vessel, and so well calculated and armed for the service that I shall want her before Tripoli. Pardon me for again urging the necessity of sending out a 32-gun frigate for this station to take her place that I might have her services."[22]

The *Argus* and Decatur arrived at Gibraltar November 1. Decatur reported to Preble and the two quickly sized up one another, the gruff, blunt commodore and the gallant, romantic lieutenant. Each liked what he saw. "I have many remarkable fine young men whose conduct promises great things to their country," Preble told Secretary Smith.[23]

The commodore had bad news, however, for the young lieutenant. Decatur, who enjoyed his brief time in command of the *Argus*, would now command the *Enterprise*. Preble needed a steadier, more experienced hand to watch Morocco and decided to send Isaac Hull on the mission. He issued orders to both men November 7, 1803, to exchange ships.

Preble, vigilant and tough, imparted those qualities to Hull in his orders:

> Experience has taught us that implicit faith cannot be placed in treaties with any of the Barbary States. You will therefore, as often as possible, appear on the coast of Morocco. . . . If you learn that any of their cruisers are fitting out for sea, you will inform yourself of the object of such equipment and take care that you repel the first aggression on their part with the greatest promptitude as an ascendancy can only be obtained over these, or any other Barbarians but by a determined mode of conduct towards them. You are to capture all vessels belonging to the Bashaw of Tripoli or his subjects and to annoy the enemy by all the means in your power.[24]

Stephen Decatur received a near-identical set of instructions, although his destination was Syracuse. Preble told him to escort the store ship *Traveller* to Sicily where it would set up the U.S. base. Decatur was also to have the *Enterprise* rerigged "and put in good condition." If the *Constitution* did not arrive by the time he accomplished those tasks, Preble told Decatur to "proceed off Tripoli and join the frigate *Philadelphia* and the schooner *Vixen* in the blockade of that place." Preble also made it clear he intended to carry the fight to the bashaw: "Continue to cruise before Tripoli until the season makes it dangerous, and then you must harbor in Syracuse, but you must even then in the worst season go out and show yourself off Tripoli occasionally if only a day or two at a time as it will have a good effect by convincing the Barbarians that [their] vessels [are] not safe in leaving port at any season of the year." He gave Decatur the same latitude he gave Hull to "capture all vessels belonging to the Bashaw of Tripoli or his subjects and to annoy the enemy by all the means in your power. You are not to suffer the vessels of any nation to enter or have commerce with Tripoli."[25]

Richard Somers, in command of the schooner *Nautilus*, received similar orders, as did Lt. Charles Stewart in command of the *Syren*. Stewart, however, also had the unpleasant task of "delivering presents and gifts" to the rulers in Algiers and Tunis before he was to join the squadron off Tripoli. The old man was about to unleash his young lions on the bashaw and they were eager for the challenge.[26] Indeed, the news that came from the *Amazon* that cool evening in November 1803 changed everything for Preble and his command.

CHAPTER 5

OFFICERS AND GENTLEMEN

T HE OFFICERS OF THE NEW UNITED STATES NAVY were an unusual bunch. At first glance, they could strike the unknowing observer as, "Young hotheads with guns, uniforms and an over-charged sense of personal honor."[1] That, however, was an oversimplification of the complicated social rules under which many of the officers lived.

To these young men, personal honor was something to defend to the very last. Honor was more than just not rolling over for an insult or protecting social position. It meant defending the name of a new nation and a new service.

The code of honor in America was an outgrowth of the code British set-tlers brought with them, especially to the southern colonies. Although duels were relatively rare during the days before the Revolutionary War, they did occur. In fact, they took place with enough frequency that Benjamin Franklin, John Adams, and Thomas Paine did their best to discourage the practice.[2]

Still, the idea of honor was something that took hold in the American psyche, although the necessity of duels was far more of a regional spin. New Englanders abhorred the practice, as did Pennsylvanians in the Mid-Atlantic. Both regions had a religious objection to the practice even though the idea of personal honor remained extremely strong. Edward Preble and Isaac Hull both despised the practice of duels. However, when it came to defending their personal honor, New England Yankees were just as zealous as were their Southern counterparts.[3]

South of the Mason-Dixon Line, there was something about the *code duello* that appealed to young men. They knew the battle that Navy advo-cates had waged just to get Congress to agree to pay for the new service and they were determined to defend the Navy's honor just as heatedly as they would defend their own. It was a difficult balance to maintain.

"Officers felt their responsibility was twofold: as gentleman they had their personal honor to uphold and as officers they had to maintain the integrity of the service and the fair name of their country," William Oliver Stephens said of the code of honor. "What a gentleman might ignore as far as it affected his own pride could not be overlooked if it threatened to disgrace his profession of arms."[4]

Although Edward Preble despised dueling, he shared with his young officers, many of them men from the Mid-Atlantic or South, a burning pride in the new U.S. Navy. Preble did his best to discourage dueling yet he almost certainly understood the reasons behind one of the more celebrated affairs of honor during the Tripoli campaign because it involved the honor of the Navy.

In 1802, while Richard Morris commanded the Mediterranean squadron, the commodore took his flagship to Malta. Two of his officers, Lt. Stephen Decatur and Midn. Joseph Bainbridge, decided to take in the sights of Valletta, the island's capital city, and went to a theater. As the show began, several British officers hurled insults in the direction of the two Americans—not at them personally, but at the United States Navy and its ineffective two-year war with Tripoli.

The Americans kept quiet until the loudest of the British officers intentionally bumped into Bainbridge twice. When he hit Bainbridge a third time, the young midshipman punched him in the face, sending the British officer sprawling to the floor. This man turned out to be a Mr. Cochran, secretary to the royal governor of Malta, Sir Alexander Ball. Cochran, an accomplished duelist, publicly challenged Bainbridge. The young midshipman, with Decatur as his second, accepted, on one condition Decatur set: instead of the usual ten paces, Decatur insisted the two men fight at four paces.

Cochran's second protested at the close range. "This looks like murder sir," he said to Decatur. "No, sir," Decatur said. "This looks like death, but not like murder. Your friend is a professional duelist, while mine is wholly inexperienced. I am no duelist, but I am acquainted with the use of the pistol. If you insist upon ten paces, I will fight your friend at that distance."[5]

Decatur's stance shocked the Englishman. Bainbridge, who was barely eighteen, looked like an easy mark. Decatur had the look of a seasoned fighter. The British officer declined Decatur's terms. "We have no quarrel with you, sir," he said.[6]

When the two parties met on the field, Cochran, unused to the close range, missed with his first shot. Bainbridge put his shot through Cochran's hat.

Decatur told Bainbridge to aim lower if he wanted to live.

Cochran missed with his second shot, while Bainbridge hit the British officer in the eye, killing him. The governor, enraged at the death of his secretary, demanded the arrest of Bainbridge and Decatur. Morris, in one of his brighter moves, sent both officers home on the next ship, keeping them out of reach of the British.[7]

It was this code of honor and ethics that drove the officers of the Navy in 1803. They beat the French under Barry and Truxtun, proving they could fight. Now, the trick was to harness that energy and marry it to naval discipline. It would be difficult. No one could fault the officers' bravery, but they were a prickly sort, extremely sensitive when it came to promotion and overly concerned with rank.

Midn. Charles Morris was less than kind in his assessment of many of his fellow officers, most of whom were not yet twenty-four years old. Some were even younger. "A very large proportion were not only men of no refinement but vulgarly profane and grossly intemperate," he said. "Very many of the midshipmen had attained an age at which their habits of thought and action had become too firmly established to be easily changed, and gave little promise of any future usefulness."[8]

The petty jealousies between the officers, coupled with their youth, did not endear them to the men they commanded. Pvt. William Ray of the U.S. Marine Corps, who served on the *Philadelphia*, shared Preble's initial feeling about the officers: "Must a brat of an officer, a boy of 12 or 14 years of age, be permitted to strike, to insult, to trample on, to swagger over grown men venerable by age and honourable by wounds in the service of their country?"[9]

However, despite their youth and sometimes unruly behavior, the officers of the squadron itched for action. Their country was at war, and they intended to gain glory from it. Midshipman Morris, who looked down on some of his peers, was quick to praise those who demonstrated "a desire to learn and advance in their profession." Those types of officers, Morris said, would go far in the service of their country.[10]

———◆◆———

Beyond a doubt, the officer everyone in the squadron expected to go far was Lt. Stephen Decatur Jr.[11] Everywhere he went, Decatur was the center of attention. There was just something about the twenty-four-year-old lieutenant from Sinepuxent, Maryland, that attracted anyone that met him.

Decatur was the son of a seaman. His father, Stephen Sr., was a privateer captain during the Revolution who went on to become a successful merchant skipper. When war with France loomed, the elder Decatur secured himself a spot in the Navy as commander of the sloop-of-war *Delaware*, and took the first prize of the Quasi-War.

Stephen Jr., born January 5, 1779, inherited his father's looks and his mother's gentleness. The elder Decatur was a descendant of French and Irish immigrants. Stephen Jr.'s mother, Ann, was Irish and raised the young boy essentially on her own while his father was at sea. Ann Decatur hoped her son would not follow in his father's wake and would make a life on land rather than at sea.

Young Stephen was a bright, inquisitive boy, but one wracked with illness. At eight he contracted whooping cough. His father thought taking the boy on a voyage might help. His mother, despite her misgivings, consented. Little Stephen went on the *Ariel* with his father, and as the ship left the dock in Philadelphia, he had another coughing spasm. It was his last one. By the time he returned, he was tanned and a little taller, and the cough was gone.

There was a need for schooling, however, before he could make a life at sea, and young Decatur attended Abercrombie's Academy in Philadelphia. There he met Charles Stewart and Richard Somers. He spent his days trying to master mathematics and Latin, while sneaking out to see the latest ship launch at Joshua Humphreys' shipyard.

Decatur earned a reputation of being intelligent and brave as a schoolboy. He once took on a crowd of angry French sympathizers who attacked him for wearing a blue cockade, a Federalist party symbol, in his hat rather than the tricolor ribbon of the French Revolution. Decatur took his lumps but gave as good as he got.

By 1796 his mother wanted him to enroll in the divinity school of the University of Pennsylvania but the call of the sea remained strong. He could not break his mother's heart—not yet—so he took a job as an accountant at Gurney & Smith, the merchant firm for which his father sailed. Decatur drank in the stories captains told of their voyages and applied himself to learning mathematics. He studied rigging, drew ships, and built models. Gurney & Smith were the naval agents for Philadelphia, and when Congress authorized Joshua Humphreys to build his frigates, Gurney & Smith handled the arrangements. John Barry, the hearty old Irishman and close friend of the Decatur family, was the captain of the frigate under construction in Philadelphia and he made sure Stephen had a hand in it as well. When the 44-gun *United States* slid down the ways July 10, 1797, young Stephen was on the quarterdeck as a guest of honor for the launching.

A year later Barry arrived at the Decatur house with Stephen Jr. in tow. His mother was not sure about the Irishman and was even more surprised to see Stephen with him. Rather than have the boy break his mother's heart, the seaman made the announcement Ann long dreaded. Stephen was about to head to sea. Barry handed Ann Decatur a rolled paper—Stephen's appointment as a midshipman on the 44-gun frigate *United States*.

When Decatur reported for sea duty, he was not yet twenty years old. As he boarded his ship, he found Charles Stewart already there, the fourth lieutenant on the *United States*. Richard Somers was also there, a fellow midshipman. The three schoolboy friends renewed their bond on the *United*

States—Stewart the senior man, Somers the middle by rank, and Decatur the junior.

In an interesting quirk of fate, when the *United States* headed out to sea in July 1798 she passed the 20-gun *Delaware*, Stephen Decatur Sr. in command. Following the *Delaware* was a sizeable brig—the *Croyable*—that the *Delaware* had captured. The Navy kept the French brig, put her into U.S. service as the *Retaliation*, and gave her to William Bainbridge to command.

Stephen Decatur Jr. sailed into manhood on that first cruise. He earned the respect of his fellow officers and the respect of his crew. He, Stewart, and Somers spent hours discussing everything from seamanship to the meaning of honor and glory. For these young officers, those two words meant the world. They did not mean a headlong pursuit of fame. Instead, honor and glory meant something more—being of service while earning respect and never shying away from a fight.

Decatur fought his first duel in 1799 against a merchant sailor who stole a group of recruits Decatur had enlisted. When Decatur demanded his recruits back, the sailor unleashed a torrent of profanity. Decatur departed without the recruits. The next day Decatur's second, Richard Somers, appeared at the merchant vessel with a challenge for the merchant sailor. The two met in New Castle, Delaware, but before they did, Decatur told his other close friend on the *United States*, Charles Stewart, that he would just wound the man. Decatur kept his word, winging the sailor in the shoulder, and his reputation began to grow.

One new midshipman, Robert Spence, quickly fell under Decatur's spell. On his assignment to the *United States*, Spence met his fellow officers. "They were pleasing, gentlemanlike men, having the characteristic air and look of sailors," he said. "But in Decatur I was struck with a peculiarity of manner and appearance, calculated to rivet the eye and engross the attention. I had often pictured to myself the form and look of a hero, such as my favorite Homer had delineated; here I saw it embodied." Spence said he turned to Somers and asked him about Decatur's character. "Sir," Somers said, "Decatur is an officer of uncommon character, of rare promise, a man of an age, one perhaps not equaled in a million."[12]

Lofty words, but it was how others saw Decatur, especially his closest friends such as Somers and Stewart. At the end of the Quasi-War, Decatur transferred first to the frigate *Norfolk*, then to the 32-gun *Essex*, which was part of the first squadron the United States sent to Tripoli. He served as the first lieutenant on the *Essex* for Capt. William Bainbridge.

Officers were not the only ones to see something special in Decatur. The lieutenant had a different way of commanding men. Bainbridge was harsh, bordering on cruel. Decatur, however, rarely used the lash or brig to get men to follow his commands. He had an air of authority about him that made him a natural leader, one that others would willingly follow. When the *Essex* was about to leave for Tripoli, Decatur addressed his men:

> Comrades—We are about to embark on an expedition which may terminate in our sudden deaths, or perpetual slavery, or our immortal glory. The event is left for futurity to determine. The first quality of good seamen is personal courage—the second, obedience to orders—the third, fortitude under sufferings; to these may be added, an ardent love of country.
>
> I need say no more. I am confident you possess them all.[13]

The words stunned the ordinary sailors, the gunners, the topmen, even the powder monkeys. Decatur addressed them as equals. He was an officer to follow.

Sometimes, however, Decatur could be too lenient with his men. Just a month after taking command of the *Enterprise*, Commodore Preble reminded the young lieutenant of his duties after the *Enterprise* crew had too good of a time onshore at Syracuse: "Your men on shore for the purpose of fitting your rigging, were this afternoon most of them drunk. This must undoubtedly have happened in consequence of the negligence of the officers in charge of them. I request you to make the necessary enquiry respecting this neglect on their part, as I shall most certainly take notice of it."[14]

As fair as he was with his crew, Decatur could be quick to take an insult yet never seemed to suffer the consequences of his at-times rash acts. His aid for Joseph Bainbridge in the Malta duel caused so much tension with the British that it forced Commodore Morris to send both officers home. Congress, rather than discipline the two officers, promoted them, making Bainbridge a lieutenant and putting Decatur in command of the *Argus*. In 1820 Decatur's last duel would cost him his life.

———— ◆ ◆ ————

Second only to Decatur in popularity was his close childhood friend, Richard Somers.[15] The two men were inseparable in youth and later in the Navy. Somers, the youngest of five children, was born September 15, 1778, in Philadelphia.[16] His father, Richard, moved the family to the city when he was appointed to represent New Jersey in the Continental Congress. In his youth, the younger Somers attended the famed Abercrombie's Academy before returning to New Jersey at age fifteen after his father died. He lived with an uncle in the family home in Egg Harbor (now Somers Point), and seemed destined for a career in the law when the fledgling U.S. Navy seized his attention.

Growing up in Philadelphia the son of a prominent lawmaker exposed young Richard to some of the top personalities in the new nation. One near-constant visitor was John Barry, then captain of the frigate *Alliance*. Another was George Washington, whom young Richard openly worshipped. His prize possession from his youth was a gold ring containing a lock of Washington's hair.[17]

When Somers returned to New Jersey to live with his uncle after his father's death, he attended a school under a Mr. Hunter in Woodbury, New Jersey. Family business ledgers show entries for Somers' lessons. By 1792 Somers was studying navigation, mathematics, and other subjects associated with a career at sea.[18] After he received news his closest friends in Philadelphia, Stephen Decatur Jr. and Charles Stewart, had applied for the fledgling U.S. Navy, Somers was eager to join as well.

As classmates at Abercrombie's Academy in Philadelphia, the three boys were inseparable. Decatur would almost always come up with their escapades, a favorite of which was to sneak out of the school and run to the Schuylkill River, where they would swim nearly a quarter-mile downstream to the confluence of the Delaware River to see the goings-on at Joshua Humphrey's shipyard.[19]

Somers' father died October 22, 1794. His estate was divided equally among his children, with Richard inheriting the homestead and other lands. In addition to attending school, Somers supervised the cutting of timber and its shipment, and in 1796, bought his first ship from his brother Constant, and began making merchant voyages along the East Coast.

Somers' mother, Sophia, died on February 3, 1797, leaving only Richard and Constant on the Egg Harbor estate. By then Somers had made up his mind to join his boyhood friends Decatur and Stewart in the U.S. Navy. Thanks to his family friendship with Commo. John Barry, Somers was assigned on board Barry's ship, the 44-gun frigate *United States*, with his two closest friends.

Although he made friends easily among his peers, his close friendship with Decatur led Somers to his first test of courage. Somers and Decatur were set to go ashore together. As they waited for their boat, Somers jokingly made fun of Decatur's dress while Decatur accused his longtime friend of "playing the fool." It was an old joke. Decatur favored simple clothes while Somers was something of a fashion plate.

Neither thought anything of their exchange, and why should they. Old friends could speak to each other any way they wanted, or so they thought. The rest of the wardroom, which overheard the conversation, thought otherwise. The other midshipmen gathered and decided Decatur had insulted Somers by calling him a fool, while Somers, by ignoring the comment and continuing to jest with his friend, was guilty of cowardice.

After the two friends returned to the *United States*, the rest of the midshipmen refused to eat or drink with them. Somers demanded an explanation and the other officers rather haughtily explained how they viewed the now two-day-old conversation. Their position shocked Somers, who immediately told Decatur. The nineteen-year-old Decatur laughed it off. Somers did not. The other midshipmen openly questioned his courage, he told Decatur. He demanded satisfaction.

Decatur thought his friend was being childish and told him so. He offered to throw a dinner for the all midshipmen at which he would not quite apologize but would say in public he meant no offense to his friend. Somers refused. Instead, the twenty-year-old challenged every midshipman to duels. All agreed, and on the appointed day Somers set out to redeem his honor.

He took a pistol ball in the arm in the first duel and a shot in the thigh in the second. By the third, he was so weak Decatur had to hold his arm up so he could fire. The loss of blood, however, was stronger than Somers. He passed out before he could get off his shot and his opponents, seeing his bravery, withdrew their charge of cowardice. The entire wardroom helped nurse Somers back to health.[20]

The affair settled any questions about Somers' strength or courage.

After a year on the frigate *United States*, Somers became the first lieutenant on the frigate *Boston* under Capt. Daniel McNeill, whose approach to command was rather different from Barry's.

A privateer during the Revolution, McNeill had the habit of ignoring orders from his superiors if he did not agree. When Richard Dale commanded the Mediterranean squadron, McNeill essentially refused to serve under him. He stretched his orders as far as he could, arriving a week early or a day too late to rendezvous with his commander, ensuring he could operate independently.

McNeill was also prone to bouts of eccentric behavior. During a port of call at Bordeaux, France, on his way back from the Mediterranean in 1802, McNeill decided to see just how fast his crew could get the *Boston* under way. It did not matter that McNeill had sent two lieutenants, William Jenks and Edward Wyer, as well as ship's purser, Charles Wordsworth, into the city to buy supplies. McNeill gave the order to slip anchor and leave. According to Midn. Ralph Izard, who was on the *Boston*, the eccentric skipper denied permission to send a boat for his officers, instead informing three French naval officers touring the ship that they were now part of his crew.[21]

McNeill eventually returned his French guests and picked up his own officers, although his example made an impression on Somers. Officers had to follow orders, but there was always a way to read some independence into those orders.

It was something Charles Stewart already knew.

——— ———

Born in July 1778, the eighth child of Irish immigrants, Stewart grew up in Philadelphia, where he attended school with Decatur and Somers. The three became fast friends whose careers intertwined throughout their lives. Stewart left Abercrombie's Academy at age twelve and, unlike his two friends, could not read or write well. When the chance came for him to get a job on a merchant vessel, Stewart seized the opportunity, securing a position as a deckhand on the merchant vessel *Lorraine* plying the Caribbean. The trader made a stop at Haiti during one of that island's revolutions in 1790. Self-styled Haitian "general" Henri Christophe wanted to visit the *Lorraine* and demanded a ladder or other means to climb on board. Stewart took a rope, shook it in the man's face, and burst out laughing.

Even though he was barely a teen, Stewart knew the childish prank was a mistake when an enraged Christophe drew his sword and demanded the captain hand the boy over for Haitian justice—a quick slice of the throat. Stewart dashed toward the galley where there was a small wardroom with a trapdoor. He dove into the small space and secured the door, making sure only he could open it. The still irate Haitians began searching the ship and soon found the trapdoor. When Christophe could not open the door, he thrust his sword into the openings around it, barely missing Stewart, who huddled as deep in the back as he could.[22]

In 1798 Stewart was among the first of the lieutenants appointed to the new United States Navy. However, there was not much to distinguish the thin-shouldered young officer from his peers other than his family connections. After his father died in 1780, his mother remarried, saying "I do" to Stephen Britton, a man of means in Philadelphia and a member of Congress. Britton was also a confidant of George Washington's, who saw to it that young Charles had the opportunity to pursue a career in the Navy.

Within a year Stewart was the first lieutenant on the frigate *United States* under John Barry. After Congress authorized the construction of the *Experiment*, a sister ship to the *Enterprise*, Barry recommended Stewart as her commander, telling Secretary of the Navy Stoddert, "I am perfectly satisfied with your appointment of Lieutenant Stewart." The commodore admitted to his boss that Stewart had few chances to distinguish himself while on the *United States* and added something of a challenge for the new skipper, saying, "I hope he will be more active when he commands than when he is commanded."[23]

Now out on his own, Stewart grew into command. He quickly captured two French privateers before smashing the ship-rigged *Diana* in a savage little battle. On board the French ship was Hyacinthe Rigaud, a general who had earned a reputation for his savage treatment of captured American merchant seaman. Stewart turned Rigaud over to Thomas Truxtun with some satisfaction.

Like the Navy's other schooner, the *Experiment* was a training ground for future captains. Stewart's first lieutenant was David Porter, while his second and third lieutenants were James Caldwell and John Trippe.[24]

Stewart had almost as much success on the *Experiment* as Shaw on the *Enterprise* enjoyed, although that success did not prevent Congress from selling off the schooner when hostilities with France ended. It seemed fitting that one of Stewart's biggest exploits during the French conflict was humanitarian rather than military.

After the end of hostilities in the Caribbean, the *Experiment* headed for home and came upon a small vessel caught on a reef. Waves threatened to turn the ship into kindling. Stewart and his crew quickly launched a rescue operation, plucking sixty-seven people, including sixty women and children, from the stricken ship. Stewart transported the survivors to Santo Domingo. The Spanish governor, Don Joaquín García, praised Stewart for his heroism and his compassion—the governor's family was among those the young lieutenant rescued.

García, in a letter to President Thomas Jefferson, said Stewart "deserves the greatest applause and consideration from me and my whole nation," for his actions, adding the young lieutenant possessed "the great humanity (the offspring of a magnanimous breast) of a military officer."[25]

As he grew into command, Stewart also determined to improve his poor writing and reading skills. Although he could be eloquent, he struggled when it came to putting his thoughts on paper. Stewart began to educate himself, battling his near-illiteracy. Before long he could command not only warships, but also the English language.

Stewart spent nearly five straight years at sea. At the end of the Quasi-War, he immediately requested duty in the Mediterranean, sailing on the *Constellation* under Alexander Murray. He remained in the Mediterranean, serving in various capacities, until January 1803, when he finally returned to the United States. On his arrival, he headed to Washington, where he testified before the Marine Committee on the need for small ships to combat the bashaw.

It was the turning point for the now twenty-five-year-old lieutenant. Stewart, who once had spelled water "warter" in a report to John Barry, was now before the national legislature, where he eloquently made the case for more brigs and schooners. Congress heeded his call and, on February 28, 1803, approved the construction of the *Syren*, *Argus*, and *Vixen*, and the purchase of the *Nautilus*. The same bill put Stewart in charge of the *Syren*.

While Stewart oversaw the construction of the *Syren*, his old friend and schoolmate Decatur was in charge of the fitting out of the *Argus*. The two struck up a friendly rivalry, with Decatur boasting how his ship would sail rings around Stewart.

It did not matter much to Stewart. He had the *Syren* ready ahead of schedule and put to sea seven days after receiving his warning order for operations. He made for the Mediterranean, but after his arrival, found himself relegated to a courier's role. He took the annual tribute to Algiers, stopped in at Tunis, and made other stops before finally arriving at Syracuse in December, where he joined with the rest of Preble's flotilla. When he arrived, William Bainbridge was already imprisoned. As a result, Stewart became the second-ranking officer in the squadron.[26]

Decatur, Somers, and Stewart stood out among Preble's junior officers. All three grew close to their commander, but they were not alone. The commodore had a stable full of young officers, all looking for glory. Normally, that would mean trouble. Under Preble, however, the twenty-somethings grew up. As his views took hold, Preble's officers grew less prone to dueling and more attentive to duty. The commodore would eventually boast to his wife, "It affords me much satisfaction to observe, that we have neither had a duel nor a court martial in the squadron since we left the United States."[27]

Those same officers took a great deal of pride in their commander, although the commodore never let on that he knew. With Decatur, Somers, and Stewart in the lead, the officers began to refer to each other as "Preble's Boys."[28]

CHAPTER 6

"CHILD OF ADVERSITY"

A MONG THE COMMANDERS in the Mediterranean was a thirty-year-old New Jersey native who earned both admiration for his ability as a mariner and condemnation for his adherence to harsh discipline. Capt. William Bainbridge was the second-oldest officer in Preble's squadron and, after the commodore, the most experienced.

Bainbridge commanded the second-most powerful ship in the squadron, the 38-gun *Philadelphia*. Preble knew Bainbridge but never sailed with him. Bainbridge was experienced, competent, and brave, although he seemed a bit unlucky. If nothing else, Bainbridge was out of his twenties, something Preble could not say about the rest of his officers.

Born too late to fight in the Revolutionary War, Bainbridge made a name for himself as a merchant captain before joining the Navy in 1797. He was tall for his time—six feet—and had jet-black hair with a pair of thick muttonchops that framed his face.[1]

Bainbridge was something of an enigma among his fellow officers. His peers, almost to a man, liked the Princeton native. No one seemed to care his parents remained loyal to the British during the Revolution. There was something about Bainbridge that seemed at odds with the man who made friends freely with other officers, though. Despite his easygoing manner in the wardroom, Bainbridge could be savage toward the ordinary seaman under his command. "I don't allow a sailor to speak to me at all," he once said. "I believe there never was so depraved a set of mortals as sailors are. Under discipline they are peaceable and serviceable. Divest them of that and they constitute a perfect rabble."[2]

Seamen that sailed under Bainbridge loathed their commander. John Rea, who served under Bainbridge on the *George Washington*, called his former captain "a man destitute of reason and humanity," and claimed he saw

Bainbridge beat one crewman with his own hands so badly the man suffered a split skull.[3]

There was something else about Bainbridge: his bravery and skill hid a dark, burning weakness. Bainbridge, officers and sailors alike whispered, was unlucky.

When the United States Navy took on the French in the Quasi-War, the Americans won just about every contest. The one loss came in 1798 when Bainbridge, in command of the brig-of-war *Retaliation*, came up against three French ships, including the 40-gun frigate *Insurgente* and the 36-gun *Volontaire*. The *Insurgente* fired a broadside at the *Retaliation*, and Bainbridge hauled down his flag. The French tossed his crew into prison while Bainbridge and his officers remained on the *Insurgente*. It was the first but not last time Bainbridge would find himself incarcerated in relative comfort while his sailors suffered.[4]

Bad luck reared its head two years later when Bainbridge took the frigate *George Washington* to Algiers to deliver America's tribute payment. Bainbridge made the mistake of sailing his ship right into the harbor, rather than anchoring out of range of the cannon lining the shore. The dey of Algiers, seeing the fine warship, shocked Bainbridge with an order, one backed up with artillery: "We receive a positive command from a despotic Dey of Algiers that we must be the porters of savage tigers and more savage Algerines Ambassadors in compliment to the Grand Signor at Constantinople," Bainbridge angrily reported. At first Bainbridge refused to comply. The dey told him, "You pay me tribute, by that you become my slaves, and them I have a right to order as I please," and pointed to the cannon now aimed at the frigate. Bainbridge grudgingly acceded to the "request," at which the Algerians hauled down the Stars and Stripes and ran up their crescent moon flag.[5]

Bainbridge did his best to make the voyage to Constantinople unpleasant for the Algerians, although his crew never forgave him for not fighting. John Rea, who was on the *George Washington*, said sailors openly wept at the insult. No matter, Bainbridge set sail for Constantinople. He managed to hamper the Muslims in their attempts to pray by tacking his ship as often as possible so they would not know in which direction Mecca was; Muslim adherents turn toward Mecca when they pray five times a day. Bainbridge had to cut the rum ration to his sailors to prevent them from attacking their "guests," but eventually pulled into the capital of the Ottoman Empire. For Bainbridge, the stain on his honor was a blot he could not forget, nor could others.

Consul William Eaton, then in Tunis, called it a "degrading exhibition." "The scene has been acted," Eaton said. "The impression is made on the world—and it will require a series of brilliant actions to blot it out."[6]

No one knew this better than Bainbridge. In a letter to Preble, he admitted, "misfortune has attended me throughout my naval career." He even called himself a "child of adversity."[7]

Now in command of the *Philadelphia*, Bainbridge yearned for the chance to change his luck and redeem himself, if only in his own eyes. He was young and aggressive and he knew Preble. The commodore was a stickler for discipline and possessed an aggressive spirit. Bainbridge knew Preble would fight the bashaw, and that was exactly what the *Philadelphia* captain wanted.

The *Philadelphia* was among the more unique ships in U.S. naval history. Philadelphia merchants had paid for the construction of the warship, then gave her to the federal government in return for a stake in any prizes the frigate might take. To build it, her backers turned to Josiah Fox, who, along with Joshua Humphreys, played a major role in the design of the Navy's first six frigates. Fox, however, disagreed with Humphreys on a number of design points. The *Philadelphia* was originally a 44-gun ship like the *Constitution*, but Fox made her slightly smaller, slightly narrower. The *Philadelphia* was faster than the *Constitution* and drew just eighteen feet of water.[8] Ultimately, the 38-gun frigate was the perfect vessel for Bainbridge and his quest for redemption.

When Bainbridge arrived on station off Tripoli on October 7, 1803, he carried explicit orders from his commander. Commodore Preble had told Bainbridge to keep the schooner *Vixen*, under Lt. John Smith, close to the frigate. Bainbridge, however, decided to ignore those orders and on October 19 he sent Smith to search for a pirate cruiser off Cape Bon, off the coast of Tunis. The *Vixen* had hardly set course when a nasty gale swept out of the desert, lashing the *Philadelphia* with sand while churning the Mediterranean into an angry green sea.

The storm gradually pushed *Philadelphia* about twenty miles from her chosen blockade spot. When the storm finally cleared on October 31, Bainbridge set course for his original location. As the *Philadelphia* tacked, her lookouts spotted a sail trying to sneak into Tripoli harbor. The *Philadelphia* gave chase—Bainbridge smelling blood.

The wind was still blowing at fifteen knots, driving the big frigate through the water. Within two hours the *Philadelphia* was close enough to open fire with her bow chasers, a pair of long-barreled cannon positioned on the front of the ship. The Arab vessel raised every scrap of canvas she had, heading in toward shore as the *Philadelphia* continued to close.

Bainbridge was on the quarterdeck, standing next to Lt. David Porter, who was in charge of the helm. The twenty-three-year-old Porter was the former executive officer on the *Enterprise*, and he drove the big frigate as though she was a schooner.

Standing just behind the officers was Marine private William Ray, a Connecticut native who watched in mounting fear as Porter pushed the frigate toward the shore. The *Philadelphia* continued to gain on the Arab vessel. Shots from the bow chasers straddled the lateen-rigged xebec as it tried to zigzag past the American ship.

Bainbridge could see waves breaking on the shore and ordered two men forward and two men amidships to keep a constant eye on the water depth. The men up front tossed a lead-weighted rope into the water, with knots every six feet. Each knot below the water level was one fathom. *Philadelphia* drew eighteen feet forward, twenty aft. The calls came steadily—ten fathoms, then seven, then ten again.

It was 11:30 a.m.[9]

The *Philadelphia* was now four miles from Tripoli. Even without a spyglass, Bainbridge and his crew could see the minarets and fortifications of the city. The xebec never pulled away, but it was clear she would reach dangerously shallow water before the *Philadelphia* could catch her. Bainbridge started to get nervous. The *Philadelphia* was running in unknown waters without a local pilot. Maybe they should back off, he said to Porter. "It was a little past twelve," Ray wrote. "Bainbridge expressed to Lieutenant Porter the danger he apprehended in pursuing any farther, and advising him to put about the ship. Lieut. Porter answered that there was no danger yet and that we would give them a few shots more." The *Philadelphia* kept up the chase for one more minute when a gut-wrenching sound and leg-bending crash sent everyone sprawling. The 38-gun frigate had landed square on Kaliusa Reef, "just as we were preparing to come about, and remained fast," Ray wrote.[10]

The *Philadelphia*'s speed caused her misery. The frigate's bow was more than six feet out of the water, although her stern remained afloat. Bainbridge tried to back his sails to put the *Philadelphia* in reverse. Gangs of sailors grabbed the lines and used brute strength to pull the sails so the wind filled them by coming over the bow rather than the stern.

Nothing happened. The frigate, in addition to being on the rocks, leaned over more than 15 degrees to port. Bainbridge ordered a boat over to inspect the damage. He remained calm despite the calamity. The sailors in the boat said it looked like they could float the frigate up if they could lighten her. Bainbridge seized on that hope.

The *Philadelphia*'s commander ordered his men to dump everything overboard. First to go were the anchors, then drinking water, finally the guns. The cannon, as precious as they were, would do little good in the battle to save the ship. The guns on the port side pointed directly into the water, thanks to the frigate's list. Those on the starboard side pointed harmlessly skyward.[11]

When the *Philadelphia* had struck the rocks, the Tripolitans probably had no idea of just how dire the situation was for the American ship. It took more than fifteen minutes before a small gunboat made its way toward the frigate.

Bainbridge tried everything to get the *Philadelphia* floating again. He ordered his men to chop away the foremast and it quickly fell over the side with a snapping of lines. Still the frigate would not move. Some of Bainbridge's officers wanted to try kedging the ship off the rocks.[12]

The approaching gunboat, however, put an end to that idea. "The impudent pirate now, for the first time, hove to and returned fire," Ray said.[13] It was not alone. Nine other gunboats converged on the *Philadelphia*, each armed with 24-pound cannon. Bainbridge, increasingly desperate, ordered his men to hack away the stern and run a couple of the frigate's remaining cannon out to keep the Arab vessels at bay. The cant of the frigate prevented anything like proper aim, and the *Philadelphia*'s salvoes flew past the Tripolitan craft.[14]

As the pirate gunboats gathered like vultures around the *Philadelphia*, Commo. Edward Preble awoke to a golden sunrise in port at Cadiz, Spain. Toward mid-morning, Preble shepherded his squadron together and weighed anchor for his next stop: Gibraltar. From there he planned to stop at Algiers and Tunis, just to let the potentates get a look at U.S. naval power. After scaring the Barbary leaders, he would sail to Tripoli.

Preble had a plan for Bashaw Karamanli, one he was sure would knock the air out of the corsair leader. In a letter to Secretary of the Navy Robert Smith, Preble rather smugly told his boss, "[W]e should have peace with Tripoli by spring." Preble planned a winter blockade of the harbor, along with incursions from his smaller vessels. Winter in the Mediterranean was the wrong time to be at sea, but with his squadron in tow, the commodore believed he could pull it off. All he had to do was make sure the rest of the Barbary nations would honor their treaties, then he could turn all of his attention to the bashaw.[15]

While Preble planned, Bainbridge pleaded with his crew to get the *Philadelphia* moving.

Nine Arab gunboats waited just outside cannon range while Bainbridge tried to find a way to save his ship, to change his luck. He continued to back the sails while the crew threw heavier objects overboard in an effort to lighten the ship. None of it worked.[16]

Just as worrisome were the Arab gunboats that would dart into range then dash out again. For four hours, "the gunboats kept throwing their balls; but they all went too high, none of them touched our hull and all but very few went through our rigging," Pvt. William Ray wrote.[17]

The *Philadelphia*, however, would not move. There was nothing more Bainbridge could do. He called his officers together. The commander, no doubt leveled emotionally by his bad luck, asked his lieutenants for their thoughts. According to Bainbridge, "they were unanimously of the opinion that it was impossible to get her off the rocks and that continuing in our present situation would be only a sacrificing of lives without effecting [*sic*] our enemy or rendering the least service to Our Country." His officers, Bainbridge said, convinced him there was only one option: surrender. "In such a dilemma too painful to relate, the flag of the United States was struck," he said.[18]

Others did not see it that way. Bainbridge, the martinet, was crumbling before their eyes, William Ray wrote, "Many of our men were surprised to see our colors down, before we had received any injury from the fire of our enemy, and begged the captain and officers to raise it again, preferring even death to slavery. The man who was at the ensign halyards positively refused to obey the captain's orders when he was ordered to lower the flag. He was threatened to be run through and a midshipman seized the halyards and executed the command, amidst the general murmurings of the crew."[19]

There was no fight left in the *Philadelphia*'s captain. "Some fanatics may say that blowing the ship up would have been the proper result," he wrote to Preble. "I thought that such conduct would not stand acquitted before God or Man, and I never presumed to think that I had the liberty of putting to death the lives of 306 souls because they were placed under my command."[20]

Bainbridge, his mind made up, decided on one final course of action while still captain of the *Philadelphia*. He ordered his carpenters and other crew to go into the bilges and cut holes in the ship's hull to sink her. The men chopped out the bottom planks and the big frigate began to settle while her magazines flooded. The crew of the *Philadelphia* sat down on deck and awaited its fate.[21]

At first, nothing happened. The Arab ships stayed out of range, waiting, believing the Americans were trying a Barbary tactic.[22] Bainbridge hauled his flag down around 3:00 p.m. The first Arabs did not board until nearly 6:00 p.m., and when they did they went wild.[23]

Tripolitan craft converged on the *Philadelphia*, bringing swarms of corsairs. One was a small ketch, the *Mastico*.[24] The Arabs, Bainbridge said, robbed the officers and men blind. "We have lost everything but what we had on our backs and even part of that was taken off," Bainbridge wrote.[25]

Sailing Master William Knight said the pirates loaded him and "20 fellow sufferers" into a boat shortly after 6:00 p.m. on October 31. "As we were going they began to rob us of watches, cravats, money and some of their coats," Knight wrote. "The captain [was] treated no better than other officers. Every article [was] taken but what they stood in."[26]

Marine William Ray and ship's surgeon Jonathan Cowdery differed over the severity of the boarders. Cowdery claimed, "[T]he Tripolitan chiefs collected their favorites and, with drawn sabers, fell to cutting and slashing their own men who were stripping the Americans and plundering the ship. They cut off the hands of some, and it is believed, several were killed."[27]

Ray, however, wrote, "It is true there was a fort of mutiny and clashing of arms amongst them; but for my part I never saw any hands amputated nor do I believe there were any lives lost."[28]

Still, even the stoic Marine said thievery among the Arabs was rampant. "As soon as we were huddled into the boats, all, or most of us, were stripped of all our clothing excepting a shirt, trousers and a hat," he wrote. "Some, however, who were in the first boat, under the eye of our officers, fared a little better and kept most of their clothes."[29]

Bainbridge tried to take stock of the latest wrong turn in his naval career. He was the only U.S. Navy captain to surrender a ship to the French during the Quasi-War. Next, he suffered the humiliation of transporting pirates to swear allegiance to their sultan. Now, he was the only captain to lose a warship to the pirates in the Barbary city-state of Tripoli.

——◆—◆——

The bashaw put Bainbridge and his officers in the home of the former U.S. consul to Tripoli. From that spot the *Philadelphia*'s officers could see the harbor and most of the city. Arabs continued to swarm over the partially sunk *Philadelphia* even as storm clouds boiled up. When the pirates took Bainbridge and his crew on shore, the highest-ranking naval officer in the bashaw's employ, High Admiral Murad Reis, accused the *Philadelphia*'s captain of cowardice. Every officer defended Bainbridge, but the accusation was there.[30]

Bainbridge chafed at the accusation. Before striking the flag on board the *Philadelphia*, Bainbridge had asked all of his officers to agree to the surrender. The next day, Tuesday, November 1, Bainbridge sent a formal note to his juniors: "Gentlemen: As I am about informing the government of our country of our late unfortunate event, and the opinion of the officers on my conduct in the distressing circumstances, may be desirous to be known by the President of the United States. You will be pleased to give me your opinions thereon; a certificate from the officers whom I esteem will in some measure alleviate my feelings which are beyond description."[31]

Lt. David Porter presented the captain with a signed note sometime later that day in which the officers, "[w]ishing to express our full approbation of your conduct concerning the unfortunate event of yesterday" believe "every exertion was made, and every expedient tried, to get her off, and to defend her, which either courage or abilities could have dictated." It was the last line, however, that probably struck Bainbridge the most. "Believe us, sir," the note ended, "that our misfortunes and sorrows are entirely absorbed in our sympathy for you."[32]

Bainbridge asked the bashaw's chief adviser, Mohammed Sidi Dgies, if he could speak with Danish consul Nicholas Nissen, who was the only friendly diplomat in the city. Dgies agreed and Nissen arrived later the afternoon of Tuesday November 1, promising to do everything he could to help the crew. The Dane also told Bainbridge that Dgies had agreed to parole the officers, which would give them some measure of liberty within the confines of the consular grounds.[33]

While Nissen visited with the rest of the officers, Bainbridge sat down to write his reports to Secretary of the Navy Robert Smith and to Preble.

His letter to Smith detailed every move the frigate had made before striking the reef, then set out his reasons for surrendering. He also began making an argument against any blame: "I am fully sensible of the loss that has occurred to our country and the difficulty in which it may further involve her with this regency and feel beyond description for the brave unfortunate officers and men under my command. I trust on investigation of my own conduct that I will appear to my government and my country, consistent to the station in which I had the honor of being placed." He also was eager to know Smith's thoughts. He wrote to the secretary, "Should you be pleased to express the opinion of the government, you will much oblige me."[34]

His report to Preble was different. Preble was a friend and a Navy man. He would understand not only what happened, but also how Bainbridge felt about losing his command.

He was also more open with his commander than he had been with Smith. The mistake, he told the commodore, was in not following Preble's orders about the schooner *Vixen*. "Had I not sent the schooner from us, the accident might have been prevented," he told the commodore. "If not we should have been able to have extricated ourselves from Barbary prison, but my motive of ordering her off Cape Bon was to grant more efficient protection to our commerce than I could by keeping her with me."[35]

———◆———

Bainbridge wrote numerous copies of his reports, giving Danish consul Nissen several copies to forward to Syracuse via the Danish consulate on Malta. He also asked Nissen to take several copies to Lt. John Smith on board the *Vixen*. Bainbridge ordered Smith to go first to Gibraltar to look for the commodore. If Preble was not there, Smith was to forward the letters to the United States via the U.S. consul. "Glory and happiness attend you and may you never experience what I have, since parting, is my present wish," he told the *Vixen* commander.[36]

The official reports, however, did not reveal Bainbridge's true state of mind. The commander wrote a letter his wife, Susan, in which he confessed his darkest fears:

> My anxiety and affliction does not arise from my confinement and deprivations in prison. These, indeed, I could bear it ten times more severe, but is caused by my absence, which may be a protracted one, from my dearly beloved Susan and an apprehension which constantly haunts me, that I may be censured by my countrymen. These impressions, which are seldom absent from my mind, act as a corroding canker at my heart.
>
> So maddened am I sometimes by the working of my imagination that I cannot refrain from exclaiming that it would have been a merciful dispensation of Providence if my head had been shot off by the enemy while our vessel lay rolling on the rocks.[37]

Marine William Ray and the rest of the crew of the *Philadelphia* did not have the same quarters as did Bainbridge and the officers. The bashaw viewed all of the *Philadelphia*'s crew—officers and men—as valuable hostages, ripe for ransom. The officers, however, were more valuable than the enlisted men. The Tripolitans put the crew into an old warehouse. Ray described the room as "about 50 feet in length, 20 in breadth and 25 in height, with a flaky front, two front grated windows. It had a most dreary appearance." Where the officers at least had mats and blankets in their quarters, the crew "had nothing to keep us from the cold, damp earth but a thin, tattered sail cloth." To make the accommodations even worse, "the floor of the prison was very uneven, planted with hard pebbles and as we had nothing but a shirt to soften our beds and nothing but the ground for a pillow and very much crowded in the bargain, the clouds of night shed no salutary repose," Ray wrote.[38]

As the officers settled into captivity in relative ease, the enlisted men learned life as a Barbary prisoner would be anything but comfortable. The bashaw expected the crewmen to work, and on their first day in captivity the Arabs separated the crew according to their skills. Carpenters, coopers, blacksmiths, and other tradesmen went to work on the various craft in the bashaw's fleet. The rest of the men worked along the shore, improving the city's fortifications and beginning construction of a battery the men dubbed "Fort American."[39]

Life in the prison was harsh. The men received two meals a day: at noon they ate a hunk of coarse bread dipped in olive oil. In the evening, they had a smattering of salt pork or salt beef, meat the Arabs had pilfered from the *Philadelphia*. When that ran out, the jailors doled out whatever was at hand. It was never enough to fill any one up, but it was enough to keep the men working.

The sailors had no idea how long they would be in jail. Certainly, their countrymen would ransom them. Then again, the whole reason for the war was so the United States would not have to pay tribute or ransom to the Barbary nations.

That first night in captivity, another storm blew in from the west. The rain lashed Tripoli and the men stayed within their prison. The storm pounded the coast for forty hours. When it blew out on November 3, the American sailors saw their worst nightmare. Floating in the harbor, minus a foremast and most of her guns, was the frigate *Philadelphia*, virtually unscathed.[40]

The storm that brought down rain on Tripoli had poured water over Kaliusa Reef, allowing the Tripolitans to float the *Philadelphia* off the rocks. The bashaw ordered the ship's carpenters, led by William Godby, to repair the holes in the bilges. Divers began bringing up the frigate's cannon. Soon, it appeared the *Philadelphia* would be ready to lead the bashaw's fleet against Preble.

For the crew, the sight of the *Philadelphia* riding at anchor in Tripoli harbor was almost too much. Their jailors made sure the Americans knew the Arabs now had the frigate in their possession; they also made sure the 307 captives in Tripoli knew their fate would be an expensive one. "The Pacha and his court did not attempt to conceal their exultation on the capture of the frigate *Philadelphia*," Dr. John Ridgeley wrote. "It was a jubilee in Tripoli. So extravagant were his calculations that he would not listen to any proposal of peace or ransom, for a less sum than one million dollars. In this condition of affairs, it would have been impolitic to have opened a negotiation. It would have been regarded as an evidence of fear and imbecility."[41] The Americans knew they would have to wait for either rescue or ransom.

———⊷⊶———

Capt. William Bainbridge could not believe his eyes when he looked out the window of the U.S. consulate on November 3 where he and his officers were prisoners of Tripoli. Workers swarmed over the decks of the *Philadelphia*, putting cannons back into carriages, scrubbing planks, and patching the holes Bainbridge's crew had made when they had tried to scuttle the ship.

For Bainbridge, it was, he thought, the final nail in his naval coffin. "I have zealously served my country and strenuously endeavored to guard against accidents, but in spite of every effort misfortune has attended me through my naval life," he wrote to Preble on November 6. "Guadeloupe and Algiers have witnessed part of them, but Tripoli strikes the death blow to my future prospects."[42]

Bainbridge knew how the Tripolitans freed *Philadelphia* from the reef, but was at a loss to explain her seeming seaworthy appearance. "Before I surrendered, I had the magazine drowned and many articles of value destroyed," he wrote to U.S. consul Tobias Lear in Algiers. "A gale from westward raised the waters on this coast and made such a sea as floated the ship off." The *Philadelphia*'s former commander also began something of a spin campaign. Claims his men had failed to resist the pirates as they boarded were untrue, he told Lear. "Would to God the attempt had been made, we should then have had a chance of convincing our country that an opportunity and not courage was wanting. Unfortunate for us they gave us no such chance."[43]

He also said there was no way to know his scuttling attempt did not work. "We were not Gods to foresee the wind and sea," he told Lear and Preble in separate letters. "Even if we knew the sea would so rise and had we been apprised at all, it could have availed us nothing for in far less time than that period, ten gunboats carrying 18 and 24 pounders, besides several vessels, which could take their station on each quarter; and not a gun of ours could be brought to bear on them, certainly would have cut is all to pieces."[44]

Bainbridge started writing letters soon after his capture, searching anywhere he could for a sympathetic ear. Letters from Tripoli went to diplomats in Algiers, Spain, and Italy, as well as to officials in the United States. He continued to write to Preble, looking for any sign the commodore could provide exoneration for the loss of the *Philadelphia*.

In return, Bainbridge had only silence. The commander sent letters to the commodore on November 11, 16, and 25, yet received no replies. The silence continued for nearly two months, adding to Bainbridge's distress. As late as February 8, he wrote to Tobias Lear, saying, "I have not yet received a line from Commodore Preble and am at a loss to account for his long silence, particularly as I have wrote him many letters and pointed out the safe channel of conveyance."[45]

What Bainbridge did not know was it would take nearly a month for the news of the *Philadelphia*'s capture to reach the commodore, and when it did, it would arrive via a British man-of-war.

CHAPTER 7

"THERE SHALL NOT BE AN IDLE SHIP"

T HE U.S. MEDITERRANEAN SQUADRON made its way slowly toward Tripoli. On November 1 Edward Preble was still in Cadiz with the bulk of his ships. The forty-three-year-old commodore had put the final touches on his plan to deal with Tripoli, although his first order of business was to secure his base at Syracuse.

Preble chose the ancient Sicilian city as his operations center mainly for its distance from British bases. The commodore was tired of repeated British attempts to induce American sailors to desert. He also wanted a place that offered supplies. The British bases at Malta and Gibraltar, although open to American ships, had little left over once they provided for Adm. Horatio Nelson's fleet.

Syracuse had the resources the Americans would need even though it was farther away from Tripoli than either British base, Preble told Secretary of the Navy Robert Smith. "This harbor is one of the best in the Mediterranean, and the country will afford us fresh meat, vegetables, fruit, candles and rice cheaper than they can be purchased in America," Preble wrote. "The inhabitants are extremely friendly and civil and our sailors cannot desert. In fact, I think it by far the best place for the squadron to rendezvous."[1]

Preble ordered Lt. Stephen Decatur and the schooner *Enterprise* to escort the provision ship *Traveller* to Syracuse to establish the base. The rest of the ships in the squadron, he decided, would rotate on blockade duty: "I shall remain off the coast as long as it is possible for any of their cruisers to keep out. I do not think it possible to cruise all winter without hazarding too much, for should any accident happen to this ship, and any of the other Barbary Powers should break out upon us, the consequences may be dreadful to our commerce on these seas."[2]

The plan was a bold one. Even the Royal Navy all but shut down its operations during the winter months. Preble, however, intended to carry the war right to the bashaw. "There shall not be an idle ship in my squadron," he told Secretary Smith.[3]

The American squadron left Cadiz, Spain, on November 8, 1803. The *Argus* headed west for Morocco. The *Enterprise* set a course for Sicily with the *Traveller*. The *Constitution* and *Syren* made sail for Tunis and Algiers.

Only the *Argus* made anything like good time. A massive storm came out of the east, pushing Hull toward Morocco while all but stalling Preble. The commodore did not reach Algiers until November 22, where he dropped off the new U.S. consul, Tobias Lear, who was to stay there. Two days later, Preble met the *Amazon* and learned what had happened October 31 off Tripoli. The news from the British warship swept through the *Constitution* in a flash. The *Philadelphia* was lost, her crew imprisoned. No one knew how Preble would react.

For the commodore, this was devastating news. The *Philadelphia* was one-third of his total strength. Now he would have to rely solely on the *Constitution* and the guns of four small ships—the *Syren*, *Vixen*, *Nautilus*, and *Enterprise*—to bring the bashaw to terms. In his fit of rage over the incident, he told his brother, Henry, he had no intention of shouldering any blame for the loss of the frigate: "If I am censured for sending the *Philadelphia* to blockade Tripoli alone it is unjust and proceeds from want of information. I sent the *Vixen* of sixteen 18-pounders, carronades, in company with her and wholly under the command of Captain Bainbridge, but he thought proper to send her to look out off the island of Lampedusa. If he had kept her with him, it is probable it would have saved his ship."[4]

Lucky for the crew, the commodore did not know the asking price for Bainbridge and his crew. The bashaw had sent word to Lear in Algiers and Richard Farquhar, the U.S. consul in Malta, that his price was a firm $3 million. Farquhar called it an "unreasonable demand." Lear thought that price could go down to as little as $450,000 or $500,000, but even he believed "this is certainly too high."[5]

At that moment, however, ransom and tribute demands did not worry Preble. The commodore had to come up with a new plan to deal with Tripoli and overcome his own anger at what had happened. Three days after learning from the *Amazon* what had happened off Kaliusa Reef, Preble received the first of Bainbridge's letters. The *Constitution* was in Malta, on her way to Tripoli. The news changed everything for Preble. "This affair distresses me beyond description and very much deranges my plans of operation for the present," he told Secretary of the Navy Robert Smith. "I fear our national character will sustain an injury with the Barbarians." Preble changed course, heading for Sicily where he could assemble his now-depleted squadron and decide on his next course of action. No one could doubt that he, Preble, would have suffered a much a different fate. "Would to God that the officers and crew of the *Philadelphia*, had one and all, determined to prefer death to slavery," he told Secretary Smith. "It is possible such a determination might have saved them from either."[6]

Still, just three days after learning of the fate of his second capital ship, the commodore's mind was working. The steel was there and now, too, was the resolve. "I do not believe the *Philadelphia* will ever be of service to Tripoli," he told Secretary Smith. "I shall hazard much to destroy her. It will undoubtedly cost us many lives, but it must be done. I am surprised she was not rendered useless before her colors were struck."[7]

———◆———

Two weeks after he had learned about the *Philadelphia*, Preble was ready to get back to sea. His anger did not boil over the way his officers might have expected three months before. Instead, there was an icy resolve about him. Preble would take the war to Tripoli no matter what.

On December 10 he gave Decatur orders to make ready to get under way. The *Enterprise*, Preble said, would join the *Constitution* on a reconnaissance of Tripoli. When the ships arrived off the pirate bastion he expected the *Syren* to be there as well. Together, those three ships would remind the bashaw that the U.S. Navy was still in business.[8]

Although his anger was palpable, Preble took the time to reply to Captain William Bainbridge. Official news moved slowly, tied to U.S.-flagged ships, and Preble waited until he received copies of Bainbridge's letter to make his own official answer to his former second-in-command. He also wrote home. The commodore, in his diary, confided his rage over the surrender and his fear it could widen the conflict: "The loss of that ship and capture of the crew with all its consequences are of the most serious and alarming nature to the United States. If it should not involve us in a war with Tunis and Algiers in consequence of the weakness of our squadron, yet still it will protract the war with Tripoli."[9]

To Preble's credit, he never showed his gloomy side to Bainbridge or his men. To Bainbridge he offered only his support. The increasingly desperate tone of Bainbridge's letters did not escape the commodore. He told Bainbridge, "I am honored with your several favors [letters]. I feel most sensibly for the misfortune of yourself, your officers and your crew." He also tried to buoy Bainbridge's spirits. "God bless and preserve you," he said. "May you have health and live to enjoy the smiles of the fickly goddess. I shall write to you often. . . . Conscious yourself of having done your duty, and the

certificate of your officers approbating your conduct and exertions the day
the ship was lost, must afford you consolation amidst your misfortunes."[10]

⎯⎯◆⎯⎯

The *Constitution* and *Enterprise* left Syracuse on December 10. Nine days
later they paid a courtesy call at Malta, where they rode out another nasty
gale that blew up out of the west. From Malta the two ships pressed on to
Tripoli. For Decatur the voyage was both good and bad. The young lieutenant was happy to be at sea and heading into action, but still somewhat
disappointed at losing command of the *Argus*, although he tried not to let
his emotion show.

While still in the United States, he had sent a letter to his close friend,
Charles Stewart, telling the commander of the brig *Syren* he planned to sail
rings around him with the *Argus*. Now, young Decatur—impetuous, proud,
and brave—was losing his first command. It was November 6 and, like the
rest of the squadron, Decatur knew nothing about what had happened off
Tripoli on Kaliusa Reef. That news would not reach him until the end of the
month when the *Constitution* arrived in Syracuse. Instead, he made a tour of
his new ship and met the officers and crew of the *Enterprise*.

The first man Decatur met was Lt. James Lawrence, his first lieutenant.
Lawrence was a New Jersey native, born October 1, 1781. He grew up the
unwanted son of the second marriage of a Tory father who remarried late in
life. His older sister, Elizabeth, raised him, and by age twelve Lawrence had
begun to talk about a career at sea. Thanks to better-than-average finances,
Lawrence went to school to learn mathematics, navigation, and astronomy.
His education earned him a spot as a midshipman on the rickety old *Ganges*
under Capt. Thomas Tingey.

The *Ganges* was not much of a warship. A converted merchantman, she
was the first armed ship the U.S. Navy sent to the Caribbean to stop French
privateers during the Quasi-War. Lawrence showed himself as a kind, intelligent officer but never had the chance to distinguish himself in combat. The
Ganges returned from a three-month cruise without engaging a single enemy.

Tingey saw something in Lawrence and had him transferred to the
24-gun frigate *Adams* as an acting lieutenant. Subsequently, the end of the
Quasi-War brought with it a downsizing in the number of ships and officers
in the Navy. Congress retained Lawrence, but kept him on as a midshipman,
not as a lieutenant. For the twenty-year-old Lawrence, it was an affront to
his honor.

The enraged Lawrence fired off an angry letter to Secretary of the Navy
Samuel Smith, who was new to the job. In it, he emphatically objected to
"the fact he must remain a midshipman. This was the first of several forceful

expressions of indignation in regard to bureaucratic decisions which affected his career."[11]

Samuel Smith, however, did not care. He told Lawrence he could take the demotion or leave the Navy. Lawrence decided to stay in the service. He eventually received his lieutenancy on April 6, 1802, and Smith's brother, Robert, who took over as Navy secretary on July 27, 1802, assigned him to the *Enterprise*.

Lawrence had roughly a year under the harsh discipline of Andrew Sterrett before Isaac Hull took command. Under Hull, Lawrence's natural abilities came through. He came to everyone's attention when he helped lead an amphibious raid on a convoy of grain-carrying *feluccas*, a cross between a lateen-rigged ship and a galley, inside Tripoli harbor.

Isaac Hull and the *Enterprise* spotted the ships the night of June 10, 1803. The *Enterprise* went inshore while Capt. John Rodgers in the frigate *New York* stayed offshore. The crews of the smaller ships beached their vessels rather than take on the American warships. Rodgers and Hull asked Commo. Richard Morris for permission to attack the vessels with a combined raiding party from each ship. Morris agreed and put Lt. David Porter in command.

Porter and six boats of men from the *New York* joined Lawrence and four boats from the *Enterprise*, as well the *Enterprise* Marine commander, Lt. Enoch Lane. All told, fifty sailors and Marines rowed toward shore in eight boats, along with two boats full of combustibles.

On shore, the Tripolitans waited. Nearly one thousand infantry and cavalry milled about the beach, with their leader riding a massive black stallion, exhorting his men with his saber. The Americans landed and immediately engaged the Arabs with pistols, muskets, and cutlasses. The landing however, was simply cover for the two boats of sailors who set fire to the *feluccas*.

The Tripolitans attempted to surround the American force, but Porter and Lawrence kept their men close to the beach. The firing became hotter and Porter went down, wounded in both legs. Lawrence took command and ably led the force off the beach and back to the *New York* and *Enterprise*. The *feluccas* burned fiercely as the Americans left the shore, although a party of Tripolitans tried to douse the flames. The *Enterprise* moved in to cover Lawrence's withdrawal and opened fire on the *feluccas*, hampering the firefighting effort.

Lawrence returned to the *Enterprise* a hero. Porter commended Lawrence for his "dashing courage and skill," and the young lieutenant was a star on the rise.[12]

Lawrence was a bit different from his peers. A quiet man, he made friends easily, and quickly became close to officers and crew alike. He also believed, as did Hull and Decatur, that flogging was wrong and that men would respond to praise more readily than to beatings.[13]

The young lieutenant was devoted to those around him. After his marriage, he made a solemn vow to write to his new bride as often as he could. Life at sea made the promise hard to keep. His wife, however, did not want excuses—she wanted mail: "My dear Julia, after the most boisterous and unpleasant passage I have ever experienced I arrived at this place yesterday without sustaining any material injury, and on landing received your rebuking tho' affectionate letter," he wrote her in one letter. "It has had such an effect on my mind, that rather than receive such another I would write a half dozen each day during my absence."[14]

Decatur liked Lawrence from the start and Lawrence returned the sentiment. Somehow the two seemed to balance each other. Both were fighters yet both would work well together.[15]

Decatur brought with him as his second lieutenant young Joseph Bainbridge. The two had been inseparable since Joseph's duel on Malta. Now that his older brother, William, was in a Tripolitan prison, Joseph Bainbridge wanted to be in the thick of any effort to help the *Philadelphia*.

The younger Bainbridge was twenty-one, born in Princeton like his older brother. Unlike William, however, young Joseph did not have a dark cloud hanging over him. His duel with the secretary of the Maltese governor earned him a reputation for courage, while his conduct as an officer appears to have been exemplary. He was devoted to Decatur and would gladly follow his commander anywhere.

Third lieutenant on the *Enterprise* was another new man, Jonathan Thorn. A midshipman on the *Constitution*, Preble liked his deportment and on November 7 ordered Thorn to join Decatur as an acting lieutenant.[16] Thorn was twenty-four, a native of Schenectady, New York. He joined the Navy on April 28, 1800, and made steady progress, especially under Preble. When he received his orders, Preble gave him a rather strong reminder of what he expected.

Preble told Thorn he was "to observe and execute the general printed instruction as what orders and directions you shall from time to time receive from your captain or any other superior officer for the United States Service." He also gave him a stern warning: "You may answer the contrary at your peril."[17]

His final officers were a pair of midshipmen, Walter Boyd and Thomas Macdonough.

Boyd was something of a roughneck. A physically imposing sailor, he enjoyed his drink, a little too much. On December 2, he went ashore and promptly drank himself into trouble. "While in this state of mind he maltreated several of the inhabitants." Decatur told Preble. "Lieut. Thorn (who was present) told him his conduct was extremely improper and ordered him on board. He replied he would comply but continued with his abuse." Lawrence then joined Thorn in subduing the angry Boyd and hauled him into a boat. Boyd tried to pull a knife on Lawrence, but the *Enterprise*'s first lieutenant, who was sober, quickly pinned Boyd's arms behind his back and knocked him into the bottom of the boat.[18]

Decatur, who disliked flogging, took the step of telling Preble about Boyd's misconduct and ordered Boyd to write to the commodore. Boyd's apology was not only sincere, but also betrayed a sense of fear. After all, Preble's anger was legendary, and the young Mr. Boyd had no wish to run afoul of the commodore: "It is with the utmost regret that I am under the necessity of addressing you a letter on so disagreeable a subject as my late misconduct on shore; confiding however to your mercy I hazard to make the request of your pardon. My superior officers whom I must confess I shamefully offended have granted me their forgiveness, and agreeably to the information of Captain Decatur, it rests entirely with you to extricate me from the evils arising from my folly."[19]

Boyd waited for an answer—and undoubtedly feared every second. Would it be censure, court-martial, or the cat-o-nine tails? When he received Preble's answer, Boyd was relieved but embarrassed: the commodore had ordered him to make a public apology to officers and crew of the *Enterprise* as well as apologize to the Sicilians he had insulted while on shore. Boyd did so, but Decatur never forgot his conduct.[20]

Macdonough was a different story. The twenty-year-old native of New Castle, Delaware, had joined the Navy at sixteen in 1799 and served on the old *Ganges* in the Quasi-War, and later on the *Constellation*. He was on the *Ganges* when she captured the French schooner *Fortune* off Cuba, but soon caught yellow fever. The disease put him in a hospital where he was able to recover from the usually fatal disease. When he arrived home, he had only the clothes on his back and a worn-our pair of shoes. He also had a burning love for the Navy.[21]

After cruising on the *Constellation* in 1802, he received orders to join the crew of the *Philadelphia*. Almost as soon as William Bainbridge arrived in the Mediterranean, the unlucky captain and the *Philadelphia* seized a prize, the Moroccan ship *Mirboka*. Bainbridge made Macdonough one of the prize officers and left him at Gibraltar. When Preble arrived at Gibraltar and returned *Mirboka* to the Moroccan emperor, Macdonough joined the *Constitution*'s crew. Then the news of the *Philadelphia*'s capture arrived. "Thus I was providentially saved from this prison and the apprehension of death which surrounded those of my shipmates in the power of a merciless foe," he wrote his parents.[22]

On December 14 Preble ordered Macdonough to join Decatur's crew. When he met Decatur, he had the same effect on his commander that Decatur had on others. They became instant friends, with Decatur calling Macdonough his "favorite midshipman."[23]

Macdonough was also a crucial source of information. He was intimately familiar with the *Philadelphia*. Decatur's father—Stephen Sr.—was the first commander of the ill-fated frigate, but Stephen Jr. had seen the ship only from a distance. In Macdonough there was an officer who knew her every board. He and Decatur would talk about the *Philadelphia* until it became Decatur's obsession.[24]

Finally, there was the crew. Nearly all agreed to remain on board when Preble made his deal to get them a bonus of two months' pay after Commodore Morris' silly decision to release the men after just six months of service. Morale was high on the little schooner, thanks to months under the steady though friendly hand of Isaac Hull. One month under Decatur proved to the crew it had another commander who cared about the welfare of the common sailor.

The Boyd incident sealed the crew's affection. Sterrett undoubtedly would have flogged Boyd before court-martialing him. Decatur made the big brawler apologize—to everyone.

As Decatur looked around his vessel, however, his keen eye saw problems. The *Enterprise* was the only ship in the U.S. Navy to see continual service since her launch, and it showed. Although the crew had replaced her rigging in Syracuse, the little schooner needed a thorough overhaul. The problem was that Preble could not spare the schooner. He needed her to work inshore of the *Constitution* off Tripoli. An overhaul, Decatur realized, would have to wait.[25]

So, too, would any reunion between the three boyhood friends. As busy as Decatur and the *Enterprise* were, Somers and the *Nautilus* were even busier. Somers cruised the Mediterranean, looking for U.S. and enemy vessels almost from his arrival. It was, his family kept telling him, his chance to equal if not surpass his old friends. "I hope when you all meet together and should be ordered by your commodore in an enterprise that the *Nautilus* and her officers may be the meteor that may light and impress the rest," his cousin wrote.[26]

—◆—

When they were together, Somers, Stewart, and Decatur formed an effective trio. That does not mean, however, that Somers was happy to sit back and watch as his closest friends reveled in the spoils of victory without him. Somers had his own plans and yearned for glory as much as any other officer in the Navy. When he took command of the *Nautilus* in March 1803, Somers made it clear to his family he intended to use his schooner as a warship, even though the *Nautilus* was somewhat small. His brother-in-law, William Jones Keen, evidently said as much to Somers, telling the new skipper he could probably outrun trouble should he meet any off Tripoli. Somers quickly set Keen straight: "I am glad to find that you think I have one advantage, that is if I can't fight I can run. But believe me dear sir [I am] far from having any such thoughts, of running while in the Mediterranean."[27]

His determination to take the *Nautilus* into battle marked something of a change in how Somers viewed his first command. The young lieutenant was not all that impressed with what he found when he first took over the schooner to supervise her conversion into a warship. "Her quarter deck is very slight, with timbers hardly stout enough to support the recoiling of the guns, only 2 inch boards," Somers wrote. "She has a trunk over the cabin and lays very low, which must be altered to keep the people from being washed off. Much work has to be done to her. The man that sold her says he will be damned if anything that ever floated can beat her sailing. After seeing her, I could say but little as it was my first visit."[28]

Henry Spencer, the shipwright behind the *Enterprise*, also built the *Nautilus*, although she was slightly smaller than the *Enterprise*. The Navy bought her from merchant Thomas Tennant of Maryland for $18,863. Somers' first task was to supervise the schooner's transformation from a trading vessel into a ship of war. According to Somers, his new command measured "one hundred and eighty-five tons, between eighty and ninety feet on deck, 26 feet beam and nine-foot-7-and-a-half-inch hold."[29]

Somers spent two months preparing the *Nautilus* for war. He had advice from William Bainbridge as the latter prepared the *Philadelphia* for her voyage to the Mediterranean. Bainbridge stressed the need for a clean spar deck and reinforced magazines, two ideas with which Somers concurred. Still, on May 15 the young lieutenant remained unsure about his new ship: "I am not much satisfied with her quarters. [The shipwright] says it has been contemplated to have netting from the rail to the gunnels and filled with wadding, which I do not approve of, for the wadding, when it becomes wet and never a chance to dry, is heavy as thin plank and cork."[30]

By late June, however, Somers was satisfied with the conversion. A gang of carpenters and joiners worked to reinforce the schooner's ribs so her deck could not only bear the weight of her armament, twelve 32-pound carronades and a pair of long 9-pound cannon, but also could take the pounding from the guns in action. The workers also swapped out many of her side timbers, exchanging the thin planks of a merchant boat for more robust timbers used in warships. As he prepared to leave for the Mediterranean, Somers' crew arrived. Among his officers was a twenty-year-old lieutenant, James Decatur, the younger brother of Stephen. Somers practically grew up with James, and told his brother-in-law "I am better pleased" to have a friend among the crew. Somers was just as happy with the rest of the officers: "There are very fine young men attached to the *Nautilus* all of good families."[31]

When James Decatur arrived on the *Nautilus*, he delivered a letter to Somers from his sister, Sarah Somers Keen. Once more, the family's expectations stoked Somers' own desires for glory, although he told Sarah he was not entirely sure just what that would mean. His sister, apparently, believed naval duty meant sightseeing, as she asked him for a variety of souvenirs from Italy and from the rest of the classical Old World. Somers tried to let her down gently as well as explain to her the realities of Navy life: "My dear sister I can't say, what I shall be able to bring, when I return from the Mediterranean. Did I say that by my orders I am to cruise for two years, from the time of weighing anchor—so that if I am fortunate I will send it all to you—for to promise two years before hand, I am sure you will think the chance but small. You no doubt will think this a long time to be gone. I should myself three years ago have thought it an age, but now only a West Indies voyage."[32]

It took him less than a month to go from Hampton Roads, Virginia, to Gibraltar. On his arrival, he almost boasted of the *Nautilus*' qualities to Preble. "The *Nautilus* has performed well, sails fast, strained nothing, is tight and strong and I have no complaint to make of her," he wrote.[33]

Somers spent his first month in the Mediterranean waiting for Preble and looking for Commo. Richard Morris' squadron. He never found Morris. He cruised from Malta to Tripoli and back to Gibraltar, thirsting for action but finding none. "I chased everything that had appearance of Tripolitan," he wrote to his brother-in-law. "I found none of our ships at Malta and but little information could get of them only that they had set sail about forty days before. From thence I proceeded off Tripoli, saw none of our ships there and but only two small vessels in Tripoli. I went in close to the batteries and fired a shot at them. Hove to for a short time, but I saw no gunboats make an appearance."[34]

It was the first time Somers and the *Nautilus* sailed into Tripoli harbor, but not the last. When Preble arrived at Gibraltar, he finally caught up with Somers and gave him orders that would keep the *Nautilus* running from one end of the Mediterranean to the other for the next three months.

CHAPTER 8

BIRTH OF A PLAN

T HE *CONSTITUTION* AND THE *ENTERPRISE* arrived off Tripoli at 8:30 a.m. on December 23. Commodore Preble ordered Decatur to take the schooner right into the harbor. From the *Constitution*'s quarterdeck, Preble could see the bashaw's fleet bobbing at anchor. To the south, however, he saw a ship trying to slip out of the harbor.

The *Constitution* hoisted a signal to the *Enterprise* and Decatur changed course and chased the vessel. Decatur, who was flying an English flag at the time, caught up to his quarry about two miles south of the *Constitution*. The ship was a ketch and was flying a Turkish flag, but something about her made the Americans suspicious.

Preble was also flying an English flag and the ketch's captain had no reason to suspect the stoppage was anything more than a Royal Navy spot check. The *Enterprise* escorted the ketch to the *Constitution*, and Preble quickly gave the Turkish captain a shock. He lowered the British ensign, hoisted the Stars and Stripes, and informed the captain he was now a prisoner of the United States Navy.[1]

The commodore and the young lieutenant took a closer look at their prize. There was not much to see. The ketch was typical of Arab and eastern Mediterranean craft that plied the waters from Constantinople to Gibraltar. At one time maybe she had been trim, but no one would call her handsome. Years of work had turned her sides a dull gray and she looked about as drab as any vessel in the region.

Her cargo hold was a different story. According to her captain, the ship was the *Mastico*. She was on her way to Benghazi when Decatur intercepted her. She carried "two cannon and some muskets, pistols and has on board a Turkish Master, seven Greeks and four Turks, sailors, and a Turkish officer," Preble wrote in his diary. While the crew piqued the Americans' curiosity, they also found "two Tripoline [Tripolitan] officers, ten Tripoline

[Tripolitan] soldiers as passengers and forty negro men, women and children which the master says was taken on board at Tripoli at the account of the bashaw . . . to present to the Pasha in Constantinople."[2]

That was not all. The search also turned up two more cannon, uniforms, and other property obviously filched from the *Philadelphia*, and a claim the ship was to pick up more "presents" at Benghazi. Only the captain had papers that appeared genuine. As the Americans examined the ketch, Dr. Pietro Francisco Crocillo took Preble aside. A Sicilian doctor, Crocillo worked for the bashaw and recently had left Tripoli. He was in the city the day the *Philadelphia* hit the reef and he told Preble he recognized not only the *Mastico*, but also her captain.

The *Mastico*, Crocillo said, flew Turkish colors that day in October, just as she had when the *Enterprise* caught her. The second the *Philadelphia* lowered the Stars and Stripes, however, Crocillo said the *Mastico* lowered the Turkish flag, hoisted the crescent moon banner of Tripoli, and landed a boarding party on the frigate. The captain, who claimed he was Turkish, was also from Tripoli. Crocillo said he was among the first to claim the *Philadelphia* for the bashaw.[3]

That cinched it for Preble. The Sicilian doctor confirmed the commodore's own suspicions. "Conceiving it improper to let her pass under all these circumstances," Preble wrote in his diary, "I ordered all the crew and passengers on board . . . and sent on board two midshipmen and several sailors to conduct her to Syracuse for further examination and have her papers translated."[4]

At 4:00 p.m. on December 23, Preble ordered Decatur and the *Enterprise* to escort the *Mastico* to Sicily. Preble wanted to remain off Tripoli as long as he could to scout the harbor and reestablish the blockade. On December 26, however, another massive storm blew in from the northeast.[5] The winds threatened to push the *Constitution* onto the rocks off the coast of the bashaw's city and Preble had no intention of losing his only other capital ship. He reluctantly turned his frigate toward Sicily. The one good effect was that the storm pushed the 44-gun ship along at top speed. The *Constitution* caught up with the speedy little *Enterprise* on December 27 and both ships, with the *Mastico* in tow, headed for Syracuse.[6]

———— ◆ ————

The *Constitution*, the *Enterprise*, and the little *Mastico* battled storms all the way back to Syracuse. When the convoy arrived at the American base on January 4, everyone needed rest—everyone, that is, but Preble. The commodore already had had ten days during his long journey to think about his prize. The ship would not fetch much, but he was not sure he wanted to surrender it.

Though the *Mastico* sailed under the Turkish flag, Preble doubted she was, in fact, a Turkish ship. Her mixed cargo and crew raised further suspicion. Still, he knew he could not keep the ship if she really belonged to the sultan in Constantinople. The key was her papers, which were in Arabic. "The papers will be translated in a day or two," he told Bainbridge in a letter. "If the captain tells the truth, I shall release her together with a Turkish officer and all the crew which the captain claims, amounting in all to twelve." Preble had different plans for the Tripolitan officers, soldiers, and slaves. "I hope to be able to exchange this cargo for some of you [*sic*] unfortunates," he told Bainbridge. Even the Turkish captain, Preble said, agreed to the idea. "He acknowledges he had no right to be transporting our enemy's officers, soldiers and property in time of war."[7]

The *Mastico* was not the commodore's only concern. Preble continued to think of how he could deal with Tripoli. He knew the key would be small vessels that could get inshore and fight the Tripolitans on their own terms. The loss of the *Philadelphia* continued to plague his preparations. Preble needed more boats. No matter, however. The commodore intended to bring the war to the bashaw with whatever force he had. "I shall make them feel the effect of my remaining force and hope soon to reduce the Bashaw's present demands to something reasonable," he told U.S. consul James Leander Cathcart in Leghorn (Livorno, Italy). "I am told he demands for peace and ransom three millions of dollars. This is a pretty good asking price. I presume our government will never accede to pay anything so extravagant." The commodore also put out the word he wanted to find "gun boats, mortar boats and . . . one or two good Bombadiers and will make their pay handsome if they understand their business."[8]

The *Mastico*, however, could also play a part. During his voyage back to Syracuse, Preble thought about one of his letters from Bainbridge. "Charter a small merchant schooner, fill her with men, and have her commanded by fearless and determined officers," Bainbridge had written. "Let the vessel enter the harbor at night, with her men secreted below deck—steer her directly on board the frigate, and then let the officers and men board, sword in hand." The captive captain had suggested using a local ship to sneak into Tripoli harbor to board and either destroy the *Philadelphia*, or sail her out of captivity.

It was a daring idea, one that could work, especially with the *Mastico*. She sailed in and out of Tripoli at will. The Arabs knew her. She would not raise suspicion.

A plan began to form in Preble's mind.[9] Before he could formulate his plan, however, he needed to know just who really owned the *Mastico*. He needed to get her papers translated. Finally, when he could not find a translator in Syracuse, he decided to head for Malta. In addition, the *Constitution* needed repairs that he could not accomplish in Sicily.

The *Enterprise* was also in dire need of repairs.

Decatur made a thorough inspection of his 12-gun ship and found numerous rotted timbers, a sprung mast, and several leaks. Although the rigging was new, the *Enterprise* needed work. "Her situation in my opinion is such as will make her cruising during the winter months [unless repaired] hazardous," Decatur told Preble. The commodore agreed. The speedy little schooner, the flotilla's "lucky little ship" would get a refit at Syracuse. It would not be the full refit Decatur wanted, but it would at least get the schooner ready for action.[10]

The refit would give the squadron a group of officers, sailors, and Marines with nothing to do, at least temporarily. Preble could look out of his quarters on the *Constitution* and see the *Mastico* riding at anchor. Now he had a daring officer and a trained crew without a ship. Still, he did not know whether he could keep the little ketch.

⎯⎯⎯ ◆ ⎯⎯⎯

Preble and a small staff boarded the schooner *Vixen* and headed for Malta. He arrived there January 13 and immediately found himself caught up in the niceties and intrigues of the Mediterranean island.[11] British governor Sir Alexander Ball treated Preble exactly as he would a Royal Navy commander. He offered Preble use of the facilities, found him a translator, and introduced him around society.

On Malta, Preble came into contact with agents for Hamet Karamanli, brother to Yusuf and, as Hamet put it, rightful ruler in Tripoli. Yusuf, it turned out, had staged a coup that ousted Hamet, sending him into exile in Egypt. Yusuf still feared his brother would raise an army and wrest Tripoli from him. On Preble's arrival at Malta, agents from both Karamanli brothers sent word they wanted to talk.

For Hamet, the topic was a coup. Yusuf, through his agents, wanted to sound out a possible peace proposal. Preble made no secret of his plans to take the war to Tripoli; the near-constant presence of American warships outside the harbor frightened the bashaw. He floated a plan that would return the *Philadelphia* to the United States, although the new nation would still have to pay for peace.

Preble angrily spurned that plan and sent Yusuf's agents on their way. As for Hamet, the commodore thought he could prove useful. Hamet boasted he could raise an army in his power base at Derna and all of Tripoli would follow him. The fact that the previous two commodores did not try to help Hamet surprised Preble. However, as the commodore told Secretary of the Navy Robert Smith, "I have less force than either with ten times the force to contend with." The commodore remained determined to find gunboats and other small craft with which to bring the war to the bashaw. "I will take Tripoli or perish in the attempt," Preble told Secretary Smith. "I am confident that it may easily be destroyed or taken in the summer with gun and mortar boats protected by our cruisers."[12]

It was this kind of talk that frightened Yusuf Karamanli and inspired Preble's squadron. The commodore, however, continued to keep his focus on the *Mastico*. He waited ten days for a Turk he hired to translate the papers found on the ship. For Preble, the choice was simple: if the papers corroborated the captain's tale that he was simply taking gifts to the sultan in Constantinople, all Preble could do was send him on his way. If, however, the captain's tale was false, Preble could seize the ship as a prize and do with it as he decided.

Once translated, the papers told a convoluted tale of ownership and mission. One fact, however, was clear to Preble: the *Mastico* was certainly a blockade runner.

The commodore set sail for Syracuse January 23 and arrived at his base two days later. Once there, he found one more piece of evidence that the *Mastico* was an enemy vessel and not a simple trade ship. Sicilian harbor pilot Salvador Catalano had worked in Tripoli. Preble had hired Catalano before he took the *Constitution* and *Enterprise* to Tripoli so the little Sicilian could keep the American ships off the rocks. Now Catalano had a story to tell.

Catalano told Preble he was in Tripoli the day the *Philadelphia* was seized. The *Mastico*, the pilot said, transported the Tripolitan admiral Mustafa Rais to the ship. The ketch flew Ottoman colors, but was a Tripolitan ship. "As soon as" the *Philadelphia* struck her colors, Catalano said, the *Mastico* "struck her Ottoman colors and hoisted the Tripoline [Tripolitan] flag."[13]

It was the final straw for Preble. He seized the *Mastico* as a lawful prize of war and sent Smith a letter informing the Navy secretary he intended to keep the ketch with his squadron. This decision was a clear violation of Preble's orders. President Thomas Jefferson wanted any prize the American squadron captured to return to the United States for condemnation. Preble used a Sicilian court to determine the status of the *Mastico* as a war prize. The commodore knew Secretary Smith would undoubtedly see Preble wanted to use the *Mastico* in his campaign against Tripoli and likely would not object. Still, just in case a congressman or senator pressed the matter, Preble sent off a note on January 28 telling Secretary Smith that the *Mastico* was "not a proper vessel to cross the Atlantic."[14]

Preble ordered Decatur and the now-idled *Enterprise* crew to begin cleaning up the *Mastico* and getting her ready for sea. It was obvious to everyone the *Mastico* was about to join Preble's flotilla.

As Decatur's men cleaned the ship, they also painted a new name on her stern. From now on, the ketch would be the *Intrepid*.

Even before Preble named the *Intrepid*, she began to figure into the future of the American squadron. Three days before Preble left for Malta, Decatur asked to see his commander to discuss an idea he had.[15]

The young lieutenant wanted to take the *Enterprise*, once refit, and repaint her to look like an Arab vessel. With his schooner disguised, Decatur said he believed he could slip into Tripoli harbor and retake the *Philadelphia*, either destroying her or sailing her right out under the pirates' noses.

Preble said no. Although he admired his young officer's yearning for action, the *Enterprise* was too valuable a ship to risk. Also, the commodore was not at all that sure the schooner could fool the Tripolitans. He thanked Decatur for his eagerness and complimented his bravery. The wily commodore also stored away the fact the captain of the *Enterprise* was willing to undertake what some might see as a one-way mission.[16]

Decatur was not alone in thinking about ways to deny the *Philadelphia* to the bashaw. The day after the *Intrepid* joined the U.S. squadron, Preble's second-in-command, Lt. Charles Stewart, paid a call on him. The twenty-six-year-old had the same idea as his longtime friend, except he wanted to use his brig, the *Syren*, to sneak into Tripoli harbor. The *Syren*, however, was less suited to sneak into the pirate cove than was the *Enterprise*. Preble was just as complimentary toward Stewart as he had been toward Decatur, but denied him permission to conduct the raid. Still, Preble felt a surge of pride in how far his cubs had developed during his few months in command. They were good lads, these young officers, Preble boasted in a letter to Tobias Lear, and they were right on the money.[17]

The *Mastico*, now named the *Intrepid*, would be the instrument to remove the *Philadelphia* from the pirates' equation.

CHAPTER 9

PRISONERS OF THE BASHAW

LIFE FOR THE OFFICERS OF THE *PHILADELPHIA* alternated between boredom and fear. Danish consul Nicholas Nissen managed to find nearly every book from the *Philadelphia* ship's library at markets in Tripoli and bought them for Bainbridge. Lt. David Porter set up a classroom for the younger officers, teaching them mathematics, navigation, and astronomy. Porter even managed to teach himself French.[1]

For Bainbridge, however, there was little to do but write letters to Preble and U.S. diplomats and watch as the Tripolitans worked on refitting his former ship. The captain spent his days on the roof of the former U.S. consulate where the bashaw kept the officers of the *Philadelphia*. From his perch, Bainbridge kept his eyes fixed on the progress the pirates made in repairing the frigate.

When the *Enterprise* and *Constitution* left Syracuse on December 10, it marked Day 41 in captivity for Bainbridge and the 306 men of the *Philadelphia*. So far, at least, Bainbridge wrote, "Our people are kept employed at various branches of their profession and labor. The Officers as yet have not been made to work, myself never will. My life is in their power but my soul is above their command."[2]

Thanks to the work of Nissen and Tobias Lear, Bainbridge had a line of credit on which he could draw. If nothing else, it meant the officers could buy food in the local markets. Still, William Bainbridge knew this was another black mark against his career. He had to find a way to erase it. He wrote to Preble, "Whatever measures my commodore you may pursue, patriotism to my country and sincere friendship to yourself will cause me to offer my fervent prayers for their success. I know they will be actuated by the purest motives and dictated by a comprehensive mind. Would to God I was this moment under its influence."[3]

While telling Preble of his surface emotions, Bainbridge tried to devise a cipher that would allow him to communicate secretly with Preble. His attempts at a code, however, failed. Instead, Bainbridge wrote in "invisible ink," using lemon juice to write secret messages between each line of the letters he sent Preble. In those messages Bainbridge did his best to tell Preble about the strength of the forces arrayed around Tripoli, including his thoughts on how to remove the *Philadelphia* from the pirate fleet.

The big frigate, Bainbridge believed, was Preble's for the taking, if he could organize an expedition to take her.[4]

For Marine private William Ray, each day in captivity was monotonously the same: "Sixteen of us were put to work boring cannon. The labor was intense and having neither bread nor anything else to eat, until 4 o'clock in the afternoon, hunger and weariness were almost insupportable."[5]

The men tried to make their lives somewhat better. Ray said some of the more industrious prisoners "began to construct what they termed cots. They were formed by fastening four pieces of timber at the corners, in the shape of a bedstead, and then weaving a net of ropes like a bed-cord. There were suspended with spikes driven in the wall, and composed a lodging much more comfortable and healthful than the moist earth, but materials for these cots being very scarce, but few of us could be provided with a luxury so rare and inestimable."[6]

While most of the prisoners tried to make the best of their incarceration, a few attempted to curry favor with the Arabs. QM John Wilson, a Swede, gained the enmity of every man when he "turned Turk" (converted to Islam) and worked directly for the bashaw.

Wilson spun wild tales for the bashaw of Bainbridge dumping bags of gold over the side of the frigate before the pirates boarded her. The bashaw questioned Bainbridge, who denied having any money on the *Philadelphia*. The bashaw sent divers to the reef and threw Bainbridge and his officers into a dungeon for a night as punishment, but he never seemed to doubt Wilson. The Swede, Ray wrote, "had turned traitor and given the enemy all the assistance of his power. He now acts as an overseer of our men. This perfidious wretch . . . spoke the lingua franca very fluently. He as yet mingled with us, and acted as a spy, carrying to the bashaw every frivolous and a thousand false tales."[7]

Bainbridge was just as angry as the men. He said Wilson was simply trying to arrange his own release: "I think that it is probable that he will be permitted to leave. If he should and any of our vessels of war meets him,

I hope they will apprehend him as a deserter to answer several capital charges which I shall bring against him."[8]

The crew itself planned its own revenge on the turncoat. One of Ray's fellow Marines beat Wilson senseless one night, only to end up in the bashaw's torture chamber. There, the unfortunate Marine suffered a typical Tripoli punishment, the *bastinado*.

According to Ray, the Tripolitan jailers would tie a man's feet together and pass them through a rope loop. One man would pin the offender on his stomach while two others raised the soles of the man's feet. A fourth would whip the man's feet with a bamboo cane. The standard punishment, Ray said, was five hundred *bastinadoes*.[9]

Torture was a constant threat for the enlisted men. However, they had a more pressing problem: Bainbridge reported the "seamen are much in want of clothing," with Ray adding they lived with just the "shirts on our backs."[10]

Despite the threat of punishment, the American sailors looked for any way they could to show their resistance. When the bashaw decided to ride past their prison one day, the *Philadelphia*'s crewmen showed their contempt for the tyrant. "Wilson came and told us that it was the Bashaw's orders that we should parade, in single file, in front of our prison, with our hats off, and when he should make his appearance we must give him three cheers," Ray said. "He presently made his entrance into the yard, and being marshaled according to orders, some of our silly asses swung their hats and brayed like the animal they personated, but the most of us refused, with a laudable spirit of indignation, this mean and sycophantic testimonial of a tyrant's applause."[11]

The sailors, however, no matter how much they might show their contempt for the bashaw, were still sailors. For Ray, that meant one thing: "To the disgrace of human nature be it said that although we all had an equal share of bread allowed us, some had the meanness, the selfishness, the brutality to steal from their companions in misery the only ligament of food and body. We frequently divided our pittance and kept one loaf overnight to eat in the morning, and often when morning came we found ourselves pillaged of our stores and nothing to silence the importunate calls of hunger."[12]

———————

Karamanli kept his American prisoners busy. He put Private Ray and the rest of the ordinary sailors and Marines to work strengthening the fortifications around Tripoli harbor.

The bashaw was no fool. In fact, everyone that met him said just the opposite. Sailing Master William Knight of the *Philadelphia* described Karamanli as "a handsome man" who was "much active." Even Ray, who despised the bashaw, commented on his keen eye and obvious intelligence.[13]

Karamanli knew the real value of his prisoners was in ransom. His initial demand for $3 million was nothing more than a feeler. The appearance of American warships outside the harbor in the middle of winter told him he now faced an adversary who would not dawdle like Dale or Morris. This Preble was someone to fear.

Using the Americans to strengthen his defenses only made sense. They were, after all, essentially his slaves. These defenses included Fort American and seven guns that the sailors and Marines were forced to drag into place.[14]

Other prisoners had it somewhat better. Surgeon Jonathan Cowdery found himself treating much of the bashaw's court. When he managed to cure the bashaw's youngest daughter of a fever, the Tripoli regent made Cowdery his personal physician. It gave Cowdery the chance to see more of Tripoli than any other officer. He did his best to see the crew, but Karamanli's tolerance did not extend that far.

Cowdery said one sailor "in a fit of despair tried to kill himself, but was prevented by the Turks when in the act of cutting his throat. The wound did not prove fatal." Cowdery also saw the Tripolitans launch a new warship— a 6-gun schooner he called "tolerably handsome." The city and its defenses were strong and Karamanli was obviously a wily opponent.[15]

What Cowdery did not know was just how clever Karamanli could be. The bashaw was already looking to cut a deal for the *Philadelphia* with one of the neighboring Barbary states. Rumors began circulating in December 1803 that the bashaw was willing to swap the American frigate for a pair of 24-gun xebecs—fast, shallow draft vessels that were perfect for raiding merchantmen in the Mediterranean. The rumors reached Preble via U.S. consul Tobias Lear in Algiers, but no one knew whether it was just talk.

According to Lear and several sources on Malta, Karamanli expected either Algiers or Tunis to make the trade, then to use the *Philadelphia* to curry favor with Morocco. The two xebecs could go to sea from either of those ports under their colors and, once at large in the Mediterranean, hoist the Tripolitan flag and raid American commerce at will. If the bashaw even knew about the loss of the *Mastico*, he probably did not care. He had the Americans' second-most powerful vessel, and now he had a plan to use it.[16]

———— ◆ ————

January 30 was just another day for Marine private William Ray and the rest of the crew of the *Philadelphia*. Ray and a gang of sailors spent yet more time working on the fortifications around Tripoli harbor. The bashaw, fully aware of Preble's intentions to bring the war to him, wanted to ring the harbor with cannon. The American captives made the perfect laborers.

Bainbridge spent the day writing letters, while his officers, under Porter's tutelage, continued their study of mathematics, astronomy, and navigation. For Bainbridge, however, there was little solace. The sight of the frigate *Philadelphia* riding at anchor under the guns of the bashaw was a constant reminder of his ill luck.

Bainbridge also noticed the state of his crew. The bashaw's jailors rather gleefully delighted in stealing their uniforms and wearing them around town, leaving the Americans with little more than undergarments to wear. Bainbridge sent several letters to Preble asking him to provide clothing for his crew; he also asked Danish consul Nicholas Nissen to see if any clothes were available.

Cowdery spent January 30 attending to the bashaw's children. Just two weeks before, the doctor said a member of the bashaw's court tried to sell the officers some of their own clothes for $600. The officers refused.

For all of the captive crew of the *Philadelphia*, even though January 30 was a Monday, there was nothing new about their routine.[17] It was a much different story on the other side of the Mediterranean.

———————

Syracuse was bustling with activity and excitement. Preble put Decatur and the crew of the *Enterprise* to work cleaning the *Intrepid*. The commodore watched the work with interest. He saw how smoothly Decatur commanded his men. There was no shouting, no swearing—just a determination about the detail that spoke volumes of the young officer.

Preble also wondered about the men Decatur commanded. The *Enterprise* crew could have been a problem—a major problem—after Commo. Richard Morris promised to release them from service after six months. Preble managed to keep the crew on by paying out an advance; under Decatur, the *Enterprise* was a model ship.

The *Intrepid*, although busy, was not in the best shape. The little ketch was dirty, smelled, and, worst of all, was infested with vermin. Everything from rats to nasty little biting insects called the ship home. Sailors would have to fumigate the ketch before anyone could use her.

Decatur's first job was to clean the ship. He put Lt. James Lawrence in charge of the operation and Lawrence quietly led his detail into the *Intrepid*'s hold. Once there, they used gunpowder, cordage, and other materials to create a smoky fire to drive out the vermin.

Lawrence did everything very carefully. Fires and wooden ship did not mix well and Lawrence knew all too well that Commodore Preble was watching. Preble had whipped a sailor when he botched a fumigation attempt on the *Constitution*, and everyone knew it.

As Lawrence's detail worked below deck, gangs of sailors worked on the *Intrepid*'s rigging. Her former owners did not pay much attention to maintenance, something Preble drilled into his officers' and men's heads. The problem Decatur faced, however, was that if he cleaned up the *Intrepid* too much, she might not look like the little merchant she always was.

Decatur's men spent all of January 30 working on the *Intrepid*.

The brig *Syren* sat alongside the *Enterprise*. Lieutenant Commandant Charles Stewart also had a solid crew, and was a steady, resourceful leader. Preble needed both on the mission he planned. His only question was who would command the assault on the *Philadelphia*.

Nathaniel Haraden, the *Constitution*'s sailing master, saw the commodore strolling alone on the quarterdeck. He also saw Stephen Decatur and Charles Stewart mounting the gangway to come on board the *Constitution*. It was 7:00 p.m.[18]

———◆———

As soon as they arrived, the two young officers—and close friends—reported to Commo. Edward Preble. They stood before him, Decatur dark-haired and resolute, Stewart slightly taller, a little leaner. They were alike in how they led and inspired their men yet different in their personalities.

Preble knew either officer could command the expedition but the decision had been made. There was simply something about Decatur that led the commodore to give the junior officer the responsibility of destroying the *Philadelphia*.[19] "I have no doubt but Lt. Decatur with the officers and men under his command will be able to take possession and destroy her," Preble said when he announced his decision to both men.[20] The men would come from the *Enterprise* and would be volunteers. Orders would follow later. For now, Decatur was to begin readying the *Intrepid* for war.

If Preble's decision bothered Stewart, he did not show it. In fact, Stewart seemed almost happy to allow his friend to command the *Intrepid*. Stewart was going with the *Syren*. He did not know the entire plan yet, but he knew he would have a part in what the squadron surmised was going to be the most daring expedition the U.S. Navy had yet attempted. Although he went to Preble with a similar mission, Stewart believed Decatur was the right man to take the *Intrepid* into Tripoli harbor.[21]

Decatur's reaction to Preble's decision was elation, then realization of just what he had to do. He was about to take a leaky old merchant ship with just a couple of cannon into a harbor ringed with 115 cannons to attack a 38-gun frigate.

The young lieutenant commandant began to think about everything he would have to do to get the *Intrepid* ready for her mission. He would wait until the last minute to select his crew. He still did not know the details of what Preble wanted.

As he made his way back to the *Enterprise*, now in overhaul, Decatur also thought about the fact his mission was to destroy the proud warship his father once commanded.

"He was aware that if the expedition should prove successful, it would render the mortification of the bashaw doubly severe," said S. Putnam Waldo, a contemporary and early biographer of Decatur, "to see a little vessel that lately belonged to his own marine force, boldly advance under the guns of his battery and castle, and destroy the largest ship in his navy."[22]

———◆◆———

Tuesday, January 31, 1804, dawned cold and blustery. A gale threatened to run over Syracuse harbor. Lt. Stephen Decatur continued to prepare the *Intrepid* for sea. Sailors swarmed over her decks, readying the ketch for an inspection by Commo. Edward Preble.[23]

All eyes were now on the former Arab ketch. An official U.S. Navy warship, the *Intrepid* was the subject of rumor and conjecture as the sailors and officers in the squadron watched Decatur's men ready her for action. They knew something was going to happen, but they did not know what.

Eyes also were on the *Syren*; Stewart was preparing his ship for sea. The lieutenant knew he would play a secondary role to Decatur, although he still was not sure of the actual logistics. Neither he nor Decatur had long to wait.

Couriers from the *Constitution* found the officers and handed sealed orders to both men. To Decatur, Preble was brief and to the point:

> Sir, you are hereby ordered to take command of the . . . *Intrepid* and prepare her with all possible dispatch for a cruise of thirty days with full allowance of water, provision etc. for a crew of seventy-five men. It is my orders that you proceed to Tripoli in company with the *Syren*, Lt. Stewart. Enter the harbor in the night. Board the frigate *Philadelphia*, burn her and make your retreat good with the *Intrepid* if possible, unless you can make her the means of destroying the enemy's vessels in the harbor by converting her into a fire ship.[24]

Preble told Decatur that to accomplish his mission he was to "provide all the necessary combustibles for destroying the ship. The destruction of the *Philadelphia* is an object of great importance and I rely with confidence on your intrepidity and enterprise to effect it." He also made it clear Decatur had to ensure the *Philadelphia* would burn. "Be sure and set fire in the gun room berths, cockpit storerooms forward and berths on the berth deck." If the commodore wanted to drop a couple of ship-name puns to ease any fear on Decatur's part, he tempered his grim humor with a warning: "On boarding the frigate it is probable you will meet with resistance. It will be well in order to prevent alarm to carry all by the sword."[25]

As for the *Intrepid*'s crew, Preble assigned Decatur "five midshipmen from *Constitution*." The remaining seventy men would come from the *Enterprise* "if that number can be found ready to volunteer their services for boarding and burning *Philadelphia*." If the crew, whose enlistments expired in just two months, would not volunteer, Preble told Decatur to "report to me and I will furnish you with men to complete your complement."[26]

As for the *Syren* and Stewart, Preble said Decatur's friend would "support you with boats of the *Syren* and cover your retreat with that vessel." Preble told Stewart his first task was to alter the *Syren*'s appearance: "You are to disguise her by changing the color of your paint, send topgallant masts on deck, rigging in the flying jib boom, housing guns, shutting in ports, raising quarter cloths to give the appearance of a merchant vessel." As soon as the two ships were outside Tripoli, Stewart was to plan for a night attack: "You will keep at a distance from Tripoli until the evening, but not so far that you can not reach the harbor by midnight. The *Intrepid* being rigged in a manner peculiar to the Mediterranean probably will not be suspected of the enemy. Of course, it will be most advisable to send her ahead." Once the *Intrepid* was alongside the *Philadelphia*, Preble told Stewart to "stand in and anchor in such a position as you, in your judgment, may think best calculated to afford her assistance in the execution of the main object, cover her retreat or destroy any of the enemy's cruisers that may be in the harbor." Preble also told Stewart to wait until he could "enter the harbor with a westerly wind as it will ensure you a safe retreat. May God prosper and succeed you in this enterprise," the commodore wrote as he finished his orders. Preble told both men to be ready to leave by February 2.[27]

As soon as Decatur returned to the *Enterprise*, he began relaying orders to prepare the *Intrepid* for her voyage. He gave Lt. James Lawrence the task of tracking down the supplies the seventy-five men would need for their mission. The list was long.

First there was water—enough water for seventy-five men for thirty days. Lawrence had to collect barrels to hold the water, fill them, and transfer them to the *Intrepid*. Next came food, and it was the usual stuff: bread and salted meat. A typical thirty-day supply was "4 barrels of pork, 1 barrel peas, 3 barrels flour, 27 barrels bread," plus molasses and rice. In addition, there were other cooking supplies—charcoal, oil, salt—as well as "spirits" or rum—to procure.[28] The business kept Lawrence and part of the crew busy throughout that Tuesday and into Wednesday, February 1.

Lawrence quickly put his detail to work, although Decatur had yet to tell even his executive officer why he needed the *Intrepid* ready for sea. That information would only come when Preble raised a signal on the *Constitution*'s mainmast.

While Lawrence had his work to perform, Decatur took a closer look at the defenses that ringed Tripoli harbor. When the *Enterprise* had accompanied the *Constitution* on her reconnaissance mission in December, Preble noted how the bashaw fortified his city. From the sea, it looked daunting. Preble counted 115 guns scattered among twelve different forts. The largest was a 19-gun battery at the mole (or breakwater) near the main city docks. The bashaw's castle mounted 10 guns while a battery he erected between his castle and the mole had 14 cannon. Tripoli also had numerous small forts for protection. Fort American, as named by the *Philadelphia* prisoners that built it, had 7 cannon, as did Fort English, another prisoner-built battery. A stone battery Preble dubbed Fort Way had 11 guns, while the Half Moon battery mounted 12. Two other fortifications—the Malta battery and West Diamond battery—each mounted 9 cannon. A small 3-gun battery guarded the main pier while a final fort, which the Americans called Fort Vixen, had 5 guns.[29]

Then there was the bashaw's little fleet. Although Karamanli had nothing that could stand up to the *Constitution*, he did have a considerable collection of smaller craft. The most dangerous were his dozen gunboats. Each mounted a long 18- or 24-pound cannon, carried a crew of fifty, and could operate in shallow water. What made them dangerous, however, was their propulsion. The bashaw had ample backs to turn into rowers and his gunboats used both sail and oar power, allowing them to operate and close no matter which way the wind blew.[30]

Decatur studied the intelligence reports throughout the day as he waited for Preble's signal. His crew, under Lawrence's watchful eye, continued to get the *Intrepid* ready. Many already guessed at her mission, but until Decatur received the commodore's signal, those guesses remained just rumors.

CHAPTER 10

VOLUNTEERS
FOR THE UNKNOWN

A SSISTANT SURGEON LEWIS HEERMAN, acting on orders from Decatur, spent February 1 assessing the health of each of the eighty-five enlisted men on the USS *Enterprise*. He found the men fit for duty, one of the benefits of the location of the U.S. base.[1] Sicily offered an abundance of fresh fruit and vegetables to the American squadron, one of the reasons Preble chose the place as his center of operations. The availability of fresh foods undoubtedly contributed to the general health of the sailors.[2]

The physicals completed, the crewmen resumed working on the *Intrepid*. Exactly where the little ship was to go and what it was to do remained a mystery, although just about everyone in the squadron had a theory. The guessing game ended February 2. Preble hoisted signal 1-1-2-9.[3] Decatur acknowledged the signal and turned to his sailors. He ordered Boatswain John Newman to pipe the entire crew of the aft to the quarterdeck.

As the men assembled, Decatur took a hard look at them. The physicals gave Decatur a good idea of which men to bring along, but, remembering Preble's orders, he had one more test to give them. Decatur trembled with excitement. His voice, normally level, grew high-pitched as the excitement of the mission filled him. The *Enterprise*, he told the crew, was not going anywhere. Instead, he needed sixty-two volunteers—almost the entire ship's complement—to board the *Intrepid*, sail into the heart of the bashaw's city, and destroy the *Philadelphia*.

When he asked for volunteers, the entire eighty-five-man crew of the *Enterprise* stepped forward. Decatur smiled. Preble's orders limited him to sixty-two men, and Decatur used the doctor's profiles to select the biggest and most agile of the crew.[4] Next, Decatur began choosing the officers. Like the enlisted men, every officer on board volunteered, and Decatur again wanted only the best.

James Lawrence, quiet, genial, had to be one of the officers selected. So, too, did Joseph Bainbridge, Decatur's constant companion. Thomas Macdonough, the former midshipman on the *Philadelphia* whom William Bainbridge had left behind in Gibraltar on the prize ship *Mirboka* and who was now an officer on the *Enterprise*, would go as well. Jonathan Thorn, third officer on the *Enterprise* and another trustworthy lieutenant, would also make the trip.

Preble sent five midshipmen from the *Constitution* to join the expedition: Charles Morris, Ralph Izard, John Rowe, Alexander Laws, and John Davis all moved from the flagship to the ketch.[5] One officer had to remain behind to command the *Enterprise* and the enlisted men that did not make the cut. Decatur chose Boyd, the brawling officer who had pulled a knife on Lawrence. The burly lieutenant had behaved like a model gentleman since the incident with Lawrence, but Decatur could not forget what had happened. Someone had to stay behind and it would be Boyd. The last man selected was Assistant Surgeon Heerman. Decatur was not sure about bringing along the doctor and thought it best to leave him behind. Heerman, however, had other ideas.

The doctor said he "felt himself bound to submit to any arrangement that might be made," yet argued his own belief that he should go. The attack on the *Philadelphia* would no doubt mean heavy casualties, Heerman argued, and his rightful place was with the men who would risk their lives to destroy the frigate. "Will the sailors not more regardlessly expose themselves, when they know professional aid is near at hand?" he asked Decatur. "Should you have many wounded, would not some confusion arise to impair your effective services?" It was all Decatur needed to hear. Assistant Surgeon Lewis Heerman would go on the *Intrepid*.[6]

Decatur now had seventy-three officers and men. Preble's orders specified seventy-five. The seventy-fourth man Decatur picked was Salvador Catalano, the Sicilian pilot who told Preble about the *Intrepid*'s—then named the *Mastico*—role in the capture of the *Philadelphia*. Catalano knew the waters around Tripoli and also spoke the local language or lingua franca, which was something of a mixture of Italian, Arabic, and Spanish. The last man Decatur selected was Midn. Thomas O. Anderson of the *Syren*. Although Preble's orders did not say Decatur could take any of Stewart's men, Decatur wanted someone who knew how his friend operated the brig.[7]

His selections complete, Decatur went over the plan with his handpicked crew. The goal of the mission was to destroy the *Philadelphia*. Preble's orders made that clear. Decatur had himself plus twelve officers to command the sixty-two enlisted men, a high ratio of officers to enlisted, but one he thought would ensure success. Next, he gave each officer his own responsibilities.

Once alongside the *Philadelphia*, the *Intrepid*'s men were to carry the frigate's gun and spar decks. After clearing the decks of pirates, Decatur, Izard, and Rowe with fifteen men would hold the area. Lawrence, leading Laws, Macdonough, and ten men, would set the berth deck and forward storerooms ablaze. Bainbridge, commanding Davis and ten men, would set fire to the wardroom and steerage. Midshipman Morris and eight sailors had the task of setting alight the cockpit and after-storeroom. Midshipman Anderson and six men would use the *Intrepid*'s cutter to keep watch for any vessels trying to intercept the *Intrepid* as well as to silence any Arabs trying to escape. Finally, Lieutenant Thorn and Gunner William Hook would pass the combustibles from the *Intrepid* to the men on the *Philadelphia*.[8]

The only officer left without a duty was Assistant Surgeon Heerman. Decatur at first told the doctor to "seek a place of safety." The mission, how-ever, excited Heerman as much as it did his commander. "I shall be pleased to obey, captain, and this place of safety, where might I find it?" he said to Decatur. His commander, almost expecting the answer, told the doctor what his role would be on the *Intrepid*: "I shall leave her in your charge with seven men, and as the enemy, where pressed hard, will be apt to retreat from the spar deck and board the ketch from the gun ports of the frigate. Your safety will consist in giving no quarter. As upon the preservation of the ketch may depend, in great measure, the success of the expedition, I shall expect you, at all events, to defend her to the last man."[9]

Every man was now set. On February 3 Decatur gave orders to slip the lines holding the *Intrepid* to the dock in Syracuse and the little ketch tacked away. Right behind her was Stewart in the brig *Syren*. As the two ships steered off into the gathering night just after 5:00 p.m., the *Constitution*'s sailing master Nathaniel Haraden watched her go: "They stood out to south-ward and are bound on some secret expedition," he wrote in the ship's log, not knowing just how right he was.[10]

The wind blowing out of the north pushed the *Intrepid* and *Syren* along at about ten knots. As the ketch and the brig sailed away from Syracuse, Decatur and Stewart expected to arrive off Tripoli in five days at most. They made good time the first full day, February 4, although they were in no real hurry. The captains knew they needed time to drill their crews in their com-ing duties. They did not shorten sail, but they made sure they "employed ourselves in the intermediate time in preparing everything for executing the intended object," Stewart wrote.[11]

Decatur used the time to continually drill his men in rushing from the *Intrepid*'s hold onto her deck while carrying swords (cutlasses), knives (dirks), pikes, and tomahawks. Stewart continued to change the *Syren*'s appearance. His goal was to make her look like the *Transfer*, an English merchant vessel

Preble said was due to arrive soon in Tripoli. The *Syren*'s crew repainted her hull and did their best to hide her gun ports.[12]

For the men on the *Intrepid*, the excitement of their mission wore off as they moved closer to Tripoli. They also had a more immediate problem to deal with: nearly all of the food on the ketch was rotten. When Decatur had captured the *Intrepid*, she carried a number of casks of dried fish. The Americans, when they loaded the *Intrepid* for their mission, reused those casks for salted beef and pork. Whoever cleaned the casks, however, botched the job and leftover fish oil turned the beef and pork rancid. Decatur ordered his men to dump the spoiled meats overboard, leaving only sea biscuits and water as rations.[13]

Despite the food shortage, the *Syren* and *Intrepid* pressed on toward Tripoli. They arrived off the bashaw's city the morning of February 7. Stewart shortened sail and allowed the *Syren* to fall off the wind, bringing her to a near stop. He did not want any sharp-eyed lookouts to spot his ship. Decatur did not have that worry. To any eye, the *Intrepid* was nothing more than another Arab craft sailing the Mediterranean.

The winds, which had been southerly, now began to blow more westerly. Heavy gray clouds scudded across the sky—"strong indications of an approaching gale," wrote Midshipman Morris. Stewart decided to confer with Decatur about their next move. The *Intrepid*'s commander ordered his ship's boat launched and Decatur, with Lawrence, Morris, and the Sicilian pilot Salvador Catalano, went on board the *Syren*.[14]

Decatur pushed to make the attack that night, despite signs of the oncoming storm. Stewart was not sure. Not only was the wind picking up, but also daylight was starting to wane. Stewart suggested sending a small boat in near the harbor mouth to check the conditions. Decatur agreed, and he ordered Morris and Catalano to make the trip. The two set off and rowed toward Tripoli in the gathering darkness.

"We went quite close to the entrance, where we found the surf breaking entirely across it," Morris reported. "My own opinion concurred with that of the pilot that no attempt ought to be made." On their return, Morris and Catalano reported to Decatur and Stewart. The Sicilian was adamant: there was no way to get into and out of the harbor that night. Morris, however, hesitated before giving his report. "I had heard many of the officers treat the doubts of the pilot as the offspring of apprehension, and the weather was not yet so decidedly boisterous as to render it certain that an attempt might not be made," he said. "Should such be the case and should it succeed, the imputations upon the pilot might be repeated upon me, and unknown as I was, might be the cause of my ruin in the estimation of my brother officers."[15]

Morris took one more look at the gathering gale, swallowed hard, and backed the pilot. His arguments failed to convince Decatur or Lawrence. "Their opinions were evidently received with much dissatisfaction by a majority, and with some murmurs," Morris wrote. Stewart put an end to the argument. He was in overall command so the decision to go was his. They would wait out the gale.[16] With that, Decatur, Lawrence, Morris, and Catalano returned to the *Intrepid* as the winds grew stronger. The *Syren* slowly turned out to sea, bucking headwinds. The *Intrepid*, despite her rig, had an even rougher time.

The ketch, never the most seaworthy craft, hammered bow down into each wave. Where the *Syren* was well built, the *Intrepid*'s very keel shuddered with each breaker. Originally built in 1798 in Marseilles, France, for the French invasion of Egypt, the *Intrepid* had a rough life while serving both the French and Tripolitans. Preble had not stretched the truth when he told Secretary Smith the *Intrepid* could never make the trip across the Atlantic. The angry Mediterranean threatened to swamp the ketch with nearly every wave.[17]

———◆———

February 8 brought little relief for the exhausted officers on the *Intrepid*. The only food and drink anyone had had the previous night were a few biscuits and some water. Sleep was almost impossible. Accommodations on any man-of-war were never the best. On board the *Intrepid*, they were downright abysmal. Morris succinctly captured the situation when he wrote, "Our situation on board was far from comfortable."[18] For all officers and crew, quarters were cramped. Stephen Decatur, James Lawrence, Joseph Bainbridge, Jonathan Thorn, and Lewis Heerman slept in "the very small cabin." Morris and his fellow midshipmen, along with the pilot, Catalano, "had a platform laid on the water casks, whose surface they covered when they lay down for sleep." The area was "at so small a distance below the deck that their heads would reach when seated on the platform."[19] The Marine detachment of a corporal and six privates slept across from Morris in similar circumstances. The rest of the crew had to make do with cramming into any available space in the hold among the barrels of combustibles the *Intrepid* carried for her mission. Adding to the misery were the vermin, both insects and rodents. The attempt to fumigate the ship in Syracuse had utterly failed. "The attacks of the innumerable vermin, which our predecessors the slaves had left behind," plagued officers and men alike.[20] Finally, due to the nature of the mission, Decatur ordered everyone but those actually sailing the *Intrepid* to remain below deck, where there was "the want of any room for exercise."[21]

For the men stuffed into the hold, the lack of food and the violent rolling of the *Intrepid* combined to hurt their morale. They were all left disappointed when they did not go on February 7. Now confined on a frail ship in a roiling sea, their growing fears "laid the foundation of apprehensions for eventual failure," Heerman wrote. Whispers were rife that the Arabs had spotted the two Americans ships and were even then preparing for battle. As Heerman put it, "The discovery by the enemy of an armed force having been anchored near the port being rendered more than probable only made the Americans more restive."[22]

Decatur and his officers never betrayed their fears. Their first concern was simply battling the gale. The *Syren* stood off roughly two miles as both ships battled the storm to move away from the coast. Stewart, on the *Syren*, ordered his crew to ready the brig's boats in case they had to rescue the crew of the *Intrepid*. The ketch was in constant danger of foundering, yet somehow managed to ride the threatening waves.

———————

The gale lashing the North African coast February 9 also pounded Syracuse. The *Syren* and *Intrepid* had left nearly a week before, and Edward Preble expected to hear at least rumors of the two vessels. Instead, the howling wind and driving rain were the only noises that came back to the commodore. When the *Syren* and *Intrepid* left, Preble busied himself with his preparations for his spring campaign against the bashaw. He wanted to find gunboats and mortar boats so he could not only mount a new blockade of Tripoli, but also bombard the town and fight the Tripolitan gunboats on equal terms.

Preble also knew he needed to watch his back. The *Constitution* and either the *Enterprise* or *Vixen* would stand off the bashaw's city. He could use the *Argus* or *Syren* and the remaining schooner to patrol the area off Cape Bon, off the coast of Tunis. He would send the leftover brig to the Adriatic to keep an eye out for Tripolitan cruisers trying to raid Sicily.[23] The more he planned, however, the more he realized he needed more ships. He sent word to Secretary Smith to send at least one more frigate and another schooner or brig. He sent word with a midshipman, Christopher Gadsden, who was on his way home after he contracted a fever. As his health grew worse, Preble decided keeping him on station was a mistake, so he discharged the young man and ordered him home on the South Carolina–bound schooner *Mary* a month before, on January 3.

Gadsden carried with him Preble's reports on the *Philadelphia*'s loss as well as the commodore's request for reinforcements. "You may depend upon my not losing a moment in going to Washington," he told the commodore in a note just before he left.[24] On February 7, though, Gadsden was only somewhere in the middle of the Atlantic, nearing the end of a six- or seven-week passage through the Mediterranean and across the ocean. More than a month had passed since Preble relayed the news to him. With no help on the horizon, Preble remained on his own, and his concern for the *Syren* and *Intrepid* grew. On February 12, when the gale finally blew itself out, Preble ordered a twenty-four-hour lookout to keep watch for the return of one or both of the ships he sent to Tripoli.

Friday February 10, 1804, brought no relief to Decatur, Stewart, or their crews. The Mediterranean continued to toss the *Syren* and *Intrepid* around. Stewart began to move farther offshore. The gale continued unabated throughout the day and into Saturday. The two American ships were now miles away from Tripoli. Finally, around 11:00 a.m. on Sunday, February 12, the storm began to ease. Stewart sent for Decatur and the two officers met on the *Syren*. They wanted to hit Tripoli that night, but were so far off course they needed first to get back on station. It took three days. On Wednesday February 15, lookouts on each ship again spotted the minarets and towers of Tripoli.

Decatur dropped anchor three miles off the harbor and waited for the *Syren*. He rowed over to speak once more with his commander. Stewart wanted to augment Decatur's force with part of his own crew "considering the possibility there was of the Tripolitans having some suspicions of our intentions." Stewart sent "an officer and nine volunteers" to the *Intrepid* in one of his boats, and had another thirty sailors readied to deploy. His plan was to follow the *Intrepid* into the harbor, then launch his own boats to cover Decatur and prevent any pirate warships from getting too close to the Americans. They would attack that night.[25]

CHAPTER 11

"THE MOST BOLD AND DARING ACT OF THE AGE"

C APT. WILLIAM BAINBRIDGE, HIS OFFICERS and the rest of the crew of the frigate *Philadelphia* knew nothing about the approach of the *Syren* and *Intrepid* or of Preble's plan. As the *Intrepid* and *Syren* battled storms to approach Tripoli, Marine private William Ray and the other enlisted men of the crew endured their continual forced labor. The officers had something of a respite as they actually managed to get out and see something of the countryside. "The bashaw gave the officers permission to walk out into the town and country, but not to visit the consuls nor the batteries," *Philadelphia* surgeon Jonathan Cowdery wrote. "Our drogerman [guard] Hamet, was ordered to walk with us and direct us where to go. We went out six at a time."[1] It turned out Lt. Charles Stewart had no reason to fear that the Tripolitans knew any more than Bainbridge, Ray, or the rest of the American captives. As night fell over Tripoli on February 15, 1804, the Americans continued to enjoy complete surprise.

The winds that had nearly swamped his ketch once more became an enemy for Lt. Stephen Decatur, only this time because they were light. The *Intrepid*, with her lateen rig, could better handle the gentle breeze than Stewart's vessel, and soon began to pull farther and farther away from the *Syren*. With darkness growing, Decatur dropped anchor in an area he believed was just outside the harbor, in a hull-down position he thought would allow the *Intrepid* to avoid detection. The *Syren* anchored roughly three miles away. Even though both commanders knew they were close to Tripoli, they were not exactly sure of their position and needed daylight to make that determination. Decatur and Stewart again postponed the attack.[2]

The sun broke over the Mediterranean at 7:52 a.m. on February 16.[3] The winds remained light and somewhat variable, keeping the *Syren* well away from the *Intrepid*. Decatur weighed anchor and ordered the *Intrepid* to make her way past the reefs. As the *Intrepid* cut through the water, Decatur raised every sail. She cleared the rocks at 11:00 a.m. and made her way into the harbor.

Almost five miles behind, the *Syren* hove into view. The *Intrepid* continued to make good speed, her lateen rig allowing her to pull away from the brig. Decatur ordered his crew to put out drags to slow the ketch. His men tossed large buckets overboard attached to heavy lines to act as water brakes, and the *Intrepid*'s speed dropped off. Decatur wanted to remain close enough to the *Syren* to exchange signals with Stewart. He also knew that by now the *Intrepid* was in plain enough view for the bashaw's lookouts to see her so he did not want to slow down too much.

Stewart did his best to keep up with the *Intrepid*, but an important part of the plan was for the arrival of the two ships to appear random. The *Intrepid*, since she was an Arab craft, could slip by without raising the alarm. The *Syren*, her brig rig clearly western built, was a tougher nut. Stewart knew he had to pass himself off as a British merchantman due in Tripoli. As the *Intrepid* pulled away, he was not sure if his plan to reinforce Decatur would work.[4]

The *Intrepid* continued to move into the harbor. As she did, the wind veered to the northwest and slackened to barely a breeze. The sheltered waters around Tripoli were still, almost glassy. The approach into the harbor took nearly six hours. As twilight neared, Decatur made his final preparations. He and his pilot, Salvador Catalano, and six others who worked the sails dressed in Sicilian clothes. The rest of the crew he ordered below.[5]

As the sun dipped below the horizon, Decatur told Catalano to adjust course. The *Intrepid* made her way through the center of the channel. Ahead, about three miles away, lay Tripoli proper. The setting sun glinted off the mosque domes and minaret towers. To his left Decatur could see a line of rocky islands and inlets. To his right rose the Maltese battery. Water broke gently over reefs off his starboard bow.

At 8:30 p.m. the breeze died completely. The *Intrepid*'s sails went slack, her blocks swinging silently. Decatur looked around in case Stewart tried to send him more men despite the distance. He could not light any lamps for the *Syren*'s boats—that would reveal his position. There was only one choice. "There was good reason to apprehend that any delay in waiting for the boats might render it very difficult for the ketch to reach the ship," Midn. Charles Morris wrote. "Decatur therefore determined to proceed without waiting." The twenty-four-year-old lieutenant whispered his decision to his crew. No one made a sound. Decatur, to lessen the blow, paraphrased from Shakespeare's *Henry V*: "The fewer the number the greater the honor."[6]

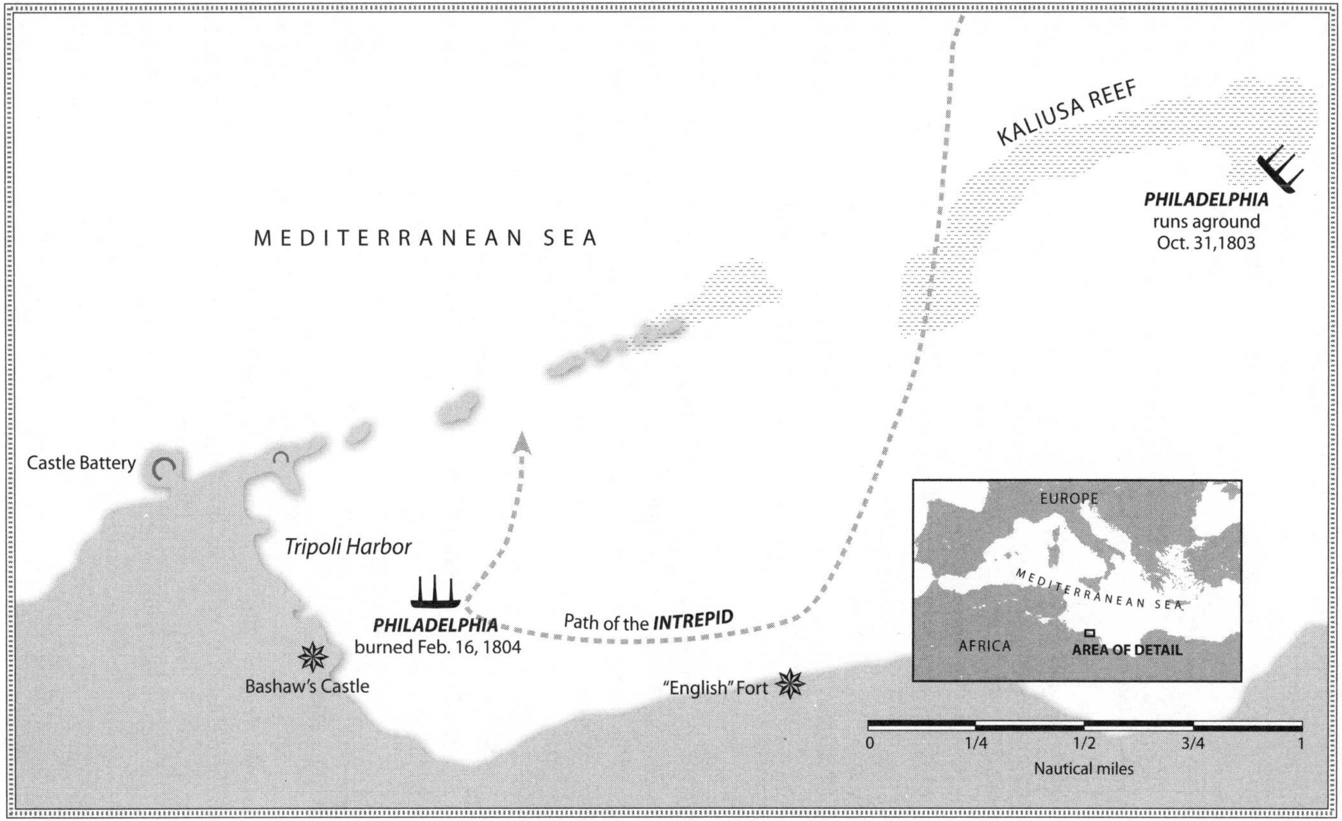

MAP 1. The Burning of the *Philadelphia*

Map by Joe Myers. Source: US Navy Heritage Center

KALIUSA REEF

PHILADELPHIA runs aground Oct. 31, 1803

MEDITERRANEAN SEA

Tripoli Harbor

Castle Battery

Bashaw's Castle

PHILADELPHIA burned Feb. 16, 1804

"English" Fort

Path of the ***INTREPID***

EUROPE

AFRICA

MEDITERRANEAN SEA

AREA OF DETAIL

0   1/4   1/2   3/4   1

Nautical miles

The *Intrepid* was now alone, two miles from the *Philadelphia*. Decatur could see the faint outline of the frigate. Even without her foremast and bowsprit, which her crew had chopped away in its desperate attempt to get off the reef, the *Philadelphia* had a look of power about her. Lanterns hung about the deck, although from his distance there was no way for Decatur to see how many Arabs guarded her. Nearby, Stewart also watched as the *Intrepid* pulled away from the *Syren*. There was nothing he could do to close the distance. As darkness fell over Tripoli, Stewart anchored the *Syren* just outside the harbor entrance.

Even though there was little chance of joining forces with Decatur, Stewart ordered Midn. Edmund Kennedy to take out a force of thirty sailors and Marines, who rowed into the darkness, in two boats. "The night was very dark and the *Intrepid* having exhibited no light to indicate her position, the boats lost their way among the rocks," Kennedy later wrote.[7] The midshipman and his party remained in open water the rest of the night while back on the *Syren*, Stewart quietly ordered his remaining crew to quarters. They kept the carronades within their ports, but removed the tampions and loaded charges. All Stewart and the *Syren* could do now was wait.

———— ◆ ————

At 9:00 p.m., February 16, 1804, the *Intrepid* ghosted her way toward the *Philadelphia*. As the ketch moved into the harbor, a thick crescent moon hung to the right of the mast, three-quarters up in the sky. The three stars of Orion's belt were directly overhead, giving Decatur some sense of bearing. Polaris, the North Star, was directly behind, providing the lieutenant with yet another reference point.[8] Although he had scouted the harbor in daylight back in December, the *Intrepid*'s commander did not know the waters. He had to depend on his Sicilian pilot, Salvador Catalano, to keep the *Intrepid* from running onto the numerous reefs and rocks that lined the harbor.

The *Intrepid* flew English colors as she approached the frigate, and so far had aroused little suspicion. From the deck, Decatur could see turbaned heads passing in front of the *Philadelphia*'s lamps. Her guns were loaded, muzzles sticking out of open gun ports. Decatur had his helmsman steer toward the frigate. The *Intrepid* slowly crept toward the *Philadelphia*. The wind shifted again, pushing the *Philadelphia* around on her mooring, the frigate's stern moving toward the ketch.

The *Intrepid*'s helmsman adjusted his own course. Decatur wanted the ketch to reach the frigate amidships to give his men the best chance to board. Catalano whispered instructions to Decatur, who passed them to the helm. The six men on the *Intrepid*'s deck wore Arab clothes. Below deck the rest of the crew waited for the word to attack. Decatur, to help his men tell friend from foe, issued a password—"Philadelphia." The question was, would anyone remember to ask for it in the heat of battle?

Midn. Charles Morris stood next to Decatur as the *Philadelphia* loomed larger off the ketch's bow. Morris looked around the *Intrepid*. The reality of their mission hit Morris, probably just as it did everyone else on the ketch as they waited for the word to board. Somewhere behind them, the *Syren* was waiting near the harbor entrance. Stewart would soon launch his boats with the supporting force. The *Intrepid*, however, would make the main assault. The *Syren*'s boats were there, Morris said, to aid any survivors from the *Intrepid*, "in case of her destruction, which was considered probable."[9] Indeed, by 9:30 p.m. the *Intrepid* was under the guns of the *Philadelphia*. At any moment, if the Arabs recognized the small ship as anything but friendly, they could blast the little ketch out of the water.

It was clear the pirates could see the *Intrepid*. Her sails hung nearly slack as she crept closer to the frigate. The English ensign on the *Intrepid* barely moved on its staff. Slowly, quietly, Lt. Stephen Decatur gathered his assault force. Most were still below deck, although men now lay prone along the rail, just out of sight. Decatur could see turbaned heads turning toward the *Intrepid*, then turning away. So far, they apparently did not think much of the weather-beaten ketch. She was a familiar sight and the few men visible on deck looked harmless enough, or so Decatur hoped. But the approach to the *Philadelphia* seemed agonizingly slow to Assistant Surgeon Lewis Heerman. The ship's doctor described it as "not without difficulty."[10] Heerman would command the *Intrepid* during the boarding and he looked around to see just where he should station lookouts. Everyone on the *Intrepid* was prepared.

Anchored near the *Philadelphia* were a pair of xebecs, and everyone on the *Intrepid* could see gunboats bobbing at the docks. Other small boats seemed to come and go with frustrating regularity. Decatur ordered Midn. Thomas O. Anderson and nine men to take one of the long boats and slip over the side. Anderson's task was "dispatching those of the enemy who might flee from the carnage of the boarders and also to give notice of and attack any of the enemy's force that might approach the ship," Heerman said.[11]

When Anderson and his men pushed off from the *Intrepid* around 9:50 p.m., the Arabs on the *Philadelphia* could clearly see the *Intrepid* now. The crescent moon—the symbol of the Ottoman Empire—hung almost overhead. The moon threw enough light to make the frigate's captors wonder just what this little ketch wanted. A hail rang out from the *Philadelphia* quarterdeck: "What ship is that?"

"*Mastico*," Catalano, who was chosen for this specificic purpose, replied. The ketch, he said, lost her anchor in the storm. That was a lie. The gale, he continued, pounded the little ship, making her nearly unseaworthy. That was true. He then asked permission to tie up near the big frigate until morning, when the ketch could work her way to the dock.[12]

The guards could see a second vessel standing off the harbor entrance. Were they together? No, Catalano replied. The ship outside the harbor was the British brig *Transfer*, which the bashaw expected to arrive any day. After a pause of a few seconds, the guards on the *Philadelphia* agreed. The Arabs launched a boat with a line to give to the *Intrepid*. Anderson, with his boatload of volunteers from the *Syren*, met the ship. Somehow, they avoided detection. The pirates passed the line to Anderson, who passed it up onto the *Intrepid*'s deck. There, the seven men in view from the *Philadelphia* made a show of hauling in the line. What the Arabs could not see were the American sailors and Marines lying prone on the deck who also hauled the line, giving the *Intrepid* more speed.

The ketch rapidly closed in on the frigate when the wind suddenly shifted. It blew the ketch slightly away from the frigate, turning her almost on her beam. The men hauling the line pulled harder, turning the *Intrepid* back toward the frigate. The distance closed from twenty yards to ten to two.[13]

The guards on the *Philadelphia* watched as the *Intrepid* closed in on the frigate. She certainly looked battered, but there was something wrong. The crewman that spoke said the ketch had lost her anchor, yet there hanging off the bow was an anchor. The ketch also closed much faster against tide and wind than any seven men could possibly haul. Bashaw Yusuf Karamanli expected an attack at any time and had warned his followers to keep a lookout. The *Intrepid* looked familiar but the situation did not add up. Suddenly, a cry rose over the harbor as the ketch touched the side of the *Philadelphia*: "*Americani!*"

Salvador Catalano turned to Decatur and in near panic shouted, "Board, captain, board!" As his crew rose to jump onto the *Philadelphia*, Decatur remained motionless. His voice then rang out. "No orders to be obeyed but those of the captain." The men froze while the *Intrepid* came up broadside to the frigate.

Decatur jumped toward the frigate, landing on the main chain plates instead of the deck. Morris, who was next to Decatur, jumped at the same time and landed on the *Philadelphia*. Decatur recovered quickly and climbed over the chain to gain the deck. He saw Morris and, for an instant, raised his cutlass to chop him down. "The enemy were already leaping over the opposite side," Morris said. "Decatur, under the supposition that he was first on board, was about to strike when I turned accidentally." A frantic

Morris shouted "Philadelphia!" just in time. Decatur stopped, then boomed out, "Board!"[14]

Commo. Edward Preble liked to walk the quarterdeck alone. By now, his officers knew better than to disturb him when he did. At 10:00 p.m. February 16, Preble paced back and forth on the quarterdeck of the *Constitution*.[15] The storm was gone, yet there was still no word from either the *Syren* or the *Intrepid*. The two vessels seemingly had vanished into the Mediterranean. Stewart and Decatur were overdue. It was more than two weeks since he had sent them off on their mission to destroy the *Philadelphia*, and there was no news.

Preble chose Syracuse because of its location away from the British. They could not tempt his crews to desert in Sicily. That did not mean, however, that Syracuse was an isolated port. Local merchantmen came and went, as did fishing boats and warships. The commodore had no way of knowing whether word had leaked out about the mission of the *Intrepid* and *Syren*. If it did, both ships could be in the bashaw's hands, their crews dead or captive. Then there was the storm. Preble had few doubts the *Syren* could weather a gale, but the *Intrepid* was another story. The commodore paced, not saying a word, while his officers and crew thought, Where were Decatur and Stewart?

Sixty men armed with cutlasses, dirks, tomahawks, and pikes swarmed onto the deck of the *Philadelphia*. With officers in the lead, they cut down anyone that stood in their way as they moved to take over the frigate. Lt. James Lawrence, leading twelve officers and men, raced forward, hacking and slashing at any pirates bold enough to stand. Most panicked and dove overboard, although handfuls of them fought back. Lt. Joseph Bainbridge and his eleven men seized the center of the frigate. Morris and eight men, along with Decatur, took the area around the helm. Midshipman Anderson and his men remained in their boat near the frigate, keeping an eye out for Tripolitans trying to retake the *Philadelphia*.

The Arabs fled as the Americans fanned out. "The Tripolitans on board her were dreadfully alarmed when they found out who we were," said Midn. Ralph Izard. "Poor fellows."[16] As they either dove overboard or died beneath the slashing blades of the Americans, the Tripolitans began "whooping and screaming," Assistant Surgeon Lewis Heerman said. Their cries "drew an almost instantaneous and continuous fire from two xebecs that lay nearby." With the pings of ricochets bouncing around the frigate, Decatur fired off a red rocket, signaling the successful completion of the first phase of the mission. The rocket, however, alerted the batteries ringing Tripoli harbor as well. "A brisk cannonade commenced," Heerman said, "and was kept up from the castle and other batteries."[17]

Below deck on the *Intrepid*, Lt. Jonathan Thorn and Gunner William Hook began passing barrels of oil, tar, old ropes, torn sails, gunpowder, and anything else that would burn to waiting hands on the *Philadelphia*. Those men quickly dumped the oil below deck, making sure to cover the cannon the frigate carried. Flames began to lick at the decks and lines of the once-proud ship.

In the cockpit below the spar deck, Midn. Charles Morris was nervous. His party had yet to return with supplies for setting fire to the frigate. Morris was about to look for his men when he spotted a turbaned head heading toward him. Morris raised his cutlass and nearly swung before he recognized Decatur. His commander gave him a glance, then continued with his inspection. Morris' men arrived right behind him and soon had a fire going.

On his way topside, Morris saw just how effective *Intrepid*'s men were at destroying a frigate. "The fire on the deck above communicated so rapidly that it was with no small difficulty and danger that our party reached the spardeck by the forward hatchways," he said.[18] By then, the *Philadelphia* was already in flames. The blaze illuminated the *Intrepid* as Decatur led his men back onto the ketch. The fire also gave the bashaw's gunners a target and more guns opened on the *Intrepid*. Their aim, however, was faulty. "The confusion of the moment probably prevented much care in their direction, and though under the fire of nearly a hundred pieces for half an hour, the only shot which struck the ketch was one through the topgallant sail," Morris said.[19]

The flames now spouting from the *Philadelphia* were far more dangerous for the *Intrepid* than were any shots coming from the city. Fires below deck shot out of open gun ports while tongues of flame ran up the rigging. The *Intrepid*'s crew let out three cheers after the men returned to the ketch, but now celebration turned to consternation. The *Intrepid* remained attached to the *Philadelphia*, tied up at the stern. Lt. James Lawrence hacked away the line with his cutlass, but the ketch remained motionless. No wind moved the *Intrepid* although there was enough of a breeze to fan the flames on the frigate. Sparks showered over the *Intrepid*, threatening to set the little ship on fire. Even worse, the *Intrepid* remained packed with powder and shot; this was ammunition Decatur wanted in case he decided to try to take the *Philadelphia* out of the harbor rather than burn her.

One look at the *Philadelphia*—and remembering Preble's explicit orders—convinced him to stick with the original plan, but his decision to carry extra powder and shot made the *Intrepid* a floating bomb. As flames whipped across the frigate, cascading over the ketch, Decatur ordered his men to man the sweeps. The *Intrepid*, like many small ships, had a set of oversized oars her crew could use to row the ship when there was no wind. Sailors and Marines put their strength behind the sweeps and the *Intrepid* slowly pulled away from the *Philadelphia*. "While urging the ketch onwards with sweeps, the crew were commenting upon the beauty of the spray thrown up by the shot between us and the brilliant light of the ship, rather than calculating any danger that might be apprehended from the contact," Morris said.[20]

There was another concern for Decatur and his men. The Arabs kept *Philadelphia*'s guns loaded and now the red-hot cannon began cooking off, sending 18-pound shot toward the ketch. Finally, a gust of wind hit the *Intrepid*'s sails, moving her ever so slowly away from the burning frigate.[21] By 10:15 p.m., less than an hour after it began, the fight for the *Philadelphia* was over.

Pvt. William Ray could see most of the harbor in Tripoli from a small window in the warehouse that served as a prison. He watched as the *Intrepid* made her way into the harbor, the light of the crescent moon glinting off the ketch. Off in the distance, he could see the *Syren*. "Our men were much rejoiced, for they were confident they were Americans, and as the season of the year was not favorable for an attack, they flattered themselves that very probably they had come with proposals of amicable accommodation," Ray said. "All our men appeared more than ordinary cheerful."[22]

Ray was right, although he had yet to guess the real intention of the two ships. The crew of the *Philadelphia* settled in for sleep, expecting the morning to bring the sound of cannon fire.

> About 11 at night we were alarmed by the screeches of women, the clattering of footsteps through the prison yard, the harsh, loud voices of men mingled with a thundering of cannon from the castle, which made our prison tremble to its base. Tumult, consternation, confusion and dismay reigned in every section of the town and castle and it was verily believed that if we had been at liberty and armed, we might with ease have taken the castle and every fort in town, for most of the people supposed we had already risen and taken the castle and were afraid to come nigh it.[23]

The captive sailors and Marines had no idea what was happening. Then someone looked out the window. There, in the middle of the harbor, was the

Philadelphia, wrapped in flames. The American prisoners cheered as they watched the frigate burn, then fell asleep.

———•—•———

The *Intrepid* pulled away from the *Philadelphia* and made her way back through the harbor. Behind her, the frigate's guns began exploding, sending shot into Tripoli, adding to the confusion on shore. Decatur took a look around him and made a head count. Sixty men had boarded the *Philadelphia*, sixty came back. "I had not a man killed in this affair," he reported to Preble, "and but one slightly wounded." The fighting on the frigate took less than five minutes. The American hacked down twenty Arabs, Decatur reported, and took one prisoner. Decatur said he was not sure how many men the bashaw had put on the *Philadelphia*, "a large boat full got off and many leapt into the sea." He turned the prisoner over to Assistant Surgeon Heerman, although he said, "From the number of bad wounds he has received [the prisoner] will not recover." In all, his crew suffered just one man slightly wounded. SN Daniel Frazier returned to the ketch with "two incised wounds on the head one of them severe; one bad wound across the wrist and seven slightly about his hands," according to Heerman's report.[24]

Across the harbor, the *Philadelphia* continued to burn. The flames ate through her anchor cable and she drifted toward shore, the fire now swirling about her main and mizzenmasts. At 11:00 p.m. just an hour after Decatur had led his men on board her, the *Philadelphia* exploded in a thunderous shower of sparks and splinters.[25]

Decatur kept his men at the sweeps until the *Intrepid* cleared the harbor. The wind was beginning to whip up once more, threatening to keep the *Intrepid* confined in the bashaw's waters. At 1:00 a.m. a voice hailed the ketch. It was a man on one of the *Syren*'s boats, asking if Decatur wanted to rig up a tow. The *Intrepid* did not need towing. Instead, Decatur jumped into one of the boats and rowed to the *Syren* where he reported to Lt. Charles Stewart, his boyhood friend and overall commander on the expedition. His news surprised Stewart: the *Philadelphia* was destroyed and not a man lost.[26]

The two ships remained just outside the harbor for an hour as the tired crews rested and watched the *Philadelphia* burn. They set sail for Syracuse at 2:00 a.m. The light of the flames from the *Philadelphia* remained brightly visible. Midn. Ralph Izard could barely withhold his joy. On both the *Syren* and the *Intrepid*, he said, "our men were in high spirits and I never saw a finer set of fellows."[27]

———•—•———

At daybreak on February 17, the men on the *Intrepid* and *Syren* could still see the flames of the burning *Philadelphia* some forty miles away. On shore, Marine private William Ray and the crew of the *Philadelphia* continued to celebrate the destruction of the frigate right under the bashaw's nose. These men were soon to pay the price of the bashaw's anger:

> Early in the morning and much earlier than usual, our prison doors were unbolted and the keepers, like so many fiends from the infernal regions, rushed in amongst us and began to beat every one they could see, spitting in our faces and hitting us like the serpents of hell. Word was soon brought that the wreck of the *Philadelphia* lay on the rocks, near the round fort, almost consumed by fire. We could not suppress our emotions nor disguise our joy at the intelligence, which exasperated them more and more so that every boy we met on the streets would spit on us and pelt us with stones.[28]

Capt. William Bainbridge and the officers of the *Philadelphia* also watched as their frigate drifted onto shore a burning hulk. To Bainbridge, the sight of his command burning along the shore was just another reminder of his own failure. "Cursed fate which deprives me of sharing in the danger and glory," he wrote Preble.[29] The bashaw revoked the officers' parole and placed them under strong guard, cutting them off from outside communication. Danish consul Nicholas Nissen, the captive Americans' constant friend in Tripoli, also saw the destruction play out in the harbor. So did Yusuf Karamanli: "The bashaw saw the whole business with his own eye," Nissen reported. "The fire ship was beyond reach before they could give orders. The frigate was totally burnt."[30]

The *Intrepid* and *Syren* set a course for Syracuse. Behind them along the shoreline of Tripoli harbor the Karamanli's most potent weapon was a burned-out wreck. The balance of power that seemed to favor the bashaw since he had captured the *Philadelphia* was now once more in the hands of Commo. Edward Preble and the United States Navy.

CHAPTER 12

STRIKE, COUNTER-STRIKE

T HE FLAMES RISING FROM THE HARBOR burned into Bashaw Yusuf Karamanli's sight. He did not particularly care how the Americans managed to destroy his greatest prize. All that mattered to the pirate leader was that the frigate was gone.

Rumors ran wild through the streets. One story said the Americans had used four ships to enter the harbor and even tried to burn the bashaw's castle. Another story claimed the Americans massacred the crew on the *Philadelphia* and mutilated the bodies.

Dutch consul Antoine Zuchet said Karamanli, "who had preened over the capture and had expected with the frigate to lay down the law to the entire universe, was deeply hit by this misfortune." The bashaw first took his fury out on the artillerymen that had failed to score a single hit on the *Intrepid* as she labored to get out of Tripoli harbor. "He beat them upside down and sideways," Zuchet said, "except those lucky ones who dared to seek refuge in a mosque."[1]

On board the *Intrepid*, the mood was much different. Despite a continued lack of food, nothing could dampen the men's spirits. Midn. Charles Morris found himself the talk of the crew, since he had been the first man to actually board the *Philadelphia*. "I was not, however, vain enough to feel that I deserved any particular merit from this accident," he said. Instead, Morris believed "I really deserved more for my faithful report against an attempt to enter the harbor when we first arrived."[2]

Lt. Stephen Decatur also could not contain his own admiration for the officers and men under his command: "Every support that could have been given I received from my officers," he said, "also . . . the brave fellows I have the honor to command, whose coolness and intrepidity was such, as I trust will ever characterize the Americans Tars."[3]

February 19, 1804, dawned crisp and clear, a stark contrast to the mood of Commo. Edward Preble. The commander of the American naval squadron in the Mediterranean, Preble had maintained a near-constant watch as he waited for the return of the *Syren* and the *Intrepid*.[4] The two ships had left February 4 for Tripoli; since they had pulled out of Syracuse harbor, there had been no information about where they were or what had happened to them.

The round trip to Tripoli should take five days at the most, Preble knew. What he did not know was whether the two ships, especially the rickety *Intrepid*, had survived a wicked four-day gale that blasted the Mediterranean.

After a week without information, he grew concerned. After two weeks, he was pacing the quarterdeck of the *Constitution* in frustration. On February 12 the commodore ordered a twenty-four-hour lookout for the two ships.[5] Still, the waiting went on and as the days ticked by, Preble grew more and more convinced both the *Syren* and the *Intrepid* had gone down in the storm.

The waiting finally ended at 10:00 a.m. on February 19. Lookouts sighted a pair of vessels rounding the cape to enter Syracuse. Preble immediately ordered a crewman to hoist a signal 2-2-7: "Have you completed your enterprise?" Once more, the commodore had to wait while the two ships came fully into view. Minutes seem to drag on as Preble waited to see a reply. Then, from the foremast of the larger of the two vessels, came a reply 2-3-2: "Completed the enterprise I was sent on."[6]

Preble breathed a sigh of relief while the rest of the squadron broke into cheers. The commodore could not contain his own relief. The mission he had feared could prove a one-way voyage was a success.

Decatur and Stewart reported to Commo. Edward Preble almost the minute they arrived in Syracuse. The little *Intrepid* showed the effects of the fire that consumed the *Philadelphia*. Black marks on the hull revealed where the flames scorched her sides, and her sails and rigging showed the effects of the Barbary fusillade as the ketch made her escape.

Nothing, however, could hide the pride of the American flotilla in Decatur's and Stewart's accomplishment. Even the normally taciturn Preble gushed in his report to President Thomas Jefferson and Secretary of the Navy Robert Smith: "Their conduct in the performance of the dangerous service assigned them cannot be sufficiently estimated. It is beyond all praise." He singled out Decatur for the lion's share of the glory: "Lieutenant Decatur is an officer of too much value to be neglected. The important service he has rendered of destroying an enemy's frigate of 40 guns and the gallant manner in which he performed it, in a small vessel of only sixty tons and four guns, under the enemy's batteries, surrounded by their corsairs and armed boats, crews of which stood appalled at his intrepidity and daring, would, in any navy in Europe, insure [*sic*] him instantaneous promotion." Preble asked

Secretary Smith to reward his young charge with a promotion to captain, despite Decatur being relatively low on the list of lieutenants: "I wish, as a stimulus, it would be done in this instance: it would, eventually, be of real service to our navy. I beg most earnestly to recommend him to the President, that he may be rewarded according to his merit."[7]

News of the raid took several months to reach the United States, and when it did it made Decatur a household name. For President Jefferson the raid's success immediately changed the gloomy outlook he had about the campaign. It took far less time for news of the raid to spread through the Mediterranean. Almost overnight, the contempt with which European navies held the American flotilla changed. The raid forced everyone, especially the British Royal Navy, to realize the days of ineptitude under commodores Morris and Dale were gone. Now Preble was in charge and he was a man of action. For Midn. Charles Morris, who was the first to set foot on the *Philadelphia*, "The Success of this enterprise added much to the reputation of the Navy, both at home and abroad. Great credit was given, and justly due to Commodore Preble, who directed and first designed it, and to Lieutenant Decatur, who volunteered to execute it, and to whose coolness, self-possession, resources and intrepidity its success was in eminent degree due," he said.[8]

Stewart, who commanded the expedition, was just as ebullient, saying, "The result shed a luster throughout Europe, over the American character, and excited an unparalleled emulation in the squadron."[9]

The British especially took notice, with none other than Admiral Horatio Nelson reputedly calling the raid, "the most bold and daring act of the age."[10]

━━━━━◆━━━━━

Lt. Richard Somers, boyhood friend of Decatur and Stewart and commander of the schooner *Nautilus*, knew nothing about the destruction of the *Philadelphia*. If he felt any disappointment in missing out on the raid, he did not have much time to think about it. On the same day his childhood friends entered Tripoli harbor to burn the frigate, Somers had his hands full with the prize vessel he had captured: The New Jersey native received orders from Preble on February 3 to sail with the schooner *Vixen* for Tunis. After delivering and picking up diplomatic mail, Preble told Somers to "proceed to the coast of Tripoli and off Cape Massurat. Cruise there 10 or 12 days and return to this port. Take on board as much provisions and water as you conveniently can and proceed to the blockade of Tripoli."[11]

For Somers, it was his second trip to the western end of the Mediterranean. On January 9, 1804, Somers sailed to Gibraltar where he met with Lt. Isaac Hull and gave the skipper of the *Argus* the now four-month-old news of the capture of the *Philadelphia*. Hull, who was still on station watching Morocco, knew nothing about the loss of the American frigate and had little to tell Somers in the way of news. That trip was something of a routine mail run for the *Nautilus*. His latest mission was far more warlike.

While returning from Tripoli on February 16, 1804, Somers and the *Nautilus* fell in with a brig flying English colors with a Sicilian crew and carrying Turkish passengers. Something about the boat did not seem quite right to Somers. The ship had a passport Preble had issued, but to the young officer the brig also carried a secret. Her cargo did not match the passport and the passengers seemed suspicious.

His reticent nature, however, cost him at first when he sent the brig ahead of him to Syracuse. He put a prize crew on the ship under command of his sailing master, Edward Cox, and dashed off a quick note to Preble:

> Sir, I have thought proper to send into Syracuse an English brig called the *Nominato Crucifisoso*, commanded by Fortunato Barbaro from Malta, bound for Jerba in Tripoli, for your examination, although having your passport to sail in Ballast and return with a cargo of bullocks. She has six Turkish men or Tripolitans and two women and a cargo consisting of bales of merchandise, wines, spars, new made sails, hemp and linen. The captain informed me he sailed for company from Malta with another brig and under convoy of an English cutter for Tripoli.[12]

At first, Somers' action enraged his commander, whose temper remained legendary among his junior officers. The ship had his passport and that meant Somers broke international conventions when he seized her. Preble was in Malta at the time, trying to broker deals for gunboats he wanted to use against Tripoli. He did not have time to deal with so-called prizes of young officers who could not follow orders. Preble "refused to have anything to do" with the *Crucifisoso*.[13] Just to complicate matters, Maltese governor Sir Alexander Ball heard about the seizure and demanded that Preble explain to him why an American ship of war had captured an English merchant vessel, especially one carrying a passport from the U.S. squadron commander.

Somers, however, believed he did nothing wrong and he stood his ground. After arriving in Syracuse on February 18, he conducted a more thorough search of the *Crucifisoso*. Locked away in the captain's cabin in the stern, under the transom boards, were more papers—papers that proved Somers' suspicions right. He told Preble the newly found documents contained "an agreement between the owner and the captain for him to sail for Jerba, Tripoli or Benghazi."[14] Without a doubt, the *Crucifisoso* was a blockade runner.

Although the new document changed Preble's mind about the capture, he was still angry with Somers. The prisoners that Somers thought were from Tripoli were, in fact, from Tunis. Preble, on March 4, told Somers to take extra care not to mistreat his prisoners and upset the ruler of Tunis, the bey, which could bring that pirate state into the war: "It will be well for you not to conduct toward the Tunisians you have on board in a manner to bring the U.S. in direct collision with the Bey of Tunis by carrying him to sea with you knowing him to be a Tunisian. I should advise you not to carry the papers of your prize to sea with you but to forward them to your prize agent in Syracuse. You have a paper relative to that prize which the governor wishes to see, viz., the contract."[15]

Preble ordered Somers to take the *Nautilus* back to Tripoli, where he was to rejoin the *Vixen* in reestablishing the blockade of the city. It would also get Somers away from Malta and more questions about the *Crucifisoso*.

There was something about Preble's note, however, that rubbed Somers the wrong way. Quiet though he might be, he was still the same officer who, to prove his courage to doubters six years prior, had fought three duels in one day against his own mess room on the frigate *United States*. Somers was not the type of officer or man to back away from a fight; when he believed he was right, he stood by his actions. On March 8 he wrote to Preble, letting the commodore know what he thought of his commander's "advice" as well as his own intention to follow his commander's orders to the letter:

> In consequence of the immediate orders received from you to proceed to sea and your verbal orders that you would not have anything to do with the brig I have captured off Tripoli, I cannot make any arrangements respecting her at present. The man I now have onboard, I now send to you. You advise me to send the papers respecting the prize to my agent in Syracuse. I have no agent in Syracuse nor have I now time to do anything further in the business, as my orders are to proceed immediately to sea, but on my return shall pay every attention the importance of the case may require.[16]

It was a dangerous tack to take with Preble. If Somers was the same, so was Preble, but the old commodore had learned to mellow somewhat in the past five months, as he and his officers had grown closer. Preble did not fly into a rage. The papers Somers found hidden on the brig proved she was up to no good, a fact even the Maltese governor acknowledged. On March 11 Preble sent a note to Secretary Robert Smith supporting Somers' actions:

"The brig captured off Tripoli by the *Nautilus*, the governor of this island acknowledges to be a fair prize, and will lay no claim to her. It will not be prudent to send her home this season of the year, as she is a dull sailor and I cannot spare men. As soon as I conveniently can, I shall send her to the United States."[17]

Somers had a prize. More important, he once again proved his courage, this time by standing up to Preble, and proved he possessed judgment as well. His willingness to stand up to his commander almost certainly added to his reputation, especially among his crew.

Somers, like Decatur and Stewart, did not believe in the harsh type of discipline the British Royal Navy enforced or the type Preble, Bainbridge, or Thomas Truxtun handed out. Although no writings exist on Somers' command philosophy, logs from the *Nautilus* show no floggings took place while he commanded the ship. There are numerous instances of Somers or his first lieutenant, James Decatur, Stephen's younger brother, putting men in the brig, but nothing to show that Somers kept order with the lash.[18]

As the *Nautilus* made her way toward Tripoli, she joined forces with the *Syren*. Stewart was already operating off the pirate stronghold and had grabbed his first prize, a Russian-flagged brig that belonged to a Maltese businessman, on March 4. Stewart captured the vessel as it tried to sneak into Tripoli harbor. The ship had a passport from Preble, but her cargo did not match her papers. It quickly raised Stewart's suspicions. So, too, did the ship's owner—Gaetano Schembri. Although the Russians protested the capture, Stewart put a prize crew on board and sent the ship to Malta.[19]

On March 6 Stewart hounded a Tunisian ship flying English colors into Malta. When the *Syren* followed the mystery vessel into the British port, he found Preble and the *Constitution* along with the *Nautilus*. The ship, it turned out, had a legitimate passport. After a quick meeting with the commodore, Stewart turned back to sea, where he planned to rendezvous with the *Nautilus* within a couple of days. Preble also told him to expect the *Vixen*, under Lt. John Smith, to join him off Tripoli.[20]

Stewart embodied the type of officer Preble liked. Young, respectful, and thoughtful, no one questioned Stewart's courage and no one doubted his leadership. He was only twenty-five but Preble had no problem putting the young Pennsylvanian in command of the blockade of Tripoli.

After sending the Tunisian vessel into Malta, Stewart, now operating in tandem with the *Nautilus* and Somers, grabbed two more prizes in the next ten days. The first was a Greek-flagged vessel, which Stewart sent to Malta and Preble released. The second was a British-built brig, the *Transfer*, which

Stewart seized on March 17. She was the same brig Stewart had imperson-
ated the night Decatur burned the *Philadelphia*. Stewart and Somers stopped
the vessel as she attempted to leave Tripoli, armed with 10 cannon and carrying a cargo of horses and oil. The ship also belonged to Gaetano Schembri.
Although she sailed under a British flag, Stewart said he believed "the violation of the blockade of the place sufficient grounds for detaining her."[21]

The brig was in good condition. Pierced for 14 guns, she only carried
10, and these were just 6-pound cannon. Despite her small size and light
armament, Preble lost no time in having his agents in Malta examine the ship
and its papers. Within a month, Preble renamed the brig the *Scourge* and
ordered her, under Lieutenant John H. Dent, to join the blockade off Tripoli.
Thanks to Stewart, Preble finally received another ship, albeit a small one,
with which to take on the bashaw.[22]

━━━━━◆━━━━━

The team of Somers and Stewart made life difficult on the pirates. Despite
having just two small vessels, the American commanders chased every sail
they spotted and turned blockade running into a dangerous hobby. When
Vixen arrived on station the day after the capture of the *Transfer*, Stewart
increased the pressure, driving his little task force right into the mouth of
Tripoli harbor.[23]

Although Stewart was not quite as close to Somers as Decatur, he and
his younger friend understood one another well, something the crewmen of
the *Syren* and the *Nautilus* could not say. On March 20 an accident nearly
knocked the *Nautilus* out of the campaign.

After dining with Stewart on board the *Syren* the night of March 19
and planning the next day's strategy, Somers returned to the *Nautilus* around
8:00 p.m. He remained on deck, going over plans and provisions with his
officers until midnight, when he went to his cabin. Lt. George Reed took
over as officer of the deck and both vessels weighed anchor and headed for
their blockade positions.

At 4:00 a.m., Reed noticed the *Syren* on a heading directly toward the
Nautilus. "I ordered the quartermaster to keep his luff which he did, bringing her nearly on our lee beam intending to shoot across her stern and wear
after her that we might pass to leeward of her," Reed said.[24]

The maneuver did not work. The *Syren* held her tack. Reed tried changing course but instead of turning away from the brig, he turned into it. Reed
said he "hailed the brig and told her to put her helm a weather but received
no answer." The lieutenant hailed a second time. This time he received an
answer—the sound of the *Syren*'s jib plowing into the *Nautilus*. The jib
caught in the main braces of the schooner's main mast. Lt. James Decatur,

ship's carpenter Robert Fell, and *Syren* carpenter John Felt examined the damage and told Somers the *Nautilus* required extensive repairs. "We are of the opinion that it is not safe to continue at sea," Decatur reported. "The damages are four of her stanchions carried away, which prevents us from setting up the rigging with sufficient security to the mast in bad weather, and at the same time prevents the use of two of the guns." The collision also tore a fourteen-foot hole in the side of the *Nautilus*.[25]

Somers dutifully reported the damage to Stewart, who told his long-time friend to "proceed to the most convenient port where you can repair the damages the *Nautilus* has sustained and refit with all possible dispatch. Return and join us on this station, provided you receive no orders to the contrary from the commanding officer of the squadron."

Stewart also told Somers to take the prisoners from the *Transfer*. The *Nautilus* limped slowly back to Messina, where she would remain for nearly a month.[26]

CHAPTER 13

BACKLASH

MARINE PRIVATE WILLIAM RAY WOKE on February 17, 1804, the day after Decatur's raid, to the sound of shouting guards and yelps of pain. The attack on the *Philadelphia* had enraged Bashaw Yusuf Karamanli, and his anger flowed down to the frigate's crew. The guards turned savage, dealing out whippings, punches, and savage kicks that rousted Ray from his makeshift bed on the floor of the old warehouse that served as the prison of the enlisted men of the *Philadelphia*.

Life as a prisoner for the enlisted men was little better than slavery. Ray and many of the nonskilled crewmen worked carrying rocks and building a pair of new forts to fend off what Karamanli plainly thought was a coming American invasion. The day after Decatur's raid, the pirate leader ordered his army to the shore. "The militia began to collect from the country," Ray said. "They were repairing their ramparts, and making every preparation to repel the expected invasion."[1]

The arrival of new troops did little to improve the lives of the prisoners. On February 18 the bashaw ordered the Americans to salvage what remained of the frigate from the rocks. The pirates also stopped the prisoners' rations, further weakening the men.

For the Americans, the already small daily diet of some bread or a bit of couscous and a few drops of olive oil was taking its toll.[2] The sailors' diet on board ship included beef and pork, sometimes fish, as well as vegetables, bread, cheese, and water. The Arab diet was completely different. Since the crewmen were all but slaves to the bashaw, they received just enough to keep a man alive. Sometimes the guards would dole out small portions of salted meat taken from the *Philadelphia*. On February 19, Ray said, even that meager portion stopped: "All hands were sent to get the remains of the frigate from the rocks, under the control of Mr. [William] Godby, who to court favor from the Turks struck several of our men, and behaved more like one of the bashaw's myrmidons [warriors] than like an American fellow-prisoner. They did not succeed in clearing the wreck, but brought off copper, bolts, spikes, &c."[3]

For the prisoners of the *Philadelphia*, life would only get worse as the bashaw used the Americans to strengthen his defenses.

Capt. William Bainbridge, Lt. David Porter, and the rest of the officers of the *Philadelphia* could no longer see the harbor of Tripoli. The morning after the raid on the *Philadelphia*, guards grabbed the officers, took them from the U.S. consul's residence that acted as their prison, and threw them into an airless room within the castle.

Bainbridge and his officers knew why, but still protested their treatment. In a letter to the bashaw, Bainbridge railed to Mohammed Dgies, the Tripolitan chief minister, against the revocation of the officers' parole and their confinement: "The walls of the city are sufficient barriers to our making the attempt of getting away and you have a much stronger bind on us that all the guards that can be placed, our parole as officers. No officer dare to break it if kept on the part of the government to whom it is given. Preventing our sending letters to our families is a restraint heavy, without the least benefit to the bashaw."[4]

The officers' new prison was a "cold, damp apartment with only one opening at the top, what was grated with iron. Through this aperture they received light and air."[5]

The bashaw also cut off all contact between Bainbridge and the enlisted men.[6] Bainbridge, however, in an act of defiance, waved and shouted out "be of good heart" to his crew as the guards led the officers to the new prison. Ray said his commander "looked very much dejected," a mood Preble noted when Danish consul Nicholas Nissen sent him a letter, confirming the officers' close confinement.[7]

There was more than a new jail on Bainbridge's mind. Although Bainbridge called his own confinement "at times quite liberal," his crew, after four months in captivity, were all but naked and in need of clothing, shoes, and blankets.[8] The new jail cell did little to brighten Bainbridge's mood. The bashaw cut the officers off from all outside contact save for the occasional visit from their longtime friend, Danish consul Nicholas Nissen.

Nissen smuggled out a pair of letters to Preble from Bainbridge. In them Bainbridge revealed another of his fears: Karamanli planned to strike back at Preble for the *Philadelphia*: "A bold attempt is in contemplation, I believe for the harbor of Syracuse, expecting to take you unguarded. They intend to disguise their crews in Christian dress."[9]

How he learned of the planned attack Bainbridge did not say, but the idea of the pirates snatching even more American prisoners or ships was something the morose Bainbridge simply could not stomach. The loss of the *Philadelphia* had consumed his thoughts during his captivity and for Bainbridge, the one lifeline he had was his correspondence with Preble. "I am quite thankful for your sympathy for me to say that I truly believe your friendship sincere and anxiously wish for an investigation of my conduct before the tribunal of our country," he told Preble, "but in spite of every effort of my own and your good advice, I cannot prevent sad reflections—my character, my loss of services to my country and my family are painful subjects to contemplate on in a close prison in Tripoli."[10]

Bainbridge also told the commodore Karamanli accused Decatur and his men of hacking down Arabs on board the *Philadelphia* after the Arabs had surrendered.[11]

There was one bright spot in all of Bainbridge's gloom. The new cell, though dank and cut off from the world, was in the lower reaches of the bashaw's castle. He could hear the surf crashing against the rocks below the lone opening. Bainbridge began to talk to his officers about that opening and the beach, and as they talked they began to form a plan.

———— ◆ ————

The destruction of the *Philadelphia* cost Karamanli more than a powerful warship. It cost him standing among other Barbary rulers. According to diplomatic mail that circled the Mediterranean in the wake of the raid, admiration for the Americans rose along with ridicule for the Tripolitans. Even more worrisome for Karamanli was the very real prospect of foreign intervention.

Sweden promised to intervene for the Americans at the court of the Ottoman sultan.[12] The French offered their services in negotiating the release of American prisoners and a new peace treaty. For Karamanli, the once-glorious capture had turned into a nightmare.

The Tripolitans apparently never planned to use the *Philadelphia* themselves. Instead, Richard Farquhar, the U.S. consul on Malta, told Preble that Karamanli was working on a deal with the Tunisians to trade the 36-gun frigate for three or four smaller vessels. The vessels would leave Tunis under that flag and, once under way in the Mediterranean, switch flags to Tripoli, giving Karamanli a seagoing strike force that could pillage American trading vessels. The Tunisians, in turn, could either keep the *Philadelphia* or sell it back to the Americans, a move Karamanli reportedly favored because he could then ask the Tunisians for a cut of the proceeds.[13]

The Decatur/Stewart raid ended that plan and sent Karamanli flying into a rage. He had lost his greatest prize in a humiliating fashion, allowing the Americans to burn the *Philadelphia* under his very nose. His tantrum also made the diplomatic news. With just a touch of irony, Thomas Appleton, an American diplomat in Italy, told Robert Livingston, U.S. minister to France and signer of the Declaration of Independence, "Nothing I am told can be compared to his unavailing anger."[14]

In addition to ordering increased labor for the enlisted men and close confinement of the officers, Karamanli came to a realization about his opponent: this Preble was different from any foe the pirate leader had faced. He was belligerent and unbending. Clearly this upstart officer from an upstart nation intended to bring the war to the bashaw's doorstep.

Karamanli had already ordered new fortifications around the city of Tripoli and put the captives to work building them. The bashaw also began to look with some fear to his east, where his older brother and one-time ruler still had a following.

———◆◆———

Yusuf Karamanli was the youngest of three brothers. He had ascended to power in Tripoli after murdering his oldest brother, Mohammed, and then deposing the next in line for power, his brother Hamet. At first, Yusuf allowed Hamet to live and rule, albeit under close scrutiny, in Derna, although he kept Hamet's wife and children in Tripoli as hostages. The elder Karamanli, however, believed his brother planned to kill him, and in 1800 he fled to Egypt and the protection of the Mameluke rulers of that country.

Now Hamet was sounding out Preble about the possibility of aiding him in taking back his throne. As early as January 1804 the idea of using Hamet to unseat Yusuf intrigued the commodore. Richard Farquhar, the U.S. consul on Malta, brought Hamet to Preble's attention, asking the commodore to meet with Hamet's representative, Salvatore Busuttil.

A Maltese businessman, Busuttil wrote to Preble on January 24, 1804, describing Hamet as the "Bashaw of Derna." He assured Preble that Hamet had "many friends and servants awaiting him in Derna" and he believed Hamet could topple Yusuf. In addition, Hamet Karamanli promised that in return for help from Preble he would free all Christian prisoners and sign a peace treaty with the United States.[15]

The idea of opening an eastern front in his campaign intrigued Preble and frightened Yusuf. The commodore believed his predecessors should have seized on the opportunity. "I wish earlier notice had been taken of this man and his views," he told Secretary Smith. "In fact, I am astonished that the first or second squadron did not oblige the Bashaw of Tripoli to sign any treaty they pleased."[16]

Yusuf knew about his brother's machinations just as he knew about Preble's search for small ships. Although the pirate leader's kingdom seemed like something out of the Middle Ages to the American prisoners, Karamanli was as shrewd as any European leader. As he watched the Americans' preparations at Syracuse with growing alarm, he began to float a series of diplomatic ideas, just to see where they landed.

Before the destruction of the *Philadelphia*, a story had circulated from Malta to Sicily that Karamanli was willing to release the 307 American prisoners in exchange for any Tripolitans Preble held, $500 per enlisted man, $1,000 per officer, and to exchange a pair of schooners for the frigate.[17] After the destruction, Karamanli raised the ransom to $1 million for the men, but left room for negotiations.[18]

Maltese businessman Gaetano Schembri held himself up as the man with whom to make those negotiations. Schembri was part player, part court jester. He called himself the Tripolitan consul on Malta, although no one was sure whether the job was really his. When Preble appeared amenable to the idea of talks, Schembri sailed to Tripoli and began to negotiate with the bashaw, saying the Americans were willing to pay up to $300,000 in ransom for the captives.

Karamanli did not buy it. Schembri was supposed to be his vassal and here he was talking for the Americans. Karamanli dismissed the businessman's overtures, but it was far from the end of the diplomatic moves. Karamanli was aware of more than Preble's preparations for war. Rumors spread about the flurry of letters between American diplomats and the outright shock the Americans had felt at the loss of the *Philadelphia*. Robert Livingston was among the most concerned. Without permission from President Thomas Jefferson, Livingston approached Napoleon Bonaparte for help from the French. The move infuriated Jefferson. "I have never been so mortified as at the conduct of our foreign functionaries on the loss of the *Philadelphia*," he told Secretary of the Navy Robert Smith. "They appear to have supposed that we were all lost now, and without resource: and they have hawked us in *forma pauperis* begging alms at every court in Europe. This self-degradation is the more unpardonable as, uninstructed and unauthorized, they have taken measures which commit us by moral obligations which cannot be disavowed."[19]

The dissension benefited Karamanli. As long as the Americans committed themselves to diplomacy, it could prevent or at least forestall either a coup attempt from his brother or an all-out assault on Tripoli. When the French decided on direct involvement, Karamanli welcomed it. If nothing else, it would buy him time to continue readying his defenses against Preble.

The sight of the *Syren* and *Nautilus* off Tripoli was a comfort to William Bainbridge. Time in the bashaw's prison weighed heavily on his mind. The commander of the now-destroyed frigate *Philadelphia* was melancholy by nature and the past few weeks had done nothing to improve his mood. His men needed clothing and better food, and his officers remained cooped up in an airless room in the bashaw's castle.

In the days after Karamanli put the officers under close confinement, several of the Arab defenders of the *Philadelphia* washed ashore. Rumor spread that Decatur's men had cut them down as they tried to surrender, sending the bashaw into even more of a rage. The pirate leader refused to allow even Danish consul Nicholas Nissen to see the Americans and completely cut off their communications with the outside world.

Word of the bashaw's actions reached Preble through Nissen, who confirmed the prisoners' condition. He also caught wind of the bashaw's accusations when Bainbridge forwarded to him a letter from the bashaw's chief adviser Mohammed Sidi Dgies. In his letter, Dgies said Preble was "far from the practice of [humanity], since three of the guards of the frigate have been found dead on the shore between Tripoli and the Mesurat covered with wounds. How long has it been since Nations massacred their prisoners?"[20]

Preble's response was swift and designed to both refute the Tripolitan charges and bolster the spirits of Bainbridge and his officers:

> I cannot conceive why the Bashaw should have changed his conduct by removing you to the castle and depriving you of the privileges you enjoyed previous to the burning of the *Philadelphia*. I had a right to burn her, but if I had not, the Bashaw would be unjust to punish you for an act of mine of which you could have no knowledge or foresight.
>
> The minister says I am wanting in the practice of humanity. Before he makes the assertion, let him inquire of his countrymen prisoners with me.[21]

As for the deaths of the guards, Preble was a little less gentle: "I regret that any lives were lost in destroying the frigate. The men who were killed in taking possession of her had a right to expect their fate from the opposition they made. People who handle dangerous weapons in war must expect wounds and death."[22]

It was exactly the type of reply Bainbridge needed to hear and one he undoubtedly enjoyed delivering to the bashaw's minister. As reassuring and confident as the note was, however, Bainbridge could not help but notice an omission. In Bainbridge's letter in which he told his commander about the bashaw's wrath and his close confinement, he included a note in lemon juice, detailing an escape plan. Bainbridge knew the American squadron was preparing its onslaught on Tripoli. When the flotilla arrived, Bainbridge wanted Preble to "ready the ship's barges" to aid some of the *Philadelphia*'s officers in an escape attempt.[23]

———— ◆ ————

The room in which the bashaw confined the officers was close enough to the shore that the officers could hear the surf pounding on the rocks. David Porter, the first lieutenant of the *Philadelphia*, organized a group of officers to attempt digging a tunnel out of their prison cell to the beach. Porter did a brief survey from memory and from a small hole he managed to poke in the wall, but quickly dropped the idea of a tunnel when he saw the distance—nearly eighty yards—was simply too great. Another problem with the tunnel idea was how to dispose of the dirt, a problem none of the officers could solve.

Although tunneling would not work, Bainbridge and Lt. Richard Jones soon found another way to escape. After opening a hole between their cell and an adjoining apartment, Jones spotted an iron-barred window on the second floor of the ruined dwelling. The floor had collapsed, leaving the window nearly twenty feet off the ground. Jones and Bainbridge believed they could reach the window and, with Porter's help, that they would be able to pry the bars off it.[24]

According to Thomas Harris, who heard the story from Lieutenant Jones, the officers used sheets, shirts—anything and everything they could scrounge—and made ropes. They planned to anchor their escape line on one of the cannon that protruded from the rampart on the roof of their prison.[25] Now, with plan and rope in hand, the officers waited for the right moment. Rumor was rife that Preble was due in the harbor at any moment for one more attempt at reaching a diplomatic solution.

As for Bainbridge, he likely had a feeling his commander would look kindly on any escape attempt. Preble knew the rigors of being a prisoner of war: and his memories of his brief stint in the British prison hulk *Jersey* during the Revolution never left the commodore. Bainbridge knew about Preble's imprisonment and believed all his officers needed was for the *Constitution* or another American warship to send a boat near shore on the day of the escape. Writing in lemon juice on March 26 between the lines of his letter, Bainbridge entreated Preble, "Pray, let me hear from you by all opportunities," as the forlorn commander of the *Philadelphia* waited the time for escape.[26]

There was, however, no escape for the 290 enlisted men from their continued forced work on the bashaw's defenses, moving rocks, building walls, and suffering from the cruel treatment of their guard.

The five months in prison had not been kind to Ray and his comrades. Bainbridge told Preble his men needed new clothes, while five of the men had died and three had "turned Turk" (converted to Islam) to curry favor with the bashaw. Finally, the men's spirits were raised on March 26 when the *Constitution* and *Vixen* hove into view of Tripoli castle.

"Our joy was increased by observing the flag which she carried to be a white one," Private Ray said. "The Bashaw soon responded to the signal, by hoisting a white ensign on the castle." Ray said none of the enlisted men knew why the *Constitution* was in the harbor, although rumors began flying almost on sight of the big frigate: "Various were the reports, and our conjectures. Some said that peace was concluded on and that the Commodore had gone to Malta, for the money to ransom us." The prisoners also had a lift from what Ray said was an about-face in how their guards treated them: "What a contemptible opinion of the Tripolitans' character must we form. Yesterday they would stone us and spit in our faces, for the burning of the frigate, which we had no hand in destroying, and today they would flatter and caress us because there appeared a pacific signal, which we had no more agency in raising than in burning the ship. As we walked the streets, the Turks would pat us on the shoulder, and say, American bono [good]."[27]

The arrival of the U.S. flagship had a similar effect on the officers. Bainbridge, Porter, and the rest of his staff knew from Danish consul Nicholas Nissen that Preble was due any day for talks with the bashaw.

The officers, unlike the enlisted men, held out little hope of those talks actually leading to their freedom. Instead, Porter, along with Lieutenant Jones and the rest of the commissioned ranks, planned to use the small window in the empty room next to their prison cell as their escape hatch. Porter and Jones had enlarged the hole and loosened the bars over it in the months' time since the bashaw moved them from the former American consul's residence to their current small room in the castle.

The officers could see the harbor and a small boat lying near the beach. With the *Constitution* in the harbor as well, Porter and Jones knew it could be their best chance to escape. They planned to scale down the castle wall on their makeshift rope and stow away on the boat. Every officer would make the attempt, except Bainbridge. The commander of the now-destroyed frigate *Philadelphia* planned to remain behind, "sharing with his crew their danger and suffering until all were liberated together."[28]

It was a complete change for the commander who once had scoffed at the idea of even speaking with an enlisted man. In fact, the frigate's crew was all too aware of its commander's worries. When Bainbridge saw the

Constitution the morning of March 26, he immediately sent Preble a note, asking the commodore about clothing and food for his men. Preble in fact had "300 sets" of uniforms as well as blankets and rations, but could not land the items without permission of the bashaw. That did not matter to Ray or the rest of the enlisted crew of the frigate. All they knew was that the same Bainbridge who once nearly beat a man to death for a slight infraction was now looking after them. Ray also said their commander, on the few occasions the enlisted men saw him, "bid us be of good heart, although he looked very much dejected himself."[29]

So Bainbridge would stay. The rest of the officers, however, began their preparations for a breakout. Around midnight on March 26, Jones and Porter removed the iron bars from the small window in the empty room. They dropped down a short distance to a rampart and crawled to a spot where they thought they could deploy their makeshift rope and descend to the harbor.

Everything hinged on the officers using a cannon as an anchor for their line. They planned to tie off on the carriage, which they knew would hold their weight. As they crawled toward a gun, the bashaw's guards decided to make their irregular rounds. Richard Jones, the lead officer, ordered everyone to halt and wait. The Arabs continued their rounds and took up posts right near the cannon the Americans wanted to use to anchor their line.

The officers waited until Jones finally ordered everyone to crawl back toward their cell, climb up a small pile of rubble, and clamber back through the window. They put the iron bars back in place and returned, "much chagrined at this disappointment."[30]

For the American officers, it was as close as they had come to freedom since their capture. Still, the streak of bad luck that seemed to follow Bainbridge hovered over the escape attempt, even if the officers did not know it. The ship on which they planned to stow away was actually a blockade runner and its captain had no intentions of going near the American flotilla.[31] There was no evidence Preble knew about the planned breakout or, if he did, that he planned to aid it.[32]

CHAPTER 14

GUNBOAT DIPLOMACY

THE FOUR CORNERS OF THE MEDITERRANEAN were rife with rumors of potential deals between the Americans and the bashaw even before Edward Preble arrived at Tripoli with three warships. Much of those rumors were Preble's doing.

The American squadron commander worked both sides of the European aisle, establishing a cordial relationship with Sir Alexander Ball, the British governor of Malta, and Sir John Acton, the British-general-turned-Neapolitan prime minister, and King Ferdinand of Naples, while also courting help with France.

Malta, although a British bastion, was an important supply point and meeting place for the American squadron. Preble's own base, Syracuse, was in the Neapolitan kingdom and he wanted Acton to push the king into loaning him the gunboats and mortar boats he needed for his summer campaign.

France, England's nemesis and America's erstwhile ally, had an amount of influence in Tripoli. The French maintained a diplomatic mission to the court of the sultan of the Ottoman Empire in Constantinople, the bashaw's nominal king. Starting in early March, Preble began dashing off notes to the French ambassador in Constantinople, asking him to tell the sultan about the capture of the *Philadelphia* and the *Mastico*. Although it was a long shot, Preble wanted the Turks to know about the Tripolitans' use of an Ottoman flag during the capture of the American frigate "and to impress on their minds the truth of this our complaint and the attendant consequence of such a flagrant violation of the laws of Nations and Humanity."[1]

Preble also invited French help in his negotiations with Ferdinand for gunboats. On March 18 he asked Robert Livingston to push the French "to influence the Neapolitan to loan or hire the gun boats we are in need of, we paying for such as might be lost and making good all damages and to furnish us with ammunition." The commodore also believed Napoleon could put pressure on the bashaw to come to terms with the Americans. He told Livingston, "The generous and friendly interference of the first Consul for the purpose of endeavoring to liberate our unfortunate citizens in Tripoli and restore peace between the United States and that regency is truly character-istic of that great man."[2]

The American commander also tried to enlist the help of the British and Swedish consuls in Tripoli. He had far less luck with them than he had with the French. Brian McDonogh, the British consul, told Preble he did not want to risk incurring the bashaw's wrath following the destruction of the *Philadelphia*: "Any urgent solicitations on my part might be construed (by people who I know their ideas) in a different light from what it was intended for and perhaps render abortive my future proceedings at another period more fit. I have therefore thought it prudent to remain at present silent until the anger of the bashaw is over."[3] The Swedish consul simply referred the matter to his government in Stockholm. The only man on whom Preble could rely was the steadfast Danish consul Nicholas Nissen, but the bashaw barred the Dane from visiting the Americans after the burning of the *Philadelphia*.

There was another avenue, one Preble tacitly allowed but in which he took no official part. Gaetano Schembri, the Maltese businessman who called himself the bashaw's consul on the British island, approached Preble and sug-gested he act as a go-between between the Americans and the Tripolitans. The commodore consented, although he gave Schembri no authority to strike any deals and in fact never gave him permission to even discuss a deal.[4]

Schembri arrived in Tripoli on February 20 and opened talks with Karamanli. He did a poor job. Schembri tried to play each side off against the other, telling the bashaw the Americans would pay up to $300,000 for the crew of the *Philadelphia* while telling Preble he could probably buy the Americans' freedom for $100,000. Neither side believed him. Karamanli ended the discussions, telling Schembri he could not strike a deal with his own envoy.

Word of the talks quickly leaked out. Bainbridge told Preble he thought Schembri "[h]as done some injury and not the best service. It is reported he offered any sum which they would demand and if he was charged by you with a commission to negotiate he did not steer in the proper channels."[5]

This was not news to Preble, who replied, "Mr. Schembri has no more authority from me than I have knowledge of him."[6]

The commodore was not done with Schembri. Not only had the Maltese businessman tried to broker a deal, but also he was—in Preble's eyes—guilty of blockade running. The onset of talks between the United States and Tripoli did not mean the end of the blockade, and Lt. Charles Stewart was tightening the noose around the bashaw's capital. His three biggest captures were vessels Schembri owned, or in which he had an interest. The latest came on March 21, when the *Syren* intercepted a Russian-flagged vessel, the *Madonna di Catapaliani*. Stewart reported she carried "bullocks, sheep and horses." However, her skipper admitted the ship also brought into Tripoli "troops, arms, goods and etc.," in violation of the blockade.[7]

The seizure prompted Schembri to write to Preble, denying any wrong-doing and claiming he was responsible for Karamanli agreeing to hold talks. He said he "gave up most part of his time and attention to discovering the sentiments of the bashaw and endeavoring by a faithful representation of the power and preparations of the United States to induce him to wave [*sic*] those pretentions to tribute." As for smuggling or blockade running, Schembri said "from the time [he] became acquainted with your intentions [he] abstain[ed] from all intercourse with the blockaded port."[8]

His pleas failed to sway the commodore. Schembri's three vessels, Preble said, "were captured only in the act of violating the laws of blockade, but in a most flagrant violation of a passport given by myself to his Excellency Governor [Alexander] Ball [of Malta]." There was more. Preble was tired of the small-time businessman with big-time aspirations: "You arrogate to yourself the possession of the 'confidence and esteem of the Bashaw of Tripoli.' Insolent Medlar! Have you sagacity enough to calculate the per-nicious consequence of your duplicity? Do you know, that your ill-timed officiousness served only to raise the sordid expectations of a Barbarian? No. . . . In addition I would advise you to be cautious in again interfering in the affairs of those who will not fail to detect your duplicity and want of common honor and honesty."[9]

While he gave the appearance of turning toward diplomacy, Preble contin-ued to plan his attack on Tripoli. He had his flagship, the 44-gun frigate *Constitution*, and the 12-gun schooners *Vixen* and *Nautilus*, but the rest of his squadron was spread around the Mediterranean, with the *Syren* off Tripoli and the *Argus* still patrolling around Morocco. His only other vessel, the schooner *Enterprise*, was in need of a major refit but the commodore simply did not have the time to have that done. Spring was approaching, and with it the good weather that would allow him to attack Tripoli.

The day after Decatur returned from his successful mission to destroy the *Philadelphia*, Preble ordered the twenty-five-year-old to take the *Enterprise* to the Neapolitan naval base at Messina "and give her such repairs as are absolutely necessary to make her a safe vessel. . . . It is expected that not a moment of time will be lost as in the latter part of March I shall sail with the squadron on an important expedition where I shall want your services."[10]

Preble did not tell Decatur what kind of "expedition" he meant. There was no need. The entire squadron was now solidly behind its commodore, and when Preble said "expedition," the officers and men knew it really meant action. The old commander, who once reviled his young officers—and vice versa—was now a hero among his men. Like him, every man in the squadron yearned to teach Karamanli a lesson. "The bashaw is a shrewd fellow but he has an equal in our commander," said Midn. Henry Wadsworth. "I have acquired a habitual hatred of the bashaw our enemy and I feel as much interested in punishing him as if he had personally insulted me. We are almost certain of peace in a few months, but whether it will be done without cannonading him (I mean his capital, Tripoli) I do not know. The officers all wish the latter."[11]

Preble had little doubt of the outcome of direct action against the pirate stronghold. Battering down the bashaw's walls, he said, would not only free Bainbridge and his crew, but also prove to everyone the worth of the U.S. Navy. "I wish to close this war with the barbarians by conduct which shall establish our naval character among them and make them have a respect for peace," Preble told his wife, Mary. "Nothing else will do."[12]

The problem Preble faced was a lack of ships. The loss of the *Philadelphia* cut his strength by roughly a third. It forced the commodore to use his smaller ships in roles Preble believed were simply too much for his brigs and schooners. He had the 18-gun *Argus*, now his second-most powerful warship after the *Constitution*, watching Morocco and guarding the Strait of Gibraltar. Preble wanted a frigate to do that job. He needed his smaller vessels to operate off and inside the harbor of Tripoli.

He had started looking for small ships even before sending Stewart and Decatur on their mission. His best chance to find gunboats and mortar boats was in Naples, capital of the kingdom of Naples and host to the U.S. base in Syracuse. The commodore sent several letters to U.S. diplomats in the Italian states, asking them for advice on how to approach the Neapolitans. Although Ferdinand IV was king, the real power lay in the hands of his prime minister, Sir John Acton, who was also commander of the kingdom's army and navy.

The commodore sent Lt. John H. Dent to Messina to find out about the Neapolitan gunboats and to recruit crews to man them. For the commodore, the approaching spring meant the time was near to take the war to the bashaw's door, and he did not want to waste any time. His orders to Dent made that clear: "Examine the gunboats and mortar boats and endeavor to know if any of the largest size are for sale. Enquire what guns or mortars can be procured, what vessels suitable for gunboats or light cruisers are for sale or charter, and at what rate. You will stay only two days and return directly to this place."[13]

It was not only the approach of warmer weather that made Preble anxious to get his flotilla together. Since January warnings had come in about Tripolitan attacks on Syracuse, pirate vessels prowling the Strait of Gibraltar, political intrigue, and news that a second Barbary state, Tunis, was ready to declare war.

The possibility of a surprise Tripolitan attack on the U.S. base in Sicily was not lost on Preble. It was why he wanted to keep at least one U.S. warship off the coast of Tripoli at all times. Now it looked like Tunis was ready to join Tripoli in its war. Preble knew he simply did not have enough strength to take on Tripoli, fight a second front against Tunis, and keep an eye on Morocco.

The commodore sent a pair of letters to Washington, DC—one to Secretary of the Navy Robert Smith and the other to his personal friend, Secretary of War Henry Dearborn.

To Smith, Preble was all business. He asked the secretary for two frigates for his immediate command and a third ship to relieve Hull and the *Argus* in monitoring Morocco. He told Smith the reinforcements would allow him to carry war right to the bashaw's palace and to cow the pirates in Tunis. The cost of sending him reinforcements, Preble told Smith, was slight compared to the gain America might reap. "Our commerce in the Mediterranean is immensely valuable and daily increasing. Should war continue between the European Powers, we may engross nearly the whole business by keeping up a respectable force to protect our vessels. I hope we never shall consent to pay Tripoli for peace or tribute, and should Tunis make war, that we never shall have peace with them but on the same terms. If we are now too economical with our naval force, it will only lead to greater expenses in the future." Three ships, Preble told Smith, was all he needed. "If you send three [ships], be assured we shall eventually be gainers by it, as it will give us a consequence with the Barbary States which we want."[14]

To his friend Henry Dearborn, Preble wrote he actually wanted two frigates and two brigs. Congress and the Navy had the frigates, but the smaller vessels were a different story. All of the U.S. Navy's fast, shallow-draft ships were already in the Mediterranean. Preble knew he had to find small ships locally. He began a diplomatic push to convince the Neapolitan ruler to loan or sell him the ships he needed. Preble asked Robert Livingston, the U.S. ambassador to France, to see what he could do to get Paris to "influence the Neapolitan to loan or hire us what gun and mortar boats we stand in need of, we paying for such as might be lost, and making good all damages and to furnish us with ammunition."[15]

As February turned to March, however, the news was always the same for Preble: nothing. John Broadbent, U.S. Navy agent in Messina, told the commodore he had met with the governor of Sicily on whether the Americans could purchase or rent gunboats and mortar boats, "but he had no authority to dispose of them without previous orders from the Court of Naples either by sale or otherwise." Broadbent promised he would contact John Acton and urge him to either loan or sell Preble the small ships he needed. Broadbent had some good news, telling the commodore the Neapolitans had agreed to open the ports of Messina and Naples to American ships.[16]

Preble received a similar message from Abraham Gibbs, the U.S. Navy agent in Palermo. The Neapolitans, Gibbs said, would almost certainly lend or rent gunboats and mortar boats to the Americans, provided Preble assured the king "they are to serve against the common enemy, Tripoli." Still, Gibbs said Preble would need Acton's permission to use the vessels.[17]

The delays rankled Preble. The commodore was a man of action and the niceties of diplomacy, though required, were not his strength. He enjoyed his trips to Malta, where the British treated him with respect, but his main wish was to close with his enemy, and to do that, Preble needed more ships.

"I want only the means to bring them to a proper sense of their situation," Preble wrote to Secretary Smith, "but if a sufficient force is not sent out immediately, the consequences may be serious."[18]

Preble, never a man of patience, was growing ever more frustrated. He knew he it would be late spring before he could use "gun and mortar boats from Naples on loan from the king, but shall not want them before the last of May as they cannot navigate these seas with safety before that time." Preble also told Smith he would have to go to Naples to pick up the ships, equip and man them, and then convoy them to Tripoli, a lengthy-sounding exercise but one in which the commodore said he would "delay no time and my route to and from there will be the best ground to fall in with the enemy's cruisers, if they should have any out."[19]

Although he spent most of his time shuttling from Sicily to Malta and engaging in diplomatic talks, Preble knew he was having an effect. On March 14 he somewhat proudly wrote to his wife, Mary:

> The winter has been tedious and would have been insufferable had I not have been constantly occupied in the necessary attention to the squadron and making arrangements for carrying on vigor in the spring the siege of Tripoli.
>
> The time is approximately near when I had expected every day to have been engaged in scenes of danger, but which I hope eventually to render influential services to our country. I have already had a principal share in affecting a peace with the Emperor of Morocco, [and] have deprived the Tripolitans of

the frigate *Philadelphia*. Success has so far crowned our efforts and the government has been sensible of the service I have rendered.[20]

Then there was Tunis.

When the *Constitution* set sail from Syracuse, Preble told Smith, there were "three Tunisian frigates from 24 guns to 32 guns and one of 32 guns, and a number of xebecs, polacres, and other war vessels at Tunis, fitting in all possible haste for sea. The object is hinted to be American commerce. I verily believe that it is the intention of Tunis to make war against us."[21]

Word was out of Tunisian displeasure at the American blockade of Tripoli. The ruler of Tunis saw an opportunity. As the new American Navy battled Tripoli, it could give the bey the chance to either extort more tribute or gain loot from pirate attacks. No one knew this better than Preble.

He received a message from Stewart on March 4 detailing an encounter the *Syren* had with a mysterious Tunisian ship. According to Stewart, the captain "could not tell how many persons there were on board neither could he show me any papers or passports from our consul at Tunis."[22]

Stewart, much to Preble's chagrin, let the ship continue on its way. Preble told Secretary Smith on March 11, "I certainly would not have suffered to let her pass without asserting the right our treaty gave us, of examining passports."[23]

Two days later, Preble himself had a run-in with a Tunisian admiral, who, "in a haughty, imperious tone, demanded that I should turn all our prisoners up for his inspection to enable him to judge if there were any Tunisians among them. I did not think the request or the manner in which it was made was very decent or proper on their part. I refused to gratify them or degrade ourselves by a compliance. They then moved off but observed that it would not be long before they should have plenty of us. It is possible they may tell truth, but I suspect they will pay dear for their bargain."[24]

Preble's fear was not just direct Tunisian intervention in the war with Tripoli—although he expected that to come by spring. His bigger fear was that Tunis would aid Tripoli with vessels and crews, allowing the bashaw to raid American commerce. He had reports from Decatur that at least one Tripolitan cruiser, with the aid of Tunis, was loose somewhere in the sea-lanes. According to Decatur, the pirate vessel boarded a Danish merchant-man "between the islands of Sicily and Sardinia."[25]

From Tunis came news of either another or the same Tripolitan vessel, now riding at anchor under that city's protection. Decatur arrived in Tunis March 3 and found the 12-gun ship apparently resupplying with Tunisian help. He received a message from Chargé d'Affaires George Davis, warning him not to linger in the harbor. The U.S. consul told Decatur the pirate captain planned to "wait for me and on my coming out, board me," a plan that suited Decatur just fine. The twenty-five-year-old skipper even spread a story his crew was shorthanded, and "what few we had were sickly."[26]

The Tripolitan captain, however, had no intention of fighting Decatur. Instead, he tried to get the Tunisians to impound the *Enterprise*, but the Americans, thanks to a tip from Davis, cut out of the port before anyone could act.

The *Enterprise* remained off Cape Bon until March 13, waiting for the corsair captain to venture out of the port. When Decatur put back into Tunis, he found the corsair ship "hauled into the mole with all his yards upon deck."[27]

Decatur told Preble the Tripolitan captain had already loaded "a very valuable cargo" on board his vessel, although he did not say what the cargo contained.[28] When the *Enterprise* returned to Tunis, the pirate captain, whose crew, Decatur said, had deserted, was busy unloading the same cargo. Without a crew and a rigged vessel, the captain was all but stranded in Tunis.

———◆———

Decatur cruised off Tunis until March 15, when he headed for Messina and the overdue overhaul on the *Enterprise*.[29]

Although Preble continued to believe Tunis planned to join the war in the spring, the bey apparently had no intention of breaking the peace. Davis, in a letter to U.S. consul Tobias Lear in Algiers, said the destruction of the *Philadelphia* "has made much noise in Tunis and is the only occasion on which I have heard our countrymen spoken of with due respect."[30]

Tunis, it appeared, had no intention of going to war, although Preble did not know it. In the commodore's mind, he faced a two-front war with just a handful of ships. He needed reinforcements and needed them soon. "The Tripolines [Tripolitans] by May will have nineteen gunboats and unless we have boats to fight them in their own way we shall not be likely to succeed," he told Secretary Smith. "I will take Tripoli or perish in the attempt. I am confident that it may be easily destroyed or taken in the summer with gun and mortar boats protected by our cruisers."[31]

The *Constitution* left Syracuse on March 22, bound for Tripoli. The commodore planned to meet with Bonaventure Beaussier, the French consul in Tripoli and through him to at least broach the idea of a peace. Failing that, Preble brought along a number of Tripolitan prisoners, most of them from ships Stewart seized, in hopes of arranging an exchange for some of the crew of the *Philadelphia*.

The American flagship pulled into Tripoli harbor the night of March 26 and dropped anchor. With her were the brig *Syren* and the schooner *Vixen*. Preble hoisted a white flag from the mainmast and waited.

———◆———

Pleasant weather greeted the crew of the *Constitution* the morning of March 27, 1804.[32] For Midn. Ralph Izard, the day began early when he reported to Commo. Edward Preble for instructions. The nineteen-year-old officer from Charleston, South Carolina, was the commodore's emissary to the bashaw as the Americans decided to try one final diplomatic push to free the captive crew of the *Philadelphia*.

Preble had no intentions of going ashore. Instead, Izard was to take the ship's barge and row ashore with messages for Mohammed Sidi Dgies, the bashaw's chief adviser, and for French consul Bonaventure Beaussier.

The first order of business was an exchange of letters on the prisoners. Dgies, in a letter March 7, accused the Americans of killing prisoners. Preble fired back a reply, denying the charges and inviting Dgies to talk to several prisoners he had brought with him. One of these prisoners had been on the *Philadelphia*. Despite receiving severe wounds—wounds at first thought fatal—the man was "now well in health" due to the "kindness and attention he has received."[33]

This news seemed to soothe the Tripolitans, although Dgies wanted the Americans to land the Tripolitan officer before he would discuss an exchange. Preble refused. "Any officer either civil or military that you may think proper to send off charged with your answer, or to converse with the prisoners I have on board shall be well treated and allowed to return whenever he may think proper."[34]

Now it was Dgies' turn to refuse; the bashaw did not care much about the prisoners the Americans held and had no plans to reduce his ransom demands for the *Philadelphia* crewmen. Dgies also denied permission to Izard to land clothing and food Preble had brought with him for Bainbridge and his men, although he said a neutral ship could land the supplies.

Running dispatches kept Izard and his small crew busy all day. As soon as Preble had a letter ready for Dgies, Izard rowed into the harbor where a Tripolitan gunboat would meet the barge and escort it to the beach. The midshipman and his men then waited, surrounded by Arab soldiers, until Dgies replied. The correspondence took hours, because, Bainbridge told Preble, Dgies had to write in French, which one of his staff then had to translate into English. If nothing else, Izard had a brief visit with Bainbridge, albeit under heavy guard, and had something else to report to his commander.

The once robust and healthy skipper of the *Philadelphia* looked gaunt, tired, and nervous. The loss of his ship and the treatment of his men, coupled with a poor diet, clearly weighed heavily on Bainbridge's mind, a fact Preble did his best to ease. "Mr. Izard tells me you are grown thin," he wrote to Bainbridge. "I fear my friend you let your misfortunes bear too heavy on your mind by which you may destroy your health. Recollect that destiny and not want of courage has deprived you of liberty, but not of honor. You will I hope 'ere long visit your native country and meet the approbation of your fellow citizens and confidence of your government."[35]

How much the stern commodore believed his own words is unclear. Privately, Preble was still the same officer who railed against the surrender of the frigate. Publicly, however, he adopted a soft tone, which had an effect on Bainbridge, who told Preble "Your friendly offers and kind assurances of your friendship I do truly estimate and regret most sincerely of being deprived of the honor of serving under your command. . . . I yet hope one day to have that pleasure." The *Philadelphia*'s captain made clear, however, he preferred prison to a peace at any price: "I hope a speedy peace will take place, but cannot expect it incompatible to the dignity of our country. Vigorous exertions may crown our wishes."[36]

On this, he and the commodore were in full agreement.

⎯⎯ ◆ ⎯⎯

Preble had put some steel back in Bainbridge. Now he turned his attention to the bashaw. The French consul, Bonaventure Beaussier, acting on orders from Napoleon, met with Karamanli March 27 on behalf of the Americans. The meeting, the Frenchman later reported, went fairly well. He told Preble the bashaw was very interested in speaking with the prisoner on board the *Constitution* "in order to interrogate him freely, as it respects the treatment he has received, also that of his comrades, and thus destroy the general credited opinion among the inhabitants that they have been massacred." In effect, Beaussier told Preble, the Americans would have to release their prisoners with no guarantee of the pirates releasing any of their captives, something the commodore refused to do. The Frenchman also told Preble he believed any deal without some sort of payment was doomed. "I think it advisable for both parties to treat peace and ransom at the same time, in so much as the bashaw intends it should be so, and will never give up the prisoners before having received the sum agreed upon. . . . Considerations make me fear that the Bashaw's pretentions will be at least $500,000."[37]

It was the final straw for Preble. The commodore broke off talks, noting dryly any payment-for-peace was simply not "proper." He was also through with the entire diplomatic process, especially when it meant outside help: "I am confident that the French, English and Swedish Consuls are all in the Bashaw's interest [and] that the Danish Consul is the only respectable character among them. We must therefore depend wholly on our exertions for effecting a peace, which can only be done by an increase of our own force, and a number of gun and mortar boats to batter down his castle and town."[38] The *Constitution* weighed anchor on March 29. The next time she appeared off Tripoli, the frigate would talk with her cannon.

CHAPTER 15

BLOCKADE

L T. RICHARD SOMERS WAS PROBABLY TIRED of seeing Syracuse. The twenty-five-year-old New Jersey native was back in Sicily after his ship, the 14-gun schooner *Nautilus*, ran smack into a late winter storm off Tripoli.

It was early April, and the second time the *Nautilus* had to limp into the U.S. base in less than a month. First, Somers spent two weeks in Syracuse following a collision off Tripoli March 20 with Lieutenant Commandant Charles Stewart and the 18-gun brig *Syren*. The collision caused damage to the *Nautilus'* main stays—the heavy lines that held her main mast in place—and tore a fourteen-foot hole in her hull. The repairs in Syracuse took ten days and Somers made his way back to the North African coast to once more take up the blockade under the command of his boyhood friend.

Stewart, however, was already gone, on his way to Tunis in company with Commo. Edward Preble and the flagship *Constitution*, and Lt. John Smith and the schooner *Vixen*. When Somers arrived on station, he worked briefly with Stephen Decatur and the schooner *Enterprise*, but Decatur could not stay long. The *Enterprise* was in dire need of a refit and Decatur was on his way to the shipyard in Messina.

Somers operated off Tripoli alone for five days. On April 6, while cruising off Cape Bon, the *Nautilus* ran into a nasty gale. Massive waves crashed into the schooner, carrying "away all my bulwarks from the gangway forward to the bridle port and filling the decks full of water so as to endanger our going down. We were obliged to heave over four of her guns for the preservation of the vessel." In a feat of seamanship, Somers managed to keep his vessel afloat and fought the storm for three days. He then turned his battered ship back toward Syracuse, where he arrived on April 11. As he inspected the *Nautilus*, he wondered just how the ship had managed to survive the storm: "On examination since my return here, I find the stanchions are generally all rotten and not able to support the recoil of the guns. I believe those that were carried away by the sea were previously broken by the recoil of the guns when firing at the gun boats."[1]

The *Nautilus* was not alone in Syracuse. Almost the entire American flotilla was back at the Sicilian port. Preble and the flagship *Constitution*, along with Stewart and the *Syren*, and Smith and the *Vixen*, returned on April 10 from Tunis.

Also at anchor was a ship many in the squadron had heard of yet had never seen: the *Argus* under Lt. Isaac Hull was finally ready to operate with the rest of the fleet.

Hull arrived in Syracuse April 9 after escorting the supply ship *Woodrop Sims* from Gibraltar to Sicily. The arrival of the *Argus* was welcome news to Preble, who desperately needed the 18-gun brig to augment his force: "I have thought prudent to keep *Argus* and have this day ordered her and the *Syren* to sail for the blockade in Tripoli. If I had two more frigates and a few gun and mortar boats I should be able to subdue [Tripoli] directly."[2]

The commodore received one new ship as he took the *Transfer*, prize to the *Syren*, into U.S. service. Preble rechristened the brig as the *Scourge* and put Lt. John H. Dent in command of her. The new vessel required a reshuffling of officers, as did sickness and resignations. Stewart lost his sailing master, Samuel Brooke, to Hull, whose sailing master, Humphrey Magrath, returned to the United States due to illness.

To replace Magrath, Preble promoted Midn. William Burrows to sailing master and assigned him to the *Syren*. Somers also lost his sailing master, Edward Cox, to illness. Preble promoted Midn. Stephen Cassin to the post.

The *Scourge* alleviated somewhat the pending loss of the *Nautilus* to repairs as well as the continued absence of the *Enterprise*. The workhorse schooner was still in Messina undergoing a complete overhaul.[3]

The shuffling of officers pointed out yet another problem Preble faced: manpower. Preble pulled enlisted men and officers off both the *Constitution* and the *Syren* to man the *Scourge*. He also faced the prospect of a potential mutiny among the crew of the *Enterprise*, whose enlistments expired in November. On April 5 the crew of the schooner sent Preble a letter, begging the commodore to release them:

> We, sir, have served America six months over our time. Some of us have been two years and three months and some more from our dearest ties while our wives and families left in an unprotected state, perhaps laboring under the most distressful circumstances but for want of that support which they have a just claim on us, but our long absence has rendered imprac-

ticable. The time has again expired that we expected would arrive and with it our discharge, but which at present we are without knowing—resting however on your goodness—we trust you will appeal to our worthy captain for his testimony of our conduct as a means of establishing ourselves in your opinion in so much so as to procure the favor of your compliance with the request of your obedient humble servants.[4]

Preble and Decatur once again made an appeal to the crew to remain until replacements arrived from the United States. All but twelve of the men agreed.[5]

The commodore had just as many problems with his officer corps. Although he and his young cubs continued to grow close, there simply were not enough experienced officers to go around. To staff the *Scourge*, Preble promoted three of the midshipmen that took part in Decatur's raid on the *Philadelphia*. Midn. Charles Morris, who beat Decatur by a step onto the frigate, became the *Scourge* sailing master. Preble promoted Midn. Henry Wadsworth to first lieutenant and Midn. Ralph Izard to second lieutenant. He also sent twenty-two seamen from the *Constitution* to the *Scourge* and gave Stewart orders to send Dent "as many men as you can spare."[6]

For Stewart, the problem was finding men he could spare. He and Somers executed their brief two-ship blockade of Tripoli so well they took four prizes. Each prize required an officer and a handful of enlisted men to take into either Malta or Syracuse. One of the prizes was the *Scourge*. He sent two other prizes back to the United States. Preble crewed those ships with midshipmen who were on the sick list and had requested leave to return home, and sailors whose enlistments had expired, but the captures taxed his limited manpower.

The commodore was also thinking about ships he did not have. He was still negotiating with the king of Naples for the loan or sale of gunboats and mortar boats. If Ferdinand and his prime minister, the British Sir John Acton, granted the request, Preble knew he would have to spread his officers and crews even more thinly to man the Italian vessels. As much as he needed the small ships, Preble wrote to Secretary of the Navy Robert Smith, "I fear I shall not succeed as the British government is working against us." The reason, Preble said, was the British and other European countries feared if the Americans forced a peace on Tripoli the bashaw would send his pirates after European traders, a situation none of the European powers could afford since they were already at war with one another.[7]

Although manpower was a problem for Preble, it was an opportunity for many of the young officers in the squadron to prove themselves to their commander. For Dent, whom Preble used as a stand-in skipper for the *Enterprise* while Decatur and Stewart led the *Philadelphia* raid, the *Scourge* was his first command.

Like many officers in the squadron, Dent was a Marylander, born in Charles County on February 22, 1782. He received his appointment as a midshipman March 16, 1798, and served under Thomas Truxtun on the *Constellation*. He was promoted to lieutenant on July 11, 1799, in recognition of his bravery during the *Constellation*'s engagements with the *Insurgente* and *Vengeance*. One of thirty-six lieutenants retained under the Peace Establishment Act of 1801, he transferred to the *Essex*, serving under William Bainbridge as part of Richard Dale's Mediterranean squadron in 1801 and on the *John Adams* in 1802. He joined the *Constitution* in June 1803 as the ship's first lieutenant.

Preble began to give Dent extra responsibilities during the winter of 1803–1804, sending him to Messina to evaluate Neapolitan gunboats and sound out the possibility of acquiring several of them. He also briefly commanded the *Enterprise*. His new command "was built for duty as a cruiser and is an excellent vessel," Preble said. The Americans increased her armament to 16 guns, although they were relatively light 6-pounders.[8]

The first lieutenant on the *Scourge* was Acting Lt. Henry Wadsworth. The only other Maine native in the squadron and the scion of a wealthy family, Wadsworth was born in Falmouth, Massachusetts (now Portland, Maine), on June 21, 1785. He received his appointment as a midshipman August 28, 1799, and served on the *Congress* during the Quasi-War. He survived the cutbacks of the Peace Establishment Act and transferred to the *Chesapeake* and served under Commo. Richard Morris before transferring to the *New York* in 1803.

Wadsworth proved his bravery while serving on the *New York*. He took part in the raid on a group of grain-carrying *feluccas*; David Porter and James Lawrence led that raid on June 10, 1803. The nineteen-year-old midshipman transferred to the *Constitution* when Preble arrived in the Mediterranean and met Morris' flagship at Gibraltar.

Midn. Charles Morris, whom Preble promoted to sailing master of the *Scourge*, said the brig was more than a mere "cruiser" to the young officer assigned to her: "More responsible duties were devolved upon me, which, at the same time, furnished means for more rapidly increasing my professional knowledge and excited me strongly to improve them."[9]

The appointments to the *Scourge*, in turn, opened doors for still more young officers. Preble had his eyes fixed on two more midshipmen, Charles

Goodwin Ridgeley, a twenty-year-old native of Baltimore, and nineteen-year-old Joseph Israel, another Maryland native. Ridgeley joined the squadron in April when he arrived on the supply ship *Woodrop Sims*. Israel was another transfer from the *New York*. Preble said both young men "stand next for promotion as they are certainly two of the smartest officers of their rank in the service."[10]

The commodore's increasingly deft touch with his officers, however, could not solve a problem Preble did not even know about, and that had nothing to with the capricious North African weather. The problem was in Washington.

President Thomas Jefferson had no idea what was happening in the Mediterranean until Midn. Christopher Gadsden reached Washington March 19 on board an American merchant vessel. Several newspapers had already hinted at a possible disaster off Tripoli during the winter. The *Hartford* (Connecticut) *Courant*, ran a story on March 14 based on the report of a merchant captain who arrived in Gloucester, Massachusetts, in February after a thirty-two-day passage from Cadiz. The merchant captain told the newspaper about the loss of the *Philadelphia*, though the *Courant* reported—somewhat inaccurately—that "Commodore Preble had purchased and equipped two vessels to be employed in an attempt to retake or destroy the frigate."[11]

The dispatches that Secretary of the Navy Samuel Smith gave Jefferson contained nothing about an attempt to destroy the *Philadelphia*. All the president knew was that his third Mediterranean commander had apparently bungled worse than his first two combined. Not only was his undeclared war dragging on, but now the pirates had another three hundred–plus American captives, something that was certain to drive up the price of any negotiated settlement.

Preble's near constant requests for reinforcements also worried the president. Instead of prosecuting the war, his latest commander seemed even more timid than the previous two. On March 20 Jefferson sent a brief message to Congress, informing both the House and the Senate of the loss of the *Philadelphia*: "This accident renders it expedient to increase our force and enlarge our expenses in the Mediterranean beyond what the last appropriation contemplated. I recommend, therefore, to the consideration of Congress, such an addition to the appropriation as they may think the exigency requires." It took the House just two days to adopt "An Act to Further Protect the Commerce and Seamen of the United States against the Barbary Powers," which authorized the president to greatly increase the naval force arrayed against Tripoli. To pay for it, the Senate on March 26 passed a special tariff that would go into a "Mediterranean Fund," which would cease three months after the United States and Tripoli signed a peace treaty.[12]

Jefferson did not stop with legislative acts. On March 28 he ordered Lt. Isaac Chauncey to prepare the frigate *John Adams* for sea. Jefferson told Chauncey to head for the Mediterranean with replacement crews for both the *Constitution* and the *Enterprise*, as well as a load of supplies. On the same day, the Department of the Navy sent orders to Capt. Samuel Barron to ready the 44-gun frigate *President* for sea. Barron, who was senior to Preble, was to command a sizable squadron with the *President*, *Congress*, *Constellation*, *Essex*, and *John Adams*. John Rodgers, who was also senior to Preble on the captain's list, was to command the *Congress*. Jefferson, with his orders, not only removed Preble from command in the Mediterranean, but also put a time constraint on his current squadron commander Preble did not know about.

Preble learned about Chauncey and the *John Adams* before most other American officials in the Mediterranean. John Gavino, American consul at Gibraltar, reported as late as April 4, 1804, that merchant vessels entering the Mediterranean had no information about reinforcements. Gavino said the ship he contracted to carry Preble's dispatches, the *Shepherdess*, ran into contrary winds, and word of the loss of the *Philadelphia* had yet to reach America. The captain of the *Woodrop Sims*, however, brought word of the *John Adams*, although the merchant skipper did not know when the frigate would sail.

The news was not exactly what Preble wanted to hear. Chauncey was sailing *en flute*—his cannon stowed as ballast—to make room for the supplies and extra men the frigate carried. Even when the *John Adams* arrived, it would be of little help until Chauncey could mount his artillery.[13]

───────

As March turned to April, little changed for the three hundred officers and men of the *Philadelphia*. William Bainbridge and the officers remained all but cut off from the outside world. "Were we only permitted to have communications with any of the consuls here, our situation would be rendered as comfortable as could be expected for prisoners," Bainbridge told Tobias Lear, the U.S. consul in Algiers, in a letter dated April 5 but that Lear did not receive until June 2.

The morose commander of the *Philadelphia* continued to work to boost the morale of his men while his own outlook alternated between resignation and despair: "It requires more than the fortitude of man to bear my daily reflections. Injurious reports, loss of services to my country, wife and child in America are painful subjects for contemplation in a close prison in Tripoli."[14]

The officers, with Lt. David Porter and Lt. Richard Jones in the lead, continued their studies while still looking for ways to break out of their prison. After the escape attempt of March 26 failed, their thoughts again turned to tunneling, although their location in the castle continued to hamper those efforts.[15]

Life for the enlisted men also went on much as it had. The bulk of the men continued their forced labor on the city's defenses, but those with skills, among them the ship's boatswain, sailmaker, and the first master's mate, all received new details, working on a set of gunboats under construction. Despite the hard labor, Pvt. William Ray of the Marine Corps said some living conditions actually had improved since Preble appeared off Tripoli in late March. The commodore extended a line of credit to Bainbridge, who used much of the money to purchase better food for his crew. The men, in turn, sold their jailor-provided dense black bread at local markets while walking to and from their labors and, combined with a small allowance from their commander, purchased vegetables, oil, and cooking utensils. "We could purchase carrots and scallions enough to make a handsome little soup. We then boiled the vegetables, threw in some bread to thicken the soup, and added salt and oil. . . . By this management we began to live more comfortably."[16]

The improved diet, however, could not eradicate months of poor food and harsh treatment. By mid-April, Bainbridge and Ray both said the total complement was down to 290 due to deaths and men "turning Turk" to curry favor with the guards. The latest crew death came April 24 when Able SN John Morrison succumbed to injuries he received while moving a load of lumber.[17]

The greatest need of the crew was clothing. "We made a most pitiable appearance," Ray wrote. "We were much affected by vermin and not having any clothes the only way we had to keep ourselves from becoming insufferably filthy was to go the beach and strip off our shirts, going naked until we washed and dried them, and then our trousers in like manner."[18]

Bainbridge did his best to get clothing for his crew, asking U.S. consuls Richard O'Brien, Tobias Lear, and John Gavino for help. Preble, in fact, had bales of uniforms ready for the crew but Karamanli refused to allow a U.S. vessel to land the supplies. The bashaw insisted the clothing come in only on a neutral, and with Tripoli under American blockade, there were few vessels willing to deliver them. If nothing else, the bashaw moved his prisoners to a new jail that was "more spacious and cleanly than the other." The Americans shared their new quarters with a hundred Neapolitan slaves, Ray said. Bainbridge told Preble the change was good for his crew, affording them more room and "more air" as the heat of summer began to descend on the city.[19]

Commodore Edward Preble, commander of the U.S. Mediterranean squadron
from 1803–1804, by an unknown nineteenth–century artist

Courtesy Naval History and Heritage Command

Stephen Decatur, depicted here as a commodore in 1815 by John Wesley Jarvis, was a lieutenant in 1804 and was the Navy's rising star.

U.S. Naval Institute Photo Archive

Captain William Bainbridge, seen here as a commodore in an 1836 engraving by George Parker, was the second in command of the Mediterranean squadron until he lost the frigate *Philadelphia* and became a captive of the corsairs of Tripoli.

U.S. Naval Institute Photo Archive

Master Commandant Richard Somers, by an unknown artist. After Decatur, Somers was the most popular junior officer in the squadron and his friendship and rivalry with Decatur pushed every officer to excel.

Courtesy Somers Point Historical Society, Somers Point, N.J.

Charles Stewart was a twenty-five-year-old lieutenant when he became the No. 2 officer under Edward Preble and commanded the blockade of Tripoli. This engraving from *Burton's Gentleman's Magazine* shows him as a full captain in 1838.

U.S. Naval Institute Photo Archive

Isaac Hull as he looked in 1812 in an engraving based on a Gilbert Stuart painting. Hull was a lieutenant in 1803 and had the task of keeping an eye on both Morocco and the entrance to the Mediterranean Sea.

U.S. Naval Institute Photo Archive

Burning of the frigate Philadelphia in Tripoli harbor, February 16, 1804, by
Charles Wellington Furlong. The oil painting shows the ketch *Intrepid*, foreground,
fleeing from the *Philadelphia* as the frigate catches fire.
Note the correct depiction of the crew using sweeps to move the ketch.

Decatur boarding the Tripolitan Gunboat, an oil painting by Dennis Malone Carter, depicts the crew of Gunboat No. 4 under Lt. Stephen Decatur boarding the second of two pirate gunboats he captured that day.

Courtesy Naval History and Heritage Command

Bombardment of Tripoli, 3 August 1804, by Michael Felice Corne. The artist incorrectly makes the *Vixen*, second ship from the left, a brig and also puts the American gunboats in the wrong position but otherwise captures the moment.

Courtesy Naval History and Heritage Command

"Blowing Up of the Fire ship Intrepid commanded by Capt. Somers in the Harbour of Tripoli on the night of the 4th Sep. 1804," a contemporary line engraving depicting the climactic action of Preble's campaign

Courtesy Naval History and Heritage Command

The better food and quarters, however, did little to improve their lives. The bashaw continued to drive the prisoners to work not only on the fortifications around the city, but also on his gunboats. Surgeon Jonathan Cowdery reported the bashaw forcibly impressed the frigate's sailmaker, boatswain, and master's mate in overseeing the construction. By the end of May, Preble reported, the bashaw had nineteen gunboats ready for combat and was working on building more.[20]

The American prisoners had another problem, one they were glad to have, however: the blockading U.S. squadron. Cowdery said the minute the American ships appeared, the bashaw put more guards around his prisoners, worried about escape attempts.[21] The American ships also began challenging the pirate warships anchored under the cover of the city's fortifications, lobbing shells at both the warships and the forts, putting the prisoner work parties squarely in the line of fire. It did not matter to the prisoners, whose "spirits were cheered by the sight." The arrival of the American squadron also told the prisoners a harsh truth, however: "We now began to abandon all hope of release through negotiations and only expected from the force of arms, carnage and emancipation."[22]

Charles Stewart arrived off Tripoli on April 22 in force. Preble's second-in-command, Stewart had the *Syren*, *Argus*, *Enterprise*, and *Vixen* all working off the city. The American vessels tried several times to lure the bashaw's gunboats out from the protection of the fortified inner harbor, but the pirates refused to budge. Stewart also looked for targets of opportunity—chasing anything with a sail or oars trying to get in or out of Tripoli—and tested the city's defenses, engaging several of the shore batteries in artillery duels. The forays were pointless as neither of Stewart's biggest ships, the *Syren* or *Argus*, had the type of cannon necessary to batter down fortifications.

The brigs carried carronades, a weapon introduced and first deployed by the British Royal Navy in 1779. Also known as "smashers" they were named after the foundry that invented them, the Carron Iron Works in Scotland. Short-barreled with a large powder chamber, carronades were a close-in weapon that could crush timbers, masts, and men. They were also lighter and cheaper to make than traditional naval artillery. Many commanders preferred carronades to normal naval guns because of their power. This was especially true on smaller ships such as the *Argus* or *Syren*, whose role was often that of a cruiser or scout ship. The powerful carronades gave smaller ships the power of a more heavily armed ship while keeping weight down. The problem with carronades was their range. A traditional 18-pound cannon—a gun that fired an 18-pound cannonball—had a range of about two thousand yards. A carronade had a range of only one-third to one-half that distance.[23]

The shortcomings of his weapons did little to stop Stewart. He boldly sailed into Tripoli harbor April 26, challenging the bashaw to send his ships out after him. The pirates refused to budge. The *Syren*, with the *Vixen* alongside, fired several broadsides at the shore fortifications but failed to cause any damage.[24]

The four ships spent several days cruising off Tripoli, strangling the city. Nothing could enter by sea, and even vessels that had passes to sail through the blockade had a rough time from Stewart. Even when Decatur left on April 28 to take U.S. diplomat Richard O'Brien to Tunis Stewart kept up the pressure.

On May 15 Isaac Hull in the *Argus* spotted a ketch trying to enter the harbor at 4:00 in the afternoon. He sent Decatur and the *Enterprise*, just back from Tunis, to intercept, bringing up the brig to support. "She proved to be a Spanish ketch from Tunis bound for Tripoli with a pass from the American consul at Tunis," Hull said. The Connecticut skipper let the ship go. Seven hours later, Stewart and the *Syren* came upon the same vessel. Stewart stopped the craft and, after thoroughly examining her papers and cargo, let her proceed. The ketch did not reach port until mid-morning the next day.[25]

The same day he intercepted the ketch, Hull twice used his ship's small boats to put landing parties ashore. Midn. Sybrant Van Schaik led the raids, which were another attempt to draw out the pirates. Once more, however, the Arabs refused to take the bait. Van Schaik's landing party fired a few shots at some troops milling about the beach, but accomplished nothing else.[26]

The harbor of Tripoli resembles a crescent moon. The points jutting out on the far east of the harbor have shoals and sand bars, with Kaliusa Reef—on which the *Philadelphia* had run aground—acting as an impenetrable guard. The main port of Tripoli sat on the western side of the basin. The medina (or "old town," an ancient walled medieval-looking city) as well as the bashaw's castle were right on the shore. A long stone mole (or breakwater) extended from the shore, protecting the city and castle. A series of rocks and shoals helped to nearly enclose the harbor, creating an inner lagoon in which the pirates kept their fleet. The only good entrance to the inner harbor was between the first set of rocks and the mole.

Bashaw Yusuf Karamanli arranged his defenses to protect the inner harbor, while Stewart ran his blockade outside the mole. Karamanli stationed his flotilla of gunboats just inside the main entrance to the inner harbor. Stewart, acting under Preble's orders, split his squadron, sending the *Argus* and *Enterprise* to the eastern side of the outer harbor and the *Syren* and *Vixen* to the west and the entrance to the inner harbor.[27]

The move quickly paid off as Hull captured a pair of ships trying to sneak out of the harbor by navigating through the shallow eastern side. The first was the same Spanish ketch he had stopped on May 15. On May 17 the little craft sailed out of Tripoli and Hull once again intercepted her. Although she carried a pass, the passengers on the ketch did not match the names on the pass. Hull seized the ship, the *Virgine del Rosario*, as a lawful prize and sent her to Malta, much to the anger of the bey of Tunis, who claimed the ketch was in Tripoli on his personal business. A week later, Hull captured a French-flagged sloop, the *St. John Baptiste*, trying to sneak into Tripoli.[28]

Stewart's blockading force grew to five ships in mid-May with the arrival of Lt. John Dent and the *Scourge*, and the return of Decatur and the *Enterprise*. The *Scourge*, however, was still short of crew, and Hull sent five seamen and two Marines from the *Argus* to help flesh out Dent's company.

The increased force only emboldened Stewart. He chased down any and every vessel trying to enter the port while doing his best to harass supply vessels that hugged the shallow coastline. He made several forays into the inner harbor, engaging the shore batteries for up to fifteen minutes at a time. On June 8 the *Syren* and *Vixen* chased a pair of grain-carrying galleys onto the beach west of the city. "We nearly got within gunshot of them after a laborious day's work," Stewart reported to Preble. He kept up the chase until 8:00 p.m., when the breeze died, allowing the galleys to escape.[29]

The galleys were lucky. Stewart stopped nearly all watercraft traffic in and out of the city. By the end of June, the bashaw's capital was a ghost town. Lt. Henry Wadsworth of the *Scourge* said the captain of a British ketch that entered the port carrying supplies for the American prisoners had a grim report: "The inhabitants of Tripoli, the skipper of the ketch says, are all moving out of the city. Famine rages and no supplies can be obtained."[30]

It was about to get much worse for the inhabitants as Preble was nearly ready to undertake his campaign against the city. "We shall attack Tripoli under many disadvantages," Preble wrote to Secretary Smith, "but as the season for action will soon pass away we must make an attempt which if it succeeds will be more glorious to the officers and seamen of the squadron."[31]

CHAPTER 16

"DREADFUL TO BARBARY"

T HE U.S. FRIGATE *CONSTITUTION* drew a crowd of onlookers as she entered the Bay of Naples on May 9, 1804. The flagship of the U.S. Mediterranean squadron was the first American warship to make an official call at the capital city of the kingdom of Naples since King Ferdinand IV, with the help of England, had defeated the French two years earlier.[1]

Commo. Edward Preble, the commander of the U.S. Mediterranean squadron, was not in Naples on a diplomatic mission. Preble arrived in the ancient city to put the final touches on a treaty that would bolster his force with a handful of Neapolitan gunboats and mortar boats as well as cannon with which he could construct floating batteries. His arrival in Naples was something of a fluke. As late as March Preble had despaired of convincing Ferdinand to give him the ships he needed to take his fight against Tripoli right to the bashaw's castle.

His attitude changed when Sir John Acton, the prime minister of Naples, wrote to U.S. consul James Cathcart on March 27: "If the commodore could take a trip to Naples, he would be accommodated with everything to his satisfaction," Acton said, provided Preble could provide a few more details on how he planned to use the gunboats and mortar boats.[2]

It was an interesting request, one to which Preble had only a hazy answer. The commodore was not sure just how he would use any ships he obtained from Naples until he saw the condition of the vessels and their armament, and measured their crews. With both gunboats and a handful of cannon, Preble told Acton, he could set up "floating batteries to go into the harbor of Tripoli with the gunboats and take position so near the shore that the guns from the Tripoline [Tripolitan] batteries cannot be brought to bear on them, but from whence they will be able effectually to destroy the bashaw's castle and also the town."[3]

The bigger question was just when the Neapolitans would make the gunboats and mortar boats—and cannon—available to the Americans. Acton did not say, which convinced Preble he would have to make a personal appeal for the vessels.[4] His problem was he had no authority to make such an appeal.

Preble's orders made no allowance for him to enter diplomatic negotiations with Naples, yet throughout April, both personally and through American diplomats, he bombarded the Italians with requests for gunboats. He told Secretary of the Navy Robert Smith he believed he had to take matters into his own hands rather than wait—possibly for months—for permission from the city of Washington to open talks with Naples about the gunboats: "The absolute necessity that something prompt and decisive should be done in order to make us respected in these seas I hope will plead my apology with the President for the measures I have adopted to procure the means."[5]

Although he displayed a deft touch with politicians and diplomats, Preble was still Preble. The forty-three-year-old Maine native had mellowed a great deal since arriving in the Mediterranean, but he still had his moments. One of them came April 22 when Preble learned the story of a sailor that deserted from the *Enterprise* while she was in Syracuse.

A French privateer had been in the port earlier in the month and her skipper induced the man to jump ship from the American schooner to the privateer. Lt. John Smith, the commander of the *Vixen* who was also in port, went to take the sailor back from the French, but the governor of Syracuse refused to allow the Americans to retrieve him. The seaman shipped out on the privateer, only to return April 21 on a prize the privateer captured. Lt. Stephen Decatur was in port when the prize arrived, and he sent a boat over to the French vessel and forcibly removed the deserter. The French immediately complained to the governor. At the same time, Lt. Richard Somers and seven other officers appeared at the governor's palace to explain what had happened. The Sicilians did not care. They arrested Somers and the other officers, threatening to hold them until Decatur agreed to release the deserter.[6]

Preble arrived in Syracuse April 22 and lost no time in settling the affair, his way. The governor "sent his aide de camp and a councilor" on board the *Constitution* to discuss the situation with the commodore. Preble was less than diplomatic. According to officers on the *Constitution*, the commodore used every swear word he knew as he stormed at the two men. In his diary, however, he simply noted he "observed to the two gentlemen that this conduct was rash and improper and an insult to our flag which I would not submit to."[7]

He ordered the *Constitution* and *Enterprise* to clear for action and trained his guns on the governor's castle, threatening to blast the Sicilian off the face of the earth unless he freed the eight Americans.[8] He also refused to release the two men the governor sent to talk to the commodore.

The governor quickly relented, "requesting that I would forgive his hasty conduct and assuring me that I might command him, on every occasion." The governor freed Somers and the other officers; Preble released his own prisoners and quickly put the incident behind him.[9]

———————

The heavy hand with the local potentates had no effect on Preble's talks with King Ferdinand or Sir John Acton. On the same day Preble threatened to level Syracuse, Acton told James Leander Cathcart that King Ferdinand would furnish the Americans with six gunboats, two mortar boats, and eight 24-pounders, plus ammunition, powder, and men to man the vessels. The caveat was that Preble would have to go Naples to accept the loan.

The commodore left for Naples on April 29, going first to Malta before sailing along the Italian coast. He left word at every port for the captain of the *John Adams*, which he expected at any moment, ordering the frigate to join the squadron off Tripoli.[10] The *Constitution* continued on her way toward Naples, sailing between the islands of Capri and Ischia on May 8 before dropping anchor off Ferdinand's capital on May 9. The commodore lost no time in contacting Acton to make arrangements for the transfer of the gunboats and mortar boats. He ended his letter with a hint of impatience: "Your Excellency's order for a prompt supply of the above requisition will ensure to His Sicilian Majesty and Your Excellency the lasting gratitude of the United States."[11]

The plea failed to move the Neapolitans. On May 13 Acton invited Preble to dine with him and King Ferdinand. Preble duly attended, where he again asked for the vessels, cannon, and supplies, handing Ferdinand a complete list of what he wanted. On May 14 Acton told Preble the king wanted to know more about just how Preble planned to use the Neapolitan vessels, but the Neapolitan prime minister also brought good news. Aside from a small reduction in the number of gunboats from eight to six, Ferdinand was ready to provide Preble with everything he needed.[12]

As the commodore prepared to leave Naples for Messina, where he was to pick up his new gunboats, he took care of another pressing issue. The commodore's mind was never far from the nearly three hundred men from the *Philadelphia* in captivity in the bashaw's stronghold, and he knew they needed clothing. He purchased fourteen "bales and boxes" of uniforms—everything from 628 shirts to 320 hats—for the enlisted men imprisoned in

Tripoli. He contracted a British vessel to carry the supplies into Tripoli since Yusuf Karamanli refused to allow an American vessel to land supplies for the prisoners.[13]

It was a whirlwind trip for the commodore and not even the trappings of a royal court made much of an impression on him. "I was so much engaged while at Naples that I did not see Pompeii, Herculaneum or any of the curiosities for which that country is so much celebrated and so much visited," he wrote to his wife, Mary. "I shall prefer a little snug parlour to all the pomp and parade of the palace." Preble also confessed to his wife his growing impatience with the seeming lack of response in Washington to his requests for help, saying he was "astonished that our government has not sent reinforcements of ships. It is now nearly eight months since the loss of the *Philadelphia* and still nothing has arrived to replace her."[14]

What Preble did not know was that reinforcements were on the way, albeit slowly.

———— ✦ ✦ ————

Master Commandant Isaac Chauncey had his hands full preparing the frigate *John Adams* for sea while Preble was in Naples negotiating for gunboats. On May 22 Secretary of the Navy Robert Smith gave Chauncey the news of his promotion from lieutenant to master commandant. In March of that year, in addition to approving the funding for and the collection of a new squadron for the Mediterranean, Congress approved Secretary Smith's plan to restore the ranks of lieutenant commandant and master commandant between those of lieutenant and captain. A week later, Smith sent Preble—via Chauncey— a list of four more officers promoted to master commandant: Charles Stewart, Isaac Hull, John Smith, and Richard Somers. Their commissions dated from May 29, although word of the promotions would not reach those four officers for another two months.[15]

Chauncey and the *John Adams* was the first vessel in a group of reinforcements destined for the Mediterranean. Chauncey, however, was not sailing to Tripoli to fight. Smith ordered him to store his cannon as ballast and pack the frigate full of supplies for Preble. The commodore knew Chauncey was coming, but he did not know when. On April 25 he left orders at Syracuse for "the commander of the *John Adams*" to resupply the blockading force off Tripoli, where the frigate would at least give the commodore another ship, albeit one essentially unarmed.[16] Preble also had word Robert Smith was assembling a larger force to send over, but again he had no idea how many vessels were coming his way—nor did he know one of the commanders of the reinforcements was Capt. John Rodgers, the same officer with whom Preble nearly came to blows back in October when he arrived on station.

Rodgers was in Norfolk, Virginia, readying the 38-gun frigate *Congress* for sea. On May 29, the same day he sent out word of the promotions of four of Preble's ship commanders, Secretary Smith sent Rodgers orders to "subdue, seize and make prize of all vessels, goods and effects belonging to the Bashaw of Tripoli or to his subjects." Secretary Smith sent similar orders to Capt. Hugh G. Campbell on the *Constellation*, and James Barron with the *Essex*. Commo. Samuel Barron was to command the squadron, with his flag on the 44-gun frigate *President*.[17]

Secretary Smith sent Preble word of the reinforcements, but that message would not reach the Mediterranean for two months. In his note, the Navy secretary tried to soften the blow of the new officers. Both Samuel Barron and John Rodgers were senior to Preble on the captain's list and, on their arrival, would take over command of the campaign against Tripoli. Secretary Smith also tried to allay any insult Preble might feel about being relieved: "Your good sense will perceive that we have thus been unavoidably constrained to supercede you in a command in which you have acquitted yourself in a manner honorable to yourself and useful to your country and in all respects perfectly satisfactory to us. The only captains in the Navy now in the United States junior to yourself are Captains James Barron and Campbell, and as the frigates cannot be commanded but by captains, we of necessity have been obliged to send out two gentlemen senior to yourself in commission."[18]

The force Secretary Smith was assembling in America, when it joined with Preble's squadron, would give Samuel Barron a massive amount of firepower. In theory, the new commodore would have five frigates, three brigs, two schooners, and the gunboats Preble was borrowing from Naples to bring against Tripoli. "A due regard to our situation with Tripoli and precautionary considerations in relation to the other Barbary Powers demanded that our forces in that quarter should be so far augmented as to leave no doubt of our compelling the existing enemy to submit to our own terms," Smith said.[19]

As strong as the new squadron was on paper, it had yet to get to sea. June 15 came and went and all of the vessels were still in port. Chauncey at least was ready to sail. On June 13 he reported from Norfolk that he was simply awaiting orders to leave—odd, since Smith's orders in April had told Chauncey to leave once he completed turning the *John Adams* into a supply ship.[20]

The remainder of the new squadron also appeared ready, except for the *Constellation*, which required new anchor cables. Rodgers and the *Congress* were ready, although Rodgers sent a scathing note to Benjamin King at the Washington Navy Yard, accusing him of providing faulty rings for the frigate's sails. "You deceived me in every promise you made and in almost every piece of work you did for the ship," Rodgers told King, although he never said whether this was why he was not ready by June 1 to sail for the Mediterranean.[21]

Although Preble did not know he was going to lose command of his squadron, Rodgers and Samuel Barron certainly did. Neither officer said why it was taking so long to prepare their ships for combat and neither seemed in much of a hurry to help a rival. Commo. Samuel Barron did not fully assemble his squadron until June 30, and did not leave port until July 4.

Capt. William Bainbridge also knew nothing of the reinforcing squadron, nor did he likely know about the dust-up between Preble and Rodgers in October 1803, and the still-simmering feud between the two. In fact, Bainbridge knew precious little of anything.

He last communicated with Preble on March 28, when the commodore somewhat half-heartedly tried negotiating for the release of the American prisoners. Since then, Bainbridge had dashed off five letters to his commander, but heard nothing in return. The former captain of the *Philadelphia* tried to keep up on current events through correspondence with diplomats around the Mediterranean, especially with Tobias Lear, the U.S. consul in Algiers. Bainbridge was particularly keen to know what people back in America were saying about his loss of the *Philadelphia*. "I feel very unhappy in not having heard from America," he told Lear.[22]

Foremost on Bainbridge's mind was whether he faced censure for his actions off Tripoli. The fear of court-martial was very real for the thirty-year-old captain. Bainbridge was all too aware of his reputation for hard luck. In the close-knit world of U.S. naval officers, nothing mattered more than the opinion of fellow captains. Soon after his capture, Bainbridge reached out to Capt. Alexander Murray, voicing his fears of how his fellow officers would react to his latest round of ill luck. Murray saw the same desperation in Bainbridge's words Preble did and the captain did his best to bolster his friend's spirits: "I have never heard you censured by any one, except a regret that the ship had not been left in such a state as to prevent her being serviceable to the enemy," Murray wrote. "I beg you will not suffer any reflections to corrode your peace but look forward to a happier change of fortune."[23]

The one happy thought Bainbridge had was of escape. The younger officers once again began tunneling and this time had more success. They continued to dig throughout April and May, and by the beginning of June they had managed to cut their way under an unused room and to make a small hole in the outside wall. Lt. Richard Jones took the risk of poking his head out of the hole and saw the new tunnel was much closer to the water than the previous try. All the officers needed, he told Bainbridge, was for a friendly vessel to dock. The officers could sneak out the hole, steal a rowboat, and make their way to the ship and stow away, only revealing themselves after they were safely away from the bashaw's guns.[24]

----◆——◆----

Master Commandant Charles Stewart still thought of himself as a lieutenant. Word of his promotion had yet to reach the Mediterranean, but rank did not matter to Stewart at this moment. The twenty-five-year-old was in charge of the blockade of Tripoli, and as he rotated his vessels on and off station, he made every day harder on the bashaw. Stewart grew more and more aggressive in his forays into the harbor to engage the Tripolitan shore batteries. On June 8 he sent the *Argus* and Hull after a group of gunboats that appeared ready to venture out of the harbor. Hull reported he "fired several shot at the gunboats which was returned by them and the batteries."[25]

That same day Stewart left Tripoli for Syracuse to resupply. As he made his way from Tripoli, his lookouts spotted a pair of galleys hugging the shoreline, trying to run the blockade. Despite headwinds, Stewart maneuvered the *Syren* "to within gunshot" of the two Arab ships, but at 8:00 p.m. the light breeze died completely and the galleys "made their escape." He then turned the *Syren* for Syracuse.[26]

Stewart's work in running the blockade immediately drew Preble's praise. At any time, Stewart had only three or four small ships with which to strangle the bashaw's commerce. He lost the *Vixen* for two weeks, May 14 to May 28, when Master Commandant John Smith took the schooner to Malta for supplies. Two days before the *Vixen* returned, Decatur and the *Enterprise* left for Syracuse for more repairs and supplies, leaving Stewart with just the *Argus* and *Scourge* to conduct the blockade. Despite having just three brigs, Stewart continued to seal off the harbor.

The blockade commander did not spend long in Syracuse. Decatur picked up a supply of wood, refilled his water casks, and turned right around for Tripoli. When he arrived there on June 14 he found Preble and the *Constitution* waiting for him.

The commodore was on his way to Tunis to check on the prince of that city once more. At the urging of diplomats Tobias Lear and James Leander Cathcart, Preble decided to give diplomacy one last try. He had Richard O'Brien on board the *Constitution*—O'Brien was also on his way to Tunis—and on June 14, the commodore hoisted a white flag from the mainmast of the *Constitution* and sailed into Tripoli harbor.

The white flag was a signal Preble wanted to talk, but the Maine native made his real intentions very clear to Bashaw Yusuf Karamanli. The *Constitution*, with the *Vixen* and *Argus* accompanying her, entered the harbor with gun ports open, cannon run out, and the tampions off. If Karamanli tried anything, Preble had the firepower to blast the city. He also kept Stewart, Decatur, and Dent operating slightly to the west of the harbor entrance to prevent any ships from using the temporary truce to leave the city.

Karamanli read every signal. He refused to see O'Brien and also refused to allow Preble to land clothing for the American prisoners, clothing the commodore knew the prisoners badly needed after the bashaw refused to allow a British vessel to deliver clothing to the prisoners in May. O'Brien spent two hours on shore, waiting. He delivered some mail for Bainbridge— letters Karamanli insisted on seeing first—and otherwise sat in the hot sun.[27]

Preble had an inkling of Karamanli's mood. The only offer he empowered O'Brien to make was $40,000 for release of the prisoners and $10,000 to chief adviser Mohammed Sidi Dgies for his "help." It was an offer he knew the bashaw would refuse. "I do not expect that these terms, or indeed any reasonable ones will be acceptable to the bashaw until we make a general attack by cannonading and bombarding the town," Preble wrote to James Monroe. "I am confident when that takes place that we shall soon have peace on conditions that we may not blush to acknowledge."[28]

On June 15 the American squadron commander called his captains together on the Constitution to update them on his plans. Preble told his young cubs he had the six Italian gunboats and two mortar boats. He also told them he planned to head to Tunis and ordered Stewart to "attend closely to the Blockade of Tripoli" until the Constitution returned. Preble ordered John Smith with the Vixen and John Dent with the Scourge to remain on blockade duty as well. However, Preble gave Stewart, his second-in-command, a pointed warning: "You will see the propriety (now we are so near the time of main attack) of not hazarding too much for the sake merely of destroying or cutting off a market or fish boat. The loss of any one of our vessels at this time would be attended with incalculable consequences to the service." The commodore informed Stewart he would have to make do with a smaller force as he planned to bring the Argus and Enterprise to Tunis just to add to the spectacle of the American arrival. His plans ready, the commodore sat down to write a letter to his forlorn friend on shore.[29]

On June 17 Capt. William Bainbridge could see the Constitution lying at anchor outside Tripoli. He had watched Richard O'Brien land on June 14 in the frigate's cutter. He waited all day to see the diplomat and watched in frustration when O'Brien rowed away from the city at 2:30 p.m. The past three days had not gone well for Bainbridge or the other officers. On June 13, when the Constitution arrived off the city, Jones had led the officers through their tunnel. When they peered out of the opening they saw the bashaw had increased the number of guards around the castle after the American frigate arrived. A pair of guards was right in front of the tunnel opening.

That did not deter Jones or the others. On June 14 they tried again. The plan was even simpler than previous attempts. The officers would scurry out of the tunnel, climb down the wall with an improvised rope, and signal to the *Constitution*. With most of the squadron on scene, the officers believed Preble could send a boat for them under the cover of American cannon.

Lt. Richard Jones again led the attempt, but this time his luck ran out. When he poked his head out of the tunnel, instead of a clear path to the beach he saw two guards, an infantry squad, and a gang of artillerymen manhandling a 42-pound cannon into place.

Jones quickly ducked back into the tunnel before anyone spotted him and relayed the bad news: there was no way for the Americans to escape.[30]

The tunnel at least allowed air into the officers' cell, which was becoming increasingly hot and stifling as the summer neared. The Americans used the tunnel as a crude sort of ventilation, but even that stopped when a guard finally saw the opening. In yet another twist of bad luck, the guard was one of the more brutal watchers. The Americans called him "Sossey," and the guard wasted no time in lining up all the officers, demanding to know who cut a hole in the "sacred walls" of the bashaw's castle. Lt. David Porter stepped forward and said he had made it. Sossey grabbed the lieutenant and dragged him from the room, to the protests of the other officers. He beat the young officer and tossed him into an airless cell, where he sat for several hours before Sossey dragged him in front of Dgies. The Tripolitan prime minister actually apologized to Porter for his treatment and ordered Sossey to return him to the officers' jail.[31]

Bainbridge tried to tell Preble about the escape in a letter on June 14 using lemon juice, but once again, the commodore probably never learned about the officers' attempts to break out of the bashaw's prison. Preble left for Tunis on June 16, taking with him the *Argus* and *Enterprise*. The commodore planned to once again impress upon the regent of that city the folly of taking on the United States before he returned to Sicily where he expected to find the newest vessels in his flotilla ready for action.[32]

———— ◆ ————

Before he left for Tripoli and Tunis, Preble went to Messina to collect the gunboats and mortar boats King Ferdinand of Naples had promised to lend. The gunboats were waiting for him, as was a treasure of supplies. The commodore picked up not only the Italian warships, but also six 24-pound cannon, "fine battering pieces," which Preble planned to use as floating batteries to smash the fortifications around Tripoli. Each gunboat came with fifteen Neapolitan sailors, powder, and shot. The king had provided a pair of "cannoneers most skilled in the use of the mortar" for the mortar boats, as well as powder and shells for those warships.[33]

The gunboats themselves were typical harbor craft—shallow draft, with a triangular lateen sail. They were not blue-water boats and Preble feared they would never survive the trip from Syracuse to Tripoli. The six gunboats and two mortar boats needed overhauls and strengthening before they could venture across the open sea.

Preble did not have the time to oversee that work, however. As he told Tobias Lear, "the want of more frigates keeps me on the fly."[34] His travels about the Mediterranean, from Naples to Tunis and back to Sicily, all took a toll on the commodore, his crew, and his flagship. Plus, the commodore knew reinforcements were on the way, although he remained in the dark about his own position and their exact strength, and he had to prepare supplies for the new ships. He believed Samuel Barron and the *President*, with two brigs, would remain at Gibraltar to keep an eye on the western Mediterranean. In addition, Preble erroneously believed Isaac Chauncey was in command of the *Essex* and that Master Commandant John Shaw—the first commander of the schooner *Enterprise*—commanded the *John Adams*. He thought those two frigates would join his force off Tripoli.[35]

As spring turned into summer, Preble spent more and more time planning his assault on Tripoli. He needed someone else to take charge of refitting the Italian gunboats, and as one officer's bad luck would have it, Preble had just the man.

⟶ ◆ ⟵

Master Commandant Richard Somers still wore the uniform of a lieutenant. Like his childhood friends Charles Stewart and Stephen Decatur, Somers had yet to hear of his promotion and was in Syracuse with the schooner *Nautilus*, which had suffered heavy damage in an April gale.

The *Nautilus* required a complete overhaul and the royal shipyard at Messina was the only place where Somers could get the work done. He arrived there in the beginning of May and watched helplessly as the Sicilian shipwrights moved agonizingly slow in their repair work of the schooner. When Preble pulled into Messina on June 3 with the six gunboats in tow, he did not want to remain there for long. The commodore needed an officer to oversee the refitting work. The job fell to Somers and his crew.

The Neapolitan gunboats were more barges than seagoing craft. They had slightly rounded bows and sterns, which made them perfect for towing across placid harbor waters but far less than ideal for operations in open water. Each vessel weighed roughly twenty-five tons, had a lateen sail and jib, and carried a long 24-pound cannon in the bow. Preble wanted Somers to strengthen the gunboats to withstand the hammer-like blows of the guns' recoil.

The gunboats also had to accommodate two crews. The king, as promised, provided gunners and sailors, but Preble wanted Americans on each gunboat. He stripped the *Nautilus* of her crew, leaving just a lieutenant, the sailing master, a boatswain, and a few men to take care of the schooner. The commodore also sent six officers from the *Constitution* to the gunboats.[36]

Somers dove into the work. He contracted seventy-two carpenters from Messina and the surrounding area to begin the work of strengthening the gunboats. He hired sailmakers, coopers, and blacksmiths. He also started training his men in handling the gunboats and in shipboard hand-to-hand combat. "Captain Somers worked with all the crew of the *Nautilus*," according to the *Constitution*'s sailing master Nathaniel Haraden. "Fifteen Sicilians are attached to each [gunboat] besides the *Nautilus*'s men," although Somers did not train the Italians for combat.[37]

The two mortar boats needed even more work. The flat-bottomed vessels required structural work so they could withstand the hammer-like blows from the 9-inch mortars they carried. Preble also wanted the mortar boats, like the gunboats, to be more seaworthy. The work on the mortar boats would take a month to complete. The gunboats, thanks to Somers' efforts, left Messina on June 3. The training did not stop in Syracuse. Preble told Somers to "exercise the men by getting under way as often as every other day and oftener if you think proper." The commodore also took steps to prevent any miscommunication between the different sailors from erupting into a major rift, telling Somers, "I wish the utmost harmony to exist between the citizens of the U.S. engaged on board [the gunboats] whether they were born in America or elsewhere."[38]

As Somers continued to work on readying the Neapolitan vessels, Preble left for Tunis on June 6 while Decatur, after a brief resupply stop in Syracuse, returned to Tripoli on June 9. The departures left Somers in command not only of the American base, but also of the better part of the squadron on which Preble would depend to defeat the bashaw. The *Nautilus* was still in Messina and Somers remained in communication with Sailing Master Edward Cox, checking on progress of the work. He also took command of the *Intrepid*, all but forgotten in Syracuse. At Preble's command, Somers converted the ketch into a hospital ship.

It was not all work for Somers and his officers. Early in June he decided to take a tour of some of the ancient sites outside Syracuse. One day Somers and two others—most likely Lt. James Decatur and Lt. George Reed—went for a walk in the countryside. According to Somers' nephew, J. B. Somers, only one of the men carried a weapon, and the armed man was not his uncle. "Five men carrying swords, who were afterwards ascertained to be soldiers of the garrison, made an attack on the party with the intent to rob," J. B. Somers wrote. The lone armed officer used his dagger to fight off and kill one of the would-be robbers while Somers, completely unarmed, went after a second. Somers "grappled with" his assailant, seizing "the blade of his antagonist's sword and was severely cut in the hand by the efforts of the robber to recover it." Richard Somers managed to pull the sword out of his assailant's hands and turned the weapon on him, killing him with one blow. Somers then turned on the other three attackers, who quickly fled. He and his officers carried the two dead men back into Syracuse where locals identified the bodies.[39]

Master Commandant Charles Stewart grew increasingly aggressive as he led the blockade of Tripoli. The second-in-command of the U.S. squadron spent all of June testing the defenses of the city, running his force of brigs and schooners in and out of the inner harbor where they could engage the shore batteries of Bashaw Yusuf Karamanli. Stewart also continued to clamp down on trade coming into and leaving Tripoli, forcing the bashaw to rely entirely on overland routes to supply his city.

On July 7 Stewart saw a chance to hit two targets at once when a galley carrying wheat tried to sneak into the harbor along the rocky shoreline under the protection of a pair of small, newly erected shore batteries. Stewart ordered the schooner *Vixen* under Master Commandant John Smith to chase the galley while he provided cover and engaged the batteries with his brig the *Syren*. He ordered Master Commandant Isaac Hull in the *Argus* and Lieutenant Commandant John Dent in the *Scourge* to provide backup.

The *Argus* and *Vixen* quickly drove the galley ashore. As her crew leaped onto the beach, the two American vessels opened fire with grapeshot and canister, and the Tripolitans replied with musket and cannon from the two forts. Despite the fire from the two American warships, the galley crew began unloading the cargo of wheat from the vessel.

Stewart decided to take the fight right to the beach. He ordered his first lieutenant, James Caldwell, and Midn. James Dorsey to take the barge and launch from the *Syren* to engage the Arabs. Caldwell placed a 12-pound carronade in the launch while the barge carried "a heavy swivel" gun. The two officers pushed their vessels right up to the beach, where they opened fire on both the galley crew and the growing number of troops on shore.

Caldwell and Dorsey quickly found themselves exposed to heavy fire from the shore batteries. The *Vixen* swept in as close as she could and opened fire, blasting away at the forts, but "the rocks formed too strong a breast work to admit of the enemy's being dislodged. The fire from both of the *Syren*'s boats and the *Vixen* sank the galley, although the crew managed to remove most of the wheat. Seeing nothing farther could be effected, I made the signal of recall that the boats might return to tow off their respective ships," Stewart said. By Stewart's estimate, his small landing party fought against "at least 1000 men," causing heavy casualties among the Tripolitans. The *Syren* suffered four casualties—Marine William Williams, who died, and three wounded. "I feel a particular degree of satisfaction in announcing to you, sir, the great bravery and exertions displayed by the officers and men employed in the boats," Stewart reported to Preble. "The enemy must have suffered severely from their great numbers."[40]

It took about a month for Somers' hand to heal. During that time, Preble returned from checking on Tunis and Decatur returned for more supplies for the schooner *Enterprise*. Decatur returned at a perfect time for the commodore. The repairs to the six gunboats, two mortar boats, and the *Nautilus* were complete by the end of June. Somers began loading supplies onto each. By July 7 the squadron was ready.

Preble gave Decatur and Somers orders to cast off with the gunboats and mortar boats. With the *Constitution* in the lead and the *Nautilus* and *Enterprise* towing the smaller vessels, Preble began the voyage to Tripoli. "I regret that we do not have another frigate or two here at the moment but it will not do to delay time as we have only about eight weeks more of this year that gun boats can remain out with safety in these seas," the commodore wrote to James Monroe. He may not have had all the ships he wanted, but the commodore had something he knew might serve him even better—his officers: "Our squadron is small but composed of young men whose anxiety to distinguish themselves gives me well-founded hopes of success."[41]

The stakes were high. George Davis, U.S. consul in Tunis, told Preble just what success—or failure—might mean to the future of American commerce and relations in the Mediterranean. The city's bey, he said, "awaits the result of your summer campaign against Tripoli and on your success there, be assured Sir depends our future respectability here. A national character has yet to be established with the states. It must be dreadful to Barbary—or we shall ever bow the neck and receive the tributary yoke of half a dozen pirates."[42]

CHAPTER 17

BATTLE LINES

THE OFFICERS OF THE UNITED STATES Mediterranean squadron packed the wardroom on board the USS *Constitution*. Their commander, Commo. Edward Preble, detailed his plan for the attack on Tripoli that would take place the next day, August 3, 1804.

The forty-three-year-old Maine native and his "cubs," as he once called them, were now a well-drilled team. His officers, whose average age was just twenty-four, had learned how to harness their zeal and energy under Preble's discipline, while the commodore had learned how to use a defter approach in dealing with his young charges. The animosity between the officers and their commander was gone. When they first met, back in the late summer of 1803, the officers, almost to a man, loathed Preble. Now they almost universally admired him. Preble was a fighter, which the young men liked. The officers had learned how to do their jobs properly and obey orders, which Preble demanded.

Lt. Joseph Tarbell, first officer on the *Constitution*, learned firsthand just how much he and his fellow officers—and Preble—had changed when he nearly ran the American flagship onto rocks outside Valletta harbor on Malta. Tarbell had the noon watch on June 5, 1804, and had orders to take the *Constitution* into Valletta. At 1:45 p.m., a midshipman interrupted Preble's lunch to tell him the frigate appeared dangerously close to the shore. "I ordered him to go on deck and tell the officer to tack ship," Preble wrote in his diary. "The helm was immediately put down and as the ship came to, I observed from the cabin ports that she was nearly on shore." The sight galvanized Preble, who said he "sprang on deck" and immediately relieved Tarbell of duty. In typical Preble fashion, he loudly accused his own first officer of neglect of duty. Preble also believed the pilot was guilty of intentionally trying to "lose the ship and he ordered his Marines to confine the man in irons."[1]

Preble remained on deck throughout the afternoon and evening, supervising her arrival in Malta while Tarbell remained below deck, no doubt anxiously awaiting his fate. Four days later, the remaining officers of the *Constitution* wrote to Preble, an act none of them would have dreamed of just six months prior. In their note, the officers told their commander, "A retrospect of his [Tarbell's] deportment heretofore, as a gentleman and correct officer, prior to this unfortunate evening of the 5th, induces us powerfully to exert ourselves that, if consistent, he may be ordered again to his duty with us as usual." The first officer's mistake, they went on, was "founded on his too great confidence in the pilot. We have always considered Mr. Tarbell to be one of our most correct officers and the circumstances above alluded to, which has incurred your displeasure, will, he says, be a lesson which he can never lose sight of."[2]

Their plea worked. Later that same day Preble formally dropped the neglect-of-duty charges against Tarbell. "I am induced to believe that too much confidence alone in the pilot might have occasioned your imprudent approach to the shore," Preble told his executive officer. "From this circumstance and a solicitation on the part of your brother officers highly honorable to you that you may still continue among them, I am induced to direct that you return to your duty in full confidence that you will in future be more guarded in your conduct."[3]

On June 10, Sailing Master Nathanial Haraden, who was the first of the officers to sign the note to Preble, made a special note in the *Constitution* logbook: "4 p.m., Mr. Tarbell had the watch."[4]

The fact that Preble was willing to relieve and charge his own first officer was yet another lesson to his young officers that he would not tolerate incompetance. For the officers, the fact their commander was willing to listen to them and take their advice was a sign of just how high in his esteem he actually held them.

The Tarbell incident was already old news by the time Preble reached Tripoli on July 28 for the much-anticipated start of his all-out assault on Tripoli. The regent of the city, Bashaw Yusuf Karamanli, still refused to accept American terms for peace. The commodore wanted to launch his summer campaign in the beginning of July to force the bashaw to accept a peace, but repairs to the pair of mortar boats Preble borrowed from the kingdom of Naples took longer than he had expected.

The *Constitution*, with the two mortar boats in tow, did not leave Syracuse until July 21, 1804. The schooners *Enterprise* and *Nautilus* sailed with the frigate, each towing three gunboats. When they arrived a week later, Preble wanted to launch an immediate attack, but a wind that blew up from the east gained strength, turning into a gale by late afternoon. The storm threatened to swamp the eight Italian craft; their flat bottoms were perfect for work inshore or in harbors, but made them difficult to handle in blue water.

The storm also forced the rest of the squadron to seek shelter, with the brigs *Argus*, *Syren*, and *Scourge* and the schooner *Vixen* all heading out to open seas to fight the gale. For three days the storm lashed the American squadron, driving the Americans away from Tripoli. When the gale finally blew itself out on July 31, Preble needed two days to reassemble his force. He set August 2 as the day for the first attack on Tripoli, and on August 1 hoisted the signal for his captains to come on board and discuss his plan.

The U.S. frigate *John Adams* usually carried 28 cannon. As she pulled into Gibraltar, however, she had just 8 guns mounted. It was all she had room for. Her crew had packed every other inch of the frigate with supplies for Preble's squadron. Normally, the frigate had a crew of 220 men, but on this trip the *John Adams* also carried more than 50 extra men, replacement crew for the squadron.

As the storm struck the American squadron, the *John Adams* rounded the massive cliffs of Gibraltar, 1,079 miles to the west of Tripoli. In addition to men and supplies, Master Commandant Isaac Chauncey carried news. Some of it Preble already knew.

Chauncey received his orders to head for the Mediterranean in March, the day after President Thomas Jefferson received word of the loss of the frigate *Philadelphia*. It took Chauncey three months to get the *John Adams* ready for the trip. The frigate left Hampton Roads *en flute* on June 28. It took her nearly a month to cross the Atlantic.

Somewhere behind the *John Adams* were four more ships, the frigates *Congress*, *Essex*, *Constellation*, and *President*, all under the command of Commo. Samuel Barron. Like Chauncey, Barron received his orders to assemble his force just days after Jefferson received news of the *Philadelphia*. Unlike Chauncey, Barron was higher on the seniority list than Preble and, on his arrival, would take command of the reinforced Mediterranean force. Preble knew about Barron and suspected he would be replaced when the more senior officer arrived.

Samuel Barron was still somewhere in the Atlantic even though he left Hampton Roads on July 1, just a week after Chauncey. Contrary winds and storms hampered the new commander's crossing, slowing it to a crawl. Chauncey made better time, arriving at the British bastion of Gibraltar on July 22. After a three-day stopover to pick up supplies for his own crew, Chauncey left for Algiers, where he was to get an update on what the dey of that city was doing, before he headed for Malta. He left letters for transmission to the Secretary of the Navy Robert Smith and Samuel Barron at Gibraltar before departing.[5]

Gibraltar was the one place in the Mediterranean where Preble had not sent his own orders for the *John Adams*. As Chauncey weighed anchor on July 28 and set a course for Algiers, Preble was anxiously awaiting the frigate off Tripoli.

Capt. William Bainbridge and the rest of the prisoners from the *Philadelphia* could plainly see the American squadron as it hove into view. July 28 was Day 270 in captivity for Bainbridge and the 294 men still alive from the frigate. Bainbridge, to keep his spirits up, spent much of his time writing—to Preble, to U.S. diplomats, to just about anyone.

The nine months in the bashaw's prison had made the normally melancholy Bainbridge even glummer. One way he tried to buoy his own spirits was to inject himself as much as possible into what was happening in the Mediterranean. The captain sent multiple letters to the American diplomats in the region, offering his thoughts on how to bring about the freedom of his crew. His moves came to nothing. In a letter to George Davis, a former purser in the Navy and then consul in Tunis, Bainbridge expressed his frustration: "I have heard in a roundabout way that the bashaw demanded one million [in ransom]. O'Brien offered forty thousand. God knows what the intention [of those talks]. I am entirely ignorant." Bainbridge also tried to send Preble tactical ideas. Even before the commodore obtained the mortar boats from Naples Bainbridge wrote Davis to tell Preble "a few shells here in this hour would have a good effect."[6] After hearing the news that the Neapolitans had agreed to loan bomb vessels to the commodore, Bainbridge wrote his commander, "I candidly believe that heaving a few shells even it was but once a week to keep them out of the town for three months and the bashaw would be induced to come to moderate terms." As for his captors, Bainbridge said the pirates "are such bad marksmen that I presume a ketch might anchor a half-mile distant from the batteries without any danger of receiving much or any damage."[7]

The other officers of the *Philadelphia* were making do, Bainbridge said, although the failed escape in May put an end to their breakout attempts. "We are so closely watched that the most desperate attempt cannot avail anything,"[8] Bainbridge wrote. If nothing else, the younger officers had their studies to keep them busy: "Our prison represents a college of students." However, it was not a comfortable college. "The officers are still penned up in close confinement, and in this hot weather feel much the want of a few windows and doors to let in some air."[9]

Bainbridge, however, had only his own thoughts to keep him company. He simply could not shake the worry he would receive censure in the United States for losing the *Philadelphia*. "I am extremely anxious to receive letters from America in answer to mine announcing the loss of the frigate *Philadelphia*," he confessed to Preble. "I cannot account for the silence of my friends."[10]

As the American squadron arrived off Tripoli on July 25, Bainbridge, from his perch in the bashaw's castle, could only wait and hope for his liberation.

Bashaw Yusuf Karamanli had plenty to keep him busy. The wily leader of Tripoli knew all about Preble's negotiations with the king of Naples, knew the Americans now had gunboats and mortar boats, and probably knew about the reinforcements set to arrive any day from the United States.[11] His best source of information was his American prisoners. Every letter William Bainbridge or any other officer wrote had to first go through Mohammed Dgies before Danish consul Nicholas Nissen could mail it to its destination. The same was true for incoming mail, which Dgies read before the Americans.

The bashaw used June and July to strengthen his defenses against an American attack. By mid-July he had a formidable force of nineteen gunboats, each mounting a long iron cannon ranging in size from 18- to 28-pounders, a pair of galleys armed with 6 cannon, two 8-gun schooners, and a brig of 10 cannon. He also built up his land defenses, with the imprisoned crew of the *Philadelphia* doing much of the work. Pvt. William Ray was one of those sent to the backbreaking labor of constructing shoreline forts for Karamanli.

The plight of the enlisted men from the *Philadelphia* worsened with each day in captivity. Their clothing, what little remained after their capture the previous fall, was all but falling off their backs. As Preble's squadron increased its blockading activity, the bashaw increased his harsh treatment, even working Americans to death. Ray said he watched helplessly as foretop captain John Morrison succumbed to injuries he sustained while loading lumber onto a wagon. Ray said the twenty-seven-year-old Morrison languished for three days before one of the guards, "an old Algerine," as Ray called him, "insisted that nothing ailed him, but that he was shamming sickness to avoid labor. He went to the dying man, told him to rise, called him an infidel and a dog, and struck him several times with his cane." Although the other prisoners "burned to immolate the ferocious villain," there was little they could do. Ray wrote that each time Master Commandant Charles Stewart led his blockading force into the harbor to engage either the shore batteries or any Tripolitan shipping, "the Turks made this a pretext for doubling their severity."[12]

By mid-July Karamanli had put the American prisoners to work on a new task. As Bainbridge told Preble, the idea of mortar shells struck terror into the pirate leader. He knew the bomb vessels could take up positions just out of range of his guns while dropping explosive shells on the city. The bashaw had no intention of being on the receiving end of any American bombardment. On July 15 he ordered the prisoners to begin clearing his belongings out of the castle. Karamanli, Ray said, now spent his nights in a small abode some two miles away from the city, well out of range of Preble's guns.[13]

After they finished the task of moving the bashaw out of Tripoli, the American prisoners settled into their jail to await developments. They saw Preble's arrival on July 25 and, like the bashaw, expected an attack right away. When the gale blew up later that day, all Ray and the enlisted men could do was continue their vigil. They continued waiting until August 1, when the storm finally cleared and the U.S. squadron sailed into the harbor, just out of range of the bashaw's guns. From their vantage point, the crew of the *Philadelphia* could easily hear as the squadron made "every preparation for an attack on the town and forts."[14]

———•—•———

A warm sun and gentle breeze greeted the American squadron at dawn on August 2, 1804.[15] The sailors and officers of the flotilla spent the morning loading supplies on their ships, paying special attention to the eight craft the Americans had borrowed from the king of Naples. The six gunboats and two mortar boats were integral parts of the plan Preble had spent more than a month devising.

At 5:30 that afternoon Preble hoisted a signal, calling for all of his commanders to convene on board the *Constitution*.[16] The commodore first went over the assignments for each of his officers. He divided the six gunboats into two divisions. Master Commandant Richard Somers commanded one division of three gunboats while Stephen Decatur Jr. commanded the other. Preble pulled Master Commandant John Dent off the *Scourge* to command one of the two mortar boats while Lt. John Robinson took the other. He stripped the *Scourge* of its crew, sending thirty men to the mortar boats while spreading the rest out among the vessels in the squadron. When he finished, the *Scourge* had three officers and a handful of sailors to man her. The brig would play no part in the upcoming battle.[17]

Each of the Italian craft had fifteen Neapolitan sailors to crew the vessels and fifteen to twenty American sailors and Marines to do the actual fighting. To find the nearly 120 men he needed for the gunboats, Preble stripped his smaller vessels. In addition to Somers, Preble pulled another five officers along with fifty men out of the schooner's complement of ninety sailors. From the *Enterprise* came another fifty sailors and Marines and four officers.[18] Preble also pulled men and officers from the *Vixen, Syren,* and *Argus.*

The Tripolitans had deployed a line of nine gunboats across the harbor entrance, using the mole as a starting point. Anchored just behind the first line were another six gunboats and a pair of galleys. Preble knew that he had to smash the enemy gunboats to get into the inner harbor.

He ordered Somers, in Gunboat No. 1 with Midn. Charles Ridgeley and Midn. William Miller of the *Nautilus,* to lead three gunboats toward the eastern end of the enemy line. Gunboat No. 2, under Lt. James Decatur and Lt. Stephen Cassin of the *Nautilus,* and Gunboat No. 3, under Lt. Joshua Blake of the *Argus,* were to accompany Somers.

Decatur, in Gunboat No. 4, was to hit the center of the line. Serving alongside the *Enterprise* skipper were Lt. Jonathan Thorn and Midn. Thomas Macdonough. Gunboat No. 5, under Lt. Joseph Bainbridge and Lt. John Davis of the *Enterprise* and Chief Boatswain William Bunker of the *Syren,* and Gunboat No. 6 under Lt. John Trippe and Midn. John Henley of the *Vixen,* were to support Decatur.

The plan was simple. The American gunboats were both bait and the anvil. They were to lure the Tripolitan gunboats into open water and then hold them in place where the *Argus, Syren,* and *Vixen* could act as the hammer, crushing the enemy vessels.

At the same time, Dent and Robinson had orders to fire mortar shells into the city to both destroy enemy batteries and sow confusion and fear among the inhabitants. After defeating the gunboats, Preble planned to sail the *Constitution, Syren,* and *Argus* into the harbor where the frigate would engage the remaining shore defenses and bombard the bashaw's castle.[19] The *Constitution,* with her long 24-pound cannon, was the only ship in the squadron with the power to engage the pirates' shore defenses. To help, Preble sent a pair of long 12-pound guns over to the *Syren,* which would allow the brig to also engage enemy land batteries.[20]

Once past the outer line of defenses, Preble's plan grew even simpler. He intended to sail the *Constitution* and his other warships into the inner harbor and, at point-blank range, "endeavor to beat and distress his savage highness into a disposition more favorable to our views than what he at present possesses." The commodore wanted to batter down not only the bashaw's castle, but also every fortification around the harbor. Only then, he believed, would Karamanli seek terms.[21]

The lack of long-range cannon and the relatively small size of all of his ships but the flagship worried Preble. With just the *Constitution* capable of close bombardment against the Tripolitan defenses, the commodore needed more frigates to fully engage his enemy. He knew Samuel Barron and Rodgers were on their way with reinforcements and expected them to arrive in July. His anxiety grew with each day they failed to show up off Tripoli. "No addition has arrived to our squadron from the U.S. since the loss of the *Philadelphia* although I anxiously expected for a long time past a frigate or two," he wrote to his wife, Mary. "I am astonished that our government has not sent reinforcements of ships."[22]

Preble, as he saw it, had little choice but to use a hammer-and-anvil strategy. The American gunboats had to either draw out or sink their pirate counterparts to open a hole for the frigate. In a letter to President Thomas Jefferson, the commodore said the layout of the harbor, coupled with the Tripolitan defenses, "renders it impossible for a vessel of the *Constitution's* draught of water to approach near enough to destroy [the gunboats] as they are sheltered by the rocks and can retire under that shelter to the shore." Everything hinged on the gunboats, Preble said, and the officers in command. "Having no vessel in the squadron excepting this ship [*Constitution*] whose cannon can make any impression on the bashaw's walls, I expect we may suffer much."[23]

As July turned to August, Preble knew he could not give the Tripolitans any more time to strengthen their defenses. He also would not wait for either Isaac Chauncey in the *John Adams* or Samuel Barron and his four frigates. Preble saw his opportunity and planned to take it. "No reinforcement has yet arrived from America as expected, I however think we shall succeed. And the less force we have, the more the honor."[24]

CHAPTER 18

BATTLE OF THE GUNBOATS

F ROM HIS JAIL CELL in the shadow of Tripoli castle, Pvt. William
Ray of the U.S. Marine Corps could see the entire harbor. It was
August 3, just before noon. Off in the distance, tacking slowly back
and forth, was the USS *Constitution*. All around the big frigate, Ray saw the
sails of the rest of the U.S. squadron. The whole city saw the American ships,
too, and the result amused the Connecticut native: "The whole town was in
an uproar. Every Turk had his musket and other weapons and wild disorder
rang through every arch."[1]

Tripolitan troops manned the batteries ringing the shore while mariners boarded the nineteen gunboats and other vessels that made up the fleet
of Bashaw Yusuf Karamanli. The leader of Tripoli could see the American
squadron and knew the long-awaited summer campaign of Commo. Edward
Preble was about to commence. For Karamanli, the American squadron was
an unknown. He had heard Preble's warlike talk, and knew the commodore
had procured mortar boats and gunboats from Naples. What he did not
know was just how much firepower the Americans would actually bring
against his city. He almost certainly expected the worst.

As early as July 15, Karamanli had moved his wife and children to an
estate outside the city. Many of the city inhabitants followed him.[2] Closer to
home the bashaw beefed up his defenses, pushing his gunboats closer to the
line of rocks that formed one edge of the harbor. Karamanli ordered nine of
the biggest gunboats to advance just outside the breakwater, creating a picket
line that could absorb any first American blow. Behind them, ten more gunboats and a pair of brigs and several oar-powered galleys waited.[3]

━━━◆◆━━━

Capt. William Bainbridge had a perfect view of the harbor, its defenses, and
the American squadron from his jail cell in the bashaw's castle. August 3 was

Day 277 in captivity for the former captain of the frigate *Philadelphia* and the sight of the U.S. squadron probably filled him with both hope and frustration.

The New Jersey native wanted nothing more than to gain his freedom, but he was torn in just how his country should win his liberty. When he first fell into pirate hands back on October 31, 1803, Bainbridge was adamant the United States should not pay ransom for the release of himself or his crew. That stance softened somewhat over his months in captivity. In June 1804, when Preble made his final attempt at mediation, Bainbridge received authorization to offer $50,000 in ransom for the crew but nothing for a peace treaty. The imprisoned skipper jumped at the chance, but knew the bashaw would reject the terms. Karamanli did, and Bainbridge remained a hostage.

Now, however, Bainbridge was growing desperate. The 277 days in captivity were beginning to take their toll. He was ready to grasp at anything that might win his release. He knew Preble would take the fight to the bashaw's door, but he had his doubts mere combat would win his or his crew's release. He wrote to Tobias Lear:

> The commodore appears sanguine on his arrangements. I hope it may prove successful. But I am of an opinion that the bashaw of Tripoli cannot be forced into terms. . . . Believe me my dear Colonel that threats will never do. I greatly respect Commodore Preble but I imagine that he is not familiar with the national character of Barbary. I love my country and sincerely feel for its honor and independence yet may see this regency in a different light and my optics are not influenced by my situation. I trust that I have the fortitude to bear my lot be it what it may.[4]

As Preble busied himself preparing for his summer campaign, the commodore's correspondence with Bainbridge grew infrequent. It did not prevent the *Philadelphia* skipper, however, from writing to his commander, offering his own insight into what Preble might attempt. In late June Bainbridge wrote to Preble: "A bomb ketch [or mortar boat] . . . to come and anchor every night or every other night and heave some bomb shells into the town would occasion all the inhabitants to leave it as they have dreadful ideas of bombs and their homes slightly built . . . this would put them to a very great inconvenience and make them extremely clamorous."[5]

Although the coming campaign was of concern, Bainbridge's chief worry continued to be how his fellow Americans would take the news of his losing the *Philadelphia* and how that would affect public opinion toward him. Bainbridge admitted to Consul George Davis, "I am extremely anxious

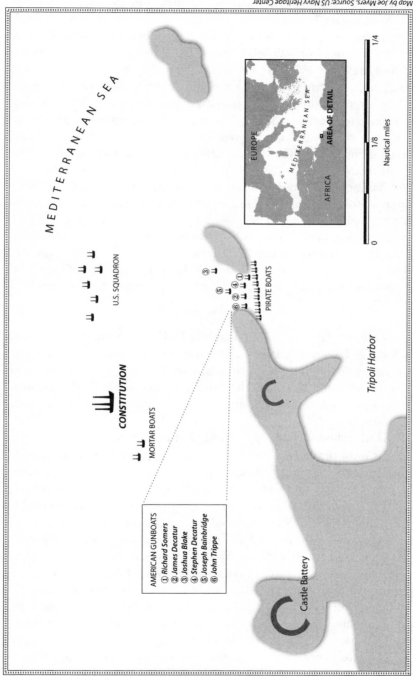

MAP 2. First Battle of the Gunboats, August 3, 1804

MEDITERRANEAN SEA

U.S. SQUADRON

CONSTITUTION

MORTAR BOATS

PIRATE BOATS

③ ⑤ ② ④ ① ⑥

AMERICAN GUNBOATS
① Richard Somers
② James Decatur
③ Joshua Blake
④ Stephen Decatur
⑤ Joseph Bainbridge
⑥ John Trippe

Castle Battery

Tripoli Harbor

EUROPE

MEDITERRANEAN SEA

AFRICA

AREA OF DETAIL

Nautical miles

0   1/8   1/4

to receive letters from America in answer to mine announcing the loss of the frigate *Philadelphia*."[6]

Davis, however, had little to tell: "I regret not being able to give you any news from America but wait with anxiety equal to your own to hear something from that quarter. All is silent as the grave." If these last words chilled Bainbridge, the captain never told the diplomat. Still, Davis gave Bainbridge some hope of a resolution to his captivity, telling the captain, "Your ransom might be affected here on admissible terms, if our affairs were brought to a decision." At the same time, however, Davis told Bainbridge not to expect too much. "The pretentions of this regency are beyond anything the government will acquiesce to."[7]

All Bainbridge could do on August 3 was watch as the sails of Preble's squadron approached the city. He had no idea of what Preble planned, nor did he know whether the American would even be able to break through the line of pirate warships. What probably hurt Bainbridge the most was that he could do nothing but watch. The captain of the once-proud *Philadelphia* could only stare out the small window in his jail cell in Tripoli castle and think about what could have happened if he had not lost his command.

◆——◆

From his spot on the deck of Gunboat No. 1, Richard Somers could not see Capt. William Bainbridge, Pvt. William Ray, or the line of pirate gunboats. In fact, Somers could not see much of anything except the towline that ran from his vessel to the *Nautilus*. The schooner was now under the command of Lt. George Reed, formerly Somers' second officer when he commanded the *Nautilus*.

The little schooner had only a handful of men on her. Commo. Edward Preble sent most of the *Nautilus* crew to man the gunboats. Somers had fifteen men from the *Nautilus* on Gunboat No. 1. Trailing behind him, he could see Lt. James Decatur on Gunboat No. 2, also with fifteen *Nautilus* crew. Lt. Joshua Blake from the *Argus* was on Gunboat No. 3, although most of his crew also came from the *Nautilus*. Reed had just fourteen officers and men to work the schooner, which towed all three gunboats closer to Tripoli harbor.[8]

As he neared the breakwater, Somers could see the *Enterprise* towing the other division of gunboats about a mile away. Like the *Nautilus*, the *Enterprise* had few of her crew left. Most were on the three gunboats that trailed behind the schooner. Stephen Decatur commanded the second division of gunboats. Decatur was in Gunboat No. 4 (in the lead), Lt. Joseph Bainbridge was in Gunboat No. 5, and Lt. John Trippe was in Gunboat No. 6. More than fifty of the crewmen in Decatur's division came from the *Enterprise*, and the rest came from the *Argus*.

Decatur also had essentially the same view as Somers. He could see his friend's division of gunboats trailing behind *Nautilus* but the *Enterprise*—and her sails—blocked his forward view. The towers and spires of Tripoli were just bumps on the horizon.[9]

The two schooners set sail with the gunboats in tow at 8:00 a.m. The vessels sailed in large, slow circles while waiting for the right wind. The gunboats were all lateen-rigged, but not even their simple triangular sails could buck the headwinds blowing out of the harbor. Sailing on either side of the schooners were the brigs *Argus* and *Syren*, keeping watch on the gunboats in case the Tripolitans tried to preempt the coming American attack with one of his own. The schooner *Vixen* sailed between the gunboat divisions. Behind the line of American warships was the brig *Transfer* towing the two mortar boats.

Under Preble's plan, the three towboats would play little to no part in the coming fight. The *Argus*, *Syren*, and *Vixen* would support the gunboats while the nimble schooners and the *Transfer*, the fastest of the brigs in the squadron, were to lay back, ready to dart into action to pull the gunboats and mortar boats out of harm's way.[10]

The commodore kept his eyes glued on the city as his squadron slowly made its way toward Tripoli. By noon, an easterly breeze pushed the Americans to within three miles of the pirate stronghold. Preble could see the bashaw's troops as they ran to their posts to man the 115 guns that ringed the harbor. He also spotted the opening for which he was waiting. The front line of nine gunboats was moving forward, outside the mole and away from the protection of the shore batteries.

The *Constitution* was in front of the columns of American ships. The big frigate moved along under easy sail, the wind shifting from east to south and back again. The easterly wind worked well for the Americans, but when the wind shifted around to the south it stopped their progress in their wakes. For two hours the ships battled the breeze, slowly sailing closer to the line of pirate gunboats. Somers was on the western side of the column, Decatur on the east. The twenty-four-year-old Decatur, like his men, was eager to fight.

"It was my intention to board if ever I had an opportunity," Decatur said in a letter to family friend Keith Spence, "and that it was my opinion that there could be no doubt as to the issue."[11]

The easterly breeze continued to push the American gunboats toward the right side of the Tripolitan warships. Decatur, with the *Enterprise* as the towboat, managed to keep his division aimed toward the middle of the harbor. The *Constitution*, with the *Nautilus* trailing behind, drifted off toward the western side of the harbor. At 2:00 p.m. Somers released the towline and ordered his crew—American and Neapolitan alike—to man the sweeps to try to get his gunboat back toward the center of the harbor. The wind and tide, however, continued to push Gunboat No. 1 toward the shoals and rocks near the mole.

Lt. James Decatur on Gunboat No. 2 saw the problems his division commander was having with the wind. As soon as he released his towline, Decatur managed to adjust course, moving more toward the center of the channel than the other craft in Somers' command.

It was not easy.

The Neapolitan craft wallowed even in small seas and easy breezes. The gunboats weighed roughly 25 tons, and had flat bottoms and rounded bows and sterns. Each was 56 foot 6 inches long, had an 18-foot beam, and drew about four feet of water. The Sicilian gunboats each carried a single 24-pound "French" cannon—a twelve-foot long iron gun that could fire solid shot, canister, and grapeshot—but no secondary armament.

Even before they could engage the enemy, the Americans found themselves in confusion. Somers remained off course as his gunboat continued to head toward the rocks on which the Tripolitans had anchored the right side of their battle line. James Decatur overcompensated for the wind and joined his brother's division of gunboats, which continued to advance toward the center of the enemy line. Lt. Joshua Blake of the *Argus*, commanding Gunboat No. 3, fell far behind Somers as he attempted to maintain his course, drifting well behind the rocks toward which Somers sailed.[12]

At 2:30 p.m. Preble hoisted the signal for the squadron to attack. The *Constitution* remained off the western side of the harbor while the *Vixen*, *Argus*, and *Syren* moved in behind the gunboats. The *Enterprise*, *Nautilus*, and *Scourge* sailed in slow circles between the American battle line and the flagship, ready to tow the gunboats and mortar boats out of danger.

———◆—◆———

Lt. John H. Dent, in command of Mortar Boat No. 2 was not having any trouble with the wind. He and Lt. Charles Robinson in Mortar Boat No. 1 easily took up position about two miles from shore, with the *Scourge* sailing circles close by. When Preble hoisted the signal to attack, Dent got off the first round of the action from the 9-inch mortar on his vessel. It fell short, landing harmlessly in the surf in front of the bashaw's castle.

The borrowed Neapolitan mortar boats looked similar in size and shape to the Italian gunboats. Each carried a brass mortar that could lob a 140-pound shell nearly two miles, or so the Americans thought. Dent was well within range of the castle with his mortar boat, but his second and third shells also fell short. He told his bombardiers—a mixed group of Neapolitans and Americans—to stop using powder the Americans had received from the Italians and instead use gunpowder made in the United States. The change did not help. Dent's next rounds also fell short and he finally ceased firing altogether around 3:30 p.m. Robinson in Mortar Boat No. 1 had the same problems. For some reason, the mortars could not reach their target and played no part in the coming action. Combined, the two mortar boats fired just fourteen rounds during the entire battle.

The gunboats in Stephen Decatur's division—with his younger brother now part of the line—had no problem finding the range. The Americans opened fire with solid shot, sending rounds crashing into the four Arab ships in front of them. Decatur and Trippe led the American charge, with Gunboat No. 5 under Joseph Bainbridge trailing close behind. James Decatur maneuvered his vessel and opened fire as well on the pirate vessels.

As the American vessels closed the range, the gunners switched from round shot to grapeshot and canister. Both were devastating antipersonnel munitions. Grapeshot consisted of eighteen or so small solid cannon balls sandwiched between two thin sheets of wood. When fired, the wood flew apart, spraying the balls across the target. Canister was a small lead can stuffed with up to a hundred musket balls. It had a shotgun effect when fired. Combined, the two munitions could sweep an enemy deck. The Americans used these weapons to telling effect.

Stephen Decatur quickly brought Gunboat No. 4 alongside the centermost Tripolitan ship. After sweeping the enemy deck with grapeshot, he ordered his men to prepare to board. John Trippe followed him, with James Decatur and Bainbridge, in Gunboat No. 5, also closing on enemy gunboats. Bainbridge, however, never had the chance to board. A shot from an enemy gun shattered the lone mast of Bainbridge's vessel, sending the lateen mainsail and the jib crashing to the deck. Bainbridge veered away from the pirate ship in front, unable to close. He continued to fire at the Tripolitans, but could not get in close enough to board.

Richard Somers also switched from solid shot to grapeshot and canister as Gunboat No. 1 closed in on the line of Tripolitan gunboats. Anchored just inside the rocks, they were impossible for the Americans to board. It did not matter. Somers squared off against five gunboats with his one, believing that Lieutenant Blake in Gunboat No. 3 was with him. Blake, however, never entered the fight.

Somers at first had no idea how many enemy vessels were in front of him. He ordered his gunners to fire as fast as they could while the rest of his American crew opened fire with muskets. Somers had a look at his odds soon after he engaged the Tripolitans. "By this time there was five of the enemy boats under way advancing and firing," Somers said. "When within point blank shot I commenced firing on the enemy with round and grape."[13]

Although Somers' gunners smashed a pair of pirate vessels, the Tripolitans refused to budge. The pirates met the Americans salvo for salvo, but their aim was faulty. Somers reported only minor damage to his vessel and continued to blast away at the enemy.

The Tripolitans tried to slip three gunboats past Somers to attack Decatur's division from the flank. Somers ordered his men to rig an anchor line and toss it into the rocks, swinging his ship around, preventing the pirates from getting past him.

———————

The shots from James Decatur's ship swept over the pirate vessel off his bow like a tidal wave. Arab sailors fell to the deck mangled and bleeding, and fire from the Tripolitan vessel completely stopped. Decatur moved to the side of his gunboat, cutlass in hand, Midn. Thomas Brown and five Marines right behind him. The pirate gunboat was strangely silent. Through the smoke, the American sailors saw an Arab hauling down the red, crescent moon flag of Tripoli. The Americans continued to pour fire into the pirate ship until the flag was completely tattered. James Decatur, flushed with victory, jumped on board the Tripolitan vessel but a split second later fell to the deck with a bullet in his head.

The Tripolitans had once more used their favorite ruse against the Americans, and this time it apparently worked. Just as they had against the *Enterprise* two years earlier, the pirates faked their surrender to lure the Americans into trying to board. Decatur—young, rash, and in search of glory like his older brother—likely forgot about the Tripolitan tactic when he leaped onto the pirate vessel.

The captain of the vessel had pulled out a pistol and shot Decatur in the temple, sending the twenty-year-old officer sprawling. The rest of the Arab crew were ready to hack the young lieutenant apart when Midn. Thomas Brown with five Marines and sailors managed to pull Decatur back onto Gunboat No. 2. Brown ordered his men to break off the attack and fell out of the battle line.

———————

Stephen Decatur and John Trippe pressed home their attacks with gusto. Neither knew what had happened to James Decatur on Gunboat No. 2 and did not seem to miss Joseph Bainbridge in Gunboat No. 5. Trippe's men hammered the gunboat in front of them with grapeshot before the Maryland native led ten sailors and Marines onto the pirate vessel. The last blast from the cannon on Gunboat No. 6 killed nearly half the Tripolitan crew. Those that remained put up a fight.

The second Trippe set foot on the Tripolitan ship he took a sword slash to the arm, then one to his back. The blows failed to stop Trippe, who led his men in a wild charge against the pirates. The pirates outnumbered the Americans twenty to eleven, but the fury of the bluejackets' charge unnerved the Tripolitans. Using pikes, tomahawks, swords, and knives, Trippe's men cut their way through the enemy crew. Each time he advanced, however, Trippe took a blow. After fifteen minutes, the pirate captain—a muscular Turkish officer—and fifteen of his crew remained alive and continued to put up a tremendous fight. Trippe closed in on the captain, who stabbed him three times with a pike. Trippe tried to use his cutlass to pry the spear out of the Turk's hands but the sword snapped at the hilt, leaving Trippe defenseless. The Turk slammed Trippe to the deck and was ready to plunge a pike into him when Marine James Ryan killed the pirate with his own boarding pike. The remaining Tripolitans surrendered, and Trippe, despite his eleven wounds and loss of blood, took command of the pirate ship. The Tripolitans lost fourteen dead and twenty-two prisoners, seven of whom were wounded. The American losses were almost miraculously slight—only four wounded, including Trippe and Ryan.

Trippe ordered his second-in-command, Midn. Joseph Henley, to take the Arab ship in tow. Trippe's men carried him back to Gunboat No. 6, and the Americans, with the pirate vessel in tow, fell out of the battle line.

Stephen Decatur and the crew of Gunboat No. 4 swept in on the Tripolitan gunboat holding the center of the line and poured in a hail of grapeshot and canister. The blast of fire cleared the deck as Tripolitans cowered below the gunnels, jumped overboard, or were killed or wounded. The smoke from the volley obscured Decatur's view, although he could hear Trippe's men boarding the pirate gunboat next to him. He did not know, however, that his younger brother James was also in the thick of the fight.

With Thomas Macdonough and Jonathan Thorn following behind, Decatur led his fourteen sailors and Marines onto the pirate gunboat. The Americans split into two groups to pass on either side of a hatchway amidships of the pirate gunboats and slammed into the massed pirate crew. Using pikes, dirks, cutlasses, and tomahawks, the Americans cut the Tripolitans apart. In just five minutes, Decatur's men killed fourteen pirates and wounded sixteen. Only five pirates escaped injury. The bluejackets took eighteen prisoners as well as the prize vessel.

The attack took less than ten minutes. Just as he returned to Gunboat No. 4, Decatur saw Gunboat No. 2 suddenly veer toward his stern. From Midshipman Brown he learned of his brother's deeds and the treacherous manner in which he had been shot. The news infuriated Decatur, who demanded to know which gunboat his brother had attacked. Brown pointed toward one of the three gunboats still firing.

It was 3:15 p.m.

Commo. Edward Preble watched the progress of the battle from the quarter-deck of the *Constitution*. Three times he ordered the *Argus*, *Syren*, and *Vixen* to enter the battle to support the two gunboat divisions. John Smith, commander of the *Vixen*, sailed the schooner right into the heat of the battle to cover Somers in Gunboat No. 1. The *Vixen* fired several broadsides into the line of pirate warships, holding them in position when they tried to encircle Somers' vessel.

Hull in the *Argus* and Stewart in the *Syren* were also in the thick of the action. Preble sent the two brigs in to cover Decatur's division just after 3:30 p.m. The two brigs prevented a second division of Tripolitan gunboats from engaging Decatur's ships and took on the enemy shore batteries that were heaving shells at the Americans.

The two brigs blasted away at the Tripolitan forts, forcing them to shift fire from the American gunboats to the larger ships. The commodore kept his flagship just outside the action, ready to move into position to provide support and cover the rest of the fleet. His concern kept shifting from Decatur's division to Somers', who continued to fight his solo battle against five pirate ships. By ordering the *Argus* and *Syren* into the gap between the two gunboat divisions, Preble effectively blocked the bashaw from sending out reinforcements. However, his order also exposed the two vessels to constant fire from Tripolitan shore batteries, and neither brig had the long-range cannon necessary to silence the forts. The commodore ordered the *Constitution* to change course toward the harbor entrance and ran out her big 24-pound cannon.

Gunboat No. 1 shook from the recoil of her gun and the near misses of pirate cannon. Despite being within pistol shot of five enemy craft, Somers' ship had yet to suffer major damage or take major casualties. Somers fought his one-ship battle for nearly an hour, raking the pirates with volley after volley. By 3:30, however, he was running low on shot. In the space of an hour, Somers' gunners had used more than two hundred pounds of powder and fired two hundred musket cartridges, twenty-five rounds of 24-pound solid shot, and fourteen stands of grapeshot.[14]

Somewhere to the left of Gunboat No. 1, Lt. Joshua Blake and Gunboat No. 3 tried in vain to get into the battle. Blake had yet to come close to the action, despite maneuvering his craft for more than ninety minutes. His gunners managed to get off just eight rounds—two of solid shot and six of grapeshot—while his sailors and Marines took just twelve shots at the pirates.[15] Blake could see Somers' ship fighting along, but never came close enough to help his commander.

The hail of fire Somers directed at the pirates had a telling effect. He crippled three of the five enemy ships he engaged and drove the other two onto the rocks. Somers, however, could not see his success. Smoke obscured his view, wreathing friend and foe alike in a smothering fog. The commander on Gunboat No. 1 also could not see a group of Tripolitan gunboats from the bashaw's second division inside the harbor moving toward Somers' lone vessel. The Americans continued to fire into the gunboats in front of them as the pirates closed in.

Commo. Edward Preble also watched Somers' engagement and could see the second line of Tripolitan gunboats advancing toward Somers with an eye toward surrounding him. He raised a signal at 4:00 p.m., ordering the *Vixen* to move in and cover Somers. The schooner swept in, raking the new line of gunboats with her carronades, stopping the pirate advance before it could even come close to Gunboat No. 1.

Stephen Decatur was in a rage when he returned to Gunboat No. 4. The close combat he experienced when he captured the pirate gunboat had combined with the news Midshipman Brown had given him of the fake surrender and shooting of his brother and sent Decatur into a fury. He ordered his crew to man the sweeps and headed toward the gunboat Brown pointed toward as belonging to the captain that shot his brother.

The maneuver took less than a minute. Gunboat No. 4 slammed into the pirate gunboat and Decatur, screaming like a wild man, leaped on board with just nine Americans behind him, including Thomas Macdonough. The odds seemed long. The ten blue-clad Americans faced a pirate crew of more than thirty, including their commander, a massive Turkish officer standing more than six feet tall. Decatur's fury impelled them. The Americans crashed into the pirates, swinging cutlasses and firing pistols. The Tripolitans fought back just as hard. The two sides battled back and forth for twenty minutes, with the Americans slowly pushing the pirates toward the stern of the gunboat. As the Tripolitans crowded together, fewer of them were able to wield their weapons and Decatur's men pressed in on them ever harder.

Decatur drove through the pirates like a wedge, hacking his way toward the enemy captain. The Turk stood his ground, urging his own men into the fight. As the American captain fought his way toward the pirate, Marine Sergeant Wren and Seaman Thomas James fell to the deck with wounds, leaving Decatur with just seven followers.[16]

It did not matter to Decatur.

He charged his opponent, swinging his cutlass. The Turkish captain blocked the American's sword with an iron boarding pike that he thrust at Decatur. The American used his cutlass to parry the blow but the sword, on striking the iron, broke at the hilt, leaving him weaponless. The pirate thrust again, and Decatur used his right arm to parry the blow. The pike rode up his forearm and struck him in the side. Decatur yanked the pike down and pulled it from the pirate's hands. The Turk then dove at Decatur and the two of them fell to the deck while a hand-to-hand melee raged all around them.

Behind the two officers, Seaman Daniel Frazier hacked and slashed his way toward his commander. He watched as Decatur managed to roll on top of his adversary just as a Tripolitan officer broke free from the fight. The pirate had just raised his sword to swing at Decatur's head when Frazier dove in front of the sword, taking the blow. The strike split open his scalp and left Frazier dazed and bleeding.[17]

Decatur and his foe continued to grapple and rolled again, this time with the Turkish officer pinning Decatur to the deck. He pulled a dagger from his belt and prepared to stab the American with his right hand while holding Decatur with his left. Decatur managed to free his left hand and grabbed the pirate's right wrist, staving off the blade. With his own left hand, he reached for a small pistol he had his in pocket, cocked it, put it in the pirate's back, and fired.

The Turk's hand with the knife went slack and his head dropped. Decatur pushed the dead pirate off him, grabbed his knife, and stood up. Macdonough and the five uninjured American sailors gathered around him and prepared to rush the remaining enemy. They did not have to. The pirates, their leader dead, surrendered.[18]

It was 4:30 p.m.

The USS *Constitution* tacked in toward Tripoli harbor, her 44 long 24-pound cannons protruding from her sides. Commo. Edward Preble ordered his flagship into the battle at 4:30, the same time he hoisted the signal for the tow-boats to move in and pick up the American gunboats and their prizes.

The big frigate swept past the line of smaller American warships, advancing toward the bashaw's castle. Preble ordered his gunners to give the pirate leaders a broadside, and the frigate's guns roared into action. The *Constitution* blasted away at the castle and surrounding buildings. Sailing Master Nathaniel Haraden later reported broadsides "drove out" defenders and inhabitants and toppled the minaret of a nearby mosque, and that he then tacked the *Constitution*, thanks to a freshening wind that veered around to the northeast.[19] The frigate now could engage the other shore batteries—those nearest the pirate flotilla as well as the pirate ships.

The American flagship moved within a half mile from shore, and at 5:00 p.m. opened fire. From her position the *Constitution* covered the withdrawal of the American gunboats and their three prizes as she fired broadside after broadside into the Tripolitan defenses. The ferocity of the attack unnerved the bashaw's gunners. Haraden reported only nine rounds managed to strike the flagship, damaging some rigging but little else, although one round caused a major scare: A lucky shot from a Tripolitan gun struck an American cannon, bursting the piece and injuring the crew. Preble was standing next to the gun when it exploded. Although unhurt, Haraden said, "The commodore's clothes were cut in several places."[20]

The *Constitution* remained in position for two hours, firing more than two hundred rounds of solid shot, grapeshot, and canister. The captains of the gunboats reported on board the *Constitution* as she engaged the shore batteries. The crew from Gunboat No. 2 also brought on board James Decatur, who was still alive despite his head wound. The younger Decatur did not live much longer, however, and within minutes died, his brother Stephen and his commander Richard Somers at his side. Decatur, overwhelmed by emotion, could only whisper a final epitaph to Charles Morris, who helped carry James onto the *Constitution*.

"I would rather see him there," Decatur said, pointing to James as he helped several men sew him into a canvas shroud, "than living with any cloud on his conduct."[21]

CHAPTER 19

Drawing Breath

C OMMO. EDWARD PREBLE MET with his officers in the hours after the battle of August 3 to take stock of what the squadron had accomplished. The Americans had captured three enemy gunboats and likely had sunk at least three more, Preble later reported.[1] His top three commanders, Stephen Decatur, Charles Stewart, and Richard Somers, had behaved coolly under fire and shown they could adapt to rapidly changing situations.

The success was almost too good for the Americans to believe. "Never was there a more complete victory," wrote Purser Noadiah Morris of the *Constitution*. "To recount every instance of personal bravery would be to name almost every officer in the squadron. The Turks were driven from their batteries in the greatest terror and confusion and I think I may say with propriety that since Charles the V of Austria never have any of the Barbary States met with so severe a check."[2]

Preble, however, was not quite as convinced of the victory as were his officers. The commodore expected more from his gunboats and wanted to know what had happened to Joshua Blake and why the *Argus* lieutenant had failed to engage any of the enemy. He also apparently expected much more from Somers and Decatur, especially Decatur. He knew of Somers' plight as the New Jersey native squared off against five enemy vessels. However, he had a less-than-clear eye on Stephen Decatur. All Preble knew was that his most daring officer, with four gunboats, had managed to capture only three of the enemy. He seemingly expected much more of a victory. The commodore was also seemingly unaware of what had happened with James Decatur and of Stephen's response.

Moments after James Decatur died on the spar deck of the *Constitution*, Preble confronted Decatur when the elder brother reported to the commodore. "Well, commodore, I have brought you out three of their gunboats,"

Decatur told his commander. Preble turned on his protégé, grabbed his uniform by the lapels, and nearly shook him. "Ay, sir and why didn't you bring me out more?" The commodore abruptly turned and disappeared into his cabin.[3]

The outburst astounded the officers on the quarterdeck, none more than Decatur. The twenty-five-year-old's right hand instinctively slipped to where he usually wore a long knife on his belt. The knife was gone— overboard when he had attacked the second Arab gunboat. The young man's anger was apparent. Somers, Stewart, and the *Constitution*'s sailing master Nathaniel Haraden all tried talking to Decatur to calm him down. Decatur, his thoughts of his younger brother still vivid, sent orders for his sailors to ready his boat to return to Gunboat No. 4.

The gathered officers talked Decatur out of leaving. They reminded him of Preble's legendary temper and that anything could set off his anger. "We despise him for his temperament," they said, but respected the commodore for his leadership and justice "in his cooler moments."[4]

The argument did little to sway Decatur, who was about to leave when Preble's steward appeared before the officer. The commodore, he said, wished to see Lieutenant Decatur. After hesitating for a second, Decatur obeyed. Several minutes passed, and the officers on deck grew uneasy. Haraden decided to go below and see what was happening. He knocked on the cabin door and entered. Preble and Decatur sat across from one another, Haraden later said, with tears streaming down their cheeks. They spoke in soft tones, almost as a father to a son. Neither mentioned the outburst again.[5]

Decatur and Preble returned to the quarterdeck, where the body of James Decatur lay. Stephen helped prepare his younger brother for a burial at sea. He cleaned the young man and helped sew his body into a canvas shroud, weighing it down with several 24-pound cannon balls. Preble officiated over the burial, calling James, "A young man who gave strong promise of being an ornament to his profession. His conduct in the action was highly honorable and he died nobly."[6]

Attention quickly turned to Joshua Blake and Gunboat No. 3. Many of the squadron officers demanded to know what had prevented the *Argus* lieutenant from joining the attack. Blake blamed contrary winds, but his argument failed to convince his peers or his commander. Preble said, "Had [Blake] gone down to [Somers'] assistance, it is probable several of the enemy's boats would have been captured."[7]

Somers apparently agreed with Preble's assessment and was among the most vocal of Blake's critics. The *Argus* lieutenant claimed he saw a recall signal flying from the *Constitution*—a young officer did in fact momentarily hoist the wrong flag—but Blake still could not answer Somers' questions as to why he did not join the fight after Preble had made sure the right signal flag was aloft.[8] Just how far Somers went with his accusations is unknown. Those accusations, however, hung over Blake and the squadron for four days. Finally, Blake decided to take matters into his own hands. "I have yet had no opportunity of conversing with Captain Somers," he told Preble on August 7, "and am therefore obliged to decline being considered attached to a gunboat. Distressing as this resignation is to my feelings, I have chosen it, as less so, than to continue under a suspicious eye." Blake said he believed that "everything done by me, as my best judgment dictated, that the Boat No. 3 was placed and continued, in *close* action, as soon and as long as signals and a prospect of being of service justified" [emphasis in original].[9]

It was undoubtedly difficult for Preble to listen to the accusations swirling around Blake. The young lieutenant was one of the first officers assigned to the *Constitution* the previous summer when Jefferson had put Preble in command. Blake helped recruit the bulk of the *Constitution*'s crew and showed promise as a leader, which was why Preble transferred him to the *Argus* when he put Hull in command. Blake did well enough on the *Argus* to merit command of one of the borrowed gunboats. Now, arguably one of his best officers, Somers, was taking out his disdain for Blake's actions public. Something had to give.

It was Blake.

The lieutenant told Preble he believed only his resignation as a gunboat commander would suffice: "With this consciousness of rectitude on my part, I feel it my duty to give place to some officer that may be more congenial to the feelings of Capt. Somers. I am placed under an additional obligation to you sir for the continuance in command, but am convinced you will think I do right by resigning it."[10]

Preble had little choice but to accept.

The Blake episode cast a small cloud over the squadron's achievements. It quickly dissipated, however, when Hull in the *Argus* intercepted a French privateer, the *Ruse*, trying to leave Tripoli. Her skipper, Pierre Blaise Mercelleise, told Preble the pirates were in shock at just how hard the Americans had hit them. The bashaw and his fighters already knew the Americans were good at gunnery—the brief battles the *Enterprise* had fought in 1802 and 1803 and Stewart's work with the brigs and schooners in enforcing the blockade had taught them about the accuracy and power behind Yankee cannon.

Close-quarters combat—hand-to-hand fighting—was supposed to be the pirates' domain. Decatur and Trippe and their bluejackets, however, beat the Tripolitans at their own game. It was not easy. As Decatur put it, "I find hand to hand is not child's play," he said. "'Tis kill or be killed." Despite the difficulty, the American victory on August 3 raised morale and spirit throughout the fleet. "I always thought we could lick them their own way and give to them two to one," Decatur wrote to his friend. "The first boat they were 36 to 20 and we carried her without much fuss. The second was 24 to 10 and they also went."[11]

There was a third opinion of why Preble's sailors fared so well against the pirates. The six Neapolitan gunboats each had fifteen Sicilian mariners on board. Although they took no part in the actual fighting, Decatur said the Neapolitans believed their actions won they day: "While we fought they prayed. They are convinced we could not have been so fortunate unless their prayers had been heard."[12]

Preble put his faith squarely in his men. In his general orders of August 3, 1804, the commodore cited most of his officers for bravery. To Stewart, Hull, and Smith he offered his "thanks for the gallant manner in which they brought their vessels into action." To Somers, Preble offered his congratulation for "the gallant conduct displayed by him in attacking five of the enemy's gunboats within musket shot of the batteries and obliging them to retreat after a warm conflict." Decatur and Trippe earned the highest plaudits from the commodore, who called their actions "particularly gratifying." To Decatur, Preble also offered his congratulations for the show of "distinguished judgment and intrepidity." The commodore also thanked James Lawrence and George Reed, of the *Enterprise* and the *Nautilus*, for handling their vessels while their commanders were off with the gunboats. Finally, Preble gave his "warmest thanks to the lieutenants, sailing master, Marine officers and other officers of the *Constitution*," as well as the "officers, seamen and Marines of the squadron," whose conduct, the commodore said, "merited the highest encomiums."[13]

Whether it was by prayer or cutlass, the Americans had gained a victory, the first combat success against the bashaw in three years of war. In addition to the three Tripolitan gunboats, the bluejackets took forty-nine prisoners, fourteen of whom were wounded. Preble prevailed upon Captain Mercelleise of the French privateer to carry the fourteen wounded pirates back to Tripoli, along with a message to the bashaw signaling Preble's willingness to negotiate with Karamanli: "While I regret the effusion of blood, humanity dictates that those who are wounded may be soothed by the presence of their friends."[14]

The commodore also sent a note to Bonaventure Beaussier, the French consul at Tripoli, telling the diplomat if he believed the attacks of August 3 made Karamanli more disposed toward negotiations, the Frenchman was welcome to reiterate the offer of $50,000 for the *Philadelphia* crew but nothing for peace. "I do not consider the terms I have offered as humiliating to the bashaw," Preble wrote, "and I am determined not to deviate much from the terms already offered." The commodore also told Beaussier to tell Karamanli he did not have long to accept the deal: "The offer is open until the arrival of our additional force of four frigates momentarily expected, after which we shall never consent to give him a cent."[15]

Three hundred miles away, the vanguard of the American reinforcements was off the city of Tunis. The 28-gun frigate *John Adams* arrived at Gibraltar on July 22 after a month-long trip from Norfolk, Virginia.[16] Master Commandant Isaac Chauncey spent three days at the British bastion before heading for Algiers. Chauncey was looking for orders from Preble as to where to find the American squadron.

John Gavino, the American consul at Gibraltar, told Chauncey to head for Malta.[17] The *John Adams* commander, however, thought it better to look along the North African coastline. He knew from conversations he had at Gibraltar that Preble was already enforcing the blockade of Tripoli. What he did not know was exactly where the commodore was holding station.

The 128-foot long frigate *John Adams* rode low in the water, despite having just eight guns in battery. The rest were in the hold as ballast to make room for the tons of supplies and the more than fifty extra men the frigate carried for the squadron. Before leaving the States, the crew had stuffed the *John Adams* full of food, dry goods, uniforms, powder, and other supplies Preble needed, as well as replacements for both the schooner *Enterprise* and the flagship.

Chauncey had more than reinforcements and supplies on board his ship. The master commandant carried news—news he knew could actually hamper the American effort. Chauncey carried official orders from Secretary of the Navy Robert Smith. These orders confirmed what Prebel already knew— he was about to lose his command.

On August 2 Chauncey and the *John Adams* were off Tunis, moving closer to Tripoli with each moment. Poor weather bounced the little frigate around off the African coast. The *John Adams* also had lost time when it gave chase to an unknown brig it spotted. Purser John Darby later said he and Chauncey at first thought the brig was the *Scourge*. When the unknown vessel failed to respond to signals, the frigate gave chase, only to lose the smaller vessel as night fell.

Chauncey continued to fight the weather as he slowly sailed closer to Tripoli. By August 3 he was past Algiers and sailing around the bulge of Cape Rosso off the western Tunisian coastline. He was four days away from Tripoli.

Almost from the second the American squadron opened fire on August 3, the American prisoners on shore felt the pirates' wrath. Marine private William Ray said the bashaw threw the crew of the *Philadelphia* back into prison and set "a formidable guard" around them. Ray saw nothing of the battle. Guards confined him and the rest of the enlisted men until the American squadron had withdrawn from the harbor. The bashaw then put Ray and the others to work cleaning the debris from Preble's attack. From his vantage point, Ray said he saw three sunk gunboats. The American enlisted men also had to suffer the wrath of the locals. "The infuriated Turks, wherever we met them, would strike, spit upon and stone us," the Marine said. "From the circumstances of our giving up the *Philadelphia* to one gunboat, without bloodshed, they had until now entertained an opinion that the Americans were all cowards, but now they were impressed with a full conviction of the skill and bravery of our tars."[18]

Capt. William Bainbridge also saw little of the battle, although he could hear the sound of American shot crashing into the city walls. Danish consul Nicholas Nissen told Bainbridge of a near miss he had when a 24-pound cannon ball from the *Constitution* slammed into the wall of his apartment.[19]

Bashaw Yusuf Karamanli received more than a rude awakening on August 3. Karamanli, like the rest of the Tripolitans, had not expected the Americans to put up much of a fight. When Preble's squadron sailed into view, Karamanli and a group of retainers went up on the roof of the castle to watch the proceedings.

The bashaw "affected to ridicule any attempt that might be made to injure either the batteries or the city. He promised the spectators that rare sport would be enjoyed by observing the triumph of his boats over the Americans." Once the battle commenced, the pirate leader quickly changed his mind, especially as American shot began to pound the city's defenses. "In a few minutes, however, he became convinced of his error and precipitously retreated with an humbled and aching heart to his bomb proof cellar."[20]

Karamanli quickly recovered from whatever shock he felt at the strength of the American attack when he received Preble's note concerning the prisoners. At first the bashaw thought it was either a sign of weakness or a trick. French consul Beaussier explained: "The commendable and humane motive in sending them was misunderstood. We had difficulty in persuading the bashaw." Once convinced, Beaussier said the bashaw showed his true colors: "I have caused him to reflect upon what he had experienced in the first attack and what he had to fear from what must follow. He declared to me that he ardently desired peace with the Americans." However, the bashaw insisted any peace treaty would cost the Americans.[21]

It was a stance Preble wanted the bashaw to take.

—◆—

The American squadron spent the days after the August 3 assault resupplying and refitting. The first order of business was distributing water.

The vital liquid was arguably the Americans' Achilles heel. Preble had filled the *Constitution* with as much water as he could when he left Syracuse, but combat used an incredible amount. Every time the Americans fired a cannon, a gunner used a wet sponge to prevent burning embers from setting off the next round. Once the sponge went into a bucket of water, the water was no longer fit or safe to drink.

Even though Preble tried to calculate just how much water he would need, there was simply no way to limit or ration water in combat. The Americans also had three new vessels they needed to provision—the captured pirate gunboats. Each would require men, officers, food, and water. The commodore's offer to return the fourteen wounded Tripolitans to the bashaw was not simply an act of kindness: they were fourteen fewer mouths to feed and fourteen injured men who would not need water the squadron's doctors could better use to treat the thirteen Americans wounded during the August 3 battle.

The squadron also needed time to refit its prizes. The Arab craft had a local lateen rig, something with which few of the bluejackets had any experience. Preble ordered his men to use spare spars and sails from the *Constitution* and *Syren* to rerig the new gunboats as sloops. The two vessels Decatur captured were identical—nearly 60 feet long (51 on deck), 14 feet wide, with a draft of 3 feet. Each carried a brass 28-pound long cannon as well as two small brass howitzers. The vessel Trippe captured was "rather smaller" than the other two, Sailing Master Nathaniel Haraden said, and carried a long 18-pound gun.[22]

The three new vessels, renamed Gunboats No. 7, No. 8, and No. 9, needed crews; once more Preble had to strip men and officers from other vessels. At the suggestion of John Smith, he put Lt. William Crane of the *Vixen* in command of Gunboat No. 7. The enlisted men came from the *Vixen* and the *Scourge*. Lt. Jonathan Thorn of the *Enterprise* took over Gunboat No. 8 with men from the schooner. The *Syren* crewed Gunboat No. 9 with the brig's first lieutenant, James Caldwell, in command, along with Lt. James Dorsey and Midn. Robert Spence. The commodore also made three command changes on the Neapolitan gunboats. He replaced Joshua Blake (who had resigned as commander of Gunboat No. 3 after his row with Richard Somers) with *Nautilus* sailing master Samuel Brooke, and replaced John Trippe (who was recovering from fourteen saber wounds) with Lt. Henry Wadsworth of the *Constitution* on Gunboat No. 6. Lt. Charles Gordon of the *Constitution* took over Gunboat No. 2.[23]

As work on the prize gunboats continued, the officers gathered on August 5 and 6 on the *Constitution* to work out a new plan. Karamanli, after the attack of August 3, moved his gunboats inside the main harbor, where his shore fortifications could cover his vessels. The Americans would have to find another way to get at the pirates, and Charles Stewart believed he had one.

The twenty-five-year-old second-in-command of the U.S. flotilla probably knew the harbor better than any officer in Preble's command. Stewart first scouted the harbor back in February prior to the attack on the *Philadelphia*. Since then, he commanded the increasingly effective blockade of the harbor, which allowed him to get to know the coast and reefs. The battle of August 3 gave him even more knowledge of the waters off Tripoli.

While protecting the gunboats, Stewart spotted a small bay on the western side of the harbor. The bay, he said, could provide the Americans with a spot from which they could bombard the town without running afoul of the bashaw's shore defenses. Decatur, Somers, and Hull also pushed for an attack from the west, pointing out that the brigs and schooners in the squadron could cut off any pirate gunboats moving to attack the American gunboats.[24]

Preble quickly agreed with the plan. An attack from the bay would open Tripoli up to an uncontested bombardment from the two mortar boats and the gunboats. If the pirates attempted to intervene, Preble would have the opportunity to destroy the bashaw's entire fleet in detail. He ordered the attack to commence the next day, August 7.

The approach from the west was not as unguarded as Stewart believed. Yusuf Karamanli was aware of the open back door to his harbor; immediately after the attacks of August 3, he had ordered the construction of a pair of gun batteries to cover the approaches to the bay. Once more, it was American slave labor that built the forts, one of five guns, the other with eight.[25]

Karamanli also apparently gave orders to his ship commanders to work more closely together. The gunboats were now moored close by Tripoli's small flotilla of schooners, galleys, and brigs directly in front of the castle, which contained the city's strongest defenses.[26] The alignment of vessels gave the pirates a slightly better chance of engaging the more powerful American ships by concentrating their firepower. Whether they would fight, however, was unknown.

———◆—◆———

Master Commandant Isaac Chauncey pulled into the harbor of Valetta, Malta, on August 4. The captain of the *John Adams* was still looking for orders and the location of the American fleet. After reaching Gibraltar and finding no orders, he decided to head for Malta by sailing along the North African coast as he also tried to locate the U.S. squadron. He reached Malta without sighting Preble's force, where he at last found letters from the commodore.

The *John Adams* arrived in Malta around 10:00 p.m. and officers from the port immediately placed the ship in quarantine for eighteen days, forbidding anyone from landing for fear the ship might carry disease.[27] The quarantine, however, did not stop news from reaching the frigate. Despite the late hour, the U.S. consul had letters for Chauncey and he delivered them almost the second the *John Adams* dropped anchor. "I have at this moment received Commodore Preble's orders from the hands of Mr. [William] Higgins [Navy agent at Malta] directing me to proceed off Tripoli without loss of time," Chauncey wrote to Secretary Smith. "In consequence, I am now getting under way for that purpose."[28]

The quick turnaround put the *John Adams* on course to reach Preble sometime around August 7. Throughout the trip, Purser John Darby said Chauncey "exercised the crew and the guns."[29] Although the *John Adams* only carried a handful of cannon for self-defense, Chauncey wanted his men ready to take part in what he believed would be an all-out assault on the city.

———◆—◆———

Gunboat No. 9 was one of three prizes the Americans had captured on August 3. Her new skipper was Lt. James Caldwell of the *Syren*. Caldwell was the first officer on the brig and had sailed with Stewart since 1801, during the Quasi-War, when both were on the schooner *Experiment*. Over the course of those three years, Caldwell and Stewart had grown particularly close and Stewart made sure to try to impart on his executive officer every bit of advice he could.

Midn. Cornelius deKrafft, one of the officers on the *Syren*, said the two huddled for hours on August 5 and 6, discussing the upcoming attack. At that time, Stewart put Caldwell in charge of rerigging the gunboat as a sloop. The work—and discussions—went on until the morning of August 7, when Preble ordered all of his commanders on board the *Constitution* for one last meeting before the assault.[30]

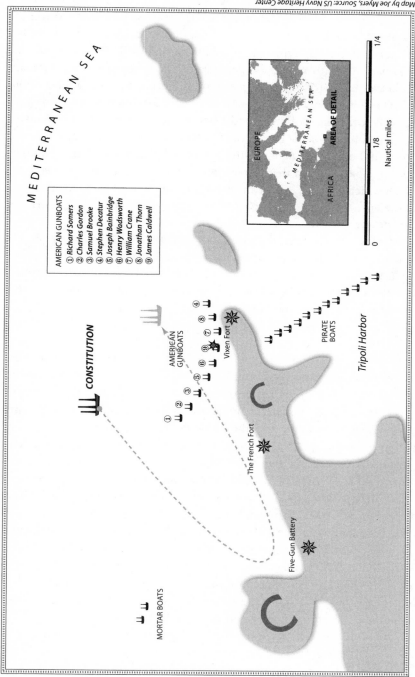

MEDITERRANEAN SEA

AMERICAN GUNBOATS
① Richard Somers
② Charles Gordon
③ Samuel Brooke
④ Stephen Decatur
⑤ Joseph Bainbridge
⑥ Henry Wadsworth
⑦ William Crane
⑧ Jonathan Thorn
⑨ James Caldwell

EUROPE

MEDITERRANEAN SEA

AFRICA

AREA OF DETAIL

Nautical miles

0   1/8   1/4

CONSTITUTION

MORTAR BOATS

Five-Gun Battery

The French Fort

AMERICAN GUNBOATS

Vixen Fort

Tripoli Harbor

PIRATE BOATS

MAP 3. Second Battle of the Gunboats, August 7, 1804

Edward Preble and his officers met at 9:00 a.m. The commodore issued his final orders for the attack from the west, although with one change: the commodore had John Smith and the *Vixen* sailing off the western approaches for a day, hoisting then "replying" to phantom signals. The idea was to mislead the bashaw as to where the Americans would strike next. Lieutenant Smith, however, spotted the new gun emplacements and told Preble about them.[31] The commodore made the new batteries the main priority of the gunboats, while ordering Robinson and Dent in the mortar boats to bombard the city. The orders for the rest of the flotilla remained unchanged.[32]

At 11:00 a.m. on August 7, the *Syren* and *Vixen* towed the gunboats and mortar boats toward the western bay. A northwesterly breeze made the approach easier, and the Americans made a great show of their advance, "to entice the enemy's boats out but without effect," Purser Noadiah Morris of the *Constitution* wrote.[33]

The nine American gunboats quickly encountered heavy fire from the shore batteries and began a hot exchange of fire with them. The new batteries, in particular, were in a position to hammer the Yankee gunboats.[34] Somers and Decatur led the line of U.S. warships to within a hundred yards of the beach forts and opened fire.

Richard Somers stood at the bow of Gunboat No. 1 as her Sicilian crew rowed the vessel into firing position. The Sicilian captain, Padrone Guardiano Tommaso Procida, stood next to Somers, translating the American officer's hand gestures into Sicilian and relaying orders to the crew.[35] It was the only way the American sailors and the Neapolitans could communicate and, though an imperfect system, Somers managed to keep his vessel on course. The same was true on the five other Sicilian gunboats—the American commanders used any means they could to show the Neapolitans where to go.

The three prize gunboats had no problems with crew. James Caldwell on Gunboat No. 9 had his own men from the *Syren* manning the oars and cannon. He bored down on the shore batteries with Gunboat No. 8 and opened fire, sending first round shot then grapeshot into the pirate forts. Midn. Robert Spence commanded the brass 28-pound main gun on Caldwell's vessel, with Gunnery Mate Joseph Kennedy second-in-command. The bow-mounted cannon spit fire once every forty seconds as the bluejackets worked to maintain a continuous barrage on the Tripolitans.

The battle between the beach forts and the gunboats lasted more than an hour. At first the Tripolitans gave as they good as they got. Somers on Gunboat No. 1 had a near miss as he brought his vessel into action. At a range of slightly less than a hundred yards, Somers engaged the pirate forts only to see a cannonball heading straight toward him. The athletic officer ducked just in time as the ball cut in half the flagstaff at the bow of his ship. "On measuring afterwards," a crewman reported, "it was rendered certain that he escaped death only by the timely removal."[36] Another shot pierced the hull of Somers' ship just above the waterline.

The engagement with the beach forts began around noon. By 2:00 p.m. the concentrated and more accurate American fire drove the Tripolitans from one of the new batteries as the 5-gun fort fell silent. The walls crumbling around them, the pirate gun crews either fled or died in the hail of American grapeshot. The gunboats, with occasional dashes from the *Syren*, *Nautilus*, and *Vixen*, then turned to engage the second new battery, the position the fleet dubbed the "*Vixen* fort."[37]

———————

Lt. John Dent and Lt. Charles Robinson maneuvered their mortar boats into position at the edge of the bay. Contrary winds hampered their efforts and the two mortar boats were not ready to fire their first rounds until 2:30 p.m. Robinson's Mortar Boat No. 1 fired the first round, dropping it squarely inside one of the shore forts engaging the American gunboats. Dent's vessel then lofted its first shot, which also found the mark.[38]

The two mortar boats drifted apart somewhat, with Dent taking up a more exposed position from which he was able to reach the bashaw's castle. The two mortar boats fired shot after shot, the Sicilian gunners straining to hoist the heavy 140-pound shells into the muzzle of the brass weapons. It was slow going. It took the Neapolitan crews more than two minutes to load and fire each mortar and another four or five minutes for the vessels to stop rocking from the recoil. The 9-inch projectiles had a slow-burning fuse that created a red tracer as it flew toward its target. The fuse touched off an interior powder charge that exploded the shell. Timing the fuse was an art, one the Neapolitans had not mastered. Preble complained that many of the shells either exploded too soon or not at all, but each had an effect.

Robinson fired twenty-eight rounds into Tripoli castle, knocking holes in the walls and destroying the quarters of a Spanish carpenter who had built most of the bashaw's fleet. Dent concentrated his fire on enemy shore batteries and succeeded in chasing the garrison of one fort from its ramparts.[39]

———————

The brig *Syren* stood slightly off to the east of the attacking flotilla. Her skipper, Charles Stewart, was in tactical command of the day's action. Stewart watched as a line of enemy gunboats with support from several galleys and schooners got under way and headed toward the American battle line.

It was exactly what Stewart hoped the pirates would do. Just after 2:30 p.m. he ordered Midn. Cornelius deKrafft to open fire on the advancing Tripolitan ships with the *Syren*'s bow chasers—a pair of long-barreled 12-pound cannon. Despite the fire from the *Syren*, the Tripolitans seemed in no hurry to close with the American gunboats. The *Syren* continued to fire and hoisted a signal that Commodore Preble on the *Constitution* quickly relayed to the rest of the squadron.

Preble ordered the *Argus*, *Vixen*, *Nautilus*, and *Enterprise* to move slightly west to get into a better position to cut off the pirate vessels if they ventured away from the main city defenses. The line of Tripolitan vessels, on seeing the American ships moving toward their rear, turned tail and returned to the safety of the city.[40]

The 8-gun stone battery the Americans called the *Vixen* fort belched fire as the line of Yankee gunboats approached. Once more the American-crewed vessels made better headway than the Neapolitan-crewed vessels. Caldwell's Gunboat No. 9 swung into action, firing both the 28-pound main gun and the two small howitzers at the enemy position. The rest of the Yankee vessels quickly joined in, and within minutes the 8-gun battery fell silent.

So, too, did the American ships because the captains believed they had destroyed the enemy fortification. The victory, however, was temporary. The Tripolitans quickly returned to their guns and reopened fire, this time using red-hot shot. Essentially a heated solid cannonball, the glowing shots hissed as they hit the water. On board Gunboat No. 9, Midn. Robert Spence and Gunner's Mate Edmund P. Kennedy urged their gun crew to load and fire as fast as possible. Robert's father, Keith, had been the purser on the *Philadelphia* and was now a prisoner in Tripoli.

The nine American gunboats fired round after round at the *Vixen* fort for nearly thirty minutes. The accuracy and power of the attack drove the pirates from their guns a second time just before 3:30 p.m. As they had the first time, the Tripolitans quickly returned to their position and opened fire, again using red-hot shot to try to rip through the hulls of the American vessels.

Midshipman Spence was ready to order his gun to fire when a shot ripped through the boat's magazine, immediately touching off her supply of powder. Gunboat No. 9 blew up in an ear-splitting roar. Ripped in half by the explosion, her bow with the main gun, remained partially intact but sank. The rest of the ship simply disintegrated, as did many of the men. "It being a red-hot shot, she instantly exploded. . . . I went up some distance in the air and lighted by the gun again; the only part remaining was that on which the gun stood. . . . Around me lay arms, legs and trunks of bodies in the most mutilated state," said Spence, who survived the explosion along with Gunner's Mate Kennedy. The nineteen-year-old Spence said it took him a couple of seconds to clear his head after the blast. The only other man he saw alive was Kennedy, and the two of them moved to the main gun, which was still loaded. "Though a little confused and bewildered by things tumbling on my head and by the prospect of death before me, for I cannot swim, I had presence of mind sufficient to know my duty and not to quit while there was still a part remaining. . . . I fired the gun and loaded her again," said Spence. However, before he could get off a second shot, the bow sank, spilling Spence and Kennedy into the water. "I gave a cheer," Spence remembered, as he went into the water, where crews from the other gunboats quickly plucked the survivors from the harbor.[41]

James Caldwell and John Dorsey died in the explosion, along with fourteen enlisted men. Spence said he saw Caldwell's body "after he came down, without arms or legs, his face so mutilated that I could not discriminate a feature. By his dress only I recognized him. He was not dead although he sank instantly."[42]

Spence and Kennedy survived the explosion virtually unscathed. Rescuers plucked six healthy and six wounded sailors and Marines from the harbor as well. The destruction of Gunboat No. 9 was the last act of the *Vixen* fort. The American gunboats knocked out seven of its eight guns and drove the pirate troops from the fort for the last time. The remaining gunboats turned their attention to the batteries closer to the castle and moved in to attack, firing their first salvoes around 4:00 p.m.[43]

Lt. John Dent inched Mortar Boat No. 2 closer to the shore with each shot. Dent could see where his shells landed and wanted to get in closer so he could hit the bashaw's castle. Each time he closed the distance, however, his vessel grew more exposed to enemy fire. At 4:30 fire from the city's main batteries grew so intense it forced Dent to move closer to Robinson's position, which was well out of range of the castle. The eight remaining American gunboats moved in closer to support the mortar boats, with the *Syren* riding herd on the smaller vessels. Gunboat No. 8 got a little too close to the big cannon on the shore and a round smashed into the ship, killing two men.[44]

The gunboats and mortar boats remained in position for another hour, more as enticement to the pirates to attack than to batter down more positions. The Tripolitan vessels maneuvered as though they would engage several times, but the proximity of the *Argus, Vixen, Nautilus,* and *Enterprise* convinced the pirates to remain inside the harbor. At 5:30 Preble ordered the tow vessels to pick up their charges and head back toward the flagship. The *Argus* remained on outboard patrol, just in case the Tripolitans decided to attack the Americans as they took the gunboats and mortar boats under tow. At 6:00 p.m. lookouts on the *Argus* spotted a strange sail on the horizon, too big to be a Tripolitan ship. Isaac Hull ordered the brig to investigate and the *Argus* slipped easily westward. Two hours later she returned, in company with the frigate *John Adams,* which finally had arrived on station.[45]

Preble's force was about to get bigger, but the commodore would now face an increasingly tight deadline for forcing the bashaw to come to terms.

CHAPTER 20

BATTLE OF TRIPOLI

APT. WILLIAM BAINBRIDGE AWOKE early in the morning on Tuesday August 28, 1804, to the sound of cannon fire smashing into the stone-and-mortar walls of his prison in Tripoli.[1] The crunching sound of iron shot grinding masonry marked the start of Day 303 of captivity for Bainbridge and the remaining 298 men of the now-destroyed frigate *Philadelphia*. After a summer of frantic letter writing and desperate escape attempts, Bainbridge appeared to have settled into life as a prisoner just as the American squadron under Commo. Edward Preble opened its long-awaited assault on Bashaw Yusuf Karamanli's city.

Although he was a talented mariner and well liked among his peers, there was a cloud that seemed to hang over Bainbridge. His loss of the *Philadelphia* on October 31, 1803, had only deepened his sense of ill luck, and the attack of August 28 did nothing to alleviate it.

The American squadron was relentlesssly hammering the bashaw. When the sound of cannon fire roused Bainbridge, he rose from his bed to peer out his small window. Just as he did so, a 28-pound ball from an American gunboat roared through the wall, showering Bainbridge with bits of stone and mortar. The shell destroyed the bed in which he had been sleeping only seconds before.[2] Almost immediately, most of Bainbridge's junior officers crowded into his room to check on their captain. The cannon ball had punched a huge hole through the wall, and through the hole they could see the Arab guards running for cover. The sight of their tormenters fleeing made the Americans cheer, then laugh.

Upon hearing the American cheers and jeers, the pirates slowly returned to their posts, where they came under fire of a different sort. The jailors, to stop the laughter of the Americans, threw stones at them through the hole in the wall. However, the ball that had crushed Bainbridge's wall created ammunition for the American officers, and with Lt. David Porter leading the way, the officers returned the fire of the guards, pelting the Arabs with stones, gravel, and pieces of mortar. The guards promptly withdrew under the hail of rocks and told the bashaw the officers were trying to escape. Sossey, the chief jailor, led a new group of guards to the Americans quarters and "threatened vengeance unless the officers conducted themselves more submissively."[3]

Bainbridge stepped in and told Sossey to take the bashaw's chief adviser, Mohammed Sidi Dgies, word of what had happened. The move put the Arabs on their heels. They agreed to do so, however, and crowded all the officers into a single room as they awaited a reply from the minister. Within a couple of hours, Dgies sent Bainbridge a note, blaming the guards for starting the rock fight and releasing the Americans from close confinement.[4]

<hr />

The delay between attacks on Tripoli was not something Commo. Edward Preble had wanted. Preble believed that the news the *John Adams* carried forced him to wait. The *John Adams* had arrived on August 7 with dispatches confirming what Preble already knew—Commo. Samuel Barron was on his way with four frigates to reinforce the Mediterranean squadron and to take command of the campaign against Tripoli. The *John Adams'* commander, Isaac Chauncey, wrote on August 7 that he thought Barron would arrive any day.[5] By August 24 there was still no word of the reinforcements and Preble had decided to get in at least one more major attack before he lost command. Although he never said it publicly, the delay gave Preble time to deal with his own frustration at losing the squadron. Whenever Samuel Barron arrived, he would succeed Preble as commodore, and Preble's rival, John Rodgers, would outrank him in seniority.

Preble knew the reason for the change came well before news of the destruction of the *Philadelphia* or the success of the blockade had reached Washington, DC. Yet when Chauncey handed Preble a packet of letters from Secretary of the Navy Robert Smith, the commodore was less than pleased, even though the secretary worked hard to soothe Preble's feelings: "We have already and repeatedly assured you, sir, of our high and unqualified approbation of your measures and your conduct. We knew that the force under your command was not adequate to carry on vigorous and effectual measures against Tripoli. . . . With a view to these important objects, and to excite among the Barbary Regencies a just idea of our national character and resources, we fitted out the armament of which you have already been advised."[6] Clearly, however, the secretary expected Preble to remain on station. He told the commodore he had approved Preble's request to send eight 32-pound carronades for the *Constitution*, which Preble wanted to use on the frigate's barge and cutter to turn those ships into small gunboats: "These will be delivered to you," Smith said.[7]

Preble had no intention of going from the squadron commander to its third-in-command officer. He turned to Sir Alexander Ball, governor of Malta, as something of a sounding board on how he should handle his pending loss of command. Although he made no official announcement, Preble knew it was next to impossible to keep a secret for long in the fleet. On August 21 he wrote to Ball, telling the governor, "You will, ere this, probably have heard I am to be superseded in the command of the American squadron in these seas. I value too highly the friendly sentiments with which you have honored me to neglect making you acquainted with the reasons assigned by the government for this (to me) unexpected measure."[8]

Preble enclosed a letter he had received the previous spring from Charles Washington Goldsborough, the chief clerk to Secretary of the Navy Smith. Goldsborough fully understood the burning desire Preble had to win glory for the Navy. He also made it clear he thought Washington could—and should—have provided more support:

> I wish you great glory because I esteem you and because I wish to see the time when the Navy shall be supported by all ranks of our citizens. The achievement of glorious deeds will render the Navy popular. If you return to this country covered with laurels, as I have no doubt you will do if an opportunity offers itself, or can be made to acquire them, there will be but one pulse in America on the subject of the Navy. If, on the contrary, you should return without having seen the whites of the enemy's eye, I should not be surprised if the Navy should lose in popularity.[9]

Ball, for his part, did his best to soothe Preble's ruffled feathers. The Maltese governor pointed out to the commodore that Secretary Smith, in his letter explaining the impending change of command, used "very flattering expressions." Quoting Smith, Ball reiterated that Preble had "acquitted yourself in a manner honorable to yourself, useful to your country and in all respects perfectly satisfactory to us." Those words, the governor said, "must satisfy your mind that nothing but imperious necessity could have caused your government to send an officer superior in rank to you."[10]

Ball was undoubtedly sad about Preble losing command for a number of reasons. The two had become friends during Preble's year in the Mediterranean, not only because the commodore could be engaging when he so chose, but also because the Americans, in prosecuting their war against

Tripoli, were keeping the pirates in check. The Barbary States were as troublesome to the British as they were to other European powers, and the Americans, for the time being, had all the pirate city-states either at peace or blockaded. The blockade of Tripoli also denied the French an important source of grain and other supplies, something that could only make the British happy. Most of all, however, Preble was an aggressive commander and a man of action, the type of commander that earned respect in all quarters and that, more than anything else, was why Ball and others were sorry he would soon lose command: "I have communicated this to all those I know," Ball told Preble. "They join me in regretting that an officer whose talents and professional abilities have been justly appreciated, and whose manners and conduct eminently fit him for so high a command should be removed from it."[11]

Preble had a difficult time keeping a lid on the news. Word spread through the squadron—likely thanks to both the crew of the *John Adams* and to the British. The Mediterranean was simply too small to keep news of Samuel Barron's impending arrival secret for any period. To their credit, the officers of the squadron acted as though they were unaware they would lose their popular commander. The cubs and the commodore had come a long way since Preble had first taken command a year earlier. Gone was the rancor and mistrust. Preble had learned to soften his approach while his aggressive spirit, and his pride in the Navy, had won over his officers and sailors alike. His young charges, in turn, won over their commander with their ability to take on any mission and succeed.

Even young John Darby, the purser of the newly arrived *John Adams*, fell under Preble's spell and was unhappy about losing the commodore, especially after the attack of August 7. "This brave and daring attack will hardly be credited by the Europeans who know the great advantage of a fort and strong fortified battery with their great superiority of gun boats, nor do I believe any other nation except the Americans would have attempted it with the same force, not even the British nation with all their boasted skill in naval tactics," Darby wrote in his journal. "I will only say that no nation could have done more than Commodore Preble with the same force."[12]

Publicly, at least, Ball's words soothed the commodore's feelings, although he lamented the fact the reinforcements had yet to arrive. "I cannot but be extremely grateful to my feelings to have my exertions thought favorably of by an officer of your Excellency's talents and experiences," Preble wrote to Ball. "I was in hopes ere this to have effected a peace in this quarter but if the reinforcement of frigates does not arrive soon, I fear we shall not succeed in bringing about so desirable an event this year."[13]

Privately, Preble seethed under the news of Samuel Barron's imminent arrival and at what he perceived as the lack of support from Washington:

"How much my feelings are lacerated by this supercedure [sic] at the moment of victory cannot be described and can only be felt by an officer placed in my mortifying position," the commodore wrote in his diary. "I cannot but regret that our naval establishment is so limited as to deprive me of the means of glory of completely subduing the haughty tyrant of Tripoli."[14]

Edward Preble was too professional to delay his assault on Tripoli because of his wounded pride. He had a much better reason for the hiatus in attacks on the city: supplies. The two attacks on Tripoli at the start of August used up far more ammunition and, above all, water, than the commodore had expected. "My ammunition is nearly expended," he wrote to Sir Alexander Ball.[15] Even the arrival of the *John Adams* with her hold bulging with supplies had not helped much.

Of greatest concern to Preble and the squadron was the lack of water. Following the attack of August 7, Preble was almost in shock at how little water remained in the squadron. On August 15 he wrote to William Higgins, the Navy agent at Malta: "Our water is nearly exhausted. I conjure you to charter two or three vessels for fear of a miscarriage of one and load them with water immediately. If one is not here in eight days I fear we shall be ruined as I only have 14 days water for the squadron."[16] Higgins ultimately managed to hire the master of a Neapolitan merchant vessel, the *Conception*, to carry supplies to the squadron and also loaded the ketch *Intrepid*, lying at port in Syracuse, with water and food. Elsewhere, Preble also sent the *Enterprise*, under Lt. James Lawrence, to Malta to pick up water. The day the *Enterprise* left, August 19, *Constitution* sailing master Nathaniel Haraden reported the squadron was down to just 13,000 gallons of water—a six-day supply even with rationing.[17]

If the *John Adams* brought bad news to Preble, it carried good news for several officers in the squadron. When President Thomas Jefferson received congressional approval to outfit Samuel Barron's reinforcing squadron, the lawmakers also approved a suggestion from Jefferson to restore several ranks to the Navy. The Peace Establishment Act of 1801 had done away with the ranks of lieutenant commandant and master commandant. Jefferson restored them and immediately promoted every ship commander in Preble's squadron. John H. Dent, John Robinson, and Charles Gordon were all promoted to lieutenant commandant. Richard Somers, John Smith, Charles Stewart, and Isaac Hull were promoted to master commandants—one step below full captain. In recognition of Stephen Decatur's destruction of the *Philadelphia*, he was promoted from lieutenant to captain, thus becoming the second-in-command in the squadron behind only Preble.

While good news to the officers, the promotions touched off a series of debates, both in Washington and in Navy circles. Jefferson had signed off on the promotions, but the Senate never approved them, which the laws of the day mandated. Legally, the promotions were nonbinding, although, just as Jefferson planned, there was simply no way to prevent the officers from accepting their new ranks.[18]

Decatur, in particular, earned the wrath of at least one fellow officer—his predecessor on the *Enterprise*, Andrew Sterrett. Still a lieutenant, Sterrett was in Virginia in May 1804 when the promotions went through; Sterrett was waiting to take command of the frigate *New York*, which was undergoing an overhaul. Sterrett was senior to Decatur on the lieutenant's list, and although he received a promotion to master commandant, he angrily resigned from the Navy in protest over Decatur's promotion ahead of him.[19]

The men in the squadron, however, had no problems with the promotions. To them, the promotions were all merited. In the atmosphere Preble had created among the usually quarrelsome junior officers, none complained nor were there any recriminations. Dueling was a thing of the past under Preble and the newly promoted officers continued in their tasks as though nothing had changed.[20]

———◆———

Preble waited for Barron's arrival—and water supplies—for two weeks before the inactivity got to him. He believed waiting was the correct action to take. "If he should arrive, the fate of Tripoli must be decided in a few hours and the bashaw completely humbled."[21] Waiting, however, did not mean doing nothing. Preble busied himself preparing to attack Tripoli with or without Barron's help. His first step was to reconnoiter the harbor, a task that nearly cost the American squadron dearly.

On the night of August 9, Preble boarded the *Argus* and ordered Hull to get in as close as possible to the castle. The brig crept into the harbor under cover of darkness, but the pirates spotted her anyway and opened fire. Every shot but one fell short. The lone hit smashed into the hull of the *Argus* below the waterline, tearing away the copper plating that sheathed the vessel's keel and carrying off part of the keel board. A few inches lower and the ball would have holed the hull, sinking the brig. Despite the damage, the *Argus* continued in service.[22]

The commodore also made use of the *John Adams*. Although she carried barely enough cannon to defend herself, Preble turned her into a decoy, stationing her at the mouth of the harbor in clear view of the Tripolitans. The frigate's crew constantly raised and lowered signal flags designed to confuse the pirates as to her mission. "From a distance," said *Constitution* sailing master Nathaniel Haraden, "she looked as though she carried her full armament and certainly must have caused alarm among the Turks."[23] Getting the *John Adams* out of the way also allowed Preble to make use of the frigate's crew, "as nearly half the crews of the *Constitution*, brigs and schooners, were taken out to man the bombs, gun boats and ship's boats."[24]

On the night of August 18, Preble ordered Master Commandant Chauncey and Capt. Stephen Decatur to make a reconnaissance of the harbor. The commodore wanted definitive information of just how much damage the attack of August 7 had caused to the bashaw's shore batteries, as well as an idea of where to place his two mortar boats to cause the most damage.

The mortar boats, so far, had been something of a bust for the Americans. Neither had caused any real damage in the first two attacks, despite throwing more than fifty shells at the city. Most of the shells either failed to explode or fell short of the range. The problem, the commodore found, was twofold. First, the gunboats themselves simply were not solid enough to withstand the recoil of the big naval mortars they carried. The Americans did what they could to strengthen the craft, but the Neapolitan vessels were structurally weak. The second, and far worse, problem was the ammunition. Preble tested the powder the Neapolitans gave him after the attack on August 7 and found it was less than half as potent as the powder he brought from America. The commodore said he believed his mortar boats suffered from sabotage of both powder and shells. The ammunition all came from a cache of supplies the Neapolitans made while their nation was under French occupation, and the shoddy workmanship, Preble believed, was a show of resistance. The sabotaged shot and shell was mixed in with properly made munitions and now was in Preble's hands.[25]

During their reconnaissance, Decatur and Chauncey found the pirates firmly anchored inside the harbor beneath the cannon of the castle and shore batteries. The Tripolitans had their vessels facing west, expecting yet another American attack from that direction. Preble sent both mortar boats into the harbor to shell the city the night of August 24. The bombards lofted fifty rounds at Tripoli, of which just three exploded.[26] In addition, the heavy recoil of the mortar on Mortar Boat No. 1 nearly broke the keel of the vessel, rendering her unserviceable.[27] After the schooners had towed the mortar boats back to the assembly point, Preble once more sent carpenters to the vessels to make yet another round of emergency repairs. The work took three days.[28]

Capt. Stephen Decatur stood at the helm of Gunboat No. 4 as the Neapolitan-built ship moved toward the main fortifications ringing Tripoli harbor. It was just before midnight the night of August 27–28, and Decatur planned a night attack on Tripoli. Looming just ahead, positioned on the rock breakwater the Americans called the mole, was an enemy battery. The bastion was dark as the gunboat crept toward it, her crew of Neapolitan sailors using the large oars, called sweeps, to row the vessel.

Decatur's contingent of Americans, all from his former command the *Enterprise*, manned the 28-pound cannon at the bow of the ship and the two howitzers on either side. Behind Decatur were four more gunboats. The crews were tired from rowing into position to attack.[29]

It took three long hours for the American gunboats to finally get into range of the pirate city and the fleet of gunboats and galleys anchored across the harbor mouth. Alongside Decatur's division of five gunboats was Master Commandant Richard Somers with three craft. Somers had just as much trouble getting his ships into position as did his friend. For Somers, a return to action also undoubtedly meant the chance to once more at least equal the accomplishments of his childhood friend, who now outranked him. Decatur, with his promotion to captain, took over as commander of the gunboats while Somers, who had commanded the gunboats in the attacks of August 3 and August 7, was second officer.

Just behind the gunboats stood the brigs *Argus* and *Syren* and the schooners *Nautilus* and *Enterprise*. The U.S. flagship *Constitution* stood off to the west of the gunboats, ready to move in between the mole and the shore to engage the forts. The *Enterprise* pulled double duty, towing Mortar Boat No. 1 into position. Carpenters from both the *Constitution* and the *John Adams* had spent three days working on the boat and had managed to repair the vessel enough that she could take part in the attack. Lt. John Robinson took command of the vessel while Lieutenant Commandant John Dent had returned from the flagship to command Mortar Boat No. 2.[30]

Although tired, the American sailors were undoubtedly happy to be back in action. After the unsuccessful bombardment of August 24, the weather had prevented the bluejackets from mounting a sustained attack. Preble had attempted to hit the city three times before the night of August 27–28, only to call off the attack each time as the wind either whipped up or was too weak.[31] Conditions that night were perfect. Even when the wind died off just after midnight, Preble ordered the ships to continue to move into position.

The *Philadelphia*'s surgeon, Jonathan Cowdery, could see the entire harbor from his apartment in Tripoli castle. Although a prisoner, Cowdery received better treatment than the rest of the bashaw's hostages thanks to his status as a physician. Early in his captivity, Cowdery had treated the bashaw's daughter, nursing her through an illness. His success earned him a position as the unofficial doctor to the Karamanli family and slightly better accommodations. He became a frequent guest at the bashaw's court, where he heard all the rumors.[32] After the attacks of August 3, the bashaw told him Lt. John Smith of the *Vixen* had led the gunboats, and that Smith and forty Americans had died in the attack. Karamanli, however, denied Cowdery permission to view the alleged dead.[33]

Cowdery, like Bainbridge, awoke on August 28 to the sound of "heavy and incessant fire of cannon and the whistling and rattling of shot all around me." He climbed out of bed and ventured to the window of his apartment: "I found that our gunboats were close in, and were firing upon the town and batteries. Every gun in Tripoli that could be brought to bear was returning the fire. The Tripolitan gunboats were close under the castle for protection."[34]

———✦✦———

The American gunboats each carried at least forty rounds of solid shot and another forty to sixty of grapeshot and canister. Decatur, Somers, and the rest of the gunboat commanders had no intention of wasting any of it. Each vessel had a full complement of fighting men: Preble had stripped the *Scourge* of most of her crew and accepted sixty volunteers from the *John Adams,* whose crew manned three smaller craft—the *Constitution*'s barge and cutter, and the *John Adams*' cutter. Each carried a small 12-pound cannon and gave the Americans added insurance against enemy attempts to board the gunboats.[35] Master Commandant Isaac Chauncey and more of the *John Adams* crew also volunteered for duty on the flagship. Chauncey took command of the frigate, freeing Preble to oversee the entire attack, and finally Preble had an attack going exactly as he wanted.

Somers, Decatur, and the other gunboat captains opened fire at 4:30 a.m. Their targets were the pirate vessels anchored in front of the castle as well as the shore fortifications: the bluejackets poured a hail of fire into both. The first enemy vessels to come under fire were a pair of large galleys anchored just in front of the pirate gunboats. From his vantage point, Cowdery watched as concentrated fire from the U.S. vessels shattered one of the galleys and drove the other on shore. The *Philadelphia* surgeon had a view no other American officer had of the battle, thanks to his perch in the castle.

Preble and his officers were not as lucky. Smoke wreathed the gunboats as the Neapolitan and American gunners sent salvo after salvo toward the line of pirate vessels and forts in a well-rehearsed ballet of destruction. The still-favorable wind, though light, blew enough of the smoke away from the U.S. ships that their captains could catch glimpses of their targets. After sighting the cannon, the Yankee seamen and their Neapolitan allies went through a series of complex movements to load and fire the 24-pound main guns on the Neapolitan ships and the 28-pound pieces on the two remaining prize gunboats.

Gunners used heavy rods—with sponges on one end and a plunger on the other—to load the guns and, after firing, to clear the weapon of still-burning embers that could set off the next charge. When it was safe, one of the "spongers" would ram down first a charge of powder weighing about two pounds, then a wad of cloth to hold the powder in place, and finally the round—solid shot, canister, or grapeshot.

After the gun captain sighted the gun using his thumbs and fingers as a crude type of sight, he removed a lead apron that covered the touchhole and primed it with powder. When everything was ready, the gun captain touched a match—a long, slow-burning fuse coiled around a rod—to the touchhole and the cannon went off. After each firing the crew went through the entire evolution again until the enemy sank or surrendered, or until enemy fire put the crew out of action. An extremely proficient gun crew could fire roughly two rounds every minute.[36]

On board the gunboats, the Italian gunners took the lead in aiming the cannon, while Americans actually manned and fired the pieces. Each blast from the gunboats sent mortar, stone, and brick flying as shots struck the shore forts or sent cascades of water and splinters whirling among the Tripolitan flotilla.

———◆———

The Tripolitan gunboats held a position guarding the western entrance to the outer harbor. Reefs and rocks studded the water to their immediate front, serving the Americans as cover for their own gunboats. The larger Tripolitan vessels were anchored just to the front of the line of gunboats until concentrated American fire smashed the two galleys.

After absorbing the American attack for more than an hour, at least one Tripolitan commander was tired of being on the receiving end. The captain of the largest gunboat ordered his vessel forward and made for Somers' division of three gunboats. The Tripolitans manned the 28-pound main gun and began firing solid shot at the Yankee vessels.

Jonathan Cowdery watched as the Tripolitans' backbone stiffened. Fire from the forts on the mole, the shoreline, and the castle intensified as the first streaks of dawn turned the eastern sky dark pink. He saw the lone gunboat break free of the line of pirate battle line and move toward Gunboats 1, 2, and 3. He also saw the American response.[37]

Master Commandant Richard Somers probably could not believe his luck. A lone Tripolitan gunboat was moving toward his three-ship division. Seizing the chance to match his friend Stephen Decatur, Somers ordered his gunners to engage the pirate ship. Lt. Charles Gordon, commander of Gunboat No. 2, also engaged the Tripolitan gunboat, as did Sailing Master Samuel Brooke on Gunboat No. 3. The American gunboats fired a volley of solid shot, then swept the advancing vessel with grapeshot and canister. Four men fell off the pirate ship dead and another two slumped to the deck wounded. The Tripolitan gunboat quickly veered off and returned to the safety of the anchorage near the castle.[38]

The gunboats continued to fire as the pink smear to the east brightened. Slowly, however, the American fire began to slacken as the gunboats expended their loads of ammunition. All told, the eight gunboats fired more than three hundred rounds of solid shot and more than two hundred rounds of grapeshot or canister.[39]

The approaching dawn was a signal to Commo. Edward Preble. His gunboats were running out of ammunition and Preble decided it was time for them to withdraw. He hoisted the signal for the brigs and schooners to move and take the gunboats and rowboats under tow. He also ordered Chauncey to move in to cover the withdrawal.

With the wind blowing east by south, the American flagship raced in toward the castle and engaged four different forts containing seventy-two cannon. At 6:30 a.m. the *Constitution* opened fire, pouring broadside after broadside into the bashaw's defenses. The result was devastating. "We silenced the bashaw's castle and half-moon battery," said Sailing Master Nathaniel Haraden. "On firing our third broadside the round battery was deserted." The frigate spent fifty-four minutes within pistol shot of the enemy defenses and fired more than six hundred rounds into them. "At every broadside we gave them showers of stone and dust would completely cover their batteries," Haraden said.[40]

A cheer went up from the crews of the retreating gunboats as the big frigate swept in to cover their withdrawal while her fight with the batteries filled the Americans with awe. "The commodore's ship when standing in and during the engagement was the most elegant sight I ever saw," said Purser John Darby of the *John Adams*. "She had the tompions [*sic*] out and matches lit and batteries lighted up [and] all hands at quarters standing right in under the fort and received a heavy cannonading from their battery. The commodore gave them several broadsides which did great injury to their battery and the houses on shore."[41]

When the *Constitution* withdrew, the bashaw's defenses were silent. Despite being at point-blank range for nearly an hour, the frigate suffered only minimal damage to her rigging and sails, and no casualties among the crew. The gunboats also reported no casualties. The men in the open boats had not been so lucky: a shot from a Tripolitan gun had struck the cutter from the *John Adams*, killing three sailors and wounding one.[42]

———— • ————

The fury of the American assault shocked Yusuf Karamanli. Until the attack of August 28, the bashaw of Tripoli had essentially escaped unscathed. The loss of several gunboats stung his pride more than his strength, and so far the one weapon the Americans had that frightened him—the mortar boats—had been ineffective, but the "attack between August 27 and 28 was more serious," said French consul Bonaventure Beaussier. "A 36-pound shot struck the castle and passed through the apartment of the prisoners, another through the sailors' prison and others struck a number of houses, especially those of the Spanish, Swedish and Dutch consuls."[43] Joseph Douglas and William Godby, sailmakers on the *Philadelphia* and prisoners in Tripoli, reported that the attack "injured a great many houses killed several Turks and drove them entirely out of three of their batteries." They also said the Tripolitans were running low on powder.[44]

Despite the damage to his city and fleet, Karamanli remained defiant. On August 29, the day after the attack, he sent word through Beaussier he would be willing to conduct a prisoner exchange—Preble had forty-two Tripolitans on board his ships—and cut a peace deal, but his asking price of $400,000 did not change and remained resolute. Beaussier said despite Karamanli's shock at the ferocity of the latest attack, "the bashaw seems to care little about the injury done to the houses by the shots. . . . Menaces have no other effect than to inflame the mind of the prince."[45]

The Frenchman also said Karamanli viewed Preble's repeated attempts to trade his prisoners for crew of the *Philadelphia* as a sign of weakness: "It must be construed to your disadvantage and tend[s] to raise the pretensions of this regency. It had been much better at the beginning to have threatened and to have followed up your attacks with energy and effect, without entering into any negotiations."[46]

Still, the French consul revealed several important details. The attack once again drove the bashaw from the city—August 29 found him at his "summer residence in the country." Karamanli also remained in constant fear of the mortars "which he fears may burn and destroy his town." There was, Beaussier said, only one option for the commodore: "Attack the town and particularly the castle without intermission. You must persevere until the pacha, harassed at all points, shall himself ask for a parley."[47]

Capt. John Rodgers was still sitting off Tangiers on August 28. The second-in-command of the reinforcing squadron that sailed under Commo. Samuel Barron was apparently in no real rush to join forces with his rival, Commo. Edward Preble. Rodgers, in the frigate *Congress*, along with Capt. James Barron and the *Essex*, had gone to Morocco to see what the emperor was planning on orders from Commodore Barron. Rodgers, when he arrived at Tangiers on August 17, found a pair of Tripolitan warships, including the *Meshouda*, "laying in ordinary"—essentially mothballed—at the port. From there, he went from port to port in Morocco searching, he said, for any sign of hostilities. He found none.[48]

On August 30 he left orders for James Barron and the *Essex* to remain off Tangier while he planned to head for Tripoli in *Congress* where he expected to "unite her services to the expedition commanded by Commodore Barron against that place."[49] However, instead of heading right to Tripoli, a two-day sail from Tangiers, Rodgers went to Gibraltar to take on supplies.[50]

Commo. Samuel Barron was no closer to Tripoli than was his subordinate. While Rodgers was keeping an eye on Morocco, Barron was doing the same at Algiers and Tunis. Interestingly, it was U.S. consul James Simpson in Tangiers, along with other American diplomats, who kept telling the officers that while the Barbary leaders are "exceedingly displeased" the American blockade prevented them from entering Tripoli, they doubted if they planned war.

On August 26 Simpson wrote Rodgers, "It does not appear to me that there is any immediate intention on the part of the emperor to act against us." The diplomat believed the emperor would likely aid the bashaw "in the manner he may think he can do it most effectually," and recommended keeping a frigate off the Moroccan coast just in case.[51] Still, the diplomats said none of the Barbary states other than Tripoli was doing anything warlike.

Whether the diplomatic traffic was an excuse or indeed gave Barron and Rodgers reason for concern, the result was the four frigates Preble desperately needed to bring Tripoli to terms, although tantalizingly close, would not arrive in time to help end the campaign.

Commo. Edward Preble did not need the French consul in Tripoli to tell him just how effective his two mortar boats could be in his campaign against the bashaw. The American commander all along planned to use the mortars as both a tactical and a strategic weapon—destroying fortifications as well as the city's will to fight. So far, however, the mortars had scored few successes. Both vessels needed repairs and Preble decided to pause his attack on the city to fix the vessels so they could participate in the next assault. Preble also wanted to wait until more supplies, especially powder, had arrived. The commodore wanted to get rid of the inferior powder he had received from the Italians and replace it with powder that would make the mortars work.

He had his wish on August 30 when a Sicilian vessel that Navy agent William Higgins chartered arrived off Tripoli carrying food, water, and ammunition.[52] The commodore also sent word to the bashaw inquiring about the prisoner exchange, but the Tripolitan leader rebuffed him. It was pretty much what Preble had expected, as the commodore had given up the idea of winning the release of the prisoners only through negotiations.

After weeks of operations off the Tripoli coast, Preble's squadron was beginning to wear out. John Smith on the *Vixen* and Decatur on the *Enterprise* both asked Preble's permission to completely overhaul their vessels.[53] The season was advancing and Preble knew his gunboats and mortar boats simply could not continue in open seas. With no idea when or even if Samuel Barron would arrive, Preble knew he had to batter the bashaw into submission now or sail away empty-handed.

While he sent word he wanted to talk to the bashaw, Preble used the time to hastily repair the mortar boats. Carpenters worked throughout the day and night August 29 and 30 to repair them, and by September 1 they were ready. John Trippe, who had suffered eleven sword wounds on August 3, returned to duty and took command of Gunboat No. 6.[54] The work on the boats progressed despite the weather, which began to turn stormy. Preble would hit Tripoli the minute the weather broke.

————◆—◆————

Mortar Boats No. 1 and No. 2 did not exactly skip over the waves as they lumbered behind the *Enterprise*. Despite light winds and flat seas, the Neapolitan-built ships wallowed in the wake of the schooner. The rounded bows and sterns and flat bottoms of the mortar boats made them ill suited for work outside of protected waters; despite the near-perfect conditions on September 3 for the rest of the American squadron, the men on the mortar boats had a less-than-enjoyable trip as the *Enterprise* towed them into position.

The previous day, September 2, the entire squadron had prepared for a surprise night assault on the bashaw's defenses, but at the last moment a change in the wind forced Preble to call off the mission. That afternoon, a Spanish ship damaged in the August 27–28 attack attempted to leave the harbor. According to her captain, the American attack caused "great havoc and destruction in the city, and among the shipping and that a vast number of people have been killed." Still, the Spaniard said the Tripolitans remained defiant, managing to salvage three of the vessels the Americans sank, although the Tripolitans were short on powder. Preble allowed the ship to continue on its journey and made up his mind to attack the bashaw the next day.[55]

On September 3 the commodore ordered the entire squadron into the attack, but wanted the mortar boats to play the major role. He once more sent his gunboats, backed by the brigs and schooners, toward the reef to the south and west of the castle, where the American ships could engage the pirate flotilla and seal off the western entrance.

Preble kept the *Constitution* to the east of the reef, opposite the castle, to cover both the gunboats and the two mortar boats, which anchored roughly a mile offshore of the city. At 3:00 p.m. the American flotilla opened fire with Somers' three gunboats concentrating on Fort English and Decatur's division of five gunboats trying to draw out the bashaw's fleet. The pirates, however, refused to budge, remaining under anchor in the shadow of the castle. The new captain turned his attention to Fort English as well as the other shore batteries. The gun battle, however, proved inconclusive. "Our boats received no injury and it is supposed we did the enemy but little damage as they were a very considerable distance from each other," said John Darby of the *John Adams*, while Charles Morris on Gunboat No. 3 said the attacks were "no particular circumstances and productive of no good effect."[56]

———— ✦ ————

Lt. Thomas Robinson and Bombardier Don Antonio Massi of the Neapolitan Navy stood near the mortar on Mortar Boat No. 1, watching as the gunners labored to load the weapon. The squat barrel did not require as much care as did the long guns on the gunboats or the *Constitution* and was far easier to clean. However, the heavy shells required four men to raise and lower into the mortar.

Each shell weighed roughly 140 pounds. Two to four men clipped chains with S-hooks at the end onto a pair of rings on the projectile. The chains dangled from an iron winch that the gunners lifted. Once in the air, the gunner shuffled to the barrel and slid the shell into place. The gunners then used wooden levers and blocks to elevate the tube under the direction of the bombardier. Once everything was ready, the bombardier touched a match to the fuse and fired the mortar. During the day, the 9-inch round projectile was nearly invisible until it neared the target. At night, the shells trailed a long, red tail of burning powder that struck fear into the defenders of Tripoli and its inhabitants alike.[57]

Lieutenant Commandant John Dent watched as his crewmen went through the same drill as the sailors and gunners on Mortar Boat No. 2. From their anchoring point, each mortar quickly found the range and began lobbing shell after shell directly on target, striking the docks near the castle as well as the bashaw's stronghold. Unlike previous attacks, each bomb that fell on the city exploded, smashing stone, wood, and bone. Cowdery recounted the attack, stating that "The two bomb ketches . . . did considerable damage to several houses and completely destroyed the house of the Spanish carpenter, the bashaw's naval contractor." The explosions created "confusion and random firing among the Tripolitans. The men, women and children ran out of the town in the utmost terror and distraction."[58]

Although each shot caused damage on shore, the constant firing also put more and more stress on the mortar boats. The concussion from each shot shook the mortar boats and pushed down on the wooden beds that held the mortars. Each blast also pushed the vessels deeper into the water, stressing the keel and timbers. Robinson, on Gunboat No. 1, watched with growing alarm as the concussion opened seams in the planks, allowing more and more water to enter the hold.

Despite the damage, both mortar boats continued to fire, and as they did so they were perfect targets for the bashaw's gunners. Spray from round shot cascaded over each vessel. Robinson's ship, in particular, had a rough time as the Tripolitans on shore found the range. Shrapnel and canister cut away nearly every shroud holding the masts in place and tore the sails to shreds. Mortar Boat No. 2 also took damage in her shrouds although she did not suffer as much as No. 1.[59]

Robinson and Dent spent an hour under direct fire from the Tripolitan shore batteries. The men on Mortar Boat No. 1 fired twenty-two shells in that time, while the crew on No. 2 fired nineteen rounds. At 4:00 p.m. the crew on Mortar Boat No. 1 stopped firing. The concussion from the mortar had knocked the weapon completely out of its bed, and Robinson reported more than two feet of water in the hold. The American and Italian sailors looked anxiously for the sight of their tow vessels coming to get them. What they saw was the flagship sweeping in to provide cover.

———— ——

The USS *Constitution* had a full breeze as she moved between the mortar boats and the shore. Master Commandant Isaac Chauncey drove the big frigate in as close to the beach as he dared. The Tripolitans, their castles and batteries only a few hundred yards away, turned every cannon they had on her and sent shot after shot toward Preble's flagship. "We were exposed to the fire of more than 80 guns," said Sailing Master Nathaniel Haraden. "The spray of the shot wet our courses nearly to the lower yards."[60] Finally, the *Constitution* answered. It was a harrowing experience according to Haraden, but "We brought to within point-blank shot of all the batteries and gave 11 broadsides of round and doublehead from our larboard [port] batteries."[61]

The *Constitution* sailed back and forth in front of the forts for forty minutes, covering the withdrawals of the gunboats and the mortar boats. Cowdery observed, "many of his shot came into the town and the castle," while Marine private William Ray, who was closer to the shore than the *Philadelphia* doctor, wrote the frigate "silenced one of the batteries. The town, castle and other batteries [were] considerably damaged."[62] But so was the American ship. The combined fire of more than 80 enemy cannon had an effect as the frigate lost her main topsail, jib, and foresail and had much of her rigging cut to shreds. Still, according to Haraden, it could have been worse. "We were not struck in the hull," he said. "The batteries fire in good direction but without judgment in elevating or depressing the guns."[63]

The gunboats also spent more than an hour under fire, with each firing forty rounds of solid shot and nearly as much grapeshot and canister. Despite the long range of their fight, the gunboats still managed to damage one pirate vessel and to cause considerable casualties among the pirate crews.[64]

The mortar boats suffered the most damage, mostly from the concussion of their own guns. Mortar Boat No. 1 was completely wrecked and would need an overhaul before she could see combat again. Mortar Boat No. 2, although not as badly damaged, also was in need of a refit.

It did not matter. Commo. Edward Preble had one final weapon to use against the bashaw, and it involved the smallest ship in the squadron: the little ketch *Intrepid* was about to see combat once more.

CHAPTER 21

An Intrepid Gamble

THE *INTREPID* LAY NEARLY FORGOTTEN in Syracuse until early August, when the supply situation off Tripoli forced Commo. Edward Preble to press the ship once more into service. Preble kept a midshipman and a couple of deckhands on the ship throughout the summer to keep it seaworthy. The small vessel was too frail to take part in any of the combat operations off Tripoli, although she made for a decent-enough hospital ship. Most of her patients came from the *Enterprise*. The enlistment terms of the schooner's crew had long expired and many of the men suffered from exhaustion. Although the bulk of the *Enterprise*'s crew chose to remain on station until replacements could arrive from America, the men needed rest. Under Assistant Surgeon Lewis Heerman of the *Enterprise*, sailors once more scrubbed down the *Intrepid* and she became something of a rest and refit vessel.[1]

As supplies ran low off Tripoli, however, Preble needed every ship he could find to take food and water to the squadron. He wrote multiple letters to William Higgins, the Navy agent at Malta, to send water, and fresh fruit and vegetables to stave off scurvy. Higgins contracted an English vessel on August 14 to carry supplies and then decided to load the *Intrepid* with water and melons and send her to the squadron as well.[2]

The *Intrepid* took three full days to reach Preble. When she arrived, the squadron was down to slim rations. At Preble's order, each man was to receive just "two quarts and two pints" of water per day, including water with which the men and officers cooked.[3] The *Intrepid* arrived carrying ten thousand gallons of water, along with a number of sheep and bullocks, and vegetables.[4]

The lengthy voyage from Sicily to Tripoli bothered Preble, who was never one to listen to excuses. He fired the unnamed midshipman commanding the *Intrepid* and put Midn. Joseph Israel in charge of the ketch, giving

Israel a field promotion to acting lieutenant.[5] Israel was a three-year veteran of the service, born sometime in 1784, most likely in Annapolis. He received his appointment as a midshipman on January 15, 1801, and served on the subscription sloop *Maryland* under the command of John Rodgers.

The *Maryland* was Rodgers' first command assignment after his promotion for his performance on the *Constellation* during the Quasi-War. The merchants of Baltimore raised the money for the 36-gun frigate and launched her in 1799. Rodgers recruited his original crew from the Baltimore-Annapolis area of Maryland.

Israel was not among the original complement. The *Maryland* spent nearly a year on the Surinam station in 1800, where she was the lone U.S. warship patrolling that area of South America. Israel joined the *Maryland* in Baltimore, where she arrived October 1, 1800, for repairs. He sailed with Rodgers and the *Maryland* on March 22, 1801, bound for France. On board was Rep. John Dawson of Virginia, who was on his way to Paris to negotiate an end to the undeclared naval war between the United States and France. The voyage was uneventful, apart from a long delay in returning home as Dawson and the French dickered over the finer points of the Treaty of Montefontaine, which ended the conflict. The *Maryland* finally pointed toward America on July 15, 1801, and arrived back in Baltimore in August. She never sailed again.

When the Quasi-War ended, Congress was quick to pass the Peace Establishment Act of 1801. The U.S. Navy had swelled to forty-six ships during the conflict, far too many for a budget-conscious legislature. The Act reduced the fleet to just twelve ships, but public outcry forced the Navy to retain the *Enterprise,* raising the total to thirteen. The *Philadelphia* was among the ships Congress retained; the *Maryland* was not.

The Act also drastically reduced the number of officers, whittling the captain's list down from thirty-one to nine, and allotted just 136 midshipmen. Rodgers left the Navy when Congress dropped his name from the captain's list. He returned to merchant service until the Tripoli conflict broke out. By an odd quirk, when he returned to the Navy, Rodgers regained his place on the captain's list, one spot ahead of Preble even though he was ten years younger. This created the setting for the feud between the two captains when Preble arrived in the Mediterranean in 1803.[6]

Israel was not part of the downsizing. When Rodgers, acting on orders, sold the *Maryland* out of the service, Israel transferred to the *Chesapeake*, which was outfitting in Baltimore as the flagship of Richard Dale's squadron headed for Tripoli. The young officer apparently did his job, but did little to merit attention. There was no mention of him in any dispatches from Dale to the Department of the Navy. When Dale returned to the *Chesapeake*, Israel joined the *New York*, the flagship of Richard Morris. He served on the *New York* throughout 1803, transferring to the *Constitution* when Preble joined forces with Morris' outgoing squadron in October 1803.[7]

Israel took on additional duties starting in July 1804, when Preble began stripping his squadron of junior officers to serve on the *Scourge* and the nine gunboats. Preble was already watching the young Marylander and mentioned him in his reports to Secretary of the Navy Robert Smith. Now he could get a look at how the twenty-year-old handled command. Israel's only task on the *Intrepid* was to keep the squadron supplied with food and water. Preble, however, had other plans for the little ketch.

After the attack on August 24 fizzled, the commodore held a council of war with his commanders.[8] The campaigning season was rapidly coming to a close and the Americans, despite their constant pounding of the bashaw, appeared no closer to winning the release of Bainbridge and his crew than they had been in the spring. Preble also knew Commo. Samuel Barron and his squadron were only days away from arriving off Tripoli. Preble wanted to wrap up the campaign before he lost command in the Mediterranean.[9]

Time was not the only enemy. After the series of defeats the Americans had inflicted on his gunboats, Bashaw Yusuf Karamanli decided to keep his vessels close to shore where his batteries could protect them. Preble's fleet could strike the town, but not the bashaw's craft. When the commodore laid out the tactical situation to his commanders, Richard Somers saw an opportunity. The bashaw kept his gunboats in a tight cluster under the guns of his castle. Although the deeper-draft American ships could not navigate that far into the harbor, the little *Intrepid* could. Somers proposed turning the *Intrepid* into a fireship, or an "infernal."

The use of fireships was an ancient tactic that was as devastating as it was simple. An opponent filled a ship full of combustibles—anything and everything that could burn and explode. The crew sailed the fireship as close as possible to the enemy, lit a fuse, and fled, leaving the fireship to complete its mission on its own. The usual method of steering the fireship was to lash the wheel. When they worked, fireships could cause havoc among an enemy. When they failed, however, they simply wasted an otherwise useful vessel.

Preble and his officers were well aware of just how devastating a fireship could be. The British had used fireships with great effect just three years before in the Battle of Copenhagen: Admiral Horatio Nelson had used a pair of fireships to break the line of Danish warships in his attack on the Scandinavian capital on April 2, 1801. Although the fireships failed to destroy any enemy vessels, their mere presence forced the Danes to open their battle lines, providing Nelson with the chance to break through the Danish defenses.[10]

Somers believed the *Intrepid* could do the Royal Navy one better. Although the pirates would likely be on the lookout for the little ketch, she was so nondescript and common, Somers argued, she could still sneak into the harbor under the guise of a blockade runner. The *Intrepid*, the master commandant said, was the perfect weapon, and Preble agreed.

The commodore, as early as the attacks of August 3 and August 7, started to think about using one of the squadron's vessels as a fireship. Preble told Secretary of the Navy Smith he had "long contemplated" using a fire-ship "to destroy the enemy's shipping and shatter the bashaw's castle and town."[11] When Somers approached him with the same idea, Preble decided to put it into action. On August 26 he ordered Israel to begin working on the *Intrepid* to turn her into a floating bomb.[12]

———•—•———

Acting Lieutenant Joseph Israel knew his superiors were talking about the *Intrepid*, but he had no idea why. It did not matter. He had work to do. He moved onto the ketch on August 22 and immediately busied his small crew unloading the supplies she carried. It was not easy. The ketch had more than six thousand gallons of water on board, as well as other supplies, and it took three stops to unload the cargo. One of them was on the night of August 24.

The squadron set out to attack the bashaw's stronghold at 9:00 p.m., only to return to its anchorage two hours later when a gale began to whip across the harbor. Preble ordered Israel to replenish water on the *Argus* and the young lieutenant navigated the *Intrepid* toward the brig. The only way to transfer the heavy water casks was to rig a crane using the boom of the mainsail. The small crew used blocks and pulleys to hoist the water casks out of the hold, then used another set of blocks and lines to manhandle the boom toward the brig, where *Argus* crewmen grabbed hold of lines and guided the water casks onto the deck. Normally a physically tough task, the heaving seas on August 24 made the job even more difficult. The fact the operation took place under the at-times unkind and overly critical gaze of Commodore Preble only added to the stress.

Israel did his best to keep the little ketch steady but the waves slammed the sixty-foot *Intrepid* into the side of *Argus* several times. Finally, Master Commandant Isaac Hull ordered Israel to cease the operation until the seas abated somewhat. Despite the difficulties, Israel managed to deliver to the *Argus* its full share of supplies and brought supplies to two other vessels, including the *Constitution*, all without earning the commodore's wrath.[13]

———•—•———

Master Commandant Richard Somers knew the mission with the *Intrepid* was his chance to finally top his close friend and rival Capt. Stephen Decatur. The battles with the gunboats had pointed out the differences between the two, and once more those differences balanced one another in combat.

Decatur built on the stature he gained after destroying the *Philadelphia* by capturing a pair of pirate gunboats. Somers gained his reputation for steadiness and courage once the U.S. squadron directly engaged the Tripolitans. After sinking three enemy vessels in the first battle on August 3, Somers followed up his victories in the battle of August 28 by sinking at least two more pirate gunboats and wrecking a handful more. Unlike the charismatic Decatur, who could captivate others by simply entering a room, Somers earned his respect from his actions. "He certainly was an extraordinary man," said Midn. Robert Spence. "He united everything that made the man or the officer, possessing more firmness and determination than any man I ever saw; sought danger in every shape—dangerous undertakings were the most pleasing ones to him."[14]

As much as they complemented one another, there were noticeable differences between the two old friends other than their success in battle. The biggest difference was in their fashion sense. Decatur usually dressed casually, unless he was to meet with Preble. Simple blue duck or white linen topped with a straw hat was his favorite uniform, and he often looked more like one of his ordinary sailors than an officer.[15] Somers cut a much sharper image. The twenty-five-year-old had money—as did Decatur—but where Decatur saved his cash for dress uniforms, Somers made sure each of his uniforms sent the message that he was an officer. While he was in Syracuse and later Messina, Somers paid several visits to tailor shops and ordered five silk uniforms, three wool uniforms, and one gingham overcoat. Something of a dandy, Somers' wardrobe also included four cashmere vests, silk drawers, a dozen silk shirts, silk cravats and handkerchiefs, and a complete set of winter clothing.[16]

No one seemed to object to his dress. There are no records that any of Somers' crew ever commented on his clothes, and when it came to his character, his crew and anyone that knew him were universal in praise. "Captain Somers was as brave and enterprising an officer as ever stepped the deck of a ship," said Purser John Darby of the frigate *John Adams*, "possessing every virtue that the human heart is susceptible of."[17]

Somers busied himself with the plan for the *Intrepid*, taking time out to once more command Gunboat No. 1 in the battle planned for September 3. He wanted to take the *Intrepid* into Tripoli harbor September 1, but poor winds prevented the expedition.[18]

Carpenters from the *Constitution* swarmed onto the *Intrepid* to transform the ketch into an "infernal." They first stripped everything they could off the ship, creating as much space as they could in the small hold and cramped cabin in which seventy-five men once hid. Once they created the space, the carpenters built a storage hold that ran from the mainmast toward the bow. The new room was the main magazine; almost as soon as it was ready, men from the *Constitution* began stowing gunpowder in the new hold.

Aft of the new hold, the carpenters laid a series of long wooden boxes that protected the fuses that ran from the gunpowder to the deck. Sailors packed the aft section full of combustibles—old rope, oil, wood, scraps—and more powder. On deck, sailors piled shells of various sizes, ranging from 18- and 36-pound exploding shells for carronades to the 9-inch shells the mortar boats had heaved at Tripoli.[19]

The last chore was laying fuses Somers could light from one spot. Decatur, Stewart, and Preble all had different ideas on what to use. Somers' two friends favored anything that would give their comrade the best chance at escape. The commodore experimented with several types of fuses, finally settling on a port-fire fuse. This was a slow-burning line. It would give Somers and his crew time to escape, but also could allow any pirates that boarded the vessel more than enough time to cut the fuse. During one meeting, Preble asked Somers whether the several minutes in which a port fire burned would give Somers enough time to escape. "I think we can sir," Somers reportedly said. Preble then asked Somers whether he wanted to shorten the port fire. "I ask for no port fire at all, sir," Somers told his commander.[20] Ultimately, Somers decided to use a simple gunpowder train and had the carpenters build wooden ducts to carry the powder throughout the ketch. The fuse would allow just a few seconds from the time Somers lit it to when the *Intrepid* would explode. It was all he believed he would need.

The short fuse was nearly synonymous with the overall mission. Somers had no intention of spending all night in Tripoli harbor. The *Intrepid* would make its way past any pirate outposts the same way she had back in February when Decatur used her to destroy the *Philadelphia*. Her familiar shape, the Americans believed, would fool the Tripolitans once more, allowing the ketch to get right into the middle of the pirate fleet.

Carpenters, under Somers' and Israel's direction, placed 115 barrels of gunpowder—roughly fifteen tons—and 150 shells on the ketch. The amount of powder and shot on the *Intrepid*, Preble believed, would destroy not only the bashaw's ships, but also a considerable portion of the town. It could also provide the pirates with a much-needed resupply if it fell into the Tripolitans' hands. Preble stressed the need to prevent the *Intrepid* from falling into the bashaw's hands.

Somers "expressed his determination not to allow himself to be captured," telling Preble he would blow up the *Intrepid* and all on board her rather than surrender. "Both were singularly quiet men in their ordinary habits," said Henry Preble in a letter to Preble biographer James Fenimore Cooper, "perfectly free from anything like noisy declarations or empty boastings of what they intended to perform, and their simply announcement of their intentions not to be taken appears to have made a deep and general impression on their brethren in arms."[21]

Although Somers was determined not to provide the bashaw with either more prisoners or a new supply of powder and shot, he did not see the mission as a one-way trip. The fuse would provide fifteen minutes for the crew to get off the ketch.[22] The *Intrepid* sailors planned to make their escape in a pair of cutters—the two fastest rowing vessels in the squadron. One, a six-oar boat, would come from the *Constitution* and the other, with four oars, would come from the *Syren*. Once they had lit the fuse, the men would board the cutters and row away, hopefully timing their escape with the destruction of the pirate fleet.

———◆ ◆———

The battles of August 28 to September 3 gave Richard Somers the chance to repeatedly rethink his plan. Everything seemed ready. After the carpenters had finished their work on the *Intrepid* on August 30, all Somers had to do was pick his crew. Preble said twelve men would sail on the *Intrepid*—two officers and ten enlisted men. Four of the enlisted men would come from Somers' ship, the *Nautilus*, while six would come from the *Constitution*. The commodore also would select the second-in-command for the mission.

The small crew was not just a reflection of the danger the mission involved. Despite the arrival of the *John Adams* in August with an extra fifty sailors for the squadron, manpower remained a problem for Preble as he tried to man the eight gunboats, two mortar boats, ships' cutters, and smaller vessels in the flotilla. The *Nautilus* would provide crew as a matter of honor to her skipper, Richard Somers, just as the *Enterprise* had provided the bulk of the men for the *Philadelphia* raid back in February under Decatur. The *Nautilus*, however, did not have that many men to spare, which is likely why Preble decided to augment the *Nautilus* crewmen with sailors from the flagship.

Because of the dangerous nature of the mission, Preble mandated anyone who went on the *Intrepid* would have to volunteer. Nearly every officer, especially the younger midshipmen and lieutenants, asked to go. The competition for the second officer spot was fiercest among the young acting lieutenants who had received a taste of command and a feel for combat on the gunboats or in independent command of one of the squadron's smaller craft.

Midn. Robert Spence, the young officer who had survived the explosion of Gunboat No. 9, asked family friend Capt. Stephen Decatur as well as his own skipper, Master Commandant Charles Stewart, to put in a word on his behalf. Both officers sent notes to Preble pushing for Spence's inclusion, but they were already too late. Lt. Henry Wadsworth, the only Maine native among the officers other than the commodore, managed to get his commander's ear and secured the coveted spot.

Wadsworth temporarily had commanded Gunboat No. 2 after James Decatur's death and continued serving on the vessel throughout August, with temporary returns to the flagship when Preble needed extra hands. He also had gained valuable experience as first officer on the *Scourge* during the spring blockade. On the morning of September 1, Wadsworth sent a note to the commodore, saying he wished "to volunteer his service on board the infernal destined for the harbor of Tripoli." At that point, no one even knew the plan, but it did not stop Wadsworth, Spence, Israel, and others from volunteering. Whether it was Wadsworth's experience on the gunboats or the hometown connection, Preble selected the twenty-year-old Maine native to sail on the *Intrepid*.[23] No one seemed to bother telling Israel. The young acting lieutenant commanded the ketch throughout the conversion work and continued in command of her through the battle on September 3.

Once he knew his second-in-command, Somers selected his four enlisted crew from the *Nautilus*. He gathered every member of the crew from Gunboats No. 1 and No. 2 as well as those men still on the *Nautilus*. Without divulging the entire plan, Somers told the assembled eighty-two sailors and officers he needed four men to volunteer for a dangerous mission on board the *Intrepid*. It was no secret the ketch was now a fireship, although no one knew exactly how the Americans planned to use her. However, for the enlisted men, like the officers, it did not matter. The mission offered a chance at glory, possibly a chance at prize money, and, most of all, a chance to strike at the heart of the enemy. Every enlisted man stepped forward when Somers asked for volunteers.

Just like Decatur half a year before, Somers would have to select the volunteers. He decided to go with four men who had served on board Gunboat No. 1 with him. All four were from Maryland and were senior rates and likely had experience in the Navy prior to enlisting on the *Nautilus*.

Quartermaster James Harris enlisted in the Navy in 1801 and served under John Rodgers—and young Joseph Israel—on the frigate *Maryland*. When Rodgers returned from France in 1802 and Congress sold the *Maryland*, Harris apparently mustered out of service.[24] He enlisted to serve on the *Nautilus* during a recruiting drive in Annapolis and was one of the crew Somers picked to serve on Gunboat No. 1.[25]

GM James Simms, BM William Keith, and Able SN Thomas Tompline also all likely had some prior naval service or military service before they enlisted on the *Nautilus* in August 1803. Like Harris, they fought with Somers on Gunboat No. 1 throughout August, distinguishing themselves enough that their commander chose them for the *Intrepid* mission.[26]

Henry Wadsworth had the task of picking the men from the *Constitution*, and, like Somers, he had plenty of volunteers. The young Maine native chose four men that had helped convert the *Intrepid* from ketch to infernal—Able SN Isaac W. Downes, SN Robert Clark, SN William Harrison, and SN Jacob Williams. SN Peter Penner also made the cut, as did a curious choice, Able SN Hugh McCormick.

McCormick was something of a hard case when he joined the *Constitution*'s crew in July 1803. Most likely a deserter from the Royal Navy, McCormick enlisted in New York and reported for duty on July 20.[27] Within just a couple of months, he had run afoul of Preble, receiving twelve lashes on October 4 for neglect of duty.[28] Two weeks later guards caught McCormick as he tried to desert while the *Constitution* was in Gibraltar. Preble ordered him confined in irons and threw him into the brig, where he languished until December 9.[29] Upon his release, McCormick was apparently a changed man. He served without problems throughout 1804 and obviously impressed young Wadsworth enough he was one of the men the lieutenant selected to go on the *Intrepid*.

The final selections gave the *Intrepid* her Preble-mandated complement of two officers and ten enlisted men. All they needed now was a decent breeze and a little bit of good fortune.

CHAPTER 22

THE INFERNAL

SEPTEMBER 4 STARTED OUT slightly better for Marine private William Ray than any day since the U.S. Navy had started launching direct attacks on Tripoli. Ray was one of the prisoners from the now-destroyed *Philadelphia*, and was the one who doled out the meager rations to the rest of the enlisted men. The prisoners' full allotment of food—which their commander William Bainbridge paid for out of his own pocket—stopped in June as the Americans tightened their blockade of Tripoli. Their rations shrank again, Ray said, when Commodore Edward "began his invasions."[1]

The captive crewmen of the *Philadelphia* were the only Americans the pirates could actually strike. Daily beatings and food denial were only part of the bluejackets' ordeal. Bashaw Yusuf Karamanli had standing orders that the Americans were to clean up the city following any attack from Preble. Karamanli did issue orders forbidding his guards from beating the Americans, but Ray said "his orders were insincere and illusive [*sic*], for the very next day [after issuing the order] he stood by and saw several of us severely beaten innocently, without the least apparent dissatisfaction."[2]

Beyond the beatings, the guards often tormented the prisoners with exaggerated claims of American losses. On August 17 the guards told the Americans that bodies of fifteen of their comrades "were found drifted ashore on the beach, westward of the town. By an epaulette on his shoulder one of them was known to be a lieutenant."[3] Although the bashaw promised the Americans they could bury their dead, their guards prevented them going to the beach and, since the "bodies" were "found" eight days after the attack of August 7, chances are the guards simply made up the story to torment their captives.

By the end of August the combination of short rations and long days of hard labor had had a telling effect of the prisoners. "A number of our men fainted and dropped beneath the weight they were compelled to sustain," Ray said. "They were brought half dead to the prison,"

Danish consul Nicholas Nissen finally managed to convince the bashaw to give the prisoners more food, and this time Nissen paid for the rations. Ray said the prisoners received a loaf of bread every day and an allotment of meat and vegetables twice a week. The new rations began to arrive on September 2. The improved food brought about a return to near normalcy among the prisoners. "This was a great alleviation to our hunger-pained breasts," Ray wrote. Two days later he helped divide the rations as he had each morning for the past month and then joined his fellow prisoners as they went to work clearing the debris from the attack the previous night.[4]

Capt. Stephen Decatur and Master Commandant Charles Stewart boarded the ketch the *Intrepid* just after noon, with Lt. Joseph Bainbridge trailing behind them. Decatur and Stewart were on the *Intrepid* at the request of their long-time friend Richard Somers. Other officers of the squadron, including two lieutenant commandants, Charles Morris and John H. Dent, were also on board, paying their respects to the commander of what the squadron expected to be the final mission against the pirates of Tripoli.

Somers somehow managed to find room in the little cabin Decatur occupied when he used the *Intrepid* to destroy the frigate *Philadelphia* in February. Although outwardly still the same ship, internally the *Intrepid* was completely different. The cabin Decatur shared with other officers back in February was now completely packed with gunpowder and combustibles. Somers squeezed himself into the small space remaining as he spoke with his friends and comrades. "Somers was grave and entirely without any affectation of levity or indifference," recalled one officer. "He maintained his usual tranquil and quiet manner."[5]

The mission on September 4 would be the third time in four nights Somers would attempt to bring the *Intrepid* into Tripoli. His first attempt was on September 1, almost the minute the carpenters finished their work converting the ketch into a fireship. At 8:00 p.m. that night the crew, including Joseph Israel, weighed anchor and sailed toward the western entrance of the harbor. Two hours later, Somers returned. The winds that were blowing out of the north had shifted around to the south, preventing even the lateen-rigged *Intrepid* from moving forward.[6]

Somers waited until later in the evening the next night. He weighed anchor at 11:00 p.m. on September 2, and made it as far as the harbor entrance. Once again the winds shifted, forcing him to turn back. Determined to carry out the assault, Somers kept the *Intrepid* off the harbor entrance for more than an hour, circling in vain to fight the wind. Finally, just after 1 a.m. on September 3, the disappointed master commandant ordered the ketch to return to the squadron assembly point. As the *Intrepid* returned to the flotilla, the pirates belatedly appeared to awaken. Midn. Charles Ridgeley reported seeing lights and hearing shouts among the defenders, but the Tripolitans never fired a shot. It was anyone's guess as to whether the defenders suspected anything.[7]

Bashaw Yusuf Karamanli knew the Americans planned another attack, but he did not know what kind. The first two assaults on his city had been primarily battles between gunboats. The next were more serious, at least for the pirate leader, as the Americans used their mortar boats to bombard the city, with the most destructive attack coming on September 3. Indeed, it was obvious to the Tripolitans that they had nothing to really challenge the American flagship in firepower. Edward Preble brought the *Constitution* within pistol shot of the city's defenses three times, and all three times the big frigate silenced batteries and caused considerable damage.

Despite the pounding, however, Karamanli remained defiant. The bashaw believed he had seen every weapon the Americans could bring against him. In addition, Karamanli was convinced the U.S. squadron was not as strong as it appeared to be. He correctly guessed the *John Adams*, which continued to sail in plain sight but took no part in combat, was armed *en flute*.[8] The belief the Americans were not as strong as they appeared emboldened the bashaw, who was "determined to encounter all of your forces in order that Europe and Africa may conceive a favorable opinion of his strength and courage," French consul Bonaventure Beaussier informed Preble.[9] Karamanli also believed Preble was up to something after the aborted mission of the *Intrepid* on September 2. Following the attack of September 3, he rearranged his defenses, putting a picket line of three gunboats close to the harbor entrance while keeping the rest in the safety of the mole.[10]

There were no illusions among the crew of the *Intrepid*. The two aborted attempts to sail the ketch into Tripoli created a near-certain belief among the bluejackets that there was little chance of them catching the pirates by surprise a third time. It did not change the Americans' determination to succeed. Indeed, to no one's surprise, when on the morning of September 4 Master Commandant Richard Somers assembled the crew of the *Nautilus* to give the four volunteers from the schooner one final chance to back out of the mission, no sailor accepted the opportunity to do so.

With his crew gathered around him on the decks, Somers shared his belief the Americans had lost the element of surprise but said that no matter what, he planned to go ahead with the mission. He added his intention to blow up the *Intrepid* rather than let the ketch, with its valuable cargo of powder, fall into the hands of the pirates, who were running low on ammunition. According to Midn. Charles Ridgeley of the *Nautilus*, Somers told the crew "no man need accompany him who had not come to the resolution to blow himself up rather than be captured and that such was fully his own determination." The crew gave its captain an immediate response—three cheers. "The gallant crew rose, as a single man, with the resolution of yielding up their lives sooner than surrender to their enemies," Ridgeley said. "Each stepped forward and begged as a favor that he might be permitted to apply the match.... It was a glorious moment...and made an impression on the hearts of all witnessing it, never to be forgotten." For Ridgeley and the other officers, the bravery of Somers and his vounteers made an indelible mark.[11]

When Somers finished and the cheers of the crew gave way to renwewed focus on the task at hand, QM James Harris, Gunner's Mate James Simms, BM William Keith, and Able SN Thomas Tompline—the four enlisted volunteers from the *Nautilus*—made their final preparations to board the *Intrepid*. They shook hands with every member of the schooner's crew, "as if they already knew that their fate was doomed," Ridgeley related. Each made his goodbye and, in a somewhat macabre scene that Ridgeley described, made their oral wills: "'I say, Sam Jones, I leave you my blue jacket and duck trousers, stowed away in my bag,' and, 'Bill Curtis, you may have the tarpaulin hat and Guernsey frock and them petticoat trousers I got in Malta—and mind boys, when you get home, give a good account of us!'" As one of the few officers left on *Nautilus*, Ridgeley said the duty of carrying out those last-minute instructions fell to him; he carried them out "to the very letter."[12]

A similar scene played out on the *Constitution* as Lt. Henry Wadsworth gathered Able SN Isaac W. Downes, Able SN Hugh McCormick, seamen Robert Clark, William Harrison, Peter Penner, and Jacob Williams, and rowed over to the *Intrepid*. With them was Joseph Israel.

———◆◆———

Capt. Stephen Decatur and Master Commandant Charles Stewart stood next to their childhood friend Richard Somers as he calmly discussed the night's work. The three friends also undoubtedly talked about their days as schoolboys in Philadelphia and their time together on the *United States* under old John Barry. The happy memories, however, provided them with only slight comfort for the impending danger Somers faced cast a heavy pall over the trio. "They all knew the enterprise was one of extreme hazard," Oliver

Hazard Perry later told Somers' nephew, J. B. Somers, "and the two who were to remain behind felt a deep interest in the fate of him who was to go."[13]

A midshipman on the *Constitution*, Perry was one of many officers who stopped on the *Intrepid*. When he shook Somers' hand, he said it was Somers and not the normally more charismatic Decatur who left a lasting impression. "He had a definite aim; he hungered and thirsted for naval distinction; it was his chief desire to be an honor to his country," Perry said. "This clearly was his ruling passion."[14] It was a passion his friends shared, although the officers that visited Somers all said Decatur looked far graver than normal. The new captain never wrote how he felt on the death of his younger brother, James, in the battle of August 3. Now, his closest friend was readying to embark on what most in the squadron believed was a one-way mission.

The bond between Decatur and Somers apparently transcended every attachment except family. Decatur had a "sweetheart," a young woman in Philadelphia, but how often he wrote to her is a matter of mystery. He certainly did not marry her. The captain, in fact, did not show much interest in romance until 1805, after he returned to the United States and met Norfolk socialite Susan Wheeler. Somers did not seem to have any one special woman waiting for him at home, although in a letter to his sister he begged her to "remember me to all the pretty young ladies."[15] Thus, those few times aside, it seemed neither friend cared much about starting his own family either while the other friend lived or while both believed they had more glory to achieve. When they were together, it seemed there was nothing they could not accomplish. As they talked on September 4 in the cramped cabin of the *Intrepid*, both almost certainly realized their world was about to change, but neither Somers nor Decatur was willing to actually voice that concern.

The talking done, Somers rose from his little chair and removed a gold ring from his left hand. The ring was a treasure to Somers. Although outwardly just a simple gold ring, it contained a lock of hair from Somers' boyhood hero, George Washington. Somers removed a small pocketknife he always carried and carefully cut the ring into three pieces. He handed a piece to Decatur and one to Stewart, and kept the third piece for himself. The three men shook hands and left the cabin.[16]

As they walked out on the deck, Decatur "admonished Somers to take care" the pirates did not board the *Intrepid*, "as it was the intention to carry to the ketch some distance within them." Somers, happy at last to have the lead position over his friend, told Decatur not to worry. He said he doubted the Tripolitans would even put up a fight based on their unwillingness to face the Americans in open combat. "The Turks have got to be so shy," he said, "they would be more likely to cut and run" on his approach than to approach and meet him.[17]

With that, Decatur and Stewart said farewell to their friend and left the *Intrepid*. The last officer to leave was Lt. George Washington Reed, the commander of the *Nautilus* while Somers was on the *Intrepid*. Reed's orders were simple: the *Nautilus* was to remain as close as possible to the *Intrepid* until she entered the harbor. Reed was then to pick up the two cutters carrying the *Intrepid* crew after they had lit the fuses."Somers was cheerful, though calm," Reed said, "and perfect order and method prevailed in the little craft."[18]

At 8:00 p.m. the *Intrepid*'s crew weighed anchor and, with the *Argus* and *Vixen* riding shotgun, the little ketch followed the *Nautilus* toward the harbor entrance. Somers expected to reach his target sometime on September 4 between 11:00 p.m. and midnight.

The *Argus* and *Vixen* made a course for the rocks at the western entrance of Tripoli harbor. From that point, the brig and schooner could cover the *Intrepid* as she sailed past the rocks into the inner anchorage. The *Nautilus* shortened sail to allow the *Intrepid* to pass, then followed the ketch toward the entrance. Midn. Charles Ridgeley took up a position on the bow. "Though it was very dark, we never lost sight of her," said Midshipman Ridgeley. "I had been directed by the first lieutenant to keep constant watch of her." Not a light showed from the *Intrepid*. All Ridgeley could see was her shape, looking ghostly in the gathering darkness. After an hour of maneuvering, the *Intrepid* slipped past the rocks.[19]

Without a pilot and using only the stars to guide him, Somers steered the *Intrepid* into the inner harbor at 9:00 p.m. Overhead Polaris guided Somers as he slowly headed east by south into the harbor. The constellation Draco, the Dragon, hung over the city, giving the *Intrepid* a perfect aiming point as the ketch approached the anchored pirate fleet.[20] It was no small feat. He had to keep the ketch almost dead center in the channel to avoid the rocks while using them to help hide the *Intrepid*'s silhouette.The shoreline was as dark, if not darker than, the sea. Behind him, the *Nautilus* remained at the harbor entrance, sailing a tight circle near the rocks. From there, Reed continued to watch the ketch as she crept closer to her prey.

Further back, the Americans tried desperately to watch *Intrepid* as she sailed into action. Master Commandant Charles Stewart stood near the helm of the brig *Syren*, peering into the darkness. Like every other officer and man in the squadron, Stewart tried his best to catch a glimpse of the *Intrepid*.

Lookouts on the *Syren* said they could just make out the shape of the *Intrepid* as she crept closer to her target ghosting her way nearer and nearer to the row of gunboats anchored under the guns of Tripoli castle.[21] At the same time, Lt. Charles Morris on the *Constitution* craned his neck along the rail to get a glimpse of anything stirring in the harbor. Like every officer, Morris said he felt a "painful anxiety" as he waited for the outcome of the *Intrepid* mission.[22] By 9:45 p.m., Midshipman Ridgeley on the *Nautilus* could barely make out the *Intrepid* as she wafted toward the bashaw's fleet. On board the *Syren*, Stewart had also nearly lost sight of the ketch as she closed in on the Tripolitan defenses.

One minute later, Midn. Michael B. Carroll, standing next to Stewart on the *Syren*, shouted, "I see a light!" and pointed toward the ketch. The officer said the light looked like, "a lantern being carried by some person in quick motion along a vessel's deck."[23] Morris, on the *Constitution*, did not see the lantern but reported hearing the firing of three cannon (Sailing Master Nathan Haraden said it was two shots). Some thirty seconds passed in utter silence.[24]

Then at 9:47 p.m a thunderous explosion shook Tripoli harbor. "For a moment the flash illumined the whole heavens around, while the terrific concussion shook everything far and near," Ridgeley said. "Then all was hushed again, and every object veiled in a darkness of double gloom."[25] The minute-long explosion filled the harbor with sparks as the shells the *Intrepid* carried launched crazily. The blast lit up the *Intrepid* for a split second and some sailors reported seeing her mast twisting in the air. All around the squadron, officers and sailors alike raced to watch the spectacle. Although they had no idea what had happened, they all knew the *Intrepid* exploded far too early.

⸺ ⬩ ⸺

Despite the premature explosion, Lt. George Washington Reed ordered the *Nautilus* to move into the entrance to Tripoli harbor after the *Intrepid* blew up. Reed's mission was to pick up the crew of the *Intrepid* as it rowed out of the harbor after detonating the ketch. As "the silence of death" cast an eery hush over his crew, Reed decided to move in and pick up any survivors whle the "din of kettle drums, beating to arms, with the noise of confusion and alarm was heard from the inhabitants on the shore." Reed ordered his crew to "Show a light" to guide any survivors from the *Intrepid* to the schooner. The minute the *Nautilus* entered the harbor with lanterns glowing, "hundreds of shot, from an equal number of guns, of heavy caliber, from the batteries near, came rattling over and around us," the midshipman said. "We heeded them not. One thought, and one feeling alone had possession of our souls—the preservation of Somers and his crew."[26]

A desperate hope consumed the remaining ships and their crews. On board the *Constitution*, Preble ordered the firing of a red rocket, a pre-arranged signal for Somers to return. He received no reply. Preble's crew repeated the signal every fifteen minutes until 9:00 a.m., but never received an answer while on the *Nautilus*, "the anxiety on board became intense," Ridgeley said. The schooner crewmen did everything they could to find their commander and comrades who had taken the *Intrepid* into Tripoli harbor, all the time exposing themselves to enemy fire. "Men, with lighted lanterns, hung themselves over the sides of the vessel till their heads almost touched the water—a position in which an object, on its surface, can be seen farthest on a dark night—with the hope of discovering something which would give assurance of its safety," Ridgeley said. "Still, no boat came and no signal was given and the unwelcome conclusion was forced upon us at last."[27] Indeed, the *Nautilus* remained at the harbor mouth until 9:00 a.m., all the time under fire from Tripolitan shore batteries. The *Argus*, *Syren*, and *Vixen* joined her as the entire squadron "lingered in vain in the hope that someone, at last, of the number might yet be rescued by us, from a floating plank or spar, to tell of his companions' fate."[28] No one from the *Intrepid* ever returned.

CHAPTER 23

"PREBLE'S BOYS"

JONATHAN COWDERY, SHIP'S SURGEON of the frigate *Philadelphia*, stood on the beach the morning of September 6 with Boatswain Lewis Heximer and watched as a group of Arabs picked through what was left of the *Intrepid*.

The day before, Cowdery said, Bashaw Yusuf Karamanli had declared an "eid" or feast in celebration of his city narrowly escaping destruction. "The bashaw and his people had a thanksgiving to Mahomet on the occasion," Cowdery said. "Their ceremony was prayer in doleful tone and singing, accompanied with the sound of an instrument made by drawing a skin over a hoop."[1]

The "doleful" sound of the celebration no doubt matched the spirits of the Americans. Capt. William Bainbridge arrived on the beach soon after Cowdery with several officers, and together they attempted to identify the remains.

It was a gruesome task. The explosion of the *Intrepid* mangled most of the bodies of her crew. The small pieces left of the ketch drifted ashore near the round battery that guarded the western entrance to the harbor. Arabs found what remained of a pair of bodies in the wreck. Another body was in the six-oared cutter Somers' crew had planned to use to make their escape. Six bodies washed ashore and another four were found floating in the harbor.

The bashaw paid his subjects one Spanish dollar in gold for each body part they produced, and by the morning of August 6 Tripolitan troops had gathered the remains of thirteen Americans. Bainbridge examined the six bodies that washed ashore and described them as "being so much disfigured, it was impossible to recognize any feature known to me or even to distinguish an officer from a seaman."[2]

Cowdery also examined the bodies and, after looking at their hands and bits of uniforms, selected three as officers. Since it turned out to be the number of officers on the *Intrepid*, no one questioned the identifications. The *Philadelphia* doctor made his determination after noticing the three officers had more "delicate" hands than the ordinary seamen, although the state of the bodies, after soaking in the harbor, rotting under the sun, and being blown up probably did not give Cowdery much with which to work.[3]

Complicating the identification, packs of dogs had gnawed on the bodies before the locals could collect them. Dutch consul Antoine Zuchet said Karamanli put the bodies on display to allow the inhabitants "to hurl curses and insults at the corpses" for three days before he allowed the Americans to bury them. Zuchet, however, claimed the pirates found fourteen bodies, thirteen of them intact, all in the wreckage of the *Intrepid*. The Dutch consul made no mention of the bounty Karamanli offered.[4]

Local accounts correlate more closely to those of Cowdery and Bainbridge than to Zuchet. According to local stories, Karamanli was in no rush to collect the remains of the American "invaders," but neither did he want them rotting on the shore. As the bodies of Somers and his crew began to wash up, the bashaw waited for at least a day before he offered the bounty. The Arab sources confirm Cowdery's story of the condition and seem to agree it was the explosion rather than dogs that caused the bulk of the damage to the corpses.[5]

After making his identifications, Cowdery received permission from the bashaw to bury the remains. A small group of American prisoners placed the ten enlisted men in a grave near the beach. They buried the three officers "southward and eastward of Tripoli castle."[6]

The loss of the *Intrepid* hit the American squadron hard. The death of Richard Somers was devastating for the bluejackets. Somers, along with Stephen Decatur, was one of the squadron's most popular officers, and his death sent a shock wave through officers and enlisted men alike.

"The loss of these brave officers was severely felt by our small squadron, being universally esteemed for their private virtues and respected for their professional talents," said Charles Morris.[7]

John Darby of the *John Adams* lamented that "the loss of those brave Officers and men are much to be regretted by their country and friends," while Commo. Edward Preble said Somers and his officers showed "conspicuous bravery, talents and merit. They uniformly distinguished themselves in action; were beloved and lamented by the whole squadron."[8]

Somers' death weighed most heavily on Capt. Stephen Decatur and Master Commandant Charles Stewart. Earlier in the campaign, Decatur's younger brother, James, had died in action. Now, his closest friend was dead.

Overnight, Decatur went from somewhat carefree to pensive; those around him were well aware of the change in his personality.

"They had so much in common, both sensitive, both proud and brave, both jealous for the service," said a fellow officer. "Decatur knew the soul of him, knew the quizzical smile, the quick retort, the manner of the man. It was impossible to believe Dick Somers was really gone. . . . Grim, Decatur gradually came to accept the fact, but meanwhile a great sadness filled him."[9]

It was the same for Charles Stewart. "A heavy sense of gloom settled in," as he absorbed the loss of "a friend who was like a brother."[10]

———◆◆———

Mixed with the grief and shock was a maelstrom of mystery surrounding the loss of Somers and the *Intrepid*. One of the first questions many of the men in the squadron wanted answered was why Joseph Israel had been on the *Intrepid*.

The twenty-year-old Marylander was not part of the original complement Preble allotted for the mission on the *Intrepid*. Israel did command the ketch for a time and helped oversee her conversion to a fireship; he also went with Somers on his first two attempts to take the *Intrepid* into Tripoli harbor.

On September 4, however, Preble reportedly denied Israel permission to join the mission. Why Preble wanted Israel to skip the mission is unknown. Perhaps the commodore, like Somers, believed the Americans had lost the element of surprise and he wanted to keep Israel safe. Preble had already tagged Israel as one of the more able midshipmen and he likely was not willing to possibly sacrifice three of his best officers.

John Darby of the *John Adams* never met Israel but said others told him he "was held high in the esteem of the commodore" and with young Henry Wadsworth "bid fare [*sic*] to be an honor to their country in the line of their profession."[11]

Charles Ridgeley summed up the surprise many in the squadron felt when word spread that Israel had gone on the mission. "To our astonishment, we learned that Lieutenant Israel, a gallant youth, had accompanied [Somers] in the expedition and had shared in his fate."[12]

The midshipman on the *Nautilus* said he heard Israel went to the *Intrepid* with final orders from Preble. Other officers, however, quickly quashed that rumor. There was simply no way Somers, who stood up to Preble regarding the first prize ship Somers took in February, would allow Israel to come on board the *Intrepid* with orders from his commander and not send the young man back to the flagship with a response.

The most likely explanation was that when Israel accompanied Wadsworth and the six volunteers from the *Constitution* as they rowed from the frigate to the ketch he simply boarded the *Intrepid* and presented Somers with a fait accompli. Somers, "admiring his determination to make the party," allowed Israel to join the crew. Whether the fact the Marylander was the ominous thirteenth man bothered Somers, he never said before he left on his mission.[13]

The biggest mystery, however, was what had happened to the *Intrepid*. Every member of the squadron knew the *Intrepid* exploded far too early, and very quickly there were three theories as to why.

The first was that someone on board the ketch had accidentally set off the explosives. The second was that gunfire had pierced the thin hull of the *Intrepid* and started a fire with disastrous results. The third theory was that pirates had tried to board the *Intrepid* and Somers, true to his word, blew up the ship rather than allow her cargo of powder to fall into the bashaw's hands.

Charles Morris seemed to believe in both the boarding and accidental theories: "I was induced to believe that the enemy had discovered her approach and made the attempt to board her. In the ensuing confusion naturally consequent upon such an action, some sparks of fire were unfortunately communicated to the train which in a moment launched both the assailer and the assailed into eternity."[14]

Nearly every officer dismissed the accident idea as quickly as it rose. It apparently started on the *Syren*, where Midshipman Carroll claimed to see a light on the *Intrepid* for a brief second. That sighting led some to think a sailor had grown careless with a lantern. However, not even the *Syren*'s commander, Charles Stewart, believed Somers would ever allow that sort of slipshod behavior on a vessel he commanded.

Most of the squadron believed Commo. Edward Preble's assessment, that Somers intentionally blew up the *Intrepid* to prevent her capture. The American commander said he saw "one of the enemy's largest gunboats was missing and three others very much shattered and damaged, which the enemy were hauling on shore." The battered and missing warships, the commodore said, were clear evidence the pirates had attempted to board the *Intrepid*. Preble said the large gunboat undoubtedly was first to approach the ketch, and "without suspecting her to be a fireship, the missing boat had suddenly boarded her." As the other vessels moved in, Preble said, the crew of the *Intrepid* had made its decision. "The gallant Somers and heroes of his party, observing the other three boats surrounding them, and no prospect of escape, determined, at once, to prefer death and the destruction of the enemy to captivity and torturing slavery," Preble said. That Somers vowed to never surrender reinforced Preble's opinion. "They declared . . . that they would put a match to the magazine and blow themselves and their enemies up; determined, as there was no exchange of prisoners, that their country should never pay ransom for them nor the enemy receive a supply of powder through their means."[15]

Several officers, however, stuck to the idea that enemy fire caused the *Intrepid* to explode. Both Morris and the *Constitution* sailing master Nathaniel Haraden reported hearing cannon fire. The *Intrepid* passed within pistol shot of several shore batteries—the same batteries that used red-hot shot to destroy Gunboat No. 8 during the battle on August 7. "Nothing is more probable than that they jealously watched the movements of a vessel that was entering their harbor after dark, necessarily passing near, if not coming directly from the American squadron."[16]

To add to the confusion, reports from the Americans in Tripoli differed as to how much damage the *Intrepid* caused and how many men actually died.

Capt. William Bainbridge wrote in his journal, "The unfortunate scheme did no damage whatever to the Tripolitans, nor did it appear to heave them into confusion."[17] Marine private William Ray also doubted the story that Somers had deliberately destroyed the *Intrepid*. "If the enemy did suffer, or were thus destroyed, should we not have been informed of it?"[18]

Ray said none of the prisoners' best sources of information—Neapolitan prisoners, Jewish residents of Tripoli, and the various consuls—told the Americans about damage or casualties among the pirates following the *Intrepid* raid. However, the Marine apparently expected to hear of "hundreds" of Turkish casualties, a number Preble never used in his report.[19]

Surgeon Cowdery said six more bodies turned up on the beach on September 6—these after the Tripolitans had already collected the remains of the *Intrepid*'s thirteen-man crew. The bashaw denied the *Philadelphia* surgeon permission to examine the bodies, which he routinely did when the dead were Tripolitans. Cowdery made no other mention of the six bodies, but if they were pirates, they could only have died in the blast that claimed the *Intrepid*.[20]

The pirates celebrated the destruction of the *Intrepid* as a great victory. Karamanli claimed his gunners holed the fragile ketch with red-hot shot, which touched off the tons of powder on board the little ship. The bashaw, however, did not say whether it was gunners from the castle or forts or those on his picket line of gunboats that had attacked the *Intrepid*.[21]

In January 1805 U.S. diplomat William Eaton might have received the most complete report of what had happened. Eaton was in Alexandria, Egypt, trying to organize a force to support a coup in support of Hamet Karamanli. On January 25, 1805, Eaton wrote to Edward Preble, telling him about a chance meeting he had with a "Turkish officer" who said he had been in Tripoli on September 4.

According to the officer, two gunboats were waiting for the *Intrepid* near the harbor entrance. The pirates, he said, were not sure when the Americans would try an attack using the *Intrepid*, but they knew it was coming. On the night of September 4, just as Somers and his men rounded the reef outside the harbor, the pirate gunboat spotted the ketch and immediately engaged. The Turkish officer said pirates from the gunboats attempted to board the *Intrepid* and Somers, true to his word, blew up his vessel, taking the two pirate ships with him.

"Stating this fact the fellow wept," Eaton said. The Turk also said, "Tripoli had lost many men in the attacks of the Americans; the town was much damaged and the inhabitants were in such a state of consternation that nobody slept in the city and that no business was conducted there."[22]

Whatever the cause of the explosion, everyone in the squadron agreed the thirteen men on the *Intrepid* willingly sacrificed their lives.

"It is certain they died meritoriously," said Ray. "While valor, patriotism, and heroic actions meet with admiration, gratitude and applause, the names of Somers, Wadsworth, Israel and their brave companions in death, will live and shine on the annals of fame, and be registered in the catalogue of American martyrs in the cause of liberty."[23]

The loss of the *Intrepid* brought an end to Commo. Edward Preble's campaign against Tripoli. With his squadron low on powder and shot and the weather becoming more and more unsettled, Preble knew his window for victory was all but shut. On September 6 he gave Master Commandant Charles Stewart orders to escort the gunboats and mortar boats back to Syracuse along with the *Enterprise*, *Nautilus*, and *John Adams*. Preble decided to remain on station with the *Constitution*, *Argus*, and *Vixen* and wait for Commo. Samuel Barron to arrive.

Before he broke up his squadron, Preble shuffled around his officers. John Dent, who had commanded both the brig *Scourge* and Mortar Boat No. 2, returned to the *Scourge*. Preble ordered him to take the brig into Syracuse, where he was to take command of the *Nautilus*. Preble promoted Thomas Robinson, who had commanded Mortar Boat No. 1, to lieutenant commandant, and gave him command of the *Enterprise*. The commodore ordered Stephen Decatur to personally return the gunboats to the king of Naples before continuing on to Messina to await further orders.[24]

The *Syren*, *Nautilus*, and *Enterprise* left for Sicily on September 7. For Preble, it was a bitter parting as he continued to think of what he might have accomplished if he had had a bigger force. "The reinforcement of four frigates from the United States have not yet arrived but they have been anxiously expected from day to day these six weeks," he told Sir John Acton. "Had they arrived before the season compelled me to send off the gun and mortar vessels, we should have forced a peace or destroyed their town and cruisers." Yet, despite what he saw as a lack of support for his campaign from America, Preble said he was proud of accomplishments, telling Acton, "I think I may safely say that these barbarians have never suffered more from any Christian power."[25]

Preble was not alone in his assessment. Marine private William Ray said he believed Preble changed the way the Barbary pirates viewed the United States and its fighting men: "He left a lasting impression on the mind of the Bashaw and all the barbarians of Tripoli, of American bravery. Such unparalleled heroism appalled their savage bosoms, and struck them with the profoundest astonishment. That a single frigate should dare venture under the batteries, in the manner that Preble did, they imputed to madness, and that she ever lived to return was ascribed by them to some superior agency's invisible protection. He was considered as a prodigy of valor, and dreaded as the minister of destruction."[26]

On September 10 Commo. Samuel Barron with the frigate *President* and Capt. Hugh McNeill in the *Constellation* finally arrived off Tripoli. Despite the presence of three frigates, Barron denied permission for an assault on the city.

Before he left Tripoli, Preble had managed to sting his enemy Bashaw Yusuf Karamanli one final time. The effectiveness of the American blockade had Tripoli on the brink of starvation. Karamanli, on seeing the American squadron disperse, decided to run grain into his capital. On September 12 three ships tried to run the blockade off Tripoli. Preble, still in command of the *Constitution*, spotted the ships and immediately chased two of them while the *Argus* and *Constellation* chased the third.

The third vessel managed to elude her pursuers but Preble made sure the other two prizes did not get away. The *Constitution* chased the pair of ships for about eight miles before finally overtaking and boarding them. Preble said his men found grain—"about 16,000 bushels of wheat"—in the ships' holds. "Tripoli is in a state of starvation and there can be no doubt but these cargoes were meant as a supply and relief to our enemies."[27]

The year-long campaign against Tripoli had cost the Navy thirty dead and twenty-four wounded.

Capt. Edward Preble set sail for Malta on September 12, 1804, with his two prizes. Before leaving, Preble made it clear to Samuel Barron he had no intention of serving longer and wanted to return to the United States in the frigate *John Adams*, which Preble had already ordered to return home. He also issued one final order. On September 18, he turned command of the *Constitution* over to Capt. Stephen Decatur Jr.: "I shall feel pleased in leaving the *Constitution* under the command of that officer whose enterprising and manly conduct I have often witnessed, and whose merits eminently entitle him to so handsome a command."[28]

The outgoing commander of the U.S. Mediterranean squadron also took a moment to reflect on just how much the rest of his officers had matured. Almost a year to the day after he had arrived on station, the commodore and his cubs were no longer at odds. Gone was the rancor and near hatred the junior officers had felt for their commander. Gone, too, was their commander's disdain for their youth and at-times impetuous behavior. "The officers of the squadron have conducted themselves in a most gallant and handsome manner," Preble said. "The conduct of the different ships' companies has merited my warmest approbation since I have had the honor to command them."[29] As for his officers, each deeply felt the loss of a commander whom at first many despised but whom all came to respect.

Charles Morris, who as a midshipman had run afoul of Preble's temper a year earlier in Boston, was particularly upset at his commander's departure. Morris continued to serve under Samuel Barron and was decidedly unimpressed with how the new commodore conducted the war: "The removal of Preble from his command, besides being unjust to him, and entirely uncalled for by any necessities of the service, was a piece of bad policy on the part of the government. [Samuel] Barron, apart from the state of his health, was in no way comparable to Preble as an officer."[30]

No matter how much others extolled his conduct, however, Preble viewed his campaign as something of a failure. He had been unable to bring Yusuf Karamanli to terms and had failed to win the freedom of the crew of the *Philadelphia*. Before he left for home, Preble wrote to Capt. William Bainbridge one final time, telling his unfortunate friend, "I sincerely regret that it has not been in my power to liberate yourself, officers and crew. Be assured no exertion on my part has been wanting which our government and the forces under my command would justify. May God bless and preserve yourself and officers, and soon restore you to all your friends, is the ardent wish of one who feels sensibly your misfortunes."[31]

As always, Preble saved his most private thoughts for his wife: "You will learn from the medium of the public papers what has been the effect our operations against Tripoli, which I presume will be satisfactory to my country, having done all in my power to annoy the enemy and indeed all that so small a squadron could have effected. It would have been pleasant to have remained in command long enough to have conquered Tripoli but be assured I shall be amply compensated for the deprivation of my command with a ten thousand fold compensation by an affectionate reception from my lovely Mary."[32]

Capt. Edward Preble stayed in the Mediterranean until November, when Isaac Chauncey and the *John Adams* were finally ready to return to the United States. He spent much of his time on Malta with his close friend, governor Sir Alexander Ball, and in Naples, where King Ferdinand feted Preble as a hero.

His greatest honor came just before he left for America. On November 4, 1804, Capt. Stephen Decatur and several other officers called on their former commander to present a simple going-away gift. Decatur handed Preble an envelope and waited while Preble opened it:

> We the undersigned officers of the squadron late under your command cannot in justice suffer you to depart without giving you some small testimony of the very high estimation in which we hold you as an officer and commander. It is under these impressions Sir, that we beg leave to apprise you, that your supercedence in a command in which you have acquired so much honor to yourself and country, is by us deeply regretted.
>
> As you are about to return to your country, we all join most cordially in wishing you a pleasant passage, and sincerely hope that our Countrymen may generously bestow on you that which your important services so richly deserve, and believe us sincere in saying that we shall largely participate in any future event that may add to your fame and happiness.
>
> We have the honor to be, with the highest respect and esteem,
>
> Preble's Boys.[33]

The first man to sign was Decatur, followed by Stewart, Hull, and thirty-four other officers of the squadron. The former commodore read the letter Decatur gave him and thanked the officers before retiring to his room, where he took pen and paper and imparted one final lesson to his officers:

> I have this day been honored with your esteemed favor of the 4th and as I have been in the highest degree gratified by the support I have received from you in a difficult and dangerous service, so am I equally flattered by your approbation of my conduct as an officer and as commander of the squadron and be assured that I should always consider my reputation as an officer secure, while my views were seconded by that [illegible] and intrepidity for which you all so eminently distinguished.
>
> As it respects my supercedence I can only say that I could not have been more gratified than being allowed to com-

mand you until the present was brought to a conclusion but rank must be attended to, and where a measure is impelled by necessity, it becomes the duty of an officer to submit with cheerfulness. This I do, convinced as I am that you will serve your country under my successor with the same ardor as here before.

There can be no question but your country will be gratefully impressed by your exertions, and be assured that I reciprocate with sincerity your kind wishes for my future fame and happiness.[34]

With that, Capt. Edward Preble left the Mediterranean, never to return.

CHAPTER 24

HOMECOMING

OPERATIONS AGAINST TRIPOLI SPUTTERED OUT soon after Commo. Samuel Barron arrived with his squadron. Despite having nearly six times the firepower of Preble's force, Barron, whose health was failing, decided to maintain a partial blockade of the harbor while preparing for operations the coming spring.

The Americans also had a back-door plan to bring down Yusuf Karamanli. William Eaton, the former U.S. consul in Tripoli, went to Egypt to organize an army to support Hamet, Yusuf's brother, in a coup attempt. In the spring of 1805, Eaton led a mixed band of mercenaries, Arab retainers, and six U.S. Marines in an epic march across the Libyan desert to Derna. With the help of the *Argus* and *Nautilus*, Eaton and Hamet captured the city in June 1805, sending a chill through Yusuf.

The combined loss of Derna and the reappearance of Samuel Barron's huge flotilla brought Yusuf Karamanli to the bargaining table once more. Col. Tobias Lear, U.S. consul in Algiers, long a proponent of purchased peace, was the main American negotiator. After several weeks of wrangling, he cut a deal for the release of the crew of the *Philadelphia* for $60,000. The settlement did not include tribute, but the Americans agreed to abandon Hamet Karamanli, despite repeated promises to Hamet not to do so.

Eaton's exploit made him a celebrity, while Lt. Presley O'Bannon and his six Marines had given the Corps an immortal feat, one enshrined in the second line of the Marines' hymn, "to the shores of Tripoli."

The treaty, however, was extremely unpopular and divided not just the government, which nearly failed to ratify the deal, but also the Navy. Samuel Barron and John Rodgers supported the deal, while James Barron and Eaton decried it. The recriminations would last for years.

So, too, would the problems with the Barbary pirates. Those problems finally came to an end in 1815 when Stephen Decatur, now a commodore, led what was then the most powerful naval force in American history to the Mediterranean to dictate peace terms to all of the Barbary powers. Algiers, Tunis, and Morocco, as well as Tripoli, agreed to end attacks on American shipping and the practice of exacting tribute. Decatur's expedition led to the permanent establishment of an American naval presence in the Mediterranean.

⸺ • ⸺

Capt. Edward Preble returned to the United States in February 1805 to a hero's welcome. News of Preble's assaults on Tripoli and the aggressive manner in which he had executed the blockade of the pirate city reached America well before the commodore and people turned out in droves to see him.

Preble went to Washington, where a much-chagrined President Thomas Jefferson, who had sacked Preble and now saw the mistake in having done so, invited him to lunch at the White House. Secretary of State James Madison threw a ball in Preble's honor, while congressmen and senators jostled to meet the former commander of the Mediterranean squadron. It was all somewhat new to the now forty-four-year-old Preble. "I cannot but be a little flattered with the reception I have met with here," Preble wrote to his wife. "The people are disposed to think that I have rendered some service to my country."[1]

He remained deeply popular with the American people, who saw Preble as the embodiment of the spirit and determination of the new nation. According to the New England Gazette, people invented toasts honoring both the commodore and the U.S. Navy, the most common of which was, "Edward Preble! Our hero before Tripoli; may the laurels he has gained in the Old World be long the pride in the New."[2]

Preble's popularity only increased when word of a peace treaty—with its price tag—reached the United States in September 1805. The treaty was deeply unpopular in Washington, where the Senate nearly refused to confirm it. Preble mostly stayed out of the national debate, although his actions while in command spoke volumes. The old commodore would never have cut a deal, and the American people knew it. He told his brother, Henry, he believed the ransom deal was "ignominious," and that Lear had cut the deal "at the sacrifice of national honor."[3]

After his return to the United States, Preble turned his attention toward Jefferson's latest naval project, the construction of gunboats. He spent two years building and testing different designs, including those of the president himself. It was good work for the commodore, but also demanding; the stomach ailment that had plagued the commodore over the years grew steadily worse, with doctors telling Preble it was "consumption" or tuberculosis. Despite his failing health, when a war scare with England broke out in the spring of 1807, Preble roused himself and reported to Secretary of the Navy Robert Smith that he was ready should the Navy need him to command a warship.

The war scare passed, and Preble's health deteriorated. By August he was almost constantly bedridden and knew the end was near. His brother, Enoch, remained by the commodore's side. "To die on a bed of glory would be something," Preble said, "but to die of stinking consumption is too bad."[4]

Commo. Edward Preble died August 25, 1807 at the age of forty-six.

Of the forty-three officers that had served under Preble in 1803–1804, thirty-seven would reach the rank of master commandant (commander) or higher, including one admiral and seven captains.

———— ◆ ◆ ————

Capt. William Bainbridge remained a prisoner of Tripoli until June 5, 1805, when he and the remaining 292 officers and men of the *Philadelphia* boarded the vessels of Samuel Barron's squadron and set off for Sicily.

Secretary of the Navy Robert Smith ordered a court of inquiry to convene in Syracuse to investigate the loss of the *Philadelphia*. Bainbridge, with his officers all backing his story, said he had no choice but to surrender the frigate. The court agreed and exonerated him.

On his return to the United States, Bainbridge asked for leave from the Navy and returned to merchant service. Once more, bad luck dogged him. While in command of the merchant brig *Minerva* out of Philadelphia in 1806, Bainbridge fell overboard trying to board the vessel of a friend. He only avoided death when his hand found a line and he managed to pull himself up. Three years later, Bainbridge was skipper of a merchant trip to St. Petersburg, Russia. Soon after entering the Baltic, Bainbridge found himself a prisoner once more, this time of Danish privateers.

William Bainbridge finally had a brief change of luck when the War of 1812 broke out between the United States and England. Bainbridge was in command of the Charlestown Navy Yard in Boston when Isaac Hull arrived with the *Constitution*, fresh from her victory over the HMS *Guerriere*.

Despite his victory, Hull asked for shore leave to attend to family matters and Bainbridge immediately took command of the 38-gun frigate. He left for a cruise to South America as commodore of a small squadron— the *Constitution* and the brig *Hornet* under the command of Master Commandant James Lawrence. On December 30, 1812, Bainbridge fell in with the British frigate *Java*; after a two-hour contest, the *Constitution* turned the 44-gun British vessel into a wreck.

Bainbridge returned to the United States a hero. However, he could not seem to shake his bad luck. The British set up a blockade of New England, confining Bainbridge to land once more. He returned to command of the Charlestown Navy Yard and oversaw the construction of the Navy's first line-of-battleship, the 74-gun *Independence*. The threat of a British invasion kept Bainbridge confined to port until news of the peace treaty ending the war with England finally reached America.

The former commander of the *Philadelphia* had his chance for revenge against Bashaw Yusuf Karamanli and the other Barbary powers in 1815 when the United States decided to put an end to pirate attacks once and for all. Algiers had declared war on America during the conflict with Britain and President James Madison ordered Stephen Decatur and William Bainbridge to lead two separate squadrons to the Mediterranean. Once he arrived on station, Bainbridge was to have overall command as the senior officer.

Decatur arrived off Algiers on June 15 and within a few weeks had completely cowed the Barbary regents. Bainbridge reached Gibraltar on August 3 only to learn of Decatur's success. It was a crushing blow to Bainbridge, who wanted more than anything to finally get the better of the Barbary leaders. He would never forgive Decatur for stealing his chance at redemption.

Five years later, Bainbridge played a strange role in Decatur's tragic death. The ongoing feud between Decatur and James Barron escalated to the point of Barron challenging Decatur to a duel. When no other naval officer would help Decatur, Bainbridge stepped up, offered to be his second, and, many said, goaded Decatur into fighting a duel he did not want to fight. Decatur died in the duel and once again Bainbridge found himself under suspicion, although he managed to avoid any direct censure for his role in Decatur's death.

William Bainbridge served in the Navy for twenty-five years, retiring in 1832. He contracted pneumonia early in 1833 and died July 28, 1833.

——◆—◆——

None of "Preble's Boys" gained more fame than Capt. Stephen Decatur Jr. The young lieutenant who had burned the *Philadelphia* and captured a pair of pirate gunboats returned to the United States in 1805 a captain and a national hero.

Decatur's accomplishments at Tripoli made him a household name throughout the United States, although it was not enough for him to keep command of the *Constitution*. Rodgers, as the senior captain on station, took command of the 44-gun frigate, giving Decatur the smaller 36-gun *Congress*. It did not matter to Decatur. At twenty-five years, five months, and twenty-four days old he was—and remains—the youngest captain in the history of the U.S. Navy.

Decatur remained in the Mediterranean until September 1805, when he turned the *Congress* toward home, arriving in Norfolk in November that same year. Among the many guests who crowded on board the frigate to meet America's newest hero was a sparklingly attractive young woman, Susan Wheeler, the daughter of the Norfolk mayor. Susan had never met Decatur and gave no indication she even wanted to until she saw a small watercolor painting of the new captain. It was love at first sight for Susan, who set out to capture her heart's desire. Decatur proved an easy target.

The two spent every day together from their first meeting November 6 until November 23, when Decatur left for Washington. There was also the matter of a woman in Philadelphia to whom Decatur had made promises when he was still a midshipman. Who that woman was remains a mystery, but Decatur, smitten, apparently jilted the Philadelphia woman and within a year married Susan.

When war with England broke out in 1812, Decatur was captain of the frigate *United States*. On October 25, 1812, the *United States* fell in with His Majesty's frigate *Macedonian*. Decatur's vessel raked the English ship with broadside after broadside, and in three hours the battle was over. Decatur put a prize crew on the *Macedonian* and, together with the *United States*, made port at New London, Connecticut; the news of his victory quickly swept through the nation.

Three years later, Decatur was once more at sea, this time as captain of the *President*. Since the victory over the *Macedonian*, Decatur had spent most of his time dodging British blockades. He spent nearly a year stuck in New York, then another year in New London. Finally, he decided to sneak out of Long Island Sound with the *President*. To do so, he would have to avoid the 56-gun *Majestic*, the 40-gun *Endymion*, and a pair of 38-gun frigates, the *Pomone* and *Tenedos*.

On December 30, 1814, the *President* slipped out of Long Island Sound into the Atlantic. Almost immediately, the British squadron pounced. Decatur did his best to split the enemy force to allow him to face each ship in one-on-one duels. The first engagement was with the *Endymion*. The daylong battle left the *President* heavily damaged and her crew weary, but the fight was not over. Two 38-gun British frigates entered the fray. As they did so, Decatur saw the *Majestic* also moving into position. He kept up the fight about fifteen minutes. With more than a fifth of his crew injured and both the mizzen and foremasts shot away, Decatur struck his colors.

Although the idea of surrendering wounded Decatur to the core, he returned to yet another hero's welcome as word spread of the damage he had caused in his unequal contest. When he petitioned the secretary of the Navy to empanel a board of inquiry to look into his actions, the board completely cleared him of any wrongdoing.

Decatur remained the nation's darling after the war. He and his wife Susan were one of the most prominent couples in Washington, DC. He gained lasting fame in 1815 when, with a squadron of seven ships, he went back to the scene of his first successes, the North African coast, and finally put an end to the deprivations of the Barbary pirates.

In May 1815 Commodore Decatur set sail with the newly built 44-gun *Guerriere*, the *Constellation*, the *Macedonian*—the same ship he had captured in 1812—the sloop of war *Ontario*, the brigs *Epervier*, *Firefly*, *Flambeau*, and *Spark*, and the schooners *Spitfire* and *Torch*. It was the largest single force the United States Navy had yet assembled.

The squadron arrived in Gibraltar on June 15 and Decatur immediately began searching for warships belonging to Algiers. The dey of Algiers had sided with England during the War of 1812 and had declared war on the United States. Decatur was there to teach the regent the error of his ways.

On June 17 his squadron overtook the Algerian frigate *Meshouda* and in twenty-five minutes forced the enemy ship to surrender. Two days later, the squadron captured the 22-gun brig *Estudio*. The two prizes handed Decatur more than five hundred prisoners, giving him even more strength in his bargaining position with the dey.

The terms Decatur dictated were simple: no tribute, no payments of any kind, and a complete end to attacks on American vessels. The Algerians took one look at the assembled squadron, and, already knowing Decatur by reputation, quickly agreed.

Decatur took his squadron to Tunis and Tripoli and quickly forced those regents to accept similar treaties. He made a stop at Tangiers, where the emperor of Morocco also accepted a treaty without payments. When Commo. William Bainbridge arrived to take command of the squadron, he found he had nothing to do. Decatur had already won the peace.

It appeared as though there was nothing Decatur could not accomplish, except to escape from his own code of honor. It led Decatur to his own death in 1820 as his ongoing feud with Capt. James Barron escalated to the point of a duel. How big of a part William Bainbridge played in goading Decatur into meeting Barron with pistols remains something of a mystery. Bainbridge refused to even speak with Decatur for five years after the two had met in the Mediterranean and yet, when he heard about the war of words between Decatur and Barron, he suddenly appeared in Washington.

The cause of the duel was complex. Decatur said several times he did not want to fight Barron—in fact, he wanted nothing to do with the man.

However, he was chronically aware of how the public viewed him and when Barron issued his challenge, Decatur believed he had to answer it.

The two men met March 22, 1820, on the dueling grounds at Bladensburg, Maryland. Both men fell wounded, Decatur mortally. He died that afternoon.

The entire nation mourned.

Master Commandant Charles Stewart outlived and out-accomplished every one of Preble's Boys. He remained in the Mediterranean for the next year, first commanding the *Syren* before taking command of the subscription frigate *Essex*. When trouble with Tunis flared up in June 1805, Stewart was the lone officer in the Mediterranean squadron that spoke out against attacking the city. Commo. John Rodgers wanted to teach the Tunisian regent a lesson but Stewart argued that only Congress could declare war. His argument won over his commander—grudgingly—but made him an instant hero in Washington.

After he returned from the Mediterranean, Stewart spent the next six years alternating between naval and merchant service. He amassed a sizeable fortune and earned a reputation as a sharp businessman and deep thinker. As war with England loomed in 1812, it was Stewart who convinced a reluctant Congress to allow the Navy to play a role in the coming conflict. Stewart also convinced the penny-pinching lawmakers that a small fleet simply could not protect the nation; on his advice, Congress approved construction of four 74-gun line-of-battleships, four more *Constitution*-class 44-gun frigates, and six sloops of war.

Stewart did not put to sea until 1814. He took command of the *Constitution* the summer of 1813 after Bainbridge's victory over the HMS *Java*, but the frigate was in need of an overhaul. He did not slip out of Boston harbor until January 1, 1814, when he steered the *Constitution* toward the Caribbean.

On February 20, 1814, the *Constitution* fell in with a pair of British warships, the 18-gun sloop *Levant* and the 32-gun frigate *Cyane*. The two British ships immediately set courses to rake the *Constitution* from the bow and stern, avoiding the American vessel's powerful broadsides. Stewart, however, was the better sailor and countered each move so skillfully he turned both British ships into wrecks. By day's end, Stewart had captured both warships.

As luck would have it, another British squadron, this one containing a 74-gun battleship, came pounding across the waves while Stewart and his prizes were in Cape Verde, a neutral harbor. Stewart lost no time in slipping out of the harbor and setting sail north for America. In the ensuing chase, he sent the *Cyane* ahead using the *Constitution* as bait to keep the British occupied. The ploy worked and the frigate safely reached the United States.

He tried the same tactic with the *Levant*, but the sloop had suffered so much damage she was simply unable to either keep up with the *Constitution* or out-run the Royal Navy. The *Levant* put back into Cape Verde, where the British cornered and recaptured her.

The *Constitution* arrived back in New York in April, and the entire city turned out to greet her. Most naval historians consider Stewart's engagement to be the finest frigate battle of the age, and his handling of the *Constitution* to be among the best of any captain in any navy.

After the war, Stewart commanded the Mediterranean squadron as a commodore, flying his pennant from the new 74-gun *Franklin*, and went on to command the Pacific squadron. His handling of the rampant piracy that accompanied revolutions in South America earned him the plaudits of Chief Justice John Marshall of the U.S. Supreme Court.

Upon his return, Stewart spent the rest of his career on land. He served on various naval boards and commissions and superintended the construction and launch of the mammoth 120-gun battleship *Pennsylvania*. By 1844 Stewart was so well regarded that the Democratic Party wanted him to run for president. He refused.

The former captain of the *Syren* went into semiretirement in the 1850s, although he remained on the active list of officers. The Navy consulted him on everything from ship design to admiralty law. In 1857 Congress awarded Stewart the rank of "senior flag officer" of the Navy, a rank he refused because, he said, he already owned the position because of seniority on the captain's list.

Stewart was eighty-three when the Civil War began in 1861 and he offered his services to the Union. In 1862 he became the first admiral in the U.S. Navy when Congress finally created the rank. He lived to see the Union victorious and the nation he had served for so long reunited.

Charles Stewart died on November 6, 1869.

◆—◆—◆

Marine private William Ray endured another seven months of captivity along with the rest of the *Philadelphia* crew until their release in the summer of 1805. Ray boarded the *Essex*—under the command of Charles Stewart—and joined the crew as the ship's clerk. He returned to the United States and lived in Essex County, New York, where he wrote poetry and dabbled in business.

In 1808 Ray published a book recounting his experiences as a prisoner of Tripoli. *Horrors of Slavery, or, The American Tars in Tripoli* earned him some local fame and also maintained his feud with Surgeon Jonathan Cowdery, whose own narrative of events while a prisoner, published in 1806, was a national best-seller. Ray used much of his book to criticize Cowdery's version of their captivity.

At the outbreak of the War of 1812, Ray commanded a small militia unit in Plattsburgh, New York. After the war he lived in several places in New York before settling in Onondaga, where he became a justice of the peace and a court commissioner. He published a volume of poetry in 1821 that earned him some acclaim.

William Ray died in Auburn, New York, in 1827.

⸻

Master Commandant Richard Somers became the stuff of legend. His family estate on the New Jersey shore became the city of Somers Point. Citizens there have spent more than two hundred years trying to convince the federal government to recover his remains and those of the rest of the crew of the *Intrepid* and return them to the United States.

So far, they have been unsuccessful.

The spot where prisoners buried Somers, Wadsworth, and Israel became the foundation of what today is the Old Protestant Cemetery in Tripoli. Commemorated in 1830 the cemetery initially was the primary burial ground for members of the diplomatic and business communities and would eventually hold graves of people from Denmark, England, France, Norway, Russia, Sweden, and the United States. In the 1920s, when Italy ruled Libya, road engineers found the bodies of the enlisted men in a mass grave and moved them to the cemetery.

They remain there to do this day, despite the efforts not only of the people of Somers Point, but also millions of Americans to convince the Department of the Navy to finally bring the crew home.

For more than a hundred years, the friendship between Stephen Decatur and Richard Somers was something taught to all American schoolchildren. They should have been rivals in every sense, but even though they yearned for and recklessly pursued glory, they never allowed their personal ambitions to disrupt their friendship. They also put the needs of the service ahead of their own; their pursuit of glory is what helped to build the United States Navy.

A monument at the U.S. Naval Academy in Annapolis commemorates the sacrifice of Richard Somers, Henry Wadsworth, Joseph Israel, James Decatur, James Caldwell, and James Dorsey, the officers that died during the

Tripoli campaign. The monument was the first war memorial erected in the United States and contains a fitting epitaph for Somers and the crew of the *Intrepid*:

> *The love of Glory inspired them—Fame has crowned their deeds—History records the event—The children of Columbia admire—And commerce laments their fall.*

NOTES

CHAPTER 1. "TO BE PREPARED FOR WAR"

1. Molly Elliott Seawell, *Decatur and Somers* (New York: D. Appleton and Co., 1894). Seawell did such a good job of blending fact and fiction that her account of certain events in the lives of Somers and Decatur as well as other officers has often confused historians as to what really happened.
2. James Fenimore Cooper, *History of the Navy of the United States*, 2 vols. (New York: Stinger and Townsend, 1856), Vol. 1, 245.
3. Muster roll of the USS *Nautilus*, Richard Somers, *Letters and Papers of Richard Somers*, Frank H. Stewart, ed. (Gloucester County, NJ: n.p., 1940) (hereafter SFP), 30.
4. Robert Smith to Edward Preble, Jun. 25, 1803, *Edward Preble Collection of Correspondence, Diaries, Logs and Other Writings* (Washington, DC: Library of Congress Manuscript Division) (hereafter EPP).
5. James Duncan Phillips, *Salem and the Indies: The Story of the Great Commercial Era of the City* (Boston: Houghton Mifflin, 1947), 59. Phillips took his trade amounts and values from newspapers of the period.
6. Thomas Jefferson, Report to Congress, Dec. 30, 1790, Annals of Congress, 1st Cong., 3d Sess., Dec. 6, 1790 to Mar. 3, 1791, *American State Papers* (Washington, DC: Gales & Seaton, 1833), 100.
7. George Washington, Address to Congress, Jan. 8, 1790, Annals of Congress, 1st Cong., 2d Sess., Jan. 4, 1790 to Feb. 16, 1790, 11.
8. George Washington, address to Congress, Dec. 3, 1793, Annals of Congress, 3d Cong., 1st Sess., Dec. 2, 1793 to Jun. 9, 1794, 21.
9. Phillips, *Salem and the Indies*, 68.
10. Edmund Randolph to David Humphreys, Jan. 20, 1794, *Letters and Papers of David Humphreys*, New Haven, CT: Yale University Manuscripts and Archives, 1776–1867 (hereafter DHC).
11. David Humphreys to Edmund Randolph, Nov. 19, 1793, DHC.

12. George Folger, *Agreeable Intelligence* (New Bedford, MA: John Spooner, Dec. 21, 1793); David Humphreys, *Miscellaneous Works* (New York: T&J Swords, 1804), 88.

13. Annals of Congress, 3d Cong., 1st Sess., Dec. 2, 1793 to Jun. 9, 1794, 154.

14. Ibid., 486–491.

15. Ibid.

16. Thomas Jefferson, Report to Congress on U.S. Commerce, Annals of Congress, 1st Cong., 1st Sess., Mar. 4, 1789 to Feb. 10, 1790, 301–303.

17. *Naval Documents Related to the Wars Between the United States and the Barbary Powers* (Washington, DC: Government Printing Office, 1935–1937) (hereafter NDBP), Vol. 1, 69–70; Third Congress, *An Act to Provide a Naval Armament, 1794* (Philadelphia: Childs and Swain, 1794). For more about the innovations of the American frigates, see Howard I. Chapelle, *The History of the American Sailing Navy* (New York: W.W. Norton and Co., 1949), 115–79.

18. Third Congress, *An Act to Provide a Naval Armament, 1794*.

19. Ibid.

20. David Humphreys to Edmund Randolph, Apr. 25, 1796, DHC.

21. George Washington to Congress, Dec. 6, 1796, Annals of Congress, 4th Cong., 2d Sess., Dec. 5, 1796 to Mar. 3, 1797, 1593–1594.

22. John Adams to Congress, May 16, 1797, Annals of Congress, 5th Cong., 1st Sess., May 15, 1797 to Jul. 10, 1797, 2240–2241.

23. For more on these events see Gardner W. Allen, *Our Naval War with France*, 27, 38–39, Michael Palmer, *Stoddert's War: Naval Operations during the Quasi-War with France, 1798–1801* (Annapolis, Md.: Naval Institute Press, 1987), 6, 18. Chapelle, *The History of the U.S. Sailing Navy*, 164. For more on ship construction see also Frederick C. Leiner, *Millions for Defense: The Subscription Warships of 1798* (Annapolis, Md.: Naval Institute Press, 2000), 60–65, 150–156.

24. Fourth Congress, *An Act to Provide a Naval Armament, 1797* (Philadelphia: Francis Childs, 1798).

25. James Fenimore Cooper, *Lives of Distinguished American Naval Officers* (Philadelphia: Carey and Hart, 1846), Vol. 1, 78–79

26. Thomas Truxtun, *Remarks, Instructions and Examples Relating to the Latitude and Longitude; Also the Variations of the Compass* (Philadelphia: T. Dobson, 1794).

27. *Naval Documents Related to the Quasi-War between the United States and France* (Washington, DC: Government Printing Office, 1935) (hereafter NDQW), Vol. 6, 483.

28. Benjamin Stoddert, *Letter from the Secretary of the Navy (Feb. 9, 1799): Accompanying Sundry Statements Relative to the Vessels of War, Employed in and Preparing for the Service of the United States, Pursuant to a Resolution of the House, of the Eighteenth Instant* (Philadelphia: J. Gales, 1799).

29. Benjamin Stoddert, Report to U.S. House of Representatives, Jan. 10, 1800.

30. John Shaw to Benjamin Stoddert, Jul. 23, 1800, NDQW, Vol. 6, 172; Cooper, *History of the Navy of the United States*, Vol. 1, 141–142.

31. Alexander Murray to John Shaw, Jan. 22, 1800, NDQW, Vol. 5, 63.

32. Benjamin Stoddert, Report to Naval Committee, NDQW, Vol. 7, 128–130. Stoddert, in his plans for the U.S. Navy, envisioned twelve 74-gun ships of the line, twelve 44- to 36-gun frigates, and up to twenty brig or ship-rigged vessels carrying a maximum of 24 guns.

33. "An Act Providing for Naval Peace Establishment," Annals of Congress, 6th Cong. 2d Sess., Nov. 17, 1800 to Mar. 3, 1801, 110–111.

34. Ibid.

CHAPTER 2. INTO THE FRAY

1. James Cathcart to James Madison, *Documents Respecting Barbary Accompanying the President's Communications to Congress*, Dec. 8, 1801 (Washington, DC: William Duane, 1802), 15.

2. David Humphreys to James Madison, May 8, 1801, Humphreys–Marvin–Olmstead Collection, Yale University Manuscripts Collection. Humphreys inaccurately reported that Tripoli declared war on Feb. 26, 1801. In a letter dated Jun. 23 to James Madison, Humphreys corrected the date.

3. Thomas Jefferson, "Proposal for War Powers Against the Barbary States," 1786, *The Thomas Jefferson Papers, Series 1, General Correspondence 1651–1827*, Library of Congress Manuscript Division (electronic version).

4. Thomas Jefferson, Annual Message to Congress 1804, Nov. 8, 1804, *Thomas Jefferson Papers*, Vol. 10.

5. Joel Barlow to Timothy Pickering, Apr. 17, 1796, NDBP, Vol. 1, 147–149; William Eaton and Richard O'Brien to Secretary of State, Feb. 22, 1799, NDBP, Vol. 1, 300–302; 3d Cong., 1st Sess., Foreign Policy, *American State Papers*, Vol. 1, 421–422.

6. Thomas Jefferson to David Humphreys, Jan. 1794, DHC.

7. David Humphreys to Timothy Pickering, Apr. 26, 1796, DHC.

8. Edward Preble, Report to Congress, EPP.

9. Cooper, *Lives of Distinguished American Naval Officers*, Vol. 2, 260–261.

10. Samuel Smith to Richard Dale, May 20, 1801, NDBP, Vol. 1, 499.

11. Richard Dale to Andrew Sterrett, May 29, 1801, NDBP, Vol. 1, 478.

12. John Gavino to James Madison, Jul. 4, 1801, NDBP, Vol. 1, 501–502; Whipple, *To the Shores of Tripoli: The Birth of the U.S. Navy and Marines* (Annapolis, MD: Naval Institute Press, 1991), 76.

13. Andrew Sterrett to Charles Sterrett, Feb. 14, 1799, NDQW, 1940, Vol. 2, 334–335.

14. Richard Dale to Samuel Smith, Jul. 3, 1801, NDBP Vol. 1, 489–491.

15. Richard Dale to Andrew Sterrett, Jul. 5, 1801, NDBP, Vol. 1, 503.

16. The U.S. Navy had yet to adopt a formal manual governing its articles of war. Instead, under Capt. Thomas Truxtun's direction, the new branch simply adopted the 1757 British Articles of War that remained in force in 1800. Truxtun also advocated flying British colors in his *Remarks, Instructions and Examples Relating to the Latitude and Longitude.*

17. The description of the battle between the *Enterprise* and *Tripoli* comes from the Report of Andrew Sterrett to Robert Smith; Report of Marine Lt. Mewton Keene; Act of Congress granting the *Enterprise* crew two months' pay as prize money for the *Tripoli*; and the *National Intelligencer and Advance* story on the combat, all contained in NDBP, Vol. 1, 535–547. See also Cooper, *History of the Navy of the United States*, Vol. 2, 152; Whipple, *To the Shores of Tripoli*, 79–80; Stephen C. Blyth, *History of the War between the United States and Tripoli and Other Barbary Powers* (Salem, MA: Salem Gazette Office, 1808. Reprint, Tripoli, Libya: Fergiani Bookshop, 1970), 89–92.

18. *National Intelligencer and Advance*, NDBP, Vol. 1, 539.

19. Ibid.

20. Andrew Sterrett to Robert Smith, Aug. 6, 1801, NDBP, Vol. 1, 535.

21. Cooper, *History of the Navy of the United States*, Vol. 2, 152.

22. Andrew Sterrett to Robert Smith, Aug. 6, 1801, NDBP, Vol. 1, 535.

23. Gardner W. Allen, *Our Navy and the Barbary Corsairs* (New York: Houghton Mifflin and Co., 1905), 120. Allen recounts the cause of a duel that comes later in this work—placing the blame squarely on the British, who, he says, engaged in their favorite pastime of insulting U.S. Naval officers. Edward Preble, in his explanations of why he chose Sicily as his base, also cited British and French tendencies to sneer at the U.S. Navy.

24. Thomas Jefferson to Robert Smith, Apr. 27 1804, *Thomas Jefferson Papers, Series 1, General Correspondence, 1651–1827*, Vol. 10.

25. William Eaton to Richard Morris, Oct. 16, 1802, NDBP, Vol. 2, 281.
26. Thomas Jefferson, *The Papers of Thomas Jefferson*, Vol. 10, Apr. 17, 1802.
27. John Rodgers to Richard Morris, Jun. 25, 1803, NDBP, Vol. 2, 465–466.
28. Annals of Congress, 7th Cong., 2d Sess., 313.

CHAPTER 3. PREBLE

1. Biographical sketch of Edward Preble assembled from the following: EPP; Cooper, *Lives of Distinguished American Naval Officers*, Vol. 1, 172–252; Christopher McKee, *Edward Preble: A Naval Biography* (Annapolis, MD: Naval Institute Press, 1972), 40–146; Fletcher Pratt, *Preble's Boys* (New York: William Sloan Associates, 1950), 13–39; Waldo Samuel Putnam, *Biographical Sketches of Distinguished American Naval Heroes in the War of the Revolution* (Hartford, CT: Silas Andrus,1818), 143, 287.
2. James Porter to William Burrows, Jan. 20, 1801, Marine Corps Correspondence, National Archives Record Group 127, Office of the Commandant of the Marine Corps, 1798–1978.
3. Edward Preble to Mrs. Dorcas Deering, Dec. 17, 1799, EPP. For more on this and the cruise of the *Essex* and events in these passages see Frances Duane Robotti and James Vescovi, *The USS Essex and the Birth of the American Navy* (Holbrook, Mass.: Adams Media Corp., 1999), 45–60; McKee, *Edward Preble*, 66–81; Leiner, 166–76.
4. Edward Preble to Samuel Smith, Apr. 17, 1801, EPP.
5. Robert Smith to Edward Preble, Jul. 14, 1803, EPP.
6. Cooper, *History of the Navy of the United States*, 175–185; Irvin Anthony, *Decatur* (New York: Charles Scribner's Sons, 1931), 104.
7. Charles Morris, *Autobiography of Commodore Charles Morris, U.S. Navy* (Annapolis, MD: Naval Institute Press, 2002), 14.
8. Edward Preble to Mary Preble, Aug. 12, 1803, EPP.
9. Logbook of the USS *Constitution*, Feb. 14, 1804, EPP.
10. Logbook of the USS *Constitution*, Oct. 4, Oct. 20, and Dec. 9, 1803, EPP.
11. Morris, *Autobiography of Commodore Charles Morris*, 18.
12. The exchange is from ibid., 19; Cooper, *Lives of Distinguished American Naval Officers*, Vol. 1, 195–196.
13. Morris, *Autobiography of Commodore Charles Morris*, 20–21.
14. Ibid.
15. Tobias Lear to Edward Preble, Sept. 18, 1803, EPP.
16. Edward Preble to James Madison, Sept. 18, 1803, NDBP, Vol. 3, 55–58.

17. Logbook of the USS *Constitution*, Sept. 16, 1803, EPP.
18. Morris, *Autobiography of Commodore Charles Morris*, 33.

CHAPTER 4. ASSEMBLY POINT

1. Logbook of the USS *Constitution*, Nov. 24, 1803, EPP.
2. Ibid., Sept. 12 to Nov. 23, 1803.
3. Ibid., Nov. 24, 1803; Edward Preble to Robert Smith, Dec. 10, 1803, EPP.
4. McKee, *Edward Preble*, 65–70.
5. Logbook of the USS *Constitution*, Nov. 24, 1803, EPP.
6. Bruce Grant, *The Life and Fighting Times of Isaac Hull* (Chicago: Peligrini and Cudahy, 1947), 74–75.
7. Ibid., 63.
8. Multiple sources discuss the relationship between Preble and Hull. However, no record of their conversations exists.
9. Edward Preble, Report to Congress, Sept. 18, 1804, EPP.
10. John Rodgers to Robert Smith, Sept. 15, 1803, *John Rodgers Papers*, Library of Congress Manuscript Division (hereafter JRP).
11. John Rodgers to Edward Preble, Sept. 15, 1803, EPP.
12. Edward Preble to John Rodgers, Sept. 15, 1803, EPP.
13. Ibid.
14. The British practice of luring American sailors to desert was almost the main pastime for Royal Navy officers. Every American commander, from Dale to Morris to Preble, complained vehemently about the British practice of poaching sailors from American men-of-war. Preble, in particular, during his stopovers in Gibraltar and Malta, wrote to the British commanders of those bases, blasting Royal Navy officers for tempting Yankee tars to desert. See Edward Preble to Robert Smith, Oct. 23, 1803, EPP.
15. Edward Preble to Robert Smith, Oct. 23, 1803, EPP.
16. Edward Preble to William Bainbridge, Oct. 1, 1803, EPP.
17. William Bainbridge to Edward Preble, Oct. 17, 1803.
18. William Bainbridge to John Smith, Sept. 23, 1803, NDBP, Vol. 3, 74.
19. Logbook of the USS *Constitution*, Oct. 27, 1803, EPP; Edward Preble to Robert Smith, Oct. 23, 1803, EPP.
20. According to a letter of Marine captain Dan McCormick to Marine Corps commandant Lt. Col. William Burrows, Oct. 15, 1802, NDBP, Vol. 2, 295, Sterrett once allowed three men to drown because they had accepted an invitation to dine on board the frigate *Constellation*.
21. Edward Preble to Robert Smith, Nov. 8, 1803, EPP.

22. Ibid.
23. Edward Preble to Robert Smith, Nov. 9, 1803, EPP.
24. Edward Preble to Isaac Hull, Nov. 7, 1803, EPP.
25. Edward Preble to Stephen Decatur, Nov. 7, 1803, EPP.
26. Diary of Edward Preble, Nov. 23, 1803, EPP (hereafter Preble diary).

CHAPTER 5. OFFICERS AND GENTLEMEN

1. Ian W. Toll, *Six Frigates* (New York: W. W. Norton, 2006), 216.
2. William Oliver Steven, *Pistols at Ten Paces: The Code of Honor in America* (Boston: Houghton Mifflin, 1940), 5–16.
3. Ibid.
4. Ibid., 50.
5. Anthony, *Decatur*, 81.
6. Ibid.
7. Anthony, *Decatur*, 79–83; James Tertiary de Kay, *A Rage for Glory: The Life of Commodore Stephen Decatur, USN* (New York: Free Press, 2004), 42–45. See also A.B.C. Whipple, *To The Shores of Tripoli: The Birth of the U.S. Navy and Marines* (Annapolis, Md.: Naval Institute Press, 1991), 89–90.
8. Morris, *Autobiography of Commodore Charles Morris*, 14.
9. William Ray, *Horrors of Slavery, or, The American Tars in Tripoli* (Troy, NY: Oliver Lyon, 1808), 63.
10. Morris, *Autobiography of Commodore Charles Morris*, 16.
11. Various sources contributed to the depiction of Decatur, including Anthony, *Decatur*, 1–81; de Kay, *A Rage for Glory*, 9–38; Pratt, *Preble's Boys*, 85–97; Cooper, *History of the Navy of the United States*, Vol. 1, 153–155; Thomas Clark, *Naval History of the United States, from the Commencement of the Revolutionary War to the Present Time* (Philadelphia: M. Carey, 1814), 148–169.
12. de Kay, *A Rage for Glory*, 36–37.
13. Anthony, *Decatur*, 70–71.
14. Edward Preble to Stephen Decatur, Dec. 14, 1803, EPP.
15. Sketch of Richard Somers' life compiled from Cooper, *Lives of Distinguished American Naval Officers*, Vol. 1, 73–122; Anthony, *Decatur*, 1–181; Pratt, *Preble's Boys*, 85–97; Clark, *Naval History of the United States*, 148–169; J. B. Somers, *Life of Richard Somers, A Master Commandant in the U.S. Navy* (Philadelphia: Collins Printer, 1886), 1–27; Edna Miriam Hoopes, *Richard Somers, Master Commandant of the U.S. Navy* (Atlantic City, NJ: n.p., 1922), 7–33.

16. Somers' birth date remains something of a mystery, with some records indicating 1778 and others 1779. A gravestone his sister erected in his memory lists his birth year as 1778 and this is the date used in this book.

17. Molly Elliott Seawell, *Twelve Naval Captains* (London: Keegan Paul, Trench and Trubner Co., 1898), 132.

18. Somers, *Life of Richard Somers*, 11–13.

19. Ibid., 136.

20. Anthony, *Decatur*, 103–104. Many authors recount the tale of these duels, although Anthony's account is the most lurid.

21. Richard Somers to William Jones Keen, undated letter, SFP.

22. Claude Berube and John Rodgaard, *A Call to the Sea: Captain Charles Stewart of the USS* Constitution (Washington, DC: Potomac Books, 2005), 7–10.

23. John Barry to Benjamin Stoddert, Jul. 30, 1800, NDQW, Vol. 6, 198.

24. Muster roll of U.S. schooner *Experiment*, National Archives and Records Administration, Old Navy Records Group 25.

25. NDQW, Vol. 7, 100.

26. Sketch of Charles Stewart's character from Berube and Rodgaard, *A Call to the Sea*, 7–34; *Biographical Sketch of Commodore Charles Stewart* (Philadelphia: J. Harding, 1830), 4–35; Pratt, *Preble's Boys*, 317–326.

27. Anthony, *Decatur*, 114.

28. Letter of squadron officers to Edward Preble, Nov. 4, 1804, EPP.

CHAPTER 6. "CHILD OF ADVERSITY"

1. Thomas Harris, *The Life and Services of Commodore William Bainbridge* (Philadelphia: Carey Lea & Blanchard, 1837), 18.

2. William Bainbridge to Edward Preble, quoted in John Rea, Letter to William Bainbridge, Esq., Formerly Commander of the U.S. Ship *George Washington* (Philadelphia: Printed by Author, 1802).

3. John Rea, *A Letter to William Bainbridge, Esq., formerly Commander of the United States Ship* George Washington (Philadelphia: n.p., 1802), 16.

4. Harris, *The Life and Services of Commodore William Bainbridge*, 25; NDQW, Vol. 2, 178–179.

5. NDBP, Vol. 1, 378.

6. Ibid., 398.

7. William Bainbridge to Susan Bainbridge, Nov. 1, 1803, NDBP, Vol. 3, 178–179.

8. Chapelle, *History of the U.S. Sailing Navy*, 161–164. See also Leiner, *Millions for Defense*, 54–68.

9. William Bainbridge to Edward Preble, reporting loss of the *Philadelphia*, Nov. 1, 1803, NDBP, Vol. 3, 174.

10. Ray, *Horrors of Slavery*, 76–77.

11. William Bainbridge to Robert Smith, Nov. 1, 1803, NDBP, Vol. 3, 171–173.

12. Kedging involved using the frigate's small boats to row an anchor into deep water. Crewmen on board the frigate would then use a capstan to winch in the anchor line, hopefully pulling the ship off the rocks. They would continue each evolution until they eventually freed the frigate.

13. Ray, *Horrors of Slavery*, 82.

14. William Bainbridge to Robert Smith, Nov. 1, 1803, NDBP, Vol. 3, 171–173.

15. Edward Preble to Robert Smith, Jan. 31, 1804, EPP.

16. William Bainbridge to Edward Preble, Nov. 1, 1803, NDBP, Vol. 3, 173–175.

17. Ray, *Horrors of Slavery*, 77.

18. William Bainbridge to Edward Preble, Nov. 1, 1803, NDBP, Vol. 3, 174.

19. Ray, *Horrors of Slavery*, 77.

20. William Bainbridge to Edward Preble, Nov. 1, 1803, NDBP, Vol. 3, 174.

21. Bainbridge testimony before a court of inquiry, Jun. 29, 1805, NDBP, Vol. 3, 190–194.

22. The pirate captains along North Africa had a tendency of faking surrender to lure ships in close. The Arab crews would then leap onto the unsuspecting ship and take it by storm. The captain of the brig *Tripoli* had tried it against Andrew Sterrett and the *Enterprise* in 1801, but the American was ready and his Marines blasted the Arab boarders.

23. *Philadelphia* sailing master William Knight to Thomas Driscoll, Nov. 1, 1804, NDBP, Vol. 3, 179–180.

24. Affidavit of Salvatore Catalano, Feb. 2, 1804, NDBP, Vol. 3, 180–181.

25. William Bainbridge to Robert Smith, Nov. 1, 1803, NDBP, Vol. 3, 173.

26. William Knight to Thomas Driscoll, November 1, 1803, NDBP, Vol. 3, 179–180.

27. Jonathan Cowdery, *American Captives in Tripoli, or Dr. Cowdery's Journal in Miniature*, NDBP, Vol. 3, 529.

28. Ray, *Horrors of Slavery*, 79.

29. Ibid., 86.

30. Ibid., 84.

31. William Bainbridge to officers of the *Philadelphia*, Oct. 31, 1803, NDBP, Vol. 3, 169.

32. Officers of the *Philadelphia* to William Bainbridge, Oct. 31, 1803, NDBP, Vol. 3, 169.

33. William Bainbridge, Report to Robert Smith, Nov. 1, 1803, NDBP, Vol. 3, 172–173.
34. Ibid.
35. William Bainbridge to Edward Preble, Nov. 1, 1803, EPP.
36. William Bainbridge to John Smith, Nov. 1, 1803, NDBP, Vol. 3, 170.
37. William Bainbridge to Susan Bainbridge, Nov. 1, 1803, NDBP, Vol. 3, 178–179; Harris, *The Life and Services of Commodore William Bainbridge*, 92.
38. Ray, *Horrors of Slavery*, 85.
39. Ibid.
40. William Bainbridge to Edward Preble, Nov. 1, 1803, NDBP, Vol. 3, 173.
41. John Ridgeley to Susan Decatur, Nov. 10, 1826, in *Documents, Official and Unofficial, Related to the Case of the Capture and Destruction of the Frigate* Philadelphia *at Tripoli on the 16th of Feb. 1804* (hereafter PDOC) (Washington, DC: John W. Towers, 1827), 24–25.
42. William Bainbridge to Edward Preble, Nov. 6, 1803, EPP.
43. William Bainbridge to Tobias Lear, Nov. 1, 1803, NDBP, Vol. 3, 177–178.
44. Ibid.
45. Ibid.

CHAPTER 7. "THERE SHALL NOT BE AN IDLE SHIP"

1. Edward Preble to Robert Smith, Oct. 23, 1803, EPP.
2. Ibid.
3. Ibid.
4. Ibid.
5. Richard Farquhar to Thomas Jefferson, Nov. 15, 1803, NDBP, Vol. 3, 222; Tobias Lear to Thomas Jefferson, Jan. 4, 1804, NDBP, Vol. 3, 292–293.
6. Edward Preble to Robert Smith, Oct. 23, 1803, EPP.
7. Ibid.
8. Edward Preble, to Robert Smith, Dec. 10, 1803, NDBP, Vol. 3, 259; orders to Decatur, Dec. 10, 1803, NDBP, Vol. 3, 260.
9. Preble diary, Nov. 5, 1803, EPP.
10. Edward Preble to William Bainbridge, Nov. 10, 1803, NDBP, Vol. 3, 280.
11. Albert Gleaves, *James Lawrence* (New York: G. P. Putnam's Sons, 1904), 37.
12. Ibid., 37–39.
13. Pratt, *Preble's Boys*, 151–156.
14. James Lawrence to Julia Lawrence, letter included in Eugene H. Pool, *"Don't Give Up the Ship": A Catalogue of the Eugene H. Pool Collection of Captain James Lawrence* (Salem, MA: Peabody Museum, 1942), 25.

15. Pratt, *Preble's Boys*, 151–153; Anthony, *Decatur*, 117–126; Lewis Deane, *The Life of James Lawrence, Esq.* (New Brunswick, NJ: L. Deane, 1813), 45–49.
16. Edward Preble to Jonathan Thorn, Nov. 7, 1803, EPP.
17. Edward Preble to Jonathan Thorn, Nov. 7, 1803, NDBP, Vol. 3, 204.
18. Pool, *"Don't Give Up the Ship,"* 5.
19. Walter Boyd to Edward Preble, Dec. 3, 1803, NDBP, Vol. 3, 252.
20. Pool, *"Don't Give Up the Ship,"* 6.
21. Pratt, *Preble's Boys*, 346–348; Rodney Macdonough, *The Life of Commodore Thomas Macdonough* (Boston: Fort Gill Press, 1909), 22–23.
22. Macdonough, *The Life of Commodore Thomas Macdonough*, 23.
23. Anthony, *Decatur*, 117.
24. Pratt, *Preble's Boys*, 116–117, 348.
25. Preble diary, Dec. 7, 1803, NDBP, Vol. 3, 254.
26. Savage Stillwell to Richard Somers, Aug. 30, 1803, SFP, 16.
27. Richard Somers to William Jones Keen, May 21, 1803, SFP.
28. Richard Somers to William Jones Keen, May 13, 1803, SFP.
29. Ibid.
30. Richard Somers to William Bainbridge, May 15, 1803, SFP.
31. Richard Somers to William Jones Keen, May 23, 1803, SFP.
32. Richard Somers to Sarah Somers Keen, Jun. 4, 1803, SFP.
33. Richard Somers to Edward Preble, Jul. 31, 1803, SFP.
34. Richard Somers to William Jones Keen, Sept. 11, 1803, SFP.

CHAPTER 8. BIRTH OF A PLAN

1. Preble diary, Dec. 23, 1803, EPP; logbook of the USS *Constitution*, Dec. 23, 1803, EPP.
2. Preble diary, Dec. 23, 1803, EPP.
3. Ibid.
4. Ibid.
5. Preble diary, Dec. 26, 1803, NDBP, Vol. 3, 298.
6. Ibid.
7. Edward Preble to William Bainbridge, Jan. 4, 1803, NDBP, Vol. 3, 310.
8. Edward Preble to James Cathcart, Jan. 4, 1804, NDBP, Vol. 3, 311.
9. There are no detailed records of exactly when Preble thought about a mission to destroy the *Philadelphia*. Many of William Bainbridge's supporters claim he gave Preble the idea. However, in a letter to his brother Henry in December after he learned of the frigate's capture, he hinted at his early thoughts to destroy the ship.

10. Stephen Decatur to Edward Preble, Jan. 11, 1803, NDBP, Vol. 3, 325.

11. Logbook of the USS *Constitution*, Jan. 13, 1804, EPP.

12. Edward Preble to Robert Smith, Dec. 10, 1803, NDBP, Vol. 3, 256.

13. Preble diary, Jan. 28, 1804, NDBP, Vol. 3, 371; Salvador Catalano affidavit, Feb. 2, 1804, NDBP, Vol. 3, 381.

14. Edward Preble to Robert Smith, Feb. 3, 1804, NDBP, Vol. 3, 384.

15. Logbook of the USS *Constitution*, Jan. 10, 1804, EPP.

16. Anthony, *Decatur*, 118; Whipple, *To the Shores of Tripoli*, 132.

17. Edward Preble to Tobias Lear, Jun. 22, 1804, EPP.

CHAPTER 9. PRISONERS OF THE BASHAW

1. David D. Porter, *Memoir of Commodore David Porter* (Albany, NY: J. Munsell Publisher, 1875), 60–61.

2. William Bainbridge to Edward Preble, Nov. 6, 1803, NDBP, Vol. 3, 176.

3. Ibid., 224.

4. Ibid., 253.

5. Ray, *Horrors of Slavery*, 99.

6. Ibid., 98.

7. Ibid., 94

8. William Bainbridge to Edward Preble, Nov. 6, 1803, NDBP, Vol. 3, 176.

9. Ray, *Horrors of Slavery*, 89.

10. William Bainbridge to Edward Preble, Nov. 6, 1803, NDBP, Vol. 3, 176; Ray, *Horrors of Slavery*, 92.

11. Ray, *Horrors of Slavery*, 93.

12. Ibid., 100.

13. William Knight to Thomas Bristoll, Nov. 1, 1803, NDBP, Vol. 3, 179–180; Ray, *Horrors of Slavery*, 81–82.

14. Fortifications on the seaboard of Tripoli (no author), NDBP, Vol. 3, 304.

15. Cowdery, *American Captives in Tripoli*, 531.

16. Tobias Lear to Edward Preble, Dec. 16, 1804, EPP.

17. Cowdery journal, Jan. 30, 1803, NDBP, Vol. 3, 531; Ray, *Horrors of Slavery*, 106–108; Harris, *The Life and Services of Commodore William Bainbridge*, 89–92.

18. Logbook of the USS *Constitution*, Jan. 30, 1804, EPP.

19. McKee, *Edward Preble*, 190.

20. Edward Preble to Charles Stewart, Jan. 31, 1804, NDBP, Vol. 3, 376.

21. *Biographical Sketch of Commodore Charles Stewart*.

22. Waldo, *The Life and Character of Stephen Decatur*, 107.

23. Logbook of the USS *Constitution*, Jan. 31, 1804, EPP.

24. Edward Preble to Stephen Decatur, Jan. 31, 1804, EPP.

25. Ibid.
26. Ibid.
27. Ibid.; Edward Preble to Charles Stewart, Jan. 31, 1804, EPP.
28. Hezekiah Loomis, *The Journal of Hezekiah Loomis, Steward on the U.S. Brig* Vixen *under Capt. John Smith* (Salem, MA: Essex Institute, 1928), 28.
29. Preble diary, Dec. 23, 1803, EPP. See also Edward Preble's Signals Book, undated, EPP.
30. Ibid.

CHAPTER 10. VOLUNTEERS FOR THE UNKNOWN

1. Anthony, *Decatur*, 126.
2. Edward Preble to Robert Smith, Oct. 23, 1803, EPP.
3. Logbook of the USS *Constitution*, Feb. 2, 1804, EPP.
4. Ibid.; de Kay, *A Rage for Glory*, 90–92; Whipple, *To the Shores of Tripoli*, 133. See also Waldo, *Life and Character of Stephen Decatur*, 107–8.
5. Stephen Decatur to Edward Preble, Feb. 19, 1804, PDOC, 5–6.
6. Anthony, *Decatur*, 126.
7. Morris, *Autobiography of Commodore Charles Morris*, 25; Anthony, *Decatur*, 127.
8. Stephen Decatur to Edward Preble, Feb. 18, 1804, EPP.
9. Anthony, *Decatur*, 127.
10. Logbook of the USS *Constitution*, Feb. 3, 1804, EPP.
11. Charles Stewart to Edward Preble, Feb. 19, 1804, NDBP, Vol. 3, 415.
12. Ralph Izard to Mrs. Ralph Izard Sr., Feb. 20, 1804, NDBP, Vol. 3, 416–417.
13. Lewis Heerman affidavit, Apr. 26, 1828, NDBP, Vol. 3, 417–419; Whipple, *To the Shores of Tripoli*, 135.
14. Morris, *Autobiography of Commodore Charles Morris*, 25.
15. Ibid., 25–26.
16. Quotes are from Morris, *Autobiography of Commodore Charles Morris*, 25–26. See also Gleaves, *James Lawrence*, 48; Charles Stewart to Edward Preble, Feb. 19, 1804, NDBP, Vol. 3, 415.
17. Lewis Heerman affidavit, Apr. 26, 1828, NDBP, Vol. 3, 418; Morris, *Autobiography of Commodore Charles Morris*, 26.
18. Morris, *Autobiography of Commodore Charles Morris*, 26.
19. Ibid.
20. Lewis Heerman affidavit, Apr. 26, 1828, NDBP, Vol. 3, 418.
21. Morris, *Autobiography of Commodore Charles Morris*, 26.
22. Lewis Heerman affidavit, Apr. 26, 1828, NDBP, Vol. 3, 418.

23. Preble diary, Jan. 6, 1804, EPP; McKee, *Edward Preble*, 192–193.
24. Logbook of the USS *Constitution*, Jan. 3, 1804, EPP; Christopher Gadsden to Edward Preble, Jan. 3, 1804, NDBP, Vol. 3, 318.
25. Charles Stewart to Edward Preble, Feb. 19, 1805, NDBP, Vol. 3, 416.

CHAPTER 11. "THE MOST BOLD AND DARING ACT OF THE AGE"

1. Jonathan Cowdery journal, Feb. 10, 1804, NDBP, Vol. 3, 532.
2. Charles Stewart to Edward Preble, Feb. 19, 1804, EPP.
3. Don Treworgy, Mystic Seaport Planetarium, Mystic, Connecticut. This and all subsequent star, moon, and sun descriptions are courtesy of a special program Mr. Treworgy created at the museum's planetarium for this work.
4. Charles Stewart to Edward Preble, Feb. 19, 1804, EPP.
5. Morris, *Autobiography of Commodore Charles Morris*, 26.
6. Ibid., 27.
7. Edmund Kennedy affidavit, Mar. 10, 1828, NDBP, Vol. 3, 420.
8. Don Treworgy, Mystic Seaport Planetarium. Dr. Treworgy graciously set up the planetarium sky as it looked the nights of Feb. 16, 1804 and Sept. 4, 1804.
9. Morris, *Autobiography of Commodore Charles Morris*, 27.
10. Lewis Heerman affidavit, Mar. 26, 1828, NDBP, Vol. 3, 418.
11. Ibid.
12. Morris, *Autobiography of Commodore Charles Morris*, 28; Lewis Heerman affidavit, Mar. 26, 1828, NDBP, Vol. 3, 418; Ralph Izard to Mrs. Ralph Izard Sr., Feb. 20, 1804, NDBP, Vol. 3, 417.
13. Ibid.
14. Morris, *Autobiography of Commodore Charles Morris*, 30.
15. Logbook of the USS *Constitution*, Feb. 16, 1804, EPP.
16. Ralph Izard to Mrs. Ralph Izard Sr., Feb. 20, 1804, NDBP, Vol. 3, 417.
17. Lewis Heerman affidavit, Mar. 26, 1828, NDBP, Vol. 3, 419.
18. Morris, *Autobiography of Commodore Charles Morris*, 30.
19. Ibid., 29.
20. Ibid.
21. Ibid.; Lewis Heerman, affidavit, Mar. 26, 1828, NDBP, Vol. 3, 419; Stephen Decatur to Edward Preble, Feb. 17, 1804, EPP.
22. Ray, *Horrors of Slavery*, 109.
23. Ibid., 110.
24. Anthony, *Decatur*, 313–314.
25. Charles Stewart to Edward Preble, Feb. 19, 1804, NDBP, Vol. 3, 416.
26. Stephen Decatur to Edward Preble, Feb. 17, 1804, EPP.

27. Ralph Izard to Mrs. Ralph Izard Sr., Feb. 20, 1804, NDBP, Vol. 3, 417.
28. Ibid., 110–111.
29. William Bainbridge to Edward Preble, Feb. 17, 1804, EPP.
30. Nicholas Nissen to Danish consul of Marseilles, NDBP, Vol. 3, 421.

Chapter 12. Strike, Counter-Strike

1. Anton Zuchet to Dutch foreign minister, Feb. 16, 1804, quoted in Richard Zacks, *The Pirate Coast: Thomas Jefferson, the First Marines and the Secret Mission of 1805* (New York: Hyperion, 2005), 82.
2. Morris, *Autobiography of Commodore Charles Morris*, 30.
3. Stephen Decatur to Edward Preble, Feb. 18, 1804, NDBP, Vol. 3, 414.
4. Logbook of the USS *Constitution*, Feb. 19, 1804, EPP.
5. Ibid., Feb. 12, 1804.
6. Ibid., Feb. 19, 1804.
7. Edward Preble to Robert Smith, Feb. 19, 1804, PDOC, 16–17.
8. Morris, *Autobiography of Commodore Charles Morris*, 30–31.
9. Charles Stewart to Susan Decatur, Dec. 26, 1826, PDOC, 22
10. Many authors use Nelson's quote about the burning of the *Philadelphia*. However, there are no actual records showing he ever commented on the Tripoli raid.
11. Edward Preble to Richard Somers, Feb. 3, 1804, EPP.
12. Richard Somers to Edward Preble, Feb. 16, 1804, SFP.
13. Richard Somers to Edward Preble, Mar. 6, 1804, EPP.
14. Ibid.
15. Edward Preble to Richard Somers, Mar. 8, 1804, EPP.
16. Richard Somers to Edward Preble, Mar. 8, 1804, SFP.
17. Edward Preble to Robert Smith, Mar. 11, 1804, EPP.
18. Logbooks and muster rolls of the USS *Nautilus*, SFP.
19. Journal of Mid. Cornelius de Krafft (hereafter de Krafft journal), Mar. 5, 1804, NDBP, Vol. 3 477.
20. de Krafft journal, Mar. 6, 1804, NDBP, Vol. 3, 480; Edward Preble to Richard Somers, Mar. 9, 1804, NDBP, Vol. 3, 482; Edward Preble to Robert Smith, Mar. 11, 1804, EPP.
21. Charles Stewart to Edward Preble, Mar. 17, 1804, NDBP, Vol. 3, 495–496.
22. Edward Preble to Robert Smith, Mar. 17, 1804; Edward Preble to Navy agents Richard O'Brien and George Dyson, Mar. 17, 1804, EPP.
23. de Krafft journal, Mar. 19, 1804, NDBP, Vol. 3, 508.
24. George Reed to Richard Somers, Mar. 20, 1804, NDBP, Vol. 3, 506.
25. James Decatur to Richard Somers, Mar. 20, 1804, NDBP, Vol. 3, 507.
26. Charles Stewart to Richard Somers, Mar. 20, 1804, SFP.

Chapter 13. Backlash

1. Ray, *Horrors of Slavery*, 111.
2. William Bainbridge to Edward Preble, Feb. 16, 1804, EPP.
3. Ray, *Horrors of Slavery*, 112.
4. William Bainbridge to Mohammed Sidi Dgies, Feb. 20, 1804, EPP.
5. Harris, *The Life and Services of Commodore William Bainbridge*, 104.
6. Ray, *Horrors of Slavery*, 113.
7. Nicholas Nissen to Edward Preble, Feb. 21, 1804, EPP.
8. William Bainbridge to Edward Preble, Feb. 22, 1804, EPP.
9. William Bainbridge to Edward Preble, Feb. 17, 1804, EPP
10. William Bainbridge to Edward Preble, Mar. 29, 1804, EPP.
11. William Bainbridge to Edward Preble, Feb. 22, 1804, EPP.
12. M. Wallen to Charles de Konig, Feb. 28, 1804, NDBP, Vol. 3, 460.
13. Richard Farquhar to Edward Preble, Mar. 15, 1804, EPP.
14. Thomas Appleton to Robert Livingston, Mar. 16, 1804, NDBP, Vol. 3, 494.
15. Salvatore Busuttil to Edward Preble, Jan. 24, 1804, EPP.
16. Edward Preble to Robert Smith, Jan. 22, 1804, EPP.
17. Tobias Lear to Edward Preble, Mar. 23, 1804, EPP.
18. Thomas Appleton to Robert Livingston, Mar. 16, 1804, NDBP, Vol. 3, 494.
19. Thomas Jefferson to Robert Smith, Apr. 27, 1804, *The Works of Thomas Jefferson in Twelve Volumes*, collected and edited by Leicester Ford (New York and London: G. P. Putnam and Sons, 1904), Vol. 10 (electronic edition).
20. Mohammed Sidi Dgies to William Bainbridge, Mar. 5, 1804, NDBP, Vol. 3, 474.
21. Edward Preble to William Bainbridge, Mar. 12, 1804, EPP.
22. Ibid.
23. William Bainbridge to Edward Preble, Feb. 16, 1804, EPP.
24. Porter, *Memoir of Commodore David Porter*, 64–65; Harris, *The Life and Services of Commodore William Bainbridge*, 73–74.
25. Harris, *The Life and Services of Commodore William Bainbridge*, 73–74.
26. William Bainbridge to Edward Preble, Mar. 26, 1804, EPP.
27. Ray, *Horrors of Slavery*, 117.
28. Harris, *The Life and Services of Commodore William Bainbridge*, 106.
29. Ray, *Horrors of Slavery*, 115.
30. Harris, *The Life and Services of Commodore William Bainbridge*, 106–107.
31. Harris, *The Life and Services of Commodore William Bainbridge*, 107; Porter, *Memoir of Commodore David Porter*, 65–66.

32. Although Bainbridge's letters to Preble with the lemon juice plans exist, there is nothing in Preble's replies that shows the commodore read that invisible ink, and so knew about the escape attempt. Bainbridge admitted as much in a letter dated June 7, 1804.

Chapter 14. Gunboat Diplomacy

1. Edward Preble to General Brune, Mar. 5, 1804, EPP.
2. Edward Preble to Robert Livingston, Mar. 18, 1804, EPP.
3. Brian McDonogh to Edward Preble, Mar. 19, 1804, NDBP, Vol. 3, 504–505.
4. Edward Preble to William Bainbridge, Mar. 12, 1804, EPP.
5. William Bainbridge to Edward Preble, Mar. 26, 1804, EPP.
6. Edward Preble to William Bainbridge, Mar. 12, 1804, EPP.
7. Charles Stewart to Edward Preble, Mar. 22, 1804, EPP.
8. Gaetano Schembri to Edward Preble, Mar. 22, 1804, EPP.
9. Edward Preble to Gaetano Schembri, Sept. 19, 1804, EPP.
10. Edward Preble to Stephen Decatur, Feb. 20, 1804, EPP.
11. Henry Wadsworth to Nancy Sloan, Mar. 17, 1804, NDBP, Vol. 3, 495.
12. Edward Preble to Mary Preble, Mar. 14, 1804, EPP.
13. Edward Preble to John H. Dent, Mar. 27, 1804, EPP.
14. Edward Preble to Robert Smith, Mar. 11, 1804, EPP.
15. Edward Preble to Henry Dearborn, in McKee, *Edward Preble*, 200–201.
16. John Broadbent to Edward Preble, Mar. 6, 1804, NDBP, Vol. 3, 478.
17. Abraham Gibbs to Edward Preble, Feb. 21, 1804, NDBP, Vol. 3, 448.
18. Edward Preble to Robert Smith, Mar. 11, 1804, EPP.
19. Ibid.
20. Edward Preble to Mary Preble, Mar. 14, 1804, EPP.
21. Edward Preble to Robert Smith, Mar. 14, 1804, EPP.
22. Edward Preble to Robert Smith, Mar. 11, 1804, EPP.
23. Edward Preble to Robert Smith, Mar. 14, 1804, EPP.
24. Ibid.
25. Stephen Decatur to Edward Preble, Feb. 26, 1804, NDBP, Vol. 4, 456.
26. Stephen Decatur to Edward Preble, Mar. 15, 1804, EPP.
27. Ibid.
28. Ibid.
29. Ibid.
30. George Davis to Tobias Lear, Mar. 9, 1804, NDBP, Vol. 3, 483.
31. Edward Preble to Robert Smith, Jan. 22, 1804, EPP.
32. Logbook of the USS *Constitution*, Mar. 27, 1804, EPP.
33. Edward Preble to Mohammed Sidi Dgies, Mar. 27, 1804, EPP.

34. Ibid.
35. Edward Preble to William Bainbridge, Mar. 27, 1804, EPP.
36. William Bainbridge to Edward Preble, Mar. 27, 1804, EPP.
37. Bonaventure Beaussier to Edward Preble, Mar. 28, 1804, EPP.
38. Preble diary, Mar. 28, 1804, EPP.

CHAPTER 15. BLOCKADE

1. Richard Somers to Edward Preble, Apr. 11, 1804, EPP.
2. Edward Preble to Robert Smith, Apr. 15, 1804.
3. Stephen Decatur to Edward Preble, Mar. 30, 1804, EPP.
4. The *Enterprise* crew to Edward Preble, Apr. 5, 1804, EPP.
5. Preble diary, Apr. 19, 1804, EPP.
6. Edward Preble to Charles Stewart, Apr. 9, 1804, EPP.
7. Edward Preble to Robert Smith, Apr. 19, 1804, EPP.
8. Ibid.
9. Morris, *Autobiography of Commodore Charles Morris*, 31.
10. Edward Preble to Robert Smith, Apr. 19, 1804, EPP.
11. *Hartford Courant*, Mar. 14, 1804, p. 3.
12. Annals of Congress, 8th Cong., 1st Sess., Oct. 17, 1803 to Mar. 27, 1804, 291–302.
13. John Gavino to Edward Preble, Apr. 4, 1804; Edward Preble to Isaac Chauncey, Apr. 23, 1804, EPP.
14. William Bainbridge to Tobias Lear, Apr. 4, 1804, NDBP, Vol. 4, 8–9.
15. Porter, *Memoir of Commodore David Porter*, 69–71.
16. Ray, *Horrors of Slavery*, 118.
17. Ibid., 119.
18. Ray, *Horrors of Slavery*, 118.
19. Wlliam Bainbridge to Tobias Lear, Apr. 30, 1804, NDBP, Vol. 4, 75–76; Ray, *Horrors of Slavery*, 121; William Bainbridge to Edward Preble, May 17, 1804, EPP.
20. Edward Preble to Robert Smith, May 15, 1804, EPP; Cowdery journal, June 27, 1804, NDBP, Vol. 4, 62.
21. Cowdery journal, April 24, 1804, NDBP, Vol. 4, 61.
22. Ray, *Horrors of Slavery*, 119–120.
23. Louis de Tousard, *The American Artillerist's Companion* (Philadelphia: C&A Conrad, 1809). Although published in 1809, de Tousard's work was simply a written version of the gun drill the U.S. Navy already used and was a derivation of the Royal Navy manual. It also included detailed descriptions and uses for each type of naval gun in use; United States

Army, History of the Development of Field Artillery Materiel (Fort Sill, OK, 1941).

24. de Krafft journal, Apr. 26, 1804, NDBP Vol. 4, 67.
25. Isaac Hull journal (hereafter Hull journal), May 15, 1804, NDBP, Vol. 4, 104–105; de Krafft journal, May 15, 1804, NDBP, Vol. 4, 103.
26. Hull journal, May 15, 1804, NDBP, Vol. 4, 105.
27. Edward Preble to Charles Stewart, Jun. 13, 1804, EPP.
28. Isaac Hull to George Dyson, Jun. 4, 2804, NDBP, Vol. 4, 149.
29. Charles Stewart to Edward Preble, Jun. 13, 1804, EPP.
30. Henry Wadsworth to Jack (no last name), Jun. 28, 1804, NDBP, Vol. 4, 233–234.
31. Edward Preble to Robert Smith, May 30, 1804, EPP.

CHAPTER 16. "DREADFUL TO BARBARY"

1. Pietro Colletta, *History of the Kingdom of Naples* (London: Hamilton, Adams and Co., 1858), Vol. 2, 441–447.
2. John Acton to James Leander Cathcart, Mar. 27, 1804, NDBP, Vol. 3, 538.
3. Edward Preble to John Acton, May 10, 1804, EPP.
4. Joseph Barnes to James Madison, Mar. 28, 1804, NDBP, Vol. 3, 542.
5. Edward Preble to Robert Smith, May 15, 1804, EPP.
6. Marcello de Gregorio, Governor of Syracuse, to Edward Preble, Apr. 22, 1804, EPP.
7. Preble diary, Apr. 22, 1804, EPP; logbook of the USS *Constitution*, Apr. 22, 1804, EPP.
8. Logbook of the USS *Constitution*, Apr. 22, 1804, EPP.
9. Preble diary, Apr. 22, 1804, EPP.
10. Edward Preble to commander, USS *John Adams*, Apr. 23, 1804; Edward Preble to commander, USS *John Adams*, May 7, 1804, EPP.
11. Edward Preble to John Acton, May 10, 1804, EPP.
12. John Acton to Edward Preble, May 14, 1804, EPP.
13. Edward Preble to James Leander Cathcart, May 13, 1804; Edward Preble order book, May 15, 1804, EPP.
14. Edward Preble to Mary Preble, Jun. 1, 1804, EPP.
15. Robert Smith to Isaac Chauncey, May 21, 1804, NDBP, Vol. 4, 106; Robert Smith memorandum, May 29, 1804, NDBP, Vol. 4, 107.
16. Edward Preble order book, Apr. 25, 1804, EPP.
17. Robert Smith to John Rodgers, May 29, 1804, NDBP, Vol. 4, 127.
18. Robert Smith to Edward Preble, May 22, 1804, EPP.
19. Robert Smith to Samuel Barron, Jun. 1, 1804, NDBP, Vol. 4, 138–140.

20. Isaac Chauncey to Robert Smith, Jun. 13, 1804, NDBP, Vol. 4, 182.

21. John Rodgers to Benjamin King, Jun. 15, 1804, NDBP, Vol. 4, 193–194.

22. William Bainbridge to Tobias Lear, NDBP, Vol. 4, Apr. 30, 1804, 75.

23. Alexander Murray to William Bainbridge, May 6, 1804, NDBP, Vol. 4, 87.

24. Harris, *The Life and Services of Commodore William Bainbridge*, 89–92; William Bainbridge to Edward Preble, Jun. 14, 1804, EPP.

25. Hull journal, Jun. 8, 1804, NDBP, Vol. 4, 170–171.

26. Charles Stewart to Edward Preble, Jun. 8, 1804, EPP.

27. Edward Preble to James Madison, Jun. 14, 1804, EPP.

28. Ibid.

29. Edward Preble to Charles Stewart, Jun. 15, 1804, EPP.

30. Harris, *The Life and Services of Commodore William Bainbridge*, 107–108; William Bainbridge to Edward Preble, Jun. 14, 1804, EPP.

31. Ibid.

32. Edward Preble to James Madison, Jun. 16, 1804, EPP.

33. Preble diary, May 15, 1804, EPP.

34. Edward Preble to Tobias Lear, Jun. 19, 1804, EPP.

35. Edward Preble to George Davis, Jun. 19, 1804, EPP.

36. Preble diary, May 29, 1804; logbook of the USS *Constitution*, May 29, 1804, EPP.

37. Logbook of the USS *Constitution*, May 29, 1804, EPP.

38. Edward Preble to Richard Somers, Jun. 3, 1804, EPP.

39. Somers, *Life of Richard Somers*, 10; Cooper, *Lives of Distinguished American Naval Officers*, Vol. 1, 87–88.

40. Charles Stewart to Edward Preble, Jul. 7, 1804, EPP.

41. Edward Preble to James Monroe, Jun. 20, 1804, EPP.

42. George Davis to Edward Preble, May 12, 1804, EPP.

CHAPTER 17. BATTLE LINES

1. Preble diary, Jun. 5, 1804, EPP.

2. Wardroom Officers of USS *Constitution* to Edward Preble, Jun. 9, 1804, EPP.

3. Edward Preble to Joseph Tarbell, Jun. 9, 1804, EPP. Joseph Tarbell would go on to reach the rank of master commandant and to command a flotilla of gunboats on the James River that defeated a British expedition in 1813. He died in 1815.

4. Logbook of the USS *Constitution*, Jun. 10, 1804, EPP.

5. Isaac Chauncey to Robert Smith, Jul. 25, 1804, NDBP, Vol. 4, 287–288.

6. William Bainbridge to George Davis, Jun. 15, 1804, NDBP, Vol. 4, 195.

7. William Bainbridge to Edward Preble, Jun. 19, 1804, EPP.

8. William Bainbridge to Edward Preble, Jul. 7, 1804, EPP.

9. William Bainbridge to Edward Preble, Jun. 19, 1804.

10. William Bainbridge to Edward Preble, Jul. 7, 1804.

11. Bainbridge and Preble were likely aware of the bashaw's interception of their mail. It was one of the reasons why they used lemon juice for "secret communications." Oddly, there is nothing in any letter explaining why the Americans insisted on communicating news they knew the bashaw would read.

12. Ray, *Horrors of Slavery*, 119.

13. Ibid., 122.

14. Ibid., 123.

15. Logbook of the USS *Constitution*, Aug. 2, 1804, EPP.

16. Ibid.

17. Logbook of the USS *Constitution*, Aug. 1, 1804, EPP.

18. Muster rolls of the *Argus*, *Syren*, *Vixen*, and *Nautilus*.

19. Edward Preble order book, Aug. 2, 1804, EPP; logbook of the USS *Constitution*, Aug. 2–4, 1804, EPP.

20. Logbook of the USS *Constitution*, Aug. 2, 1804, EPP.

21. Preble diary, Jun. 14, 1804, EPP.

22. Edward Preble to Mary Preble, Jul. 8, 1804, EPP.

23. Edward Preble to Thomas Jefferson, Aug. 4, 1804, EPP.

24. Edward Preble to James Leander Cathcart Jul. 5, 1804, EPP.

CHAPTER 18. BATTLE OF THE GUNBOATS

1. Ray, *Horrors of Slavery*, 371.

2. Ibid., 355; William Bainbridge to George Davis, Jul. 15, 1804; Cowdery journal, Jul. 19, 1804, NDBP, Vol. 4, 62.

3. Ray, *Horrors of Slavery*, 371; logbook of the USS *Constitution*, Aug. 3, 1804, EPP.

4. William Bainbridge to Tobias Lear, Jul. 10, 1804, NDBP, Vol. 4, 264–265.

5. William Bainbridge to Edward Preble, Jun. 22, 1804, EPP.

6. William Bainbridge to George Davis, Jun. 24, 1804, NDBP, Vol. 4, 213–214.

7. George Davis to William Bainbridge, Jul. 16, 1804, NDBP, Vol. 4, 271–272.

8. Logbook of the USS *Constitution*, Aug. 3, 1804, EPP; Richard O'Brien, "Narrative of Attacks on Tripoli," NDBP, Vol. 4, 341–343.

9. Ibid.

10. Logbook of the USS *Constitution*, Aug. 3, 1804, EPP; Edward Preble, Report to Congress, Sept. 18, 1804, EPP.
11. Stephen Decatur to Keith Spence, Jan. 8, 1805, NDBP, Vol. 4, 346.
12. Richard Somers, Stephen Decatur Jr., Joshua Blake, Henry Wadsworth, Robert T. Spence, Noadiah Morris, Lewis Heerman, and Jacob Boston, Reports to Edward Preble, NDBP, Vol. 4, 341–367; Edward Preble, Report to Congress, Sept. 18, 1804, EPP; logbook of the USS *Constitution*, Aug. 3–4, 1804, EPP; logbook of the USS *Argus*, Aug. 3, 1804, EPP; Cooper, *Lives of Distinguished American Naval Officers*, Vol. 1, 90–94; Ray, *Horrors of Slavery*, 124–128. Unless otherwise noted, all descriptions of the battle of August 3 come from these sources.
13. Richard Somers to Edward Preble, Aug. 3, 1804, NDBP, Vol. 4, 382.
14. Ibid.
15. Joshua Blake to Edward Preble, Aug. 3, 1804, NDBP, Vol. 4, 383.
16. Assistant Surgeon Lewis Heerman to Edward Preble, Aug. 3, 1804, EPP.
17. Many early sources identified the sailor as Reuben James. However, James did not report any wounds from the battle. Assistant Surgeon Lewis Heerman's report of the wounded lists Daniel Frazier with a deep head wound from which he would recover. Lewis Heerman, Report to Edward Preble, Aug. 3, 1804, EPP.
18. Numerous sources recount the tale of Decatur's duel with the pirate captain. A reprint of Alexander Slidell Mackenzie's account, which he based on the secondhand narrative of two of Decatur's friends, J. K. Hamilton and Francis Gurney Smith, is found at NDBP, Vol. 4, 347–348. Decatur himself never provided a firsthand report of his encounter.
19. Logbook of the USS *Constitution*, Aug. 3, 1804, EPP.
20. Ibid.
21. Morris, *Autobiography of Commodore Charles Morris*, 44.

Chapter 19. Drawing Breath

1. Edward Preble, Report to Congress, Sept. 18, 1804, EPP.
2. Noadiah Morris to unnamed recipient, Sept. 7, 1804, NDBP, Vol. 4, 353–354.
3. Cooper, *History of the United States Navy*, Vol. 1, 216–218. Cooper was the first to report on the outburst and meeting between Preble and Decatur. There are no other accounts of the encounter from any officers then on the *Constitution*. Cooper's version is the basis for several biographies of Decatur, most notably Irvin Anthony's. However, there is no other corroboration. Cooper also does not use Haraden's name, referring only to an officer "older than the officers" and "who could presume

on rank" (Cooper, 218). This could only be the *Constitution*'s sailing master.

4. Ibid.

5. Ibid.

6. Edward Preble, Report to Congress, Sept. 18, 1804, EPP.

7. Ibid.

8. Logbook of the USS *Constitution*, Aug. 3, 1804, EPP.

9. Joshua Blake to Edward Preble, Aug. 7, 1804, EPP.

10. Ibid.

11. Stephen Decatur to Keith Spence, Jan. 9, 1804, NDBP, Vol. 4, 346.

12. Ibid.

13. Edward Preble, General Order, Aug. 3, 1804, EPP.

14. Edward Preble to Mohammed Sidi Dgies, Aug. 4, 1804, EPP.

15. Edward Preble to Bonaventure Beaussier, Aug. 4, 1804, EPP.

16. Isaac Chauncey to Robert Smith, Jul. 22, 1804, NDBP, Vol. 4, 260.

17. Isaac Chauncey to Robert Smith, Jul. 25, 1804, NDBP, Vol. 4, 292.

18. Ray, *Horrors of Slavery*, 128.

19. Harris, *The Life and Services of Commodore William Bainbridge*, 112.

20. Ibid., 112–113.

21. Bonaventure Beaussier to Edward Preble, Aug. 6, 1804, EPP.

22. Logbook of the USS *Constitution*, Aug. 5, 1804, EPP.

23. Ibid., Aug. 7, 1804, EPP.

24. Ibid., Aug. 5, 1804, Aug. 6, 1804, EPP.

25. Ray, *Horrors of Slavery*, 133; Charles Stewart to Edward Preble, after-action report, Aug. 7, 1804, EPP.

26. Ray, *Horrors of Slavery*, 133.

27. Journal of John Darby, NDBP, Vol. 4 (hereafter Darby journal), Aug. 4, 1804, 364.

28. Isaac Chauncey to Robert Smith, Aug. 4, 1804, NDBP, Vol. 4, 364.

29. Darby journal, Aug. 7, 1804, NDBP, Vol. 4, 370.

30. de Krafft journal, Aug. 7, 1804, NDBP, Vol. 4, 375–376.

31. Logbook of the USS *Constitution*, Aug. 6, 1804, EPP.

32. Preble diary, Aug. 7, 1804, EPP.

33. Noadiah Morris, letter to unnamed recipient, Sept. 7, 1804, NDBP, Vol. 4, 354–356.

34. Edward Preble, Report to Congress, Sept. 18, 1804, EPP.

35. Muster roll of Neapolitan gunboats, Aug. 7, 1804, NDBP, Vol. 4, 259–260.

36. Somers, *Life of Richard Somers*, 21.

37. Edward Preble, Report to Congress, Sept. 18, 1804, EPP.

38. Ibid.

39. Edward Preble, Report to Congress, Sept. 18, 1804, EPP; logbook of the USS *Constitution*, Aug. 7, 1804, EPP.

40. de Krafft journal, Aug. 7, 1804, NDBP, Vol. 4, 375–376; Edward Preble, Report to Congress, Sept. 18, 1804, EPP.

41. Robert Spence to Mrs. Keith Spence, Nov. 23, 1804, NDBP, Vol. 4, 351–352.

42. Ibid.

43. Logbook of the USS *Constitution*, Aug. 7, 1804, EPP.

44. Ibid.

45. Logbook of the *Argus*, Aug. 7, 1804; logbook of the USS *Constitution*, Aug. 7, 1804, EPP.

CHAPTER 20. BATTLE OF TRIPOLI

1. Nicholas Nissen to George Davis, Aug. 29, 1804, NDBP, Vol. 4, 495.

2. Ibid.

3. Harris, *The Life and Services of Commodore William Bainbridge*, 113–114.

4. Ibid.

5. Isaac Chauncey to Edward Preble, Aug. 7, 1804, EPP.

6. Robert Smith to Edward Preble, Aug. 7, 1804, EPP.

7. Ibid.

8. Edward Preble to Alexander Ball, Aug. 21, 1804, EPP

9. Charles W. Goldsborough to Edward Preble, Mar. 5, 1804, EPP.

10. Alexander Ball to Edward Preble, Aug. 28, 1804, EPP.

11. Ibid.

12. Darby journal, Aug. 28, 1804, NDBP, Vol. 4, 385–385.

13. Edward Preble to Alexander Ball, Aug. 28, 1804, EPP.

14. Preble diary, Aug. 8, 1804, EPP.

15. Edward Preble to Alexander Ball, Aug. 21, 1804, EPP

16. Edward Preble to William Higgins, Aug. 15, 1804, EPP.

17. Logbook of the USS *Constitution*, Aug. 19, 1804, EPP.

18. Cooper, *Lives of Distinguished American Naval Officers*, 97–100.

19. Naval Registry, 52; F. Stanhope Hill, *The Lucky Little Enterprise and Her Successors in the United States Navy, 1776–1900* (Boston: n.p., 1900), 13–14.

20. Cooper, *Lives of Distinguished American Naval Officers*, Vol. 1, 100.

21. Edward Preble, Report to Congress, Sept. 18, 1804, EPP.

22. Ibid.

23. Logbook of the USS *Constitution*, Aug. 17, 1804, EPP.

24. Edward Preble, Report to Congress, Sept. 18, 1804, EPP.

25. Cooper, *History of the Navy of the United States*, 394–395.
26. Ibid.
27. Logbook of the USS *Constitution*, Aug. 24, 1804, EPP.
28. Ibid., Sept. 1, 1804, EPP.
29. Ibid., Aug. 28, 1804, EPP.
30. Edward Preble, Report to Congress, Sept. 18, 1804, EPP.
31. Darby journal, Aug. 27, 1804, NDBP, Vol. 4, 470.
32. Cowdery, *American Captives in Tripoli*, 6.
33. Ibid., 10.
34. Cowdery journal, Aug. 28, 1804, NDBP, Vol. 4, 64.
35. Darby journal, Aug. 28, 1804, NDBP, Vol. 4, 475–476; Cowdery journal, Aug. 28, 1804, NDBP, Vol. 4, 64; logbook of the USS *Constitution*, Aug. 28, 1804, EPP.
36. de Tousard, *The American Artillerist's Companion*.
37. Cowdery journal, Aug. 28, 1804, NDBP, Vol. 4, 64.
38. Ibid.; Edward Preble, Report to Congress, Sept. 18, 1804, EPP.
39. Gunboat commanders, Report to Edward Preble, Aug. 28, 1804, EPP.
40. Logbook of the USS *Constitution*, Aug. 28, 1804, EPP.
41. Darby journal, Aug. 28, 1804, NDBP, Vol. 4, 475–476.
42. Logbook of the USS *Constitution*, Aug. 28, 1804, EPP; gunboat commanders, Report to Edward Preble, Aug. 28, 1804, EPP; Isaac Chauncey to Edward Preble, Aug. 28, 1804, EPP.
43. Bonaventure Beaussier to Edward Preble, Aug. 29, 1804, EPP.
44. Joseph Douglas and William Godby to Edward Preble, Aug. 28, 1804, EPP.
45. Bonaventure Beaussier to Edward Preble, Aug. 29, 1804, EPP.
46. Ibid.
47. Ibid.
48. John Rodgers to Robert Smith, Aug. 30, 1804, JRP.
49. John Rodgers to James Barron, Aug. 30, 1804, NDBP, Vol. 4, 486.
50. John Rodgers to Robert Smith, Aug. 30, 1804, JRP.
51. James Simpson to John Rodgers, Aug. 26, 1804, NDBP, Vol. 4, 464.
52. Logbook of the USS *Constitution*, Aug. 30, 1804, EPP.
53. John Smith to Edward Preble, Aug. 25, 1804, EPP.
54. Logbook of the USS *Constitution*, Sept. 1, 1804, EPP.
55. Edward Preble, Report to Congress, Sept. 18, 1904, EPP.
56. Darby journal, Sept. 3, 1804, NDBP, Vol. 4, 501; Charles Morris journal (hereafter Morris journal), NDBP, Vol. 4, 510–511.
57. Bonaventure Beaussier to Edward Preble, Aug. 9, 1804, EPP.
58. Cowdery journal, Aug. 28, 1804, NDBP, Vol. 4, 64.

59. Logbook of the USS *Constitution*, Sept. 3, 1804, EPP.
60. Ibid.
61. Ibid.
62. Cowdery journal, Aug. 28, 1804, NDBP, Vol. 4, 64; Ray, *Horrors of Slavery*, 139.
63. Logbook of the USS *Constitution*, Sept. 3, 1804, EPP.
64. Ibid.

Chapter 21. An Intrepid Gamble

1. Preble diary, Jun. 1, 1804, EPP.
2. William Higgins to Edward Preble, Aug. 14, 1804, EPP.
3. Edward Preble order book, Aug. 20, 1804, EPP.
4. Logbook of the USS *Constitution*, Aug. 20, 1804, EPP.
5. Edward Preble to Joseph Israel, Aug. 20, 1804, EPP.
6. Sixth Congress, *An Act Providing for a Naval Peace Establishment*; Charles Oscar Paullin, *Commodore John Rodgers* (Cleveland, OH: Arthur H. Clark, 1910), 53–68. Different sources classify the *Maryland* as anything from a 20-gun sloop to a 36-gun frigate. Cooper, *History of the U.S. Navy*, Allen, *Our Naval War with France*, and Leiner, *Millions for Defense* all classify the *Maryland* a 20-gun sloop; Larry J Sechrest, in a journal article in the *Independent Review* titled, "Privately Funded and Built U.S. Warships in the Quasi-War of 1797–1801," rates the *Maryland* as a 26-gun ship even though he quotes heavily from Liener. The official U.S. Navy history of the *Maryland*, contained in the *Dictionary of American Fighting Ships*, says *Maryland* carried 36 guns, which would push her out of the sloop class and into the frigate class. The discrepancies may be because captains tended to add cannon to their ships. The *Constitution*, for example, though rated as a 44, carried up to 56 guns. American designers, unlike their European counterparts, also refused to count carronades mounted on the spar deck or quarterdeck as guns. There are, however, no papers in the John Rodgers Collection that say Rodgers, the only commander of the *Maryland*, added carronades to ship's armament.
7. Register of Officer Personnel United States Navy and Marine Corps and Ship's Date, 1801–1807 (Washington, DC: Government Printing Office, 1945), 28. Robert Smith wrote to Edward Preble in August 1803 giving him permission to "remove from the New York such men and officers as your service might require" (Aug. 9, 1803, EPP). The muster book of the *Constitution* also notes Israel's arrival on the *Constitution* as a transfer from the *New York*.

8. Logbook of the USS *Constitution*, Aug. 25, 1804, EPP.
9. Preble diary, Aug. 28, 1804.
10. Journal of Sir Hyde Parker, Apr. 2, 1801, T. Sturgis, ed., *Logs of the Great Sea Fights, 1794–1805* (London: Navy Records Society, 1900), 87–92.
11. Edward Preble, Report to Congress, Sept. 18, 1804, EPP.
12. Logbook of the USS *Constitution*, Aug. 29, 1804, EPP.
13. Ibid., Aug. 24, 1804; logbook of the USS *Argus*, Aug. 24, 1804, EPP.
14. Robert Spence to Mrs. Keith Spence, Nov. 23, 1804, NDBP, Vol. 4, 351–352.
15. Morris, *Autobiography of Commodore Charles Morris*, 40.
16. Inventory of Richard Somers' belongings, Sept. 5, 1804, SFP, 33–34.
17. Darby journal, Sept. 4, 1804, NDBP, Vol. 4, 506.
18. Logbook of the USS *Constitution*, Sept. 3, 1804, EPP.
19. Ibid., Aug. 29, 1804, EPP; Cooper, *Lives of Distinguished American Naval Officers*, Vol. 1, 102.
20. Cooper, *Lives of Distinguished American Naval Officers*, Vol. 1, 102.
21. Henry Preble to James Fenimore Cooper, in *Correspondence of James Fenimore Cooper*, James Cooper, ed. (New Haven, CT: Yale University Press, 1922), Vol. 1, 133–35.
22. Edward Preble, Report to Congress, Feb. 20, 1805, EPP.
23. Henry Wadsworth to Edward Preble, Sept. 3, 1804, EPP; Robert Spence, Nov, 23, 1804, NDBP, Vol. 4, 351–352; Edward Preble, Report to Congress, Sept. 18, 1804, EPP.
24. Muster roll of the USS *Maryland*, JRP.
25. Muster roll of USS *Nautilus*, SFP.
26. Ibid.
27. According to a letter from recruiting officer Lt. John Robinson to Capt. Edward Preble, July 23, 1803, most of the men enlisting in New York were deserters from the Royal Navy or were from British merchant boats. John Robinson to Edward Preble, Jul. 23, 1803, EPP.
28. Logbook of the USS *Constitution*, Oct. 4, 1803, EPP.
29. Ibid., Sept. 20, 1803 and Dec. 9, 1803.

CHAPTER 22. THE INFERNAL

1. Ray, *Horrors of Slavery*, 132.
2. Ibid.
3. Ibid.
4. Ibid., 134–135.

5. Cooper, *Lives of Distinguished American Naval Officers*, Vol. 1, 106.

6. de Krafft journal, Sept. 1, 1804, 495; Darby journal, Sept. 1, 1804, NDBP, Vol. 4, 494.

7. Charles L. Ridgeley, Account of the Destruction of USS *Intrepid*, NDBP, Vol. 4, 508.

8. Bonaventure Beaussier to Edward Preble, Sept. 1, 1804, EPP.

9. Ibid.

10. Charles L. Ridgeley, Report, Account of the *Intrepid*, NDBP, Vol. 4, 508; Cooper, *Lives of Distinguished American Naval Officers*, Vol. 1, 105.

11. Charles L. Ridgeley, Account of the *Intrepid*, NDBP, Vol. 4, 508.

12. Ibid.

13. Somers, *Life of Richard Somers*, 28.

14. Ibid., 35.

15. Richard Somers to Sarah Keen, undated, SFP.

16. Cooper, *Lives of Distinguished American Naval Officers*, Vol. 1, 105–106; Somers, *Life of Richard Somers*, 27.

17. Cooper, *Lives of Distinguished American Naval Officers*, Vol. 1, 106.

18. Ibid., 107.

19. Charles L. Ridgeley, n.d., Account of the USS *Intrepid*, NDBP, Vol. 4, 509.

20. Personal communication, Don Treworgy, Mystic Seaport Planetarium.

21. de Krafft journal, Sept. 4, 1804, NDBP, Vol. 4, 506; Cooper, *Lives of Distinguished American Naval Officers*, 108.

22. Morris journal, Sept. 4, 1804, NDBP, Vol. 4, 512.

23. Cooper, *Lives of Distinguished American Naval Officers*, Vol. 1, 108.

24. Morris journal, Sept. 4, 1804, NDBP, Vol. 4, 512; logbook of the USS *Constitution*, Sept. 4, 1804, EPP.

25. Charles L. Ridgeley, Account of the USS *Intrepid*, NDBP, Vol. 4, 507–508.

26. Ibid., 509.

27. Charles L. Ridgeley, Account of the USS *Intrepid*, NDBP, Vol. 4, 509; Logbook of the USS *Constitution*, Sept. 4, 1804, EPP.

28. Ibid.

CHAPTER 23. "PREBLE'S BOYS"

1. Cowdery journal, Sept. 6, 1804, NDBP, Vol. 4, 64.

2. William Bainbridge journal, date unknown, in Cooper, *Lives of Distinguished American Naval Officers*, 109.

3. Cooper, *Lives of Distinguished American Naval Officers*, 111.

4. Journal of Antoine Zuchet, quoted in Richard Zacks, *Pirate Coast* (New York: Hyperion Books, 2005), 105–106. In his very brief account of

Preble's campaign, Zacks got several dates of battles wrong and failed to challenge Zuchet's claim that the Arabs found fourteen bodies in the wreckage of the *Intrepid*.

5. Abdu-Ihakim Amer Al-Tawil, *Secrets of the Old Protestant Cemetery* (Tripoli: Libyan Center for Historical Studies, 2008; translated informally), 133–140, 264, 334–370.

6. Al-Tawil, *Secrets of the Old Protestant Cemetery*, 133–140, 264, 334–370; Cooper, *Lives of Distinguished American Naval Officers*, 111. Sometime later, either the Libyans or their Italian conquerors reburied the ten men initially interred near the beach. The graves of the three officers became the foundation of what today is the Old Protestant Cemetery. According to a Libyan history of the cemetery, all of the men are buried in the cemetery, although some historians claim bodies remain buried near the highway the Italians built in the 1920s. Since 1844 the families of Somers and Wadsworth have tried to recover the remains of the crew, but have found apathy and the U.S. government blocking them. A new effort is under way to recover the remains. For more information on this effort, go to www.richardsomers.org.

7. Morris journal, Sept. 4, 1804, NDBP, Vol. 4, 514.

8. Darby journal, Sept. 4, 1804, NDBP, Vol. 4, 508; Edward Preble, Report to Congress, Sept. 18, 1804, EPP.

9. Anthony, *Decatur*, 152.

10. Berube and Rodgaard, *A Call to the Sea*, 50.

11. Darby journal, Sept. 4, 1804, NDBP, Vol. 4, 506.

12. Charles L. Ridgeley, Account of the USS *Intrepid* NDBP, Vol. 4, 509.

13. Cooper, *Lives of Distinguished American Naval Officers*, 105–106.

14. Morris journal, Sept. 5, 1804, NDBP, Vol. 4, 513.

15. Edward Preble, Report to Congress, Sept. 18, 1804, EPP.

16. Cooper, *Lives of Distinguished American Naval Officers*, Vol. 1, 115–116.

17. Ibid., 118.

18. Ray, *Horrors of Slavery*, 139.

19. Ibid.

20. Cowdery journal, Sept. 6, 1804, NDBP, Vol. 4, 64.

21. Al-Tawil, *Secrets of the Old Protestant Cemetery*, 315–334.

22. William Eaton to Edward Preble, Jan. 25, 1805, EPP.

23. Ray, *Horrors of Slavery*, 144.

24. Edward Preble to John H. Dent, Sept. 4, 1804, EPP; Edward Preble to Thomas Robinson, Sept. 4, 1804, EPP; Edward Preble to Stephen Decatur, Sept. 6, 1804, EPP.

25. Edward Preble to John Acton, Sept. 6, 1804, EPP.

26. Ray, *Horrors of Slavery*, 149.

27. Edward Preble, Report to Congress, Sept. 18, 1804, EPP.

28. Ibid.

29. Edward Preble, Report to Congress, Sept. 18, 1804, EPP.

30. Morris, *Autobiography of Commodore Charles Morris*, 34–35.

31. Edward Preble to William Bainbridge, Oct. 28, 1804, EPP.

32. Edward Preble to Mary Preble, Nov. 12, 1804, EPP.

33. Squadron Officers to Edward Preble, Nov. 4, 1804, EPP.

34. Edward Preble to Squadron Officers, Nov. 4, 1804, EPP.

CHAPTER 24. HOMECOMING

1. Edward Preble to Mary Preble, Feb. 25, 1805, EPP.

2. *New England Gazette*, Mar. 26, 1805.

3. Edward Preble to Henry Preble, Sept. 21, 1805, EPP.

4. McKee, *Edward Preble*, 354.

BIBLIOGRAPHY

PRIMARY SOURCES

Third Congress. *An Act to Provide a Naval Armament*. Philadelphia: Childs and Swain, 1794.

Third Congress. *Marine Committee Report: The Naval Force Necessary for the Protection of the Commerce of the United States, Against the Algerine Corsairs: An Estimate of the Expense of Such a Force; and the Ways and Means for Defraying the Said Expense*. Philadelphia: Childs and Swain, 1794.

Fourth Congress. *An Act to Provide a Naval Armament, 1797*. Philadelphia: Francis Childs, 1797.

Sixth Congress. *An Act Providing for a Naval Peace Establishment*. Washington, DC: n.p., 1804.

Seventh Congress. "Committee Report on the *Enterprise*." Washington, DC, 1802.

Annals of the Congress of the United States, Third Congress, Philadelphia, 1794.

Annals of the Congress of the United States, Fourth Congress, Philadelphia, 1796.

Annals of the Congress of the United States, Fifth Congress, Philadelphia, 1798.

Annals of the Congress of the United States, Sixth Congress, Washington, DC, 1800.

Annals of the Congress of the United States, Seventh Congress, Washington, DC, 1802.

Annals of the Congress of the United States, Eighth Congress, Washington, DC, 1803.

Annals of the Congress of the United States, Ninth Congress, Washington, DC, 1804.

Annals of the Congress of the United States, Tenth Congress, Washington, DC, 1805.

Congress of the United States. *American State Papers: Documents, Legislative and Executive, of the Congress of the United States, from the First Session of the First to the Second Session of the Twenty-Second Congress*. Washington, DC: Gales & Seaton, 1833.

Blyth, Stephen Cleveland. *History of the War between the United States and Tripoli and Other Barbary Powers*. Salem, MA: Salem Gazette Office, 1808. Reprint, Tripoli, Libya: Fergiani Bookshop, 1970. Citations refer to both editions.

Burney, William. *A New Universal Dictionary of the Marine*. London: T. Cadell & Davies, 1815.

Cathcart, James Leander. *Tripoli: First War with the United States. Letter Book*. LaPorte, IN: Herald Print, 1901.

Cooper, James Fenimore. *Correspondence of James Fenimore Cooper*, edited by James Cooper. New Haven, CT: Yale University Press, 1922.

Cowdery, Jonathan. *American Captive in Tripoli, or Dr. Cowdery's Journal in Miniature*. Boston: Belcher & Armstrong, 1806. Also NDBP, Vol. 3.

Documents Respecting Barbary Accompanying the President's Communications to Congress, Dec. 8, 1801. Washington, DC: William Duane, 1802.

Documents, Official and Unofficial, Relating to the Case of the Capture and Destruction of the Frigate Philadelphia at Tripoli on the 16th February 1804. Washington, DC: John W. Towers, 1850.

Decatur, Stephen, Jr. *Letters and Papers*. Philadelphia: Pennsylvania Historical Society, Manuscript Division, multiple years.

de Krafft, Cornelius. *Journal*. Washington, DC: National Archives, 1803–1804.

Dent, John H. *Letterbook*. Washington, DC: Library of Congress Manuscript Division, 1801–1804.

Eaton, William. *Interesting Detail of the Operations of the American Fleet in the Mediterranean Communicated in a Letter from W. E. to His Friend in the County of Hampshire*. Springfield, MA: Bliss & Brewer Printers, 1805.

———. *The Life of the Late Gen. William Eaton: Several Years an Officer in the United States' Army, Consul at the Regency of Tunis on the Coast of Barbary, and Commander of the Christian and Other Forces That Marched from Egypt Through the Desert of Barca, in 1805*. Brookfield, MA: E. Merriam, 1813.

Enterprise Deck Logs, 1800–1805. Washington, DC: National Archives.

Folger, George. *Agreeable Intelligence*. New Bedford, MA: John Spooner, 1793.

Foss, John. *A Journal of Captivity and Suffering of John Foss.* Newburyport, MA: Angier March, 1798.

Hoxse, John. *The Yankee Tar: An Authentic Narrative of the Voyages and Hardships of John Hoxse.* Northampton, MA: John Metcalf, 1840.

Hull, Isaac. *The Papers of Isaac Hull,* edited by Gardner W. Allen. Boston: Boston Athenean, 1929.

Humphreys, David. *Letters and Papers of David Humphreys.* In the Humphreys–Marvin–Olmstead Collection. New Haven, CT: Yale University Manuscripts Collection, 1776–1867.

———. *Miscellaneous Works.* New York: T&J Swords, 1804.

Inderwick, James. *Journal of Surgeon James Inderwick of the Cruise of the U.S. Brig* Argus *in 1813,* edited by Victor Hugo Paltsits. New York: New York Public Library, 1917.

Jackson, Thomas Sturgis, ed. *Logs of the Great Sea Fights, 1794–1805.* London: Navy Records Society, 1900.

Jefferson, Thomas. "Message from the President of the United States, Communicating to Congress, A Letter Received from Capt. Bainbridge, Commander of the *Philadelphia* Frigate: Giving Information of the Wreck of That Vessel, on the Coast Of Tripoli, and That Himself, His Officers, and Men Had Fallen into the Hands of the Tripolitans." March 19, 1804, Washington, DC.

———. *The Papers of Thomas Jefferson.* Washington, DC: Library of Congress, 1999.

———. *The Thomas Jefferson Papers, Series 1, General Correspondence, 1651–1827.* Library of Congress Manuscript Division.

———. *The Works of Thomas Jefferson in Twelve Volumes.* Collected and edited by Leicester Ford. New York and London: G. P. Putnam and Sons, 1904 (electronic edition).

Lawrence, James. *Letters and Papers of James Lawrence.* New York: New York Historical Society, n.d.

Loomis, Hezekiah. *The Journal of Hezekiah Loomis, Steward on the U.S. Brig Vixen under Capt. John Smith, USN.* Salem, MA: Essex Institute, 1928.

Marine Corps Correspondence. National Archives Record Group 127, Records of the Office of the Commandant of the Marine Corps, 1798–1978.

Morris, Charles. *Autobiography of Commodore Charles Morris, U.S. Navy.* Annapolis, MD: Naval Institute Press, 2002.

Naval Documents Related to the War Between the United States and the Barbary Powers. 6 vols. Washington, DC: Government Printing Office, 1935–1937.

Naval Documents Related to the Quasi-War Between the United States and France. 6 vols. Washington, DC: Government Printing Office, 1936–1945.

Naval Documents of the American Revolution. 6 vols. Washington, DC: Government Printing Office, 1972.

O'Brien, Richard. *Message from the President of the United States, Communicating the Copy of a Letter from Richard O'Brien, Late Consul of the United States, at Algiers: Giving Some Detail of Transactions before Tripoli.* Washington, DC: Duane & Sons, 1804.

Pool, Eugene H., Ed. *"Don't Give Up the Ship": A Catalogue of the Eugene H. Pool Collection of Captain James Lawrence.* Salem, MA: Peabody Museum, 1942.

Porter, David D. *Memoir of Commodore David Porter.* Albany, NY: J. Munsell, 1875.

Preble, Edward. *Edward Preble Collection of Correspondence, Diaries, Logs and Other Writings.* Washington, DC: Library of Congress Manuscripts Division.

Preble, Henry. *Letters to James Fenimore Cooper.* New Haven, CT: Yale University Beineke Museum of Western Americana Manuscripts Collection.

Ray, William. *Horrors of Slavery, or, The American Tars in Tripoli.* New York: Oliver Lyon, 1808.

Rea, John. *A Letter to William Bainbridge, Esq., formerly Commander of the United States Ship* George Washington. Philadelphia: n.p., 1802.

Register of Officer Personnel United States Navy and Marine Corps and Ship's Data, 1801–1807. Washington, DC: U.S. Government Printing Office, 1945.

Rodgers, John, Papers, Library of Congress Manuscript Division. Unpublished.

Somers, Richard. *Letters and Papers of Richard Somers*, edited by Frank H. Stewart. Gloucester County, NJ: n.p., 1940.

Stoddert, Benjamin. *Letter from the Secretary of the Navy (Feb. 9, 1799): Accompanying Sundry Statements Relative to the Vessels of War, Employed in and Preparing for the Service of the United States, Pursuant to a Resolution of the House, of the Eighteenth Instant.* Philadelphia: J. Gales, 1799.

Truxtun, Thomas. *Remarks, Instructions and Examples Relating to the Latitude and Longitude; Also the Variations of the Compass.* Philadelphia: T. Dobson, 1794.

U.S. Department of the Navy. *American Naval Policy as Outlined in Messages of the Presidents of the United States, From 1790.* Washington, DC: Government Printing Office, 1922.

SECONDARY SOURCES

Al-Tawil, Abdu Ihakim Amer. *Secrets of the Old Protestant Cemetery.* Tripoli: Libyan Center for Historical Studies, 2008. Translated informally.

Allen, Gardner W. *Naval History of the American Revolution.* Boston: Houghton Mifflin Company, 1913.

Anthony, Irvin. *Decatur.* New York: Charles Scribner's Sons, 1931.

Bailey, Isaac. *American Naval Biography.* Providence, RI: H. Mann, 1815.

Berube, Claude G., and John A. Rodgaard. *A Call to the Sea: Captain Charles Stewart of the USS* Constitution. Washington, DC: Potomac Books, 2005.

Biographical Sketch of Commodore Charles Stewart. Philadelphia: J. Harding, 1830.

Chapelle, Howard I. *The History of American Sailing Ships.* New York: W. W. Norton, 1935.

———. *The History of the U.S. Sailing Navy: The Ships and Their Development.* New York: W. W. Norton and Sons, 1949.

Clark, Thomas. *Naval History of the United States.* Philadelphia: M. Carey, 1814.

Colletta, Pietro. *History of the Kingdom of Naples.* 2 vols. London: Hamilton, Adams, 1858.

Cooper, James Fenimore. *History of the Navy of the United States.* 2 vols. New York: Stinger and Townsend, 1856.

———. *Lives of Distinguished American Naval Officers.* 2 vols. Philadelphia: Carey and Hart, 1846.

Deane, Lewis. *The Life of James Lawrence, Esq.* New Brunswick, NJ: L. Deane, 1813.

De Kay, James Tertius. *A Rage for Glory: The Life of Commodore Stephen Decatur, USN.* New York: Free Press, 2004.

de Tousard, Louis. *The American Artillerist's Companion.* Philadelphia: C&A Conrad, 1809.

Dictionary of American Fighting Ships. 2 vols. Washington, DC: Government Printing Office, 1963.

Gleaves, Albert. *James Lawrence.* New York: G. P. Putnam's Sons, 1904.

Grant, Bruce. *The Life and Fighting Times of Commodore Isaac Hull.* Chicago: Pellegrini and Cudahy, 1947.

Harris, Thomas. *The Life and Services of Commodore William Bainbridge.* Philadelphia: Carey Lea & Blanchard, 1837.

Hill, Stanhope F. *The Lucky Little Enterprise and Her Successors in the United States Navy, 1776–1900.* Boston: n.p., 1900.

Hollis, Ira N. *The Frigate* Constitution. Boston: Houghton Mifflin Company, 1931.

Hoopes, Edna Miriam. *Richard Somers, Master Commandant of the U.S. Navy.* Atlantic City, NJ: n.p., 1922.

Kimball, Horace. *American Naval Battles.* Boston: Charles Gaylord, 1837.

Macdonough, Rodney. *The Life of Commodore Thomas Macdonough.* Boston: Fort Gill Press, Samuel Usher, 1909

MacManemin, John A. *Early Warships of the U.S. Sailing Navy:* Alliance, Essex *and* Enterprise. Spring Lake, NJ: Ho Ho Kus, 1997

Maloney, Elbert S., Ed. *Chapman Piloting and Seamanship*, 65th edition. New York: Hearst Books, 2006.

Maloney, Linda M. *The Captain from Connecticut: The Life and Naval Times of Isaac Hull.* Boston: Northeast University Press, 1986.

McKee, Christopher. *Edward Preble: A Naval Biography.* Annapolis, MD: Naval Institute Press, 1972.

Nelson, James L. *Benedict Arnold's Navy.* Camden, ME: McGraw-Hill, 2006.

Niles, John M. *The Life of Oliver Hazard Perry.* Hartford, CT: Oliver D. Cooke, 1821.

Palmer, Michael A. *Stoddert's War: Naval Operations during the Quasi-War with France, 1798–1801.* Annapolis, MD: Naval Institute Press, 1987.

Paullin, Charles Oscar. *Commodore John Rodgers.* Cleveland, OH: Arthur H. Clark, 1910.

Phillips, James Duncan. *Salem and the Indies: The Story of the Great Commercial Era of the City.* Boston: Houghton Mifflin Company, 1947.

Pratt, Fletcher. *Preble's Boys.* New York: William Sloane Associates, 1950.

Putnam, Waldo Samuel. *Biographical Sketches of Distinguished American Naval Heroes in the War of the Revolution.* Hartford, CT: Silas Andrus, 1818.

Roosevelt, Theodore. *The Naval War of 1812.* New York: G. P. Putnam and Sons, 1882.

Seawell, Molly Elliott. *Decatur and Somers.* New York: D. Appleton, 1894.

———. *Twelve Naval Captains.* London: Keegan Paul, Trench and Trubner, 1898.

Somers, J. B. *Life of Richard Somers, A Master Commandant in the U.S. Navy*. Philadelphia: Collins Printer, 1886.

Steven, William Oliver. *Pistols at Ten Paces: The Code of Honor in America*. Boston: Houghton Mifflin, 1940.

Toll, Ian W. *Six Frigates*. New York: W. W. Norton, 2006.

Waldo, Putnam S. *The Life and Character of the Late Commodore Stephen Decatur*. Middletown, CT: Clark and Lyman, 1822.

Whipple, A. B. C. *To the Shores of Tripoli: The Birth of the U.S. Navy and Marines*. Annapolis, MD: Naval Institute Press, 1991.

Zacks, Richard. *The Pirate Coast: Thomas Jefferson, the First Marines and the Secret Mission of 1805*. New York: Hyperion Books, 2005.

INDEX

ABOUT THE AUTHOR

CHIPP REID is a veteran journalist and historian with more than twenty years' experience writing for newspapers. He covered the wars in Iraq and Afghanistan and won awards for his coverage of homeland security issues and racial tensions in New England as well as for sports writing. He works in Washington, D.C., and lives in Annapolis, Md.

THE NAVAL INSTITUTE PRESS is the book-publishing arm of the U.S. Naval Institute, a private, nonprofit, membership society for sea service professionals and others who share an interest in naval and maritime affairs. Established in 1873 at the U.S. Naval Academy in Annapolis, Maryland, where its offices remain today, the Naval Institute has members worldwide.

Members of the Naval Institute support the education programs of the society and receive the influential monthly magazine *Proceedings* or the colorful bimonthly magazine *Naval History* and discounts on fine nautical prints and on ship and aircraft photos. They also have access to the transcripts of the Institute's Oral History Program and get discounted admission to any of the Institute-sponsored seminars offered around the country.

The Naval Institute's book-publishing program, begun in 1898 with basic guides to naval practices, has broadened its scope to include books of more general interest. Now the Naval Institute Press publishes about seventy titles each year, ranging from how-to books on boating and navigation to battle histories, biographies, ship and aircraft guides, and novels. Institute members receive significant discounts on the Press's more than eight hundred books in print.

Full-time students are eligible for special half-price membership rates. Life memberships are also available.

For a free catalog describing Naval Institute Press books currently available, and for further information about joining the U.S. Naval Institute, please write to:

Member Services
U.S. Naval Institute
291 Wood Road
Annapolis, MD 21402-5034
Telephone: (800) 233-8764
Fax: (410) 571-1703
Web address: www.usni.org